AFTER
IDEOLOGY

David Walsh

AFTER
IDEOLOGY

Recovering the Spiritual
Foundations of Freedom

The Catholic University of
America Press • Washington, D.C.

First published in 1990 by Harper San Francisco, A Division of Harper Collins
Publishers.

Copyright © 1990, 1995 by David Walsh
All rights reserved
Printed in the United States of America

The paper used in this publication meets the minimum requirements of American
National Standards for Information Science—Permanence of Paper for Printed Library
materials, ANSI Z39.48-1984.
∞

Library of Congress Cataloging-in-Publication Data
Walsh, David, 1950–
    After ideology : recovering the spiritual foundations of freedom / David Walsh.
        p.   cm.
    "First published in 1990 in a cloth edition by Harper San Francisco, a division of
Harper Collins Pub."—Pub. info.
    Includes bibliographical references.
    ISBN 0-8132-0833-5 (pbk : alk. paper)
    1. Sociology, Christian.   2. Christianity—Philosophy.   3. Political science—
Philosophy.   4. Christianity—Philosophy.   5. Conservatism.   6. Liberty.
7. Freedom (Theology)   8. Ideology.   9. Postmodernism—Religious aspects—
Christianity.   I. Title.
BT738.W332   1995
261.7—dc20   95-40683

To Gail

Contents

Preface to this Edition

The appearance of a new edition is a welcome opportunity for an author to add some thoughts in light of the response to a book that is now five years old. Originally written in the late eighties, *After Ideology* was published just as the Berlin Wall came down and the countries of Eastern Europe were released from the Soviet empire. Communism in the Soviet Union had not yet fallen, but clearly its days were numbered, as the collapse of its inner legitimacy was already fully evident. It was only a matter of time before such processes were completed, as indeed they are bound to continue in the remaining countries where residual communist regimes still hold sway. What was clear was that we were at a turning point, at which the last of the great ideological movements of the twentieth century was making its historic exit. The momentous significance of these events still remains to be digested, and this is the principal area in which I hope that *After Ideology* can make some small contribution.

Among the obstacles to the recognition that the age of great ideologies has passed is the failure to distinguish clearly between them and the multiplicity of lesser ideological enthusiasms that continue to proliferate. For there is all the difference in the world between the great ideological systems—such as communism, fascism, nazism, positivism, nationalism—that were carriers of revolutionary political movements and the low intensity preoccupations of globalism, environmentalism, feminism, or multiculturalism. The latter represent the changing winds of social convictions and concerns more than any attempt at radically reshaping the human condition. Unlike the militant ideological movements of an earlier era, they do not contain the promise of universal human emancipation; they do not assert a comprehensive explanation of the whole of reality and history; and, most important of all, they neither call for nor attempt to justify a total violent conflict in the name of the cause. No one will die for multiculturalism. What they often share with the great ideologies is a pattern of thinking or, rather, of not thinking. The ideological style is the refusal to entertain questions that might jeopardize one's convictions. Such failure will, I suspect, remain a permanent human temptation. It is the disappearance of an apocalyptic drive behind the passion that has been the major transformation of our time.

The result is that we are confronted with the more ordinary range of human conflicts and prejudices that are accessible to the ordinary political processes of resolution. The challenge we face is to restore a common framework of reason within a setting where a history of ideological conflict has pretty well eviscerated it. Ordinary political resolution of conflicts through processes of persuasion and negotiation and compromise presuppose a shared understanding of what is fair and reasonable. The reconstruction of that shared human understanding is the principal intellectual task we confront today. Its difficulty, especially in light of the continued prevalence of ideological styles of thinking, has caused more than a few observers to declare the task well nigh impossible. Needless to say, I am more sanguine about the prospects, chiefly because I recognize that the residual ideological attitudes we still encounter are little more than what Mao referred to as paper tigers. They derive from no immovable passions and, given sufficient resistance, will prove accessible to honest critique.

The deepest reason for hope, however, lies not in the weakness of the forces of irrationality but in the possibility of recovering a publicly authoritative understanding of the moral order in which we live. The disintegration that seems to characterize the end of modernity need not be the last word. Fragmentation can give way to meaning if we are willing to meditate on the crisis through which our civilization has passed. *After Ideology* is in the manner of an appeal to resist forgetfulness, the temptation to pass too readily over the horrors to which the intellectual and political movements of our century brought us. This is the great danger of museums to the various holocausts of our era. We reduce them to objective dimensions that separate us from them. We fail to recognize ourselves within such nightmare events or to acknowledge that they are in some way representative of the modern civilization that gave them birth. We are in danger of losing the most precious gift that the millions of sufferers can bequeath to us: the recognition, not of such platitudes as the inhumanity of man, but of the reality of the struggle between good and evil that is unending within every human heart. A reorientation of our whole civilization is possible from that very elementary recognition.

The endless philosophical discussions of the impossibility of discovering a foundation to morality are cut through in the recognition that we are inescapably engaged in a moral struggle even from the beginning. There is no way for human beings to step outside of their condition in order to verify its sources. All our reflections must take place in the rush of life itself. The illusion of stepping beyond good and evil, of man becoming a law unto himself, of providing himself with his own values, is no more than that. It is an illusion that portends the endless self-destruction of man. There is no freedom to be attained by stepping beyond the boundaries of ordinary morality, where, rather, we discover the abyss of domination and cruelty without restraint. Preservation of our humanity crucially depends on a recognition of the limits within which a human being lives and, above all, of the givenness of that order in which we find ourselves but of which we are surely not the source.

Acknowledgment of such philosophic insights at the end of the twentieth century no longer depends on the intellectual arguments. They are more powerfully the fruit of life experience itself. In a curious way, the reflections of philosophers have still to catch up with the developments that have become dramatically plain in actual history. I have written this book to help bridge that connection between theory and life by drawing attention to the life whose clarity is considerably in advance of the world of theory. We do not have to wait for philosophers to solve the problem of the moral sources of our order, because they have already been exemplified in the lives and reflections of the human beings who have confronted and surmounted the disorder of the age. That is why this book is not about philosophical ideas but about individuals who have lived out the moral exigencies of human life and thereby revealed the ideas with a force that is unsurpassed by philosophy.

The germ of a truly postmodern order is revealed in the individuals who have confronted the darkness of the modern project of human self-creation and self-perfection. Within the struggle with the abyss of evil unleashed by the effort to overstep the boundary of our humanity, they discovered the power of a spiritual reality infinitely stronger than the strength of ideological illusions. In the process they revealed the structure of a moral order that reaches into human existence, but whose roots lie beyond the realm of all that is under finite control. The moral intimations that draw us are a touch of that other, divine reality whose redemptive self-revelation within history is the ultimate drama within which human

existence is enacted. By refusing to be mastered by the deforming forces
of totalitarian ideology, such individuals discovered the reality of goodness that remains stronger than the power of evil. They discovered the
power of truth that dissolves the falsehood of ideology and provides the
only real foundation for the common order that shelters human beings
within politics and history.

Debates about foundations are superseded by the undeniable witness
of an inexorable moral exigence within human life. Even the elaborate
denial of its presence by the great ideological systems, and the apparently irresistible backing of the power of the totalitarian state, was not
enough to obliterate the consciousness of its reality. What could not be
eliminated by the power of that hideous strength can hardly be endangered by the shifting uncertainties of our current fragmented social
debates. But there is a risk that we will lose the clarity attained in that
most dramatic confrontation with the extremity of human self-assertion.
In losing sight of this epic struggle against the totalitarian spirit, we will
also lose sight of the truth about the human condition that became inexorably clear within the conflict. This would surely be the ultimate tragedy
for a tragic age. For it is indisputably the existential demonstration of the
power of moral truth that is the most precious philosophic achievement
of the century. The fate of the next century is intimately bound up with
our capacity to meditatively retrieve the insight into the human condition
that has been purchased at such a supreme price.

June, 1995

Preface

When I began the research for this book in 1984 it seemed to me that our world had reached a turning point. Now the sense of living in a transitional phase has become pervasive, especially in light of the widening disintegration of Communism. The last of the great ideological movements has lost its self-confidence and its sense of invincibility. Fast on the heels of this inner collapse is the fall of its external political claim to legitimacy. We all find ourselves wondering how political parties that no longer believe in themselves can continue to hold a monopoly on public authority. How much longer can defunct political movements retain the reins of political power? Will they be succeeded by vastly different forms of government? Or will the Communist parties metamorphose along liberal democratic lines? What kind of world will we be living in?

This is a time, in other words, for some profound reflection on the world in which we have been living in order to take the measure of the changes that are upon us. The great danger is that we will be misled by the surface appearances of events or that we will relapse into outmoded patterns of thought. Unable to find the appropriate intellectual perspective to illuminate our time, we will fail to rise to the epochal challenges presented by our historical moment. Instead of being the generation that undertook the decisive reorientation of our civilization, we will continue to drift half-consciously through the disintegrated fragments of modernity. We cannot transcend what we have not understood. Never have we been so much in need of a clear-eyed understanding of ourselves and of the world that has shaped us.

We cannot know if Communism is dead unless we know what the innermost essence of Communism has been. What is it that has constituted the core of the Communist movement, without which it preserves only its outward trappings? More important, what does the demise of this ideological movement signify for the age of ideology that has produced it and all the others? What of that most successful and most universal of all ideologies, faith in the virtually limitless power of technology? Are we beginning to see it shaken? Has the imperious standing of *homo faber* been dislodged, and what is to replace the omnipotence of humanity at the center of our world? Is there room yet for the God who creates the world that humans so desperately strive to dominate? Have we reached the point where we can admit that we can only manipulate the rich and wonderful reality we have received but have not created?

It has been to answer questions such as these that I have turned to the thinkers who are the focus of this book. They have been selected because of the depth of their penetration of the spiritual and political crisis that has defined our era. Theirs is an insight that has been achieved by living through the crisis, confronting the darkness at its core and surmounting it by means of the spiritual truth beyond it. As a consequence, they not only provide an analysis of the problems but also demonstrate the alternative vision of order capable of resolving them. Indeed, the degree to which they have won through to an order of existence beyond the ideological madness has made the depth of their understanding possible. Only someone who has broken out of the restricted horizon of ideology can see clearly what has been left behind. And only those who have fully contemplated the abyss can be sure of having attained the spiritual truth capable of overcoming it.

The task is clearly not for the faint of heart. It requires an existential descent to the depths in order to discover the reality that draws us up to the transcendent height. The ascent from the depths is not an abstraction, an idea or literary symbol. It is first and foremost a living reality that we must undergo if we wish to make contact with a wider world than the inhumanly closed logic of ideology. For this reason our study, if it takes its subject seriously, cannot confine itself to the ideas about politics or order presented by these writers. This book is not a work of literary criticism, nor of political theory, nor even of theology in the conventional sense. Primarily, it is a study of the existential search for order in soul and society by some of the most profound thinkers of the contemporary world. Our interest is less in the literary or political form of what they said, than in the illumination it can provide for an understanding of ourselves and the time in which we live.

Inevitably this more engaged reading of the texts runs the risk of misunderstanding, especially the risk that I may have lost critical distance or objectivity toward the subject matter. In response, it must be noted, first, that I have chosen the writers I have because I believe they are closer to the truth than any of their contemporaries. For this reason I will very often appear to be in agreement with them. But this is not the same as endorsing everything they say, or claiming that they have reached *the* truth. Besides, what other procedure can we follow if we are interested not in doing scholarly studies, but in getting as close to the truth about human existence in society and history as we can? Second, the purpose in undertaking a sympathetic reading of an author is always to see how far his or her understanding can be applied. What other way is there to determine its limits, if not by treating it as a guide to the world of our common experience? Finally, we are ourselves bereft of all understanding unless we are willing to place ourselves under the guidance of those who have gone before us. Few of us are up to the task of discovering the spiritual order of existence on our own. Nowhere is this more evident than in the attempt to free ourselves from the climate of ideology that has shaped us.

Understanding is always a collaborative enterprise. Beyond the broad and deep debt that I owe to those who have gone before me to open the way, I would like to acknowledge certain more particular debts. I began the research for this book shortly after my arrival at the Catholic University of America to take up a position in Christian Political Thought. I am grateful to then chair Claes Ryn for his wisdom in defining such a position, which is perhaps unique among American political science departments. In addition, the support provided by succeeding chair Jim O'Leary and by my colleagues and students in the department and at the University has been an invaluable source of sustenance. The manuscript was read in its entirety by Brendan Purcell of University College Dublin, and his perceptive suggestions were of great assistance in eliminating some of the more egregious errors. My editors at Harper & Row, especially Bill Newell, performed a like service in improving a text that would otherwise have had many more defects than it still does. Lee Cheek cheerfully assisted in the compilation of the index. I am grateful for the financial support for the research and writing provided by a Summer Stipend and a Fellowship from the National Endowment for the Humanities, and by a Summer Research Fellowship from the Earhart Foundation and for manuscript preparation by a grant from the Catholic University Research Fund. I acknowledge the permission granted by the editor of *The World and I* to publish the material on Nietzsche that originally appeared in that journal.

Finally, my deepest thanks go to my wife, Gail, who has been the constant support of all my work. I dedicate this book to her as a token of my love.

Abbreviations Used in Text

I have consulted the original texts of all of the sources used, but generally make reference only to the currently available English translation. I have adopted this procedure in the belief that it will best serve the interests of a majority of readers and avoid the more cumbersome appearance of multiple references to the same text. Those who are capable of consulting the original sources will undoubtedly have no difficulty in locating the equivalent references.

In general, I have used the already available translations, but I have not hesitated, where I felt it necessary, to modify such translations for the sake of greater accuracy. Most of the translation problems arise in relation to Solzhenitsyn. A great many of his works were rushed to publication under the pressure of his initial notoriety and since then the project of further translations seems to have slowed considerably. The new ninety-six-chapter version of *The First Circle*, for example, has still not appeared in English. This has made it necessary for me to refer to the available English edition and, where the germane material is not included, to the Russian text. We are fortunate that the final expanded version of *August 1914*, the first "knot" of his *Red Wheel*, has finally appeared in translation. But the second "knot," *October 1916*, has not yet been translated and so reference can only be made to the Russian text. However, in all such cases I have also included a chapter reference to facilitate consultation of future translations.

All titles without an abbreviation code were consulted, but not cited directly, and are included in this list for the reader's reference.

Albert Camus:

E   *Essais*. Edited by R. Quilliot and L. Faucon. Paris: Pléiade, Gallimard, 1965.

       Théâtre, récits et nouvelles. Edited by R. Quillot and L. Faucon. Paris: Pléiade, Gallimard, 1962.

MS   *The Myth of Sisyphus and Other Essays*. Translated by Justin O'Brien. New York: Vintage, 1955.

R   *The Rebel*. Translated by Anthony Bower. New York: Vintage, 1956.

RRD   *Resistance, Rebellion, and Death*. Translated by Justin O'Brien. New York: Vintage, 1960.

N   *Notebooks* Vol. 1 (1935–42). Translated by Philip Thody. Vol. 2 (1942–51). Translated by Justin O'Brien. New York: Knopf, 1963, 1965.

       Carnets. Vol. 1 (1935–42). Vol. 2 (1942–51). Paris: Gallimard, 1962, 1964.

P   *The Plague*. Translated by Stuart Gilbert. New York: Vintage, 1948.

F   *The Fall*. Translated by Justin O'Brien. New York: Vintage, 1956.

       Caligula and Three Other Plays (*The Misunderstanding, The State of Siege, The Just*). Translated by Stuart Gilbert. New York: Vintage, 1958.

       Exile and the Kingdom. Translated by Justin O'Brien. New York: Vintage, 1957.

Fyodor Dostoevsky:

       Polnoe Sobranie Sochinenii [*Collected Works*]. Leningrad: Navka, 1966–77.

DW   *The Diary of a Writer*. Translated by Boris Brasol. Santa Barbara: Peregrine Smith, 1979.

HD   *The House of the Dead*. Translated by H. Sutherland Edwards. New York: Everyman, 1962.

LFU   *Letters from the Underworld*. Translated by C. J. Hogarth. New York: Everyman, 1968.

CP   *Crime and Punishment*. Translated by Constance Garnett. New York: Everyman, 1963.

I   *The Idiot*. Translated by Henry and Olga Carlisle. New York: Signet, 1969.

P   *The Possessed*. Translated by Andrew R. MacAndrew. New York: Signet, 1962.

A   *The Adolescent*. Translated by Andrew R. MacAndrew. New York: Norton, 1971.

K   *The Brothers Karamazov*. Translated by Constance Garnett. New York: Modern Library, 1950.

Friedrich Nietzsche:

    Gesammelte Werke [*Collected Works*]. 23 vols. Munich: Musarion, 1920–29.

GM   *On the Genealogy of Morals and Ecce Homo*. Translated by Walter Kaufmann and R. J. Hollingdale. New York: Vintage, 1967.

BGE   *Beyond Good and Evil*. Translated by Walter Kaufmann. New York: Vintage, 1966.

GS   *The Gay Science*. Translated by Walter Kaufmann. New York: Vintage, 1974.

Z   *Thus Spoke Zarathustra*. Translated by Walter Kaufmann. New York: Penguin, 1978.

WP   *The Will to Power*. Translated by Walter Kaufmann. New York: Vintage, 1967.

TI   *Twilight of the Idols*, in *The Portable Nietzsche*. Edited and translated by Walter Kaufmann. New York: Viking, 1968.

AC   *The Anti-Christ*, in *The Portable Nietzsche*.

DAY   *Daybreak*. Translated by R. J. Hollingdale. New York: Cambridge University Press, 1982.

Alexander Solzhenitsyn:

    Sobranie Sochinenii [*Collected Works*]. Paris: YMCA Press, 1978–86. Eighteen volumes have so far appeared.

OC *The Oak and the Calf*. Translated by Harry Willets. New York: Harper & Row, 1979.

GA *The Gulag Archipelago*. Vol. 1. Translated by Thomas Whitney. Vol. 2. Translated by Thomas Whitney. Vol. 3. Translated by H. T. Willetts. New York: Harper & Row, 1974, 1975, 1978.

ID *One Day in the Life of Ivan Denisovich*. Translated by Ralph Parker. New York: New American Library, 1963.

CW *Cancer Ward*. Translated by Nicholas Bethell and David Burg. New York: Bantam, 1969.

FC *The First Circle*. Translated by Thomas Whitney. New York: Bantam, 1968.

  V Kruge Pervom. Sobranie Sochinenii, Vols. 1–2. 1978. This is the expanded ninety-six-chapter version of *The First Circle*. A French translation is available, *Le premier cercle*. 2 vols. Paris: Laffont, 1982.

  Krasnoe Koleso. Sobranie Sochinenii, vols. 11–18. This is Solzhenitsyn's multi-volume history of the Russian revolution, *The Red Wheel*. Three of the "knots" have so far appeared, *August 1914*, *October–November 1916*, *March 1917*, and a fourth is projected, *April 1917*.

AUG *August 1914*. Translated by H. T. Willets. New York: Farrar, Strauss, Giroux, 1989.

  Avgust Chetyrnadtsatogo. Sobranie Sochinenii, vols. 11–12. This is the final expanded version of *August 1914*. New York: Bantam, 1974.

OCT *Oktiabr' Shestnadtsago. Sobranie Sochinenii*, vols. 13–14. A French translation is available, *Novembre seize*. Paris: Fayard, 1985. [The title and all of the dates were changed, presumably in accordance with the author's wishes, to conform to the Western or Gregorian calendar. An English translation, when it appears may be called *October–November 1916*.]

  Lenin in Zurich. Translated by H. T. Willetts. New York: Bantam, 1976. This contains three chapters from *August 1914*, *October 1916*, and *March 1917*.

UR *From Under the Rubble*. Translated by A. M. Brock et al. Chicago: Regnery, 1981.

WSA *A World Split Apart*. Translated by Irina Ilovayskaya Alberti. New York: Harper & Row, 1978.

Detente: Prospects for Democracy and Dictatorship. New Brunswick: Transaction, 1980.

DOC *Solzhenitsyn: A Documentary Record*, 2nd ed. Edited by Leopold Labedz. Harmondsworth: Penguin, 1974.

Stories and Prose Poems. Translated by Michael Glenny. Harmondsworth: Penguin, 1971.

Letter to the Soviet Leaders. Translated by Hilary Sternberg. New York: Harper & Row, 1974.

The Mortal Danger. Translated by Michael Nicholson and Alexis Klimoff. New York: Harper & Row, 1981.

Eric Voegelin:

OH I *Order and History*. Vol. 1; *Israel and Revelation*. 1956.

OH II *Order and History*. Vol. 2; *The World of the Polis*. 1957.

OH III *Order and History*. Vol. 3; *Plato and Aristotle*. 1957.

OH IV *Order and History*. Vol. 4; *The Ecumenic Age*. 1974.

OH V *Order and History*. Vol. 5; *In Search of Order*. 1987. Baton Rouge: Louisiana State University Press.

NSP *The New Science of Politics*. Chicago: University of Chicago Press, 1952.

AN *Anamnesis*. Translated by Gerhart Niemeyer. Notre Dame; IN: University of Notre Dame Press, 1978.

ER *From Enlightenment to Revolution*. Edited by John H. Hallowell. Durham; NC: Duke University Press, 1975.

SPG *Science, Politics and Gnosticism*. Translated by William J. Fitzpatrick. Chicago: Regnery, 1968.

AR *Autobiographical Reflections*. Edited by Ellis Sandoz. Baton Rouge: Louisiana State University Press, 1989.

Introduction

A shift of far-reaching significance is presently taking place within Western civilization. The dominant self-understanding of social and political order is in the process of breaking down and is on the verge of being replaced by a very different conviction. No longer can we naively subscribe to the fundamental conceit from which modernity began: that human beings are capable of providing their own moral and political order. The conception of a secular society, existing without reference to any transcendent source and drawing its legitimacy entirely from humanity's autonomous self-determination, has begun to lose its appeal. That experiment has run its course. Having been brought to its limits in the twentieth century, its bankruptcy has become fully exposed. Virtually everywhere we look, the old confidence in secular rationality has been broken and the first tentative outlines of a very different understanding of order can already be discerned.

That alternative is in the direction of a rediscovery of the transcendent foundation of order. Faced with the evident inability of reason to provide the ultimate justification and motivation for order, modern human beings have again begun to look toward the source of order that lies beyond the self. A remarkable opening of the soul is taking place, as we increasingly come to realize that we are not the self-sufficient ground of our own existence. Right at the heart of contemporary secular civilization the recognition is emerging of our participation in an order of being utterly beyond our control. The old arrogance has disappeared and there are the first faint glimmerings that, perhaps, it is only through participation in the order of this transcendent source that the existence of individuals in society and history partakes of goodness and truth and reality. A widespread sense that a particular phase has reached its conclusion now prepares us to contemplate again the God who for so long has been displaced at the center of our existence. The historian James Billington has described our situation well. Reflecting on what it means to have reached the end of the modern revolutionary era with its driving passion for messianic self-salvation, he observes that he is inclined to believe that

the end may be approaching of the political religion which saw in revolution the sunrise of a perfect society. I am further disposed to wonder if this secular creed, which arose in Judeo-Christian culture, might not ultimately prove to be only a stage in the continuing metamorphosis of older forms of faith and to speculate that the belief in secular revolution, which has legitimized so much authoritarianism in the twentieth century, might dialectically prefigure some rediscovery of religious evolution to revalidate democracy in the twenty-first.[1]

That ironic sequel to the modern revolutionary and totalitarian convulsion is the subject of this book.

After Ideology is the story of how modern human beings rediscovered their oneness with God at the limit of their despair. When the cup of misery of the twentieth century had been drained of its bitterest dregs, the miracle of life and hope sprang forth anew. The possibility of resurrection has dawned for modern civilization now that the abyss of evil contained within it has been confronted and surmounted. A struggle for spiritual growth has been the indispensable means of overcoming the spiritual crisis endemic to our world. This is the startling development so little noticed amid the din and distraction, the endless competition for attention, that is the forum of discourse in contemporary society. We sense that something has changed, but we are apt to overlook its most significant dimensions. Unless it is identified for us we may not recognize the full implications of what has occurred. Such is the purpose that has inspired and informed this book.

My intention is to select those instances in which the process has been carried through to its conclusion. In them the dramatic nature of our contemporary historical moment is most fully revealed. What is occurring is nothing less than the definitive resolution of the spiritual crisis of the modern world. For this is no piecemeal effort of resistance to the erosion of moral standards, or to the expansion of individual egotism, or even to the spread of political oppression. It is a liberation from the spirit of the age that has furnished the justification for the unprecedented cruelty and the unlimited menace of our own time. This liberation has at last become possible as a result of the recognition that the evil is not simply the responsibility of this or that dictator, political system, or specific set of circumstances. The problems lie deeper in the nature of modern civilization itself. The spiritual vacuum at its core has finally been confronted. Modernity has been overcome.

Of course, it goes without saying that this recognition has not yet become a widespread social admission. As a society we are only aware of certain vague changes taking place. We understand that our historical direction is no longer that of unending technological, industrial, social, and political "progress," which is the picture that has dominated the Western imagination ever since the Enlightenment. We have not yet comprehended the degree to which we have separated ourselves from the spirit of modernity itself; we do not yet recognize the extent to which we have become in the deepest sense postmodern. That is the fascination of the thinkers who are the focus of this book. For they are distinguished from all their contemporaries by the depth of their penetration of the problems confronting us. The struggle, they realized, is not against this or that symptom of the contemporary upheaval, not even against the specific forms that tyranny and injustice may temporarily have assumed, but against the historical abyss of evil that ultimately lies at their core. As a consequence, the victory they attained is not over particular manifestations of inhumanity or vacuity, but over the underlying spirit of revolt from which these phenomena derive.

This is what makes the experiences of Dostoevsky, Camus, Solzhenitsyn, and Voegelin of more than individual importance. The problems they surmounted are the very ones with which we are faced, so that their successful resolution is not merely an interesting or edifying biographical aside. It is pregnant with significance for the future of our civilization. Insofar as some individuals have managed to extricate themselves from the ideological chaos of our time, they have uncovered the means by which all others may undergo the same liberation. They have become exemplars of the resolution of the spiritual crisis within our civilization. By their confrontation with the extremity of evil in our century, they have understood its relationship to the revolt against God at the root of the modern world. Through their successful resistance to its destructive force, they rediscovered the power of transcendent Love, from which a genuine restoration of order can begin. They have completed the course that remains to be chosen by our civilization.

What separates them even from the many others who have undergone the same kind of cathartic regeneration is precisely this elaboration of the larger philosophical significance of their experience. This is what makes them the spokesmen for the great multitude of twentieth-century human beings who have found spiritual truth, God, in the midst of suffering. Concentration camp memoirs are filled with such accounts of personal transformation under conditions of extreme suffering.[2] More generally, there are the accounts of the rediscovery of faith in the struggle with the forces of totalitarian oppression.[3] And beyond that are the many instances of conversion, which occur in our own time as much as at any time previously, where human beings undergo the opening of the soul as a result of the ordinary vicissitudes of human life.[4] All such accounts are of inestimable value in awakening us from our "public unconsciousness" of spiritual reality. They draw us up to the recognition of the higher reality of which we are today only dimly aware. But they are all in danger of being dismissed as idiosyncratic or personal experiences, unless they are taken up by individuals who have the artistic and philosophical capacity to make clear their broadly representative character.

Individual catharsis must be elaborated as the existential foundation for a new or renewed civilizational order. The relationship between the experience of rebirth within the soul and the ordering principles of social and political order must be fully articulated. This is the essence of the project undertaken by Dostoevsky, Camus, Solzhenitsyn, Voegelin, and the others who come before us with the authority of profound personal truth. They speak with a voice that arises from the truth of "living life". Yet they go beyond a merely personal perspective. Ultimately they are recognized as sources of moral authority by their contemporaries, because they give expression to the authoritative divine reality glimpsed by every human heart. That is the answer to the seemingly insoluble problems of our relativistic and immanentist age. More authentically than Heidegger they can declare that "only a god can save us," for they have opened themselves to the pull of transcendent reality.[5] All of their writings have been a convergence of attempts to make this truth transparent as the source of order in the individual, society, and history.

Their achievement might be characterized as the existential rediscovery of classical philosophy and Christianity, although they did not begin with this intention in mind. Rather, they began as human beings concerned with their own descent and that of their societies into the darkness of disorder. In the process of resistance, of mounting a critique and articulating the direction in which the alternative lies, they ended by recovering what is in essence philosophic Christianity. The big difference, however, is that they recovered it precisely in response to the crisis of the modern world. Theirs is not a revival of something in the past. but the discovery of a living truth in the present. Philosophy and Christianity have entered the modern world because they have emerged within that world, as the fullest unfolding of its own aspiration to live in the order of being and as the definitive antidote to the destructive illusions of self-perfection. From having been on the defensive for the past five hundred years, philosophy and Christianity have regained a centrality and authority within the contemporary world that is hardly short of epochal.

Because this paradigmatic shift has primarily occurred through the unfolding of an existential catharsis, the focus of this book is on the experiential foundations for order. That is inevitable but it can also be misleading. A consistent emphasis on experiences and symbols might be mistaken as a disparagement of the importance of conceptual definition and critique. No interpretation could be more inaccurate. The permanent validity of abstract or doctrinal elaboration must be acknowledged as a given. Control of meaning is virtually impossible if we operate simply on the level of experiences and symbols. There is not only the history of the Church, but also the history of philosophy to confirm this. Without the increasing precision of dogma, the content of faith and experience is forever in danger of distortion and evaporation. However, doctrines and ideas remain secondary or derivative. They have no reality unless they arise from and constantly refer back to the immediacy of lived experience. This is as true for the life of reason as for the life of faith. Whether it is desirable to recover the original engendering experience or preferable to articulate the definitional content, is entirely dependent on the circumstances of the social context.

The presupposition of this book is that our own historical moment requires a return to the primary experiences and symbols of order. Conceptual or doctrinal elaboration continues to be of value, but it cannot obviate the need to restore the existential foundations for all subsequent discourse. Intellectual critiques of ideology and theoretical defenses of virtue perform a vitally important role. But they remain ineffective as long as the opposing sides merely assert an arbitrary adherence to their respective first premises. What is required is a confrontation with those existential experiences that always and everywhere provide the foundation for order. When agreement on first principles is no longer possible, then the only option remaining is a rejuvenation of the self-evident experiences of participation in the order of reality that no human being can deny. Given our contemporary situation, we have no choice but to assign priority to the formative experiences of order. This priority should not be taken as indicative of any devaluation of the struggle for doctrinal truth.

In the same way, the fact that I do not begin with a defense of philosophy and Christianity should not be interpreted as an effort to stand outside of them. There is no third or independent perspective from which I attempt to sit in judgment over them. Rather my intention is to follow the existential course by which the concrete truth of philosophy and Christianity has been rediscovered in the contemporary world. Inevitably, this means that we must arrive at philosophy and Christianity, as so much of our society must, from the outside. The tradition has been lost as a source of public authority. It can only be recovered by undertaking a genuine effort of rediscovery. We must begin from the position of late modern men and women as we find ourselves today. Philosophy and Christianity can become a living source of order for society as a whole only if their truth is drawn out from the experiences of our own modern world. A doctrinal or discursive exposition will no longer work. Instead, the effort to communicate must be in the mode of an existential drama. Truth must be seen to arise from the unfolding of the crisis within the modern project itself. Through the confrontation with its inner contradictions, the nature of the choices before us will be laid bare, and the correlative movement of repentance and redemption can emerge into its fullest reality. An alternative title is the one selected by Henri de Lubac for his own earlier study of the culmination of the modern crisis. His *Drama of Atheist Humanism* is in many respects a model of the kind of nonjudgmental exploration of the existential logic of the problems I have in mind.[6] If my own efforts come at all close to this precedent, the result will, I believe, be of service to philosophy and Christianity.

Besides, a defense of philosophy and Christianity, even if it were not so likely to be ineffective, would probably be superfluous. Philosophy and Christianity contain the evidence for their truth within themselves, and would not have functioned as the pillars of Western civilization for so long if that were not the case. A much more fruitful approach is to take up the struggle for order in the present. We must begin with the problems to which philosophy and Christianity are the answer. In the process of grappling with the spiritual crisis of our world, we are eventually brought back to the recognition of the symbolisms by which they can be resolved. Rather than attempting to demonstrate the truth of philosophy and Christianity, we confront the problems of order today that reveal the truth of philosophy and Christianity. We do not begin with the presupposition that philosophy and Christianity are the solution. Instead, we pursue the inner logic of the problems, which arrives, inexorably, at the conclusion that only a philosophic-Christian response can adequately provide what is needed. We do not ask whether it is possible to be a Christian or a philosopher in the modern world. Our impulse is to remain faithful to the nature of the world we live in. Then the question becomes whether it is possible any longer to be conscientiously modern without reaching up to the horizon of philosophic Christianity.

NOTES

1. James H. Billington, *Fire in the Minds of Men: Origins of the Revolutionary Faith* (New York: Basic Books, 1980), 14.

2. From the Nazi camps there are Viktor E. Frankl, *Man's Search for Meaning*, trans. Ilse Lasch (New York: Washington Square Press, 1963), and Etty Hillesum, *An Interrupted Life: The Diaries of Etty Hillesum 1941–43* (New York: Washington Square Press, 1983). The Soviet camps have produced, besides Solzhenitsyn, Walter J. Ciszek, S. J., *He Leadeth Me* (New York: Doubleday, 1973); Natan Sharansky, *Fear No Evil*, trans. Stefani Hoffman (New York: Random House, 1988); and Irina Ratushinskaya, *Grey Is the Color of Hope*, trans. Alyona Kojevnikov (New York: Knopf, 1988). Even Castro's Cuban gulag made its contribution to the literature on spiritual rebirth, in Armando Valladares, *Against All Hope*, trans. Andrew Hurley (New York: Ballantine, 1986). The Chinese experience has produced Nien Cheng, *Life and Death in Shanghai* (New York: Grove Press, 1987).

3. See for example, Nadezhda Mandelstam, *Hope against Hope*, trans. Max Hayward (New York: Atheneum, 1970); and Tatiana Goricheva, *Talking about God Is Dangerous*, trans. John Bowden (New York: Crossroad, 1986).

4. C. S. Lewis provides a well-articulated case in *Surprised by Joy* (New York: Harcourt Brace Jovanovich, 1955) and *A Grief Observed* (New York: Bantam, 1963). Or there is the narrative of Thomas Merton, *The Seven Storey Mountain* (New York: Harcourt Brace Jovanovich, 1948).

5. "If I may answer briefly, and perhaps clumsily, but after long reflection: Philosophy will be unable to effect any immediate change in the current state of the world. This is true not only of philosophy but of all purely human reflection and endeavor. Only a god can save us. The only possibility available to us is that by thinking and poetizing we prepare a readiness for the appearance of a god, or for the absence of a god in [our] decline, insofar as in view of the absent god we are in a state of decline." Martin Heidegger, "'Only a God Can Save Us': The *Spiegel* Interview (1966)," in *Heidegger: The Man and the Thinker*, ed. Thomas Sheehan (Chicago: Precedent, 1981), 57.

6. Henri de Lubac, *The Drama of Atheist Humanism*, trans. Edith M. Riley (New York: New American Library, 1950). A parallel approach is developed by Nicolai Chiaromonte: "A return to reality after mind and soul have been beclouded can only take place through disillusion and despair. Yet this suffering will remain sterile and the recovery of reason impossible unless a true conversion takes place." *The Paradox of History* (Philadelphia: University of Pennsylvania Press, 1985), 148.

CHAPTER 1

The Dead End of Modernity

We are living in a time when the crisis of the modern world has reached its denouement. All that has been present from the inception of modernity has now been unfolded, and we are privy to consequences that our predecessors could only glimpse as they launched us on this great collaborative experiment. What appeared to them as the way toward a future of uninterrupted happiness is now before us as a reality that falls far short of total satisfaction. The age that began with the glory of the Renaissance, the bright expectations of the Enlightenment, and the energies of the scientific, industrial, and political revolutions has devolved into the horror, vacuity, and mediocrity of the twentieth century. So sharp is the contrast that we are left wondering whether there is indeed any connection between these developments. Is there a necessary link between the promise of universal human progress and the reality of persistent human failure, between the vision of a brave new world and the recognition of its staggering spiritual costs, between the vast expansion of human power and the equally vast abuse of power in our own time? This question more than any other gives us the sense of living, if not at the end of the modern age, at least at a decisive turning point within it. For the question indicates the extent to which we have lost faith in the modern experiment and its Promethean myth.[1]

We no longer look toward the future in a state of wide-eyed anticipation. A spirit of weariness and wariness has set in as a result of the cumulative disillusionments of recent history. Nowhere is this decline more evident than in the disintegration of the ideological mass movements. When one considers the level of support and the degree of respect enjoyed by movements such as Marxism, national socialism, fascism, positivism, and Freudianism in the early part of the century and the extent to which their appeal has now either evaporated or severely eroded, the change has been nothing short of revolutionary. The collapse has been so decisive that it is no longer possible, outside a few remaining enclaves, to be taken seriously as a thinker if one is an ideologist. This is not to say that such movements do not continue to exercise considerable intellectual and political influence, but the tendency is entirely in the opposite direction and away from their original systematizing impulse. For there is all the difference in the world between regarding Marxism as a critique of the problems of early capitalism or of the economic rationalizations that are found to conceal them, and the assertion that it provides the indispensable means for the realization of universal human emancipation. We live in a post-ideological age to the extent that we have lost faith in all systems and, with it, the faith that had inspired system builders from Descartes on: in the power of humanity to dominate reality as a whole.

The force that has accomplished this revolution has been none other than the relentless pressure of reality itself. No matter how often explanations and predictions are revised, the real world refuses to be confined within the limits of a system, and the attempt to act on such a basis has repeatedly led to the most bitterly disappointing results. What has shifted this experiment to a new level in the contemporary period is the attainment of political power by the carriers of these ideological faiths. The horrors of our time have been attributable not so much to the perennial lusts, stupidities, and misunderstandings that have always plagued the relationships of human beings, but more to a quite novel passion to compel recalcitrant reality to fit within the perimeters of one or another intellectual system. That most "twentieth century" of phenomena the concentration camp, with its attendant instruments terror and the totalitarian state, has as its goal not some finite political objective but the final and irrevocable transformation of human nature itself.[2] It is not enough that the enemies of the regime be subdued, but friends and foes alike must be completely remade to become the perfect ideological automata, carrying out the role that is required of them without residual personal expression. The point is, as one of Solzhenitsyn's characters ironically remarks, to demonstrate the truth of Marx's famous dictum that "circumstances determine consciousness" (FC, 291). By means of total domination, the ideological blueprint can be imposed on receptive human material in which "each and every person can be reduced to a never-changing identity of reactions, so that each of these bundles of reactions can be exchanged at random for any other."[3]

The sheer scale of this catastrophe in which totalitarian governments have so far killed, apart from those who have perished in wars, more than 100 million people,[4] has finally begun to provoke a far-reaching revision of our conception of the modern world and of the ideological movements that have dominated it. Even the most universalistic and successful of these movements, Communism, has now been unmasked and linked so irrevocably with extermination and repression that the Soviet term *gulag*, no longer needs translation into any of the Western languages.[5] For although rational critiques of the ideologies have been available almost from their first appearance, and demonstrations of their unworkability and unreality, even warnings of the disastrous consequences of putting them into practice, have been equally abundant, all of this has been to no avail.[6] What understanding and persuasion could not accomplish has now come about through experience. Even countries that are officially committed to an ideological construction are seeking ways to edge themselves away from the damaging impractical results (albeit without dismantling their ideology). A prolonged exposure to the consequences appears to have been the only way to break the infatuation with these systems. Individuals can be persuaded but, as Eric Voegelin observes, a whole society "probably has to go through all the misery of revolutions and world wars until even the most stupid person understands that he doesn't get anywhere that way. It is our critical situation today that these revolutionary communal experiences which started in the eighteenth century have run to their death now."[7]

We have had, in other words, long enough for the fever of ideology to wear itself out. The nonoccurrence of the Parousia has always caused the fire of apocalyptic expectations to cool and compelled a readjustment to the conditions of continued existence in an unregenerate world. We are now at a stage where all of the great ideological systems have been created and found wanting, and there are no more new ones waiting to be tried. For the past two hundred years "every possible locale where one could misplace the [divine] ground has been exhausted," whether the key has been sought in race, economics, science, sexual desire, or nationality. This is why Voegelin is so confident in predicting that "nobody will be a great thinker of the type of Marx or Hegel or Comte in the future, because that has all been done once. There will be no further ideological thinkers of any stature. We have had them all."[8] What remains of their appeal after the intellectual deficiencies have been exposed has been overwhelmed by the confrontation with the practical consequences they have produced. We know where

such systematizations lead and it is no longer possible to be an ideologist "without making oneself a silent accomplice in every atrocity in
Auschwitz or in the Gulag Archipelago."[9]

Power beyond Good and Evil

The struggle to break free of the influence of ideology requires that we
engage in more than ineffectual hand-wringing. It makes it necessary
that we take account of the significance of ideology within the structure
of modern civilization as a whole. We must recognize that the ideological mass movements represent not an isolated or idiosyncratic reversion to barbarism, a random interruption of an otherwise smoothly
progressing civilization, but the logical outcome of the direction we
have been following since the Renaissance. After all, these have been
the major intellectual movements of the past two hundred years, and
the murderous consequences of their social expansion could be clearly
foreseen by such perceptive nineteenth-century thinkers as Dostoevsky
and Nietzsche.[10] Moreover, they have clothed themselves in the authority of the most successful branch of our civilization—modern science—
as befitted the original connotation of the term *ideology*. It was coined
to describe the application of the methods of the natural sciences to the
study of the individual and society; the intention was to reduce all
human behavior to a single causal system that could be fitted within
the comprehensive science of zoology.[11] But most telling of all is that
the ideological thinkers have sought no more than to carry out the
central modern project of, in the words of Francis Bacon, applying the
power of science for "the relief of man's estate." Such a realization
compels us to confront anew and even more resolutely the question
with which we began: How can the pursuit of universal human well-
being result in so much universal human misery? How can an age that
sets itself up to surpass all predecessors in satisfying the needs of humanity surpass all others in the suffering inflicted on human beings?

The answer cannot lie in ignorance, error, or accident, but in something that has been integral to the humanitarian project from the start.
Within the dream of limitlessly expanding power in the service of humanity are the seeds of the nightmarish abuse of that power in the
destruction of human beings. For it is not something incidental, but an
essential consequence that as humanity's power has increased the capacity to virtuously guide its use has declined. In the beginning this
was hardly noticeable as men like Galileo and Bacon sought to shake
off the Aristotelian and scholastic understanding of the universe, in

order to make room for a mathematical experimental science that lifted us "from the closed world to an infinite universe."[12] Before long, however, it became apparent that the new science, which in Bacon's conception identified knowledge with power, was premised on a rejection of the fundamental teleological perspective on reality that had formed the worldview of Western civilization since antiquity. Teleology had provided the foundation not only for the understanding of nature but for the ethical and political order of human life as well. Now that knowledge had become identified with the power of making, all fixed points of reference were lost. Of what do we even have knowledge? It is certainly not of fixed natures with determinate ends, since it is precisely that which is to be determined. Humanity has set itself above nature and must choose its ends in freedom. The Faustian bargain, by which a vast new power is given to us at the cost of the soul that alone can provide the wisdom for its use, is the problem that lies at the very beginning of the modern world.

From one aspect the history of the succeeding centuries can be regarded as a progressive unfolding of the logic of this starting point. Once the authority of the ancient worldview had been undermined, it was inevitable that the challenge should spread to the symbols of reason and revelation that were the very core of the philosophic-Christian conception of order. Called upon to justify the "innate ideas" of order that were the foundation of its hierarchy of ends, the classical understanding of reason was found deficient and demoted to its modern truncated counterpart as an instrument of the passions.[13] A similar test was applied to the truth of revelation, as the sacred Scriptures became the focus of scrutiny by the new empirical science. Not too surprisingly, their meaning also proved elusive when the texts were pressed for the factual contents of the experiences behind them, and treated by the methodologies of analysis used for any intramundane historical documents.[14] This is the background that ultimately lies behind the infamous conflicts of science and religion over the past three hundred years. While the surface disputes may in retrospect appear inconclusive and exaggerated, what was at stake was the very existence of reason and revelation as authorities independent of science.[15] A similar type of issue is involved in the conflict between romanticism and rationalism, insofar as the romantics sought to emphasize the knowledge of nature that is necessarily excluded in an exploitive analytic approach.

In all these areas the tensions still remain, although by virtue of its pragmatic success science has attained the preponderance of public authority. That is, until now. A new phase of the problem has opened up with the revolutionary developments in the biological sciences, where attention is increasingly directed not only to the control of nature in general but also of human nature in particular.[16] For it is when we ponder the techniques and possibilities of genetic engineering and behavioral control that the radical lostness of our situation becomes clear. When we possess the capacity to make a person into whatever we wish him or her to be, by what absolutes of value or right are we to be guided? We know what is to be produced in this person so that everything of value within him or her is something that we have imparted. There is nothing inherently worthwhile in the person as an end-in-himself or -herself apart from what has been given; there is certainly nothing that is prior to the very existence of the individual. The quest for the "relief of man's estate" has here clearly reached a limiting point, once the human being who is to be benefited has no existence apart from the benefits that are bestowed. Whose estate in this case is to be relieved? Inevitably, we find ourselves drifting toward some functional or utilitarian justification. What is certain is that nothing is being done for the sake of the concrete human being before us.

This state of affairs is not too surprising given that contemporary science, once it turned its attention toward the person as its object, has tended more and more to eliminate the notion of the "distinctively human." Viewed from the perspective of biological evolution, biochemical processes, psychological conditioning, and social influences, a human being appears to be "nothing but" the finite processes and structures that constitute him or her. The tendency to slip into reductionistic fallacies is very great when such unintegrated and partial perspectives are regarded as the authoritative understanding of the concrete person. But the temptation becomes irresistible in the absence of any countervailing spiritual vision that would emphasize, with St. Augustine, that "man is an abyss so profound as to be hidden to him in whom it is."[17] At the same time, the fragmentary analyses of the sciences are held to be validated by the immediate pragmatic success of their manipulations. "Here, perhaps," Leon Kass has observed, "is the most pernicious result of technological progress—more dehumanizing than any actual manipulation or technique, present or future. We are witnessing the erosion, perhaps the final erosion, of the idea of man as something splendid or divine, and its replacement with a view of man, no less than nature, as simply more raw material for manipulation and homogenization."[18]

Among the first to recognize the peculiar helplessness of modern humans before our own newfound power was the Belfast-born scholar

C. S. Lewis. In an incisive short essay, *The Abolition of Man*, he explained what the notion of our conquest of nature "must always and essentially be." Regardless of whether it is used wisely or foolishly, by good persons or evil, "what we call Man's power over Nature turns out to be a power exercised by some men over other men with Nature as its instrument."[19] The danger becomes progressively more acute as we seek to control ever more completely the nature and development of human life. If that goal of total domination were to be attained then we would have broken the link with any conception of the human good to be served. The "conditioners," in Lewis's terminology, would be left to determine what kind of humanity to create and what kind of good is to define it.

However far they go back, or down, they can find no ground to stand on. Every motive they try to act on becomes at once a *petitio*. It is not that they are bad men. They are not men at all. Stepping outside the *Tao*, they have stepped into the void. Nor are their subjects necessarily unhappy men. They are not men at all: they are artifacts. Man's final conquest has proved to be the abolition of Man.[20]

Without rational criteria to guide their choices, the conditioners would be left with nothing but whim, impulse, or chance to guide them. "Nature, untrammelled by values, rules the Conditioners and, through them, all humanity. Man's conquest of Nature turns out, in the moment of its consummation, to be Nature's conquest of Man."[21]

Having confronted thus the end point of the process, we begin to see what is involved as the essence of the modern project: to liberate humanity from the shackles of traditional morality in order to expand limitlessly our power of subordinating the whole of existence to our fulfillment. The "arrogance of humanism," to borrow the phrase of David Ehrenfeld, can brook no principle of opposition to its Promethean drive.[22] Nothing can be allowed to stand in the way of attaining human happiness, least of all humanity itself. It is in this sense that the demand for new technological developments and for their immediate implementation becomes an all-conquering pressure, against which it is sheer fantasy to erect the paper barriers of ethical codes and safeguards. We are constantly reminded of the necessity for science to have an ethical basis and repeatedly harangued on the importance of using the power of science for exclusively beneficial purposes. But if it were so easy, surely this could have been achieved long ago? The dream of "concerned scientists," of employing nuclear power for peaceful purposes alone, arises from a blindness to the reality that power once it has been made available remains forever available to do evil as well as good. It allows those who possess it to forever threaten, withhold, or inflict it on those who do not. There can be no such thing as a power for good that does not also include the power to do evil. It is in the illusion that the development of power will be sufficient in itself to realize all the blessings of happiness, that the chief error of our technological age consists. A belated attempt to insert occasional moral provisos will not be enough to overcome it.

Seen against this background of faith in the efficacy of power, the modern ideological movements and their totalitarian offspring do not appear so unrepresentative. They are simply the most extreme manifestations of this faith, for they are founded on the conviction of possessing the means of bringing about the final perfection of human life in society and history. Supremely confident in the rightness of their goal, the ideologists skip blithely over the traditional conventions of morality; they are no longer bound by the outmoded moral sense of a world that through their actions is soon to be left far behind. The result is identical to Lewis's description of the conditioners. With nothing but the absolute goal of the future to guide them they act on the basis of whim, impulse, or self-interest—in short, they are invaded by the forces of evil that for millennia human beings have sought to resist. The only difference is that it is no longer recognized as evil, and that makes its influence all the more insidious. Ideological activism consists in the exercise of power not only without moral restraints, but also without even the inhibiting recognition that such restraints should apply. This explains the extraordinary phenomenon of our time that Camus has called "logical crime." "On the day when crime dons the apparel of innocence," he goes on to say, "it is innocence that is called upon to justify itself" (R 4). When evil is systematically committed in the name of good, it is clear that any residual influence of morality in the exercise of power has been thoroughly evacuated. We live in a world where might really does *make* right.

That this outcome is no mere aberration is emphatically brought home to us by the realization that it is the end deliberately envisaged by the most far-seeing modern thinkers. The representative Hegelian project, for example, of overcoming all the diremptions of our human existence in the final universal self-reconciliation of Spirit in his System, is intended to bring about the end of history. It abolishes all higher courts of judgment other than the now comprehensively revealed order of all that is. This is the "universal and homogeneous" state announced by Hegel's most astute twentieth-century reader, Alexander Kojève. The latter recognized the extent to which the completion of all things would also mean the abolition of the restless, inquiring, searching creature that is the human. Reflecting on what human life could be when all the fundamental questions had been settled, Kojève speculated that it could only mean a return to natural animal existence, as in contemporary American consumerism, or the elaboration of a snobbish formalism without content, as in Japanese Shintoism.[23] In either case there is nothing further to be attained; when all possibilities have been realized then nothing is any longer of value. We exist beyond good and evil. It is no wonder therefore that Kojève once fancied that it was Stalin and not Napoleon, as Hegel thought, who had brought about the end of history and that he, Kojève, was the messenger charged with proclaiming this final comprehensive truth.[24] In his urbane untroubled acceptance of all the horrors of our time we encounter the supreme expression of the logic of the closed system. For however much we may dislike his conclusions, as Barry Cooper has pointed out, Kojève's explication of Hegel provides the clearest account of much of the self-understanding of the contemporary world. It is a vision that extends from the efficiency of the multinational enterprise to the rationality of the Gulag Archipelago, that comprehends the pervasiveness of the technological society as well as the ubiquity of the terror of nuclear destruction.

The Collapse of Every Moral Response

Nevertheless, it would be a mistake to identify modern civilization only with its most manifest disasters. Besides the murderous grotesque of totalitarianism there are many achievements in which we can take a legitimate pride of accomplishment. Not the least of these have been the hitherto successful efforts to resist and subdue the worst excesses of the totalitarian spirit. The very real achievements of the sciences and technology are not to be minimized, nor the fact that they have made it possible for the earth to support a larger number of people, enjoying greater health, abundance, and leisure than have ever existed before. There has even been a heightened awareness that this ever-increasing freedom from material necessity is not an end in itself, but should provide the means for modern men and women to pursue the higher ends of the good life for themselves and all others. Along with the emphasis on extending the range of rational instrumental control there has always been a countermovement within modernity, of dissatisfaction with power as a self-sufficient principle. The great philosophic minds of the preceding centuries have been profoundly aware of the vacuum created by the disappearance of the classical and Judeo-Christian worldview. They have consistently sought to provide the spiritual foundation for the new moral and political order that now exists without benefit of its traditional religious underpinnings.

It is to the outcome of this aspect of the modern experiment that we must turn if we wish to take the full measure of the crisis that is upon us. For by definition a civilization is in a state of crisis not when its order has broken down for one reason or another, but when the attempt to restore the authoritative order of society is itself ineffective and thereby serves only to exacerbate the original problem. Such is precisely the case with most of the attempts to provide a rational vindication of morality from Locke to the present. They have been undertaken by thinkers who have wished to preserve the traditional Christian understanding of the virtues, although on a different foundation. If even they have not been able to make the case persuasive, then the individual and political good is left without a justification. The way is then open for the untrammelled exercise of power without restraint, since no basis exists for a principled opposition to totalitarianism. In the failure of modern philosophy to provide an alternative to the foundational role of religion, we can recognize both the clearest illumination of the collapse of modernity and one of its central constitutive causes.[25]

The story has already been well worked over and we need only refer to some of the highlights covered in Alasdair MacIntyre's recent survey of the problem. He correctly identifies the initial awareness of the crisis in the seventeenth century and the great attempts at a rational resolution with the thinkers of the Enlightenment and their successors.[26] In many ways Locke, although not discussed by MacIntyre, is the one who sets the terms of the problem because he provides the empiricist tools by which the classical-Christian foundations are removed, and by means of which the new autonomous humanist order is proposed to be established. Beyond the mere proposal, however, Locke was unable or unwilling to go. The first to develop one of the possible alternatives was David Hume, who, having rejected instrumental reason as a source of moral purpose, sought the foundation of morality in the life of the passions. But this compelled him to resort to various subterfuges, including the assertion of an innate wellspring of sympathy, as the only way of disguising the lack of any adequate moral ground. Immanuel Kant took up the challenge of Hume's failure and sought to find a basis in reason. His "categorical imperative" was among the most successful attempts (witness its continuities to the present), but it too was ultimately unable to transcend its formalism to provide a basis for substantive rules of morality. The problem is, as MacIntyre among others points out, "I can without any inconsistency whatsoever flout it; 'Let everyone except me be treated as a means' may be immoral, but it is not inconsistent and there is not even any inconsistency in willing a universe of egotists all of whom live by this maxim."[27] As a consequence, the search is eventually reduced to Kierkegaard's notion of a radical choice. We *choose* the reason that is to establish our moral principles even though it can no longer claim to have any foundation in rationality. The final admission in this endeavor is, as even Kant was brought to conclude, that morality cannot ultimately dispense with the theological "postulates" of God, human freedom, and the immortality of the soul.

Moral philosophy, insofar as it sought a rational foundation in the post-Kantian period, looked first toward a pseudo-objective ultimate such as Bentham's "greatest happiness of the greatest number." But Mill's analysis of the utilitarian conception of happiness exposed its purely subjective character. He demonstrated the incommensurability of different pleasures and the impossibility of determining what the principle is to mean. Utilitarianism degenerated in philosophical circles into intuitionism and emotivism, and the subsequent recognition that it could be used to justify virtually any course of action has removed it from the list of respectable options. More recent attempts have searched for a neo-Kantian foundation in the concept of rights. The only difficulty is that they have either presupposed the existence of a social order recognizing rights and hence have not found a universal basis in reason, or they have conceded that rights cannot be demonstrated and yet gone on to assert them as the universal starting point for any discussion of order.[28]

The intriguing feature of MacIntyre's presentation of this largely Anglo-American tradition in philosophy—one in which he is himself clearly steeped—is that he follows through to the practical social consequences of the theoretical wasteland. To a considerable extent, the true nature of the situation has not been recognized because of an unwillingness to admit the philosophic bankruptcy of our whole moral outlook. The conviction remains that human beings "ought always to be treated as ends-in-themselves and never as a means," but we can no longer give an adequate reason for it. We take refuge in a host of "moral fictions" such as intuitionism, appeals to self-evidence, and (in the case of the UN Declaration on Human Rights) simply silence. Those who wield authority in society must stake their claim to it on technical expertise and efficiency, not on a knowledge of the human good, because the subjective realm of values has irrevocably separated from the objective world of facts. And since none of the purportedly "factual" justifications are valid—there is no science to demonstrate the alleged effectiveness of either the manager or the therapist—the effect is to leave us "without any genuine distinction between manipulative and nonmanipulative social relations."[29] This accounts, in MacIntyre's view, for the interminability and incommensurability of moral debate in contemporary society. No commonly understood foundations exist by means of which such debate can be settled. We vacillate between an individualistic profession of rights and a bureaucratic assertion of utility without ever approaching a conclusion. "The mock rationality of the debate conceals the arbitrariness of the will to power at work in its resolution."[30] It forces MacIntyre to conclude at the end of his examination that a "new dark age" is upon us, in which once again "politics is civil war carried on by other means."[31]

The Crisis of Nihilism Exposed: Nietzsche

The characterization of the present as a new dark age is reminiscent of the prophetic reflections of Friedrich Nietzsche at the dawn of the contemporary period. It is moreover no accident that MacIntyre's analysis derives a good deal, as even the language indicates, from the most penetrating diagnostician of the modern world. He correctly regards Nietzsche as "the Kamehameha II of the European tradition," an analogy with the king who abolished the defunct taboos of Polynesian society through his own declarative utterance. For like the Hawaiian king, Nietzsche did nothing more than express a truth that everyone else sought to avoid; he recognized that the morality and ideology in which European society had tried to clothe itself were nonexistent. The values, beliefs, and systems that they held onto were already crumbling and were soon to disappear. They were based on a rejection of life itself that could only be self-defeating. In Nietzsche's view, modern men and women denied the very source from which the strength of any conviction must of necessity be derived: that it leads toward more life or a more real life, and not less. The contemporary political movements, whether liberalism, socialism, utilitarianism, positivism, or anarchism, were, despite their differences, united around their commitment to ideas, to an unreal future, to abstraction, as a reality superior to the force of living life itself. In all of them Nietzsche discerned the same "will to negate life" (*WP*, 77) that belied the humanitarian espousals of their proponents.

He compared the preachers of equality with tarantulas, for they aim at poisoning the very core of human nature itself. By seeking to restrain and break the strong in the name of protecting the weak, they undermine the only source of strength from which human beings, whether strong or weak, can hope to attain whatever life, light, and joy is afforded to us by the harsh exigencies of existence. At the same time they reveal the extent to which their own motivations arise from a hatred of life and the desire to work their revenge upon it. *Ressentiment*, the resentment of the strong by the weak, is the sentiment that Nietzsche sees as the universal perversion of the instinctive will to power that is present in all things; the only consolation it contains is that as a rejection of life it is self-defeating and will lead to its own overcoming. The drive for equality, for example, is betrayed by the self-assertive individualism (whether individually or collectively expressed in liberalism or socialism) with which it is pursued (*WP*, 411–12). All of the ideological systems will when pushed to the logical extreme reveal the will to power that remains their only genuine root.

Nietzsche flatly rejected the possibility of a moral source because he refused to admit the existence of morality as such. What humanity calls morality is only one more form assumed by the will to power. If we take one of the most impressive modern attempts to demonstrate the existence of moral principle, Kant's categorical imperative, we find according to Nietzsche that it too is without foundation. To the firmness and unconditionality of the assertion that "here everyone must judge as I do", Nietzsche responds; "Rather admire your *selfishness* at this point. For it is selfish to experience one's own judgement as a universal law; and this selfishness is blind, petty, and frugal because it betrays that you have not yet discovered yourself nor created for yourself an ideal of your own, your very own—for that could never be somebody else's and much less that of all, all" (*GS*, 265). Like the more generally acknowledged foundation, the voice of conscience, the question is repeatedly begged of Why should I consider this right? What impels me to regard it in this way? Behind every appeal to reason and truth is the self that has adopted this means to the enlargement of its power. This is why Nietzsche regards morality as self-contradictory, because the very selflessness that it touts is motivated wholly by the love of self, by the desire to feel superior to the world and to others, and by the will to power.[32] His most profound insight was that morality, when it is carried far enough and required to submit to its own law, "will bring about its own destruction through an act of self overcoming" (*GM*, 161).

So ends the modern experiment in creating an autonomous morality, preserving Christian morality without God. In Nietzsche's view, it was doomed to fail. He took it as axiomatic that the realization that "God is dead" would lead to the collapse of everything that had been built upon the Christian faith, including "the whole of our European morality" (*GS*, 279). Kant had already demonstrated that morality cannot do without faith in God, freedom, and immortality (*GS*, 264). Now the modern movements such as liberalism and socialism were about to show that, despite their character as "this worldly" religions (*WP*, 20) or "heirs of Christianity" (*BGE*, 116), they could not ultimately sustain their commitment to the absolute worth of human beings without a sense of their transcendent significance.[33] "At bottom, man has lost faith in his own value when no infinitely valuable whole works through him" (*WP*, 12). And more generally, Nietzsche goes on to explain that "every moral value system (that of Buddhism, for example) ends in nihilism: this is to be expected in Europe. One still hopes to get along with a moralism without religious background: but that necessarily leads to nihilism. In religion the constraint is lacking to consider *ourselves* as value-positing" (*WP*, 16). He reserves his severest criticism for those who, like the English, believe that morality is possible without Christianity. For they refuse to see that they are still so Christian that they have merely overlooked the very "conditional character" of their own value judgments (*TI*, 515–16). Without a transcendent authorization, moral principles can only be validated by human choice.

The collapse of the modern project of creating a secular humanist order is, however, only the final act of a much greater drama that has been unfolding in Western civilization since its inception. It is testimony to the depth of Nietzsche's vision that he saw the modern crisis as part of the crisis in philosophic Christianity itself. He recognized that "the anarchist and the Christian have the same origin," together with all of the political movements that lie between them (*AC*, 647).[34] This is why the analysis of the contemporary chaos led Nietzsche to explore its roots in the Platonic-Jewish-Christian rejection of life and its natural values. In his most polemical work on the subject, *The Anti-Christ*, he traced the roots of the crisis back, not to Christ, but to the Christianity invented by his followers—above all to the priestly character of Paul that was defined by a hatred of life and the power of fate. Nietzsche regarded Christ as a preacher of a religion of love, someone who sought to overcome the separation between human beings and reality by the kind of childlike self-surrender embodied in Dostoevsky's figure of the idiot. "In truth, there was only one Christian, and he died on the cross" (*AC*, 612). Nietzsche regarded it as a "world-historic irony" (*AC*, 609) that Christ's death, which had sought to demonstrate his superiority over *ressentiment*, should have been distorted by his followers into an expression of their vengeful longing to escape existence. By inventing a faith in immortality, they shifted the center of gravity from this life to one beyond it. They thereby gave rise to the spirit of asceticism that in the last resort "would rather will nothingness than not will" (*GM*, 163). It is not merely the disconnection of philosophic Christianity as either the explicit or implicit basis for morality and politics that constitutes for Nietzsche the crisis of the modern world. It is the realization of the hollowness that was at the core of those ancient symbolisms from the start.

Nietzsche did not coin the term nihilism (it had already appeared by 1862 in Turgenev's *Fathers and Sons*), but he did adopt it as the label best suited to the character of the present age. When he spoke of relating the history of the next two centuries, he described it as "the advent of nihilism" (*WP*, 3). It is "the end of Christianity at the hands of its own morality," when "the sense of truthfulness, developed highly by Christianity, is nauseated by the falseness and mendaciousness of all Christian interpretations of the world and of history" (*WP*, 7). Nihilism is, in Nietzsche's definition, the point that is reached when "the highest values devaluate themselves" (*WP*, 9). The confession is finally wrung from us or perhaps exultantly proclaimed by us: "Nothing is true, all is permitted" (*Z*, 274; *GM*, 150). Having contemplated thus the abysmal emptiness at its core Nietzsche could foresee the catastrophe toward which European culture had been moving and which has been so abundantly realized within the twentieth century. It has perfectly fulfilled his prediction of being externally an "age of tremendous wars, upheavals, explosions," and internally "even greater weakness of man, events as excitants" (*WP*, 79–80). At the same time, Nietzsche was more than an acute observer of the sickness of Western civilization, for he also sought a remedy by suffering through the disease himself and overcoming it. He referred to himself as "the first perfect nihilist of Europe who, however, has even now lived through the whole of nihilism, to the end, leaving it behind, outside himself" (*WP*, 3). As a consequence, he left his own mark on the unfolding of the crisis, and it is in Nietzsche's own struggle to transcend nihilism that we confront the modern problem at its deepest level.

He sought to free himself from the contrived and self-serving nature of the values that humanity has so far adopted, in order to return to

the one indubitable reality that is behind them all in the force of life
itself. For no matter how much a particular value system might reject
life explicitly, implicitly it cannot avoid affirming the truth of life that
is its own ultimate source. This is moreover not a mask for some ulterior purpose, but the simple recognition that beyond all appeals to purpose stands the inescapable and impenetrable purpose of life itself. The
desolate emptiness of nihilism can be overcome by returning to the
innocent childlike unity with life, the playful creation of values that is
no longer disturbed by the intrusion of reflection and separation (Z,
"Three Metamorphoses"). It makes no sense to ask the meaning of life.
"One would require a position *outside* of life, and yet have to know it
as well as one, as many, as all who have lived, in order to be permitted
even to touch the problem of the *value* of life: reasons enough to comprehend that this problem is for us an unapproachable problem" (*TI*,
490). It is in terms of life that other values are to be justified, for "life
itself forces us to posit values" (*TI*, 490). The goal of making contact
with this one reality that is serenely and supremely beyond question
was the intention that guided Nietzsche's tortured search for a truth
beyond nihilism.

It first led him back to the force that he had discerned as the reality
behind all religion and morality: the will to power. From there it
brought him to the discovery of this very will as the inexhaustible procreative will of life. "And life itself confided this secret to me: 'Behold,'
it said, 'I am *that which must always overcome itself*'" (Z, 115). Nietzsche
was always careful to insist that this is not a mere will to life or survival
(as in Darwin), but a will to power in which life sacrifices itself for
power. It is the drive that he found in all living things, human and
nonhuman, and even in the hearts of those who claimed to pursue a
dogmatic abstraction contrary to it. In the forthright acceptance of the
will to power he felt he had found the means of transcending nihilism,
by overcoming the spirit of *ressentiment*, of cruelty and revenge, that
had been inspired by the terror of the meaninglessness of existence.
For once we have ceased to be revolted by the sufferings, burdens, and
harshness of life, then we have already become superior to it in a way
that is the fulfillment of life itself. In the elaboration of this vision,
especially the evocation of the new higher human who would be its
realization, Nietzsche provided his principal response to the spiritual
crisis of the age.

The Übermensch or overman proclaimed by Zarathustra is the representative of a new race, a true aristocracy, whom Nietzsche foresees
as the future rulers of the earth. What lifts them beyond the human

level is the titanic or Napoleonic strength of soul that they possess, as a result of their annihilation of all values and the acceptance of a life that is beyond good and evil. It is not that they are immoral, although Nietzsche frequently leaves us with this impression,[35] but that such categories no longer apply to humans who have definitively transcended the artificiality of all values. The nihilism of the devaluation of all values is for them no more than a starting point; they have succeeded in overcoming the need for purpose through the indomitable strength of their will to power. Indeed, it has been the confrontation with the disappearance of all possible principles of meaning that has enabled them to reach this final, all-affirming, unconditional Yes to life.

This is the insight Nietzsche claimed to have obtained from the Greeks and the reason he referred to himself as "the last disciple of the philosopher Dionysus" (*TI*, 563). "Say Yes to life even in its strangest and hardest problems, the will to life rejoicing over its own inexhaustibility even in the very sacrifice of its highest types—*that* is what I call Dionysian, that is what I guessed to be the bridge to the psychology of the *tragic* poet" (*TI*, 562). Such an experience of cosmic affirmation is necessarily an affirmation of the eternity of all things, since to will the all-conquering joy of life is at the same time to will its continuance and eternal return. "Here [in the Dionysian festivals] the most profound instinct of life, that directed toward the future of life, the eternity of life, is experienced religiously—and the way of life, procreation, as the holy way" (*TI*, 562). This is the positive side of the eternal return that in *Zarathustra* Nietzsche presents as the great test of the strength of the *Übermensch*, as he contemplates not only the absence of meaning but also the continual recurrence of all things, including the "last man." Only by refusing to be mastered by this most dreadful prospect does the *Übermensch* emerge, and the eternal return is transformed into an unbounded joy. The "most extreme form of nihilism: the nothing (the 'meaningless') eternally" (*WP*, 36) has been transcended by "a Dionysian affirmation of the world as it is, without subtraction, exception, or selection—it wants the eternal circulation" (*WP*, 536).

Yet despite the vigor with which Nietzsche gives expression to this climactic experience, it is also clear to his readers that his profession of faith is ringed with uncertainties. It seems to be more in the nature of a promised land that is glimpsed from afar, than one that has been securely seized and occupied by the author. For all of his insistence on the joy of embracing the nihilistic return of all—indeed, *because* of it— we are left with the impression that it is still not finally established if "joy is yet deeper than agony" (*Z*, 322). What is certain is that the experience is not truly Greek, for the tragedians lived with a trust in the embracing order of the cosmos that they never doubted, however much its mystery remained impenetrable to them. Nietzsche, as Karl Löwith points out, is too much part of the Christian differentiation of a meaning beyond history to ever really be assured that its meaning can be sufficiently contained within time.[36] The anguish that Nietzsche exhibits before a disenchanted universe would have been quite alien to the Greek experience of the cosmos.

Like Zarathustra, Nietzsche too is "a seer, a willer, a creator, a future himself and a bridge to the future—and alas, a cripple at this bridge" (Z, 139). Even the transformation of Zarathustra into the higher human is more announced than attained at the end of the account of his development. The *Übermensch* remains more of an evocation than a reality, and in the "Night Song," which Nietzsche also included in his self-commentary *Ecce Homo*, we begin to see the reason why.

> Night has come; only now all the songs of lovers awaken. And my soul too is the song of a lover.
>
> Something unstilled, unstillable is within me; it wants to be voiced. A craving for love is within me; it speaks the language of love.
>
> Light am I; ah, that I were night! But this is my loneliness that I am girt with light. . . . I live in my own light; I drink back into myself the flames that break out of me. I do not know the happiness of those who receive; and I have often dreamed that even stealing must be more blessed than receiving. This is my poverty, that my hand never rests from giving. . . . Many suns revolve in the void: to all that is dark they speak with their light—to me they are silent. Oh, this is the enmity of the light against what shines: merciless it moves in its orbit . . . Alas, ice is all around me. (Z, 105–7)

The indomitable will to power begins to crack just at the moment of its highest achievement. It recognizes that it is still a will to nothingness in which the power it has attained can serve no purpose beyond itself, and thus is condemned to a life of vigilant defiance in the face of its own futility. This is the point at which the soul utters the heartrending cry of Zarathustra's "Night Song." In it we see the extent to which Nietzsche's resolve to accept the reality disclosed by life without misconstruction or resentment, was overshadowed by his concurrent desire to attain a position of dominance over the whole in which he would have no superior. The fatal flaw that doomed his project from the start makes him the paradigmatic figure of the modern tragedy.

But the understandable compassion we feel before such a fate must not be allowed to cloud our analysis of the structure of the experience involved. The tragedy was after all self-consciously undertaken, and

Nietzsche himself is the one who reveals the closure of the soul that has sought to prove its superiority to existence. If his lament were genuine, Eric Voegelin has observed, then he would not assert his own nonreception of grace as a superhuman ideal and would remain silent. "But Nietzsche is not in the least speechless; and his eloquence is convincing proof that the lament is only an act of sympathetic understanding, that has not been allowed to touch the core of his existence in rebellion against God."[37] Behind the self-deception and self-laceration of becoming the *Übermensch* is the deeper will to persist in it despite the awareness of its falseness. Indeed, Nietzsche goes as far as to explain that existence in untruth is precisely his aim. He had already explained in *Beyond Good and Evil* that he regarded the ideal of the superior value of truth over falsity to be a mere moral prejudice and "even the worst proved assumption there is in the world" (*BGE*, 46). Nor did he regard the falseness of a judgment as necessarily an objection to it; "the question is to what extent it is life-promoting" (*BGE*, 11). Even his repeated assertion that there is only "perspective knowing," from which it is impossible to eliminate the influence of will altogether (*GM*, 119), cannot be taken as his final word on epistemology; it hardly applies to the truth-value of this assertion itself. No alternative remains except to acknowledge that in some fundamental respects Nietzsche knew what truth was but chose to disregard it. We have only to return to his own self-revelation of his strategy for confirmation superior to what can be obtained in any commentary. He explains in *The Will to Power* that "we shall conquer and come to power even without truth. The spell that fights on our behalf, the eye of Venus that charms and blinds even our opponents, is the *magic of the extreme*, the seduction that everything extreme exercises: we immoralists—we are the most extreme." (396).

The persistence in transparent deception can only be attributed to a force deeper than the will to power. It presupposes an indifference to the success or failure of the enterprise, because it ultimately arises from a stratum of the soul that burns with the raging passion of revolt: the revolt against God. There is in Nietzsche not only the observation that God is dead as a recognition of the social decline of faith, but also an admission that God has been murdered as a necessary prelude to the consummation of human power. The "ugliest man," who murders God, could not bear the limitation that divine compassion imposed upon him (*Z*, 263–67), and in general we must cease to be believers so that humanity will no longer be the kind of dependent being who "cannot posit *himself* as an end, and who cannot posit any end at all by himself"

(*AC*, 638). This is the secret finally disclosed when Zarathustra decides to "reveal my heart to you entirely, my friends: *if* there were gods, how could I endure not being a god!" (*Z*, 86). Nietzsche cannot be touched by divine grace, not because it is not offered, but because he has already resolved to extend grace to himself (*DAY*, sec. 79). It is not that "we find not God . . . [that] differentiates us, but that we experience what has been revered as God, not as 'godlike' but as miserable, as absurd, as harmful, not merely as an error but as a *crime against life*. We deny God as God. If one were to *prove* this God of the Christians to us, we should be even less able to believe in him" (*AC*, 627). This hatred of God, even if Nietzsche is wrong, represents the limiting expression of the spirit of revolt.

What needs to be emphasized, however, is that this hatred of God arises from only one stratum of the soul of Nietzsche, albeit a controlling one, and that the truth disclosed within the other phases of his inquiry remains as valid as before. For it is the profound spiritual sensitivity of Nietzsche that makes his final choice of closure all the more tragic. At the same time, it is his resolute determination in seeking the unvarnished truth of existence that makes his work the proper starting point for a contemporary opening toward reality. His rejection of all ideologies, his distrust of all constructions of reality as masks for the will to power, his refusal to sacrifice living human beings to the abstractions of a religious or political absolute must be taken seriously if we wish to reestablish contact with the bedrock of life. He understood that the advent of nihilism had undermined the possibility of resuscitating any of the traditional sources of meaning. The strength to live life to its fullest would now have to be derived from the experiential truth that survives the furnace of ideological critique. This is the "honesty" that— despite what he also says about the illusoriness of truth—is the virtue of "we free spirits" whom he calls upon not to be "weary of 'perfecting' ourselves in *our* virtue, the only one left to us" (*BGE*; also *GS*, sec. 335). A fierce and unyielding honesty is the only way, Nietzsche was convinced, to attain the one ultimately self-justifying reality whose sheer joyfulness would obliterate even the hint of nihilistic doubt. It would be the final *fröliche Wissenschaft* that conquers all.

The conflict between this opening toward reality and the correlative desire to dominate is palpable in many of Nietzsche's discussions of the need for truth. He recognized that his trust in the power of truth to lead toward life was the same as the faith he had rejected. Speaking of the modern faith in science, he remarked that "even we seekers after knowledge today, we godless antimetaphysicians still take our fire, too, from the flame lit by a faith that is thousands of years old, that Christian faith that was also the faith of Plato, that truth is divine" (*GS*, 283). This is the paradox of Nietzsche, that it was his very commitment to truth that caused him to place the existence of truth in question.[38] With good reason, he acknowledged that he was still to be numbered among the pious. The unemployed last pope, whom Zarathustra encounters in his wanderings, calls him "the most pious of all those who do not believe in God" because it is "your piety itself that no longer lets you believe in God" (Z, 260, 262). He thereby provides a glimpse of the other Nietzsche that might have been.

For the critique of moral and religious faith with which Nietzsche began need not have led to a rejection of truth or goodness or God as a whole. It could as easily have resulted in the rejection of certain defunct forms of faith. Indeed the very principle of the critique, as Nietzsche acknowledged, presupposes a criterion of truth or morality, although a higher one. The self-overcoming of Christian morals and dogma does not necessarily mean their abolition; it could more correctly signify the transition to a higher, more demanding level. What he objected to in Christianity was not so much the falsity of its ideals as the persistent failure to live up to them. He proposed the *Übermensch* as an answer to this hypocrisy. The individual who has so overcome the spirit of revenge within himself or herself will be the first to love sincerely, without seeking self-promotion in return. Their very abundance of power is what purifies their motive so that they can love without superiority, for they know that "all great love is even above all pity" (Z, 90).[39] Such a love comes very close to the Christian ideal and is present within Nietzsche as the true standard by which all other love must be measured. It is known without mediation or argument in the imperious pull of experience toward a goal that might have been quite different, had it not been derailed by the self-contracting resolve of the *libido dominandi*, the will to power. Besides the deformation, Nietzsche also shows us the reality capable of overcoming it.

In this sense his example is definitive of the contemporary crisis because he has explored it to the limits through his own participation in it. The spiritual disease of the modern world, of yielding to the fascination of power without purpose, stands revealed within Nietzsche's exposition for what it is; the concomitant dream of humanity constituting the *telos* of its own existence has been carried to the point of transparent self-deception within his response; and, most important of all, the persistence in the attempt has brought to light the element of atheistic revolt that is the source of its spell. From the sear-

ing honesty of Nietzsche's analysis, an honesty that can hardly be surpassed, it is unmistakable that something more than critique is required
in order to break the fatality of power. One can scarcely dissuade someone from a conviction that he or she already knows to be false.
Nietzsche himself was aware that the process of discursive reason rests
on a prior underlying disposition to view reality in a certain way, and
that it is this innermost orientation of the soul that must be touched
before the opening toward transcendent reality can take place.

The Necessity of Penetrating the Existential Core

Nietzsche makes the nature of the modern crisis inescapably clear. He
provides us with a glimpse of the powerful spiritual forces that are
ultimately its motivating source. We begin to understand the convictions and sentiments behind the upheaval more adequately than
through the methods of the empirical social sciences. Such phenomenal
approaches are notoriously deficient in estimating the depth and intensity of the reality they study; at best they resort to intuitive guesswork.
Only an individual who has both the capacity to enter fully into the
reality and at the same time reflectively analyze the processes at work
within it, can provide us with an insight into the inner structure of the
phenomenon. This is why Nietzsche's analysis is such an invaluable
guide to the contemporary ideological chaos. Within his thought all
scientific, historical, political, and humanitarian explanations have been
stripped away, to reveal the irreducible will to power that is their animating force. Moreover, he goes on to show how this will has exceeded
the perennial human inclination to wield power over others. In its ideological manifestation, the will to power is rooted in a hatred of reality
and a revolt against its divine source.

This accounts for the demonic imperviousness of the modern ideological movements. Contrary empirical evidence, demonstrations of inner inconsistency, or appeals to humanitarian impulses all fall on deaf
ears. Nietzsche has shown us that knowledge of the futility of the enterprise is insufficient to dissolve its fascination. Hatred of reality can
become so intense that nothing can deflect the determination to bring
about the illusory transfiguration of existence. In the final analysis
Marxism, national socialism, fascism, positivism, and the others have
less to do with economic, political, or scientific aspirations than they
do with an impenetrable will to transform the human condition forever.
This is what has made them so long-lasting, and so difficult to remove
or remediate through rational persuasion.[40] They display a tenacity that

only the natural processes of exhaustion and decline seems to be able to dislodge. Marxism, for example, has survived for more than a century despite its abject failure as a predictive science, its abysmal achievements as an economic system, and its irrefutable connection with totalitarian repression. The hollowness of the intellectual system is eventually acknowledged by all.

What furnishes the ideological movements with their "hideous strength" (to use C. S. Lewis's phrase) is that this recognition has no effect upon them. When all rationalizations have fallen away, Nietzsche has shown, the exercise of the will to power is capable of providing its own end. Even the recognition that power cannot bring about any profound change in human nature cannot alter the determination. The will to power endures despite its futility in producing the *Übermensch*. This is why one cannot convince a terrorist, a totalitarian, or a conditioner that the mutilation of human beings will not bring about the global spiritual transformation they espouse. Their souls have already been steeled to commit the most cruel actual injustice in the name of their most exalted ideal of justice. Objections to the self-contradictoriness of their actions have no effect. They have fully resolved to surmount such objections through the sheer force of will.

Real communication is possible only if we can penetrate to the existential core of the ideologue. There in the *anima animi*, the innermost center of the person, the fascination with power must be broken. Then it will be possible to see the real consequences of our actions, to take responsibility for them, to repent for our excesses, and to live in the world of common humanity again. But how can such true communication take place? It can only occur when the will to power is no longer confronted merely by critique, but also by the positive reality capable of replacing it. The nihilistic perseverance in futility must be overcome by the sense of true life, vastly more real than the impoverished substitute now being pursued. Only contact with transcendent Being can provide this overwhelming sense of reality. Nihilism disappears when it is rendered obsolete. In the discovery of unending reality and life, it finds that of which Nietzsche and all the others were ultimately in search.

Without this replacement of nihilism by the truth of living life, the critique is itself vitiated. It fails to lead us beyond the state of lostness that is identical with nihilism. We may have abandoned our faith in one ideology, but we are vulnerable to the attractions of a host of others. As a consequence we drift according to the pressures of the moment, from one system of false premises to another, all of them equally illusory. The net result is often a preference for deception over truth. What is so wrong, we are asked, with the destruction of human reason or freedom if it brings about the final age of universal happiness and peace? Eventually we no longer have any basis for objecting to the abolition of human nature. For even the critiques become questionable when the criteria by which ideological falsity is judged are nowhere clearly articulated.

This is the problem that now confronts us, surrounded as we are by a wealth of critical analyses of modernity but a dearth of suggestions as to how to overcome it. One need only consider the most famous and devastating satires of ideology by Zamyatin, Huxley, and Orwell, which can hardly be improved on as critiques, to realize that they provide us with little illumination as to how to proceed from here. Or there is the whole contemporary literature of the absurd with its endless analyses of the emptiness of life, yet almost nothing on what a meaningful form of existence might be. Even scholars of the stature of Karl Löwith are afflicted by this sense of exhaustion. His studies of the ideological constructions of history as attempts to bring about an innerworldly eschaton, have fully exposed their inadequacies but left the alternative understanding of history that is to replace them in a state of obscurity.[41] There is the philosopher Paul Ricoeur, who correctly diagnoses the "new level of anguish" of our era resulting from the collapse of the Hegelian culmination of history within time, but who cannot visualize any way out of it.[42] In general, these thinkers remain too much a part of the problems they describe to pursue the possibility that was also rejected by Nietzsche: that of articulating the reality of order that is immediately experienced as the standard by which to judge the contemporary disorder.

Even thinkers who have broken free of the restrictive horizon of nihilism are prone to a similar problem, in their failure to explicate the experiential source of their conviction of an "objective" moral order. They merely oppose their assertion of universal truth to the nihilistic assertion of subjective will and, as a consequence, do not really take up the challenge of the radical closure to transcendence in the modern world. It is not enough to identify the inadequacies, errors, and self-contradictions of modern intellectual history. We must also seek to understand why such mistakes have occurred, why they have not been corrected, and why they are persisted in even after their falsity has been demonstrated. If we do not wish to become the creators of "secondary ideologies," defining ourselves largely in terms of that to which we are opposed, then we must be willing to pursue the questions to their end.

Only in this way will we be able to take the full measure of the contemporary upheaval as rooted in a spiritual crisis and retain any possibility of a resolution on a fundamental level. The problems must be traced to their experiential motivation if we are to obtain any sense of how the reality of transcendent Love is ultimately capable of dissolving them.

Unfortunately, the habits of doctrinal thinking die hard. It is difficult to move to the underlying experiential level, as the example of much twentieth-century philosophy indicates. Alasdair MacIntyre, for example, illustrates the difficulty as well as any. Following the first half of his book, in which he presents his excellent analysis of the problems upon which we have already drawn, he sets out an impressive argument for a restored teleological perspective as the only adequate foundation of order. His strategy consists in showing that a teleological order is implicit in the search for excellence in any human practice. We cannot succeed in any endeavor (learning to play chess, for example) unless we presuppose the presence of virtues (such as honesty) that define the limiting purpose of life; they are the sine qua non without which all other goods become worthless. His provisional conclusion is that "the good life for man is the life spent in seeking the good life for man, and the virtues necessary for the seeking are those which will enable us to understand what more and what else the good life for man is."[43] The problem with this argument is not that it is incoherent, but that its coherence would have little impact on the Nietzschean question of why one should seek to be consistent with oneself. It still smacks of "superfluous teleological principles" (BGE, 21) to a man who asks why consistency should be elevated into an absolute. Why not dissimulate and deceive, even oneself?

The difficulty is that MacIntyre can speak only to those who share his starting point of rationality. When the possibility of argument has broken down, when we are confronted with the persevering unreason of the ideological thinkers, then the response must touch a deeper level. It must not only bring forward the principles of right order, but also show what it is that makes them right as an overwhelmingly self-justifying reality. The analysis must recognize that the closure is motivated at root by the revolt against God, and that it is only the grace of divine reconciliation that can finally overcome it. If the problem could be resolved through the discovery of an acceptable intellectual formulation then it would have been remedied long ago; it would not have been a spiritual crisis, in which it is precisely the refusal to acknowledge what we know we should acknowledge that constitutes the crux of the issue. While MacIntyre is very persuasive in developing a teleological order independent of Aristotelian naturalism, he completely neglects the experiences in which the luminously joyful *telos* of life comes into view.[44]

The same limitation mitigates the efforts of that remarkable group of scholars who have sought to restore the tradition of classical political philosophy, as a deliberate counterweight to the widespread disintegration caused by the unraveling modern experiment. Even as revered a figure as Leo Strauss has tended to base his rejection of modern views of nature, politics, and human life merely on a juxtaposition of the opposing conceptions derived from the ancient world. When called upon to defend his conviction of a right moral order against the positivist and historicist relativisms of the age, he responds by referring to "those simple experiences regarding right and wrong which are at the bottom of the philosophic contention that there is a natural right."[45] Moreover, he is surely correct in seeing the assignation of primacy to power over knowledge, whether in the utilitarian science of nature or in the new institutional science of politics, as the source of the moral decline that eventually debouches into the radical nihilism of Nietzsche. But whether a return to "the classical principles as stated and elaborated by the classics" will, even when translated into the vastly different circumstances of our world, be sufficient to overcome the Promethean fire is extremely doubtful.[46]

No less problematic have been the efforts of those who have sought to bring the light of Christianity, as well as philosophy, to bear on the contemporary situation. Jacques Maritain may be taken as representative of this movement, which received its impetus from the encounter with fascism, national socialism, and communism in the decade before the Second World War. His innovative and influential attempt to show how Christianity can provide the indispensable theoretical foundation to liberal democracy spoke directly to the time. It showed how the liberal defense of the inviolable freedom and dignity of the individual could be based on the natural law that had its origins in Christianity, but did not depend on an explicit affirmation of faith for its persuasive effect. He evoked the image of a "new Christianly inspired civilization" as the only viable alternative to the destruction of humanity wrought by the prevailing "totalitarian spirit."[47] The only difficulty was that the rightness of Christianity and of its view of human nature and the political order remained an assumption or a starting point, and not a discovery of experiential truth resulting from the struggle with the profound spiritual crisis of the age. It is not enough to assert Christian or philosophic principles as right; their rightness must be grasped as a participation in the highest living reality that is.

The focus must shift from the level of doctrines to the experiential bases for holding them. Only then can we understand the strength of the revolt against God that makes the ideological constructions so impervious to rational critique. Conversely, it is only through the countermovement to revolt that we can discover the experiential divine reality beyond it. The necessity of responding adequately to the crisis of the age requires us to descend to its deepest level. Other approaches, such as the development of analytic critiques or the elaboration of universal principles, remain essential. But they are not sufficient when it is precisely a crisis in our ability to reason or to apprehend first principles that is at issue. The response must penetrate to the formative spiritual level at which the intellectual capacities are ultimately shaped. It must touch the inner orientation of the soul from which everything else follows. That is the challenge presented by Nietzsche and the larger civilizational convulsion foreseen and foreshadowed by him.

It is a challenge that has been accepted, as we have seen, by relatively few of those who wish to oppose the destructive tendencies of modernity. For although there has been a prodigious array of movements of resistance to "the universal and homogeneous state," virtually none have succeeded in articulating the roots of their own convictions. Fewer still are the thinkers or institutions that have made their positions intelligible in contemporary terms. The survival of premodern spiritual traditions has been a force of inestimable social significance, but by their nature these traditions lack the means of achieving a definitive resolution of the problems. This is what makes the thinkers who are the object of this book so significant. Fyodor Dostoevsky, Albert Camus, Alexander Solzhenitsyn, and Eric Voegelin are perhaps the most prominent among a select group of men and women who have plumbed the depth of response required by the contemporary crisis. They are distinguished from other opponents of modernity in finding within modernity itself the grounds of their opposition. They exemplify the cathartic resolution of the crisis that finally allows the possibility of transcending it.

This is not to claim that these four are the only ones to have gone through a catharsis. But they are among its most articulate exponents and thereby the ones who make the experience representative for our civilization as a whole. In the novels of Dostoevsky and Solzhenitsyn, or the philosophical reflections of Camus and Voegelin, we can discern the movement toward a definitively postmodern viewpoint. It is postmodern precisely because it has emerged from the most profound involvement with the spirit of modernity. The answer with which these four have returned is one that has been found in the struggle itself. Nothing has been imposed or asserted arbitrarily. All that has emerged is the truth of living life, which even their opponents are compelled to acknowledge. For this reason, they represent more than one more voice of dissension within the contemporary bedlam of debate. They are the authoritative guides toward a postmodern order.[48]

Key to the success of these four in each instance has been the willingness to follow problems to their ultimate roots. These individuals have not remained at the level of conventional generalities or doctrinal preconceptions, but have plunged into the churning sea of experience within the human soul. Nor have they been reluctant to confront the question of the modern revolt against the divine ground. Like Nietzsche, they have been willing to contemplate the abyss of evil from which the destructive convulsion has erupted. But unlike him, they have not been seduced by its fascination. Their responsive unfolding of the movement of resistance to disorder has led them toward the transcendent reality of order beyond the demonism of revolt. The truth experienced even by Nietzsche as the measure has at last received its unfolding. By accepting his call to unremitting honesty, the cathartic thinkers have carried through his opening toward reality, without derailing into the self-contracting resolve to dominate it.

As a result, they have regained the experiential infrastructure of the great spiritual symbolisms of the past, especially philosophy and Christianity, with a freshness that is virtually unrivaled. In their work, philosophy and revelation have become a living reality again, not simply an object of a scholarly or antiquarian revival. The rediscovery of philosophy and revelation has become a matter of experience, rather than of ideas or abstractions. This has been possible because of the postmodern recognition that the problems do not simply lie on the level of reason. But what accounts for the extraordinary depth of these thinkers' recovery of the ancient symbolisms is that they have discovered philosophy and revelation within the crisis of our civilization itself. Christian and classical thought are not introduced from outside, as incidental or extraneous to the problems at hand. Instead, they are apprehended within the movement of resistance to disorder. The grace of Christ is discovered as the reality that alone is capable of overcoming the spirit of revolt. Classical philosophy is recognized as the definitive articulation of the order within soul and society. What makes these symbolisms a powerful living reality is that they have now emerged precisely in response to the most profound confrontation with the abyss of contemporary disorder.

The problem with Christians today, Voegelin has observed, is not that they do not have the answer but that they have lost the question to which it is the answer.[49] In sharp distinction from all such self-contained solutions, the postmodern thinkers have been prepared to explore the depths of our terrifying darkness, wherever these may lie. From this darkness they have regained the living spiritual truth that alone contains the power of surmounting the chaos. This is the secret both of their recovery of philosophic Christianity and of their authoritative public expression. For theirs is no merely private or idiosyncratic viewpoint, but a realization that has emerged from the crisis of disorder experienced by a whole century. Like Nietzsche, the postmoderns understood the necessity of going through the worst flames of nihilistic critique if we are to regain anything of value. But unlike him, they discovered the reality of life that is capable of withstanding the test. In this reappropriation of transcendent spiritual truth within the postmodern catharsis, we encounter perhaps the final ironic consequence of the abyss so thoroughly exposed within Nietzsche's reflections.

NOTES

1. Christopher Booker, *The Seventies: The Decade That Changed the Future* (New York: Stein & Day, 1980); Marshall Berman, *All That Is Solid Melts into Air* (New York: Simon & Schuster, 1982); Paul Johnson, *Modern Times* (New York: Harper & Row, 1983); Tilo Schabert, *Gewalt und Humanität: Über philosophische und politische Manifestationen von Modernität* (Freiburg/Munich: Carl Alber, 1978).

2. The term *concentration camp* was first used in its contemporary sense by Lenin in August 1918, to indicate a way of dealing with a whole group of people within one's own society. Terror is of course the technique of exercising power that was brought to perfection by Stalin, then Hitler and subsequently a wide variety of imitators in the twentieth century. And the totalitarian state is, according to Hannah Arendt, the only new political form to have emerged since the appearance of the nation-state.

3. Hannah Arendt, *The Origins of Totalitarianism* (1951; reprint, New York: Harcourt Brace Jovanovich, 1973), 438.

4. According to the latest count by Professor R. J. Rummel on the basis of minimum estimates within each country of the world. See R. J. Rummel, "War Isn't This Century's Biggest Killer," *Wall Street Journal*, July 7, 1986.

5. The most dramatic example of the impact of Solzhenitsyn's account of the Soviet "sewage disposal system" is that of a whole group of "new philosophers" in France who came to reject their sixties attachment to Marxism as a result of reading *The Gulag Archipelago*. See Bernard-Henri Lévy, *Barbarism with a Human Face*, trans. George Holoch (New York: Harper & Row, 1979; French original, 1977); Andre Glucksmann, *La cuisiniére et le mangeur d'hommes: Essai sur les rapports entre l'état, le Marxisme et les camps de concentration* (Paris: Seuil, 1975); Philippe Nemo, *L'homme structurel* (Paris: Grasset, 1975).

6. Solzhenitsyn mentions his surprise at discovering after his expulsion that more than forty books had already been published in the West since the 1920s on the purges, camps, and exterminations within the Soviet Union. We might also recall the limited impact of such famous exposés as Arthur Koestler's *Darkness at Noon* and Merleau Ponty's *Humanisme et terreur*. A similar failure of response to available critiques is well documented for the Nazi case. See Martin Gilbert's comprehensive work *The Holocaust* (New York: Holt, Rinehart & Winston, 1985). And there is the continuing influence of Freudianism despite the devastating critique of Philip Reiff, *Freud: The Mind of a Moralist* (1959; reprint, Chicago: University of Chicago Press, 1979).

7. Eric Voegelin, *Conversations with Eric Voegelin*, ed. R. Eric O'Conner (Montreal: Thomas More Institute, 1980), 109.

8. Ibid., 16.

9. Ibid., 148.

10. The madness was also glimpsed in other remarkable ways, as, for instance, by Goya, who, while producing his courtly neoclassical paintings, was simultaneously engaged in creating the series of etchings populated by monsters. The most famous of the latter is undoubtedly the picture of a man sleeping, with horrible winged creatures emanating from his head, entitled, "The Sleep of Reason Produces Monsters." Francisco Goya, *Los Caprichos* (New York: Dover, 1969), no. 43. Similarly, there is something peculiarly self-revealing in the motto Freud selected for his *Interpretation of Dreams*: "If I cannot bend the higher powers, I will move the infernal regions." Another such self-transparent commentator is Baudelaire in *Les fleurs du mal*. And in their own ways, Jacob Burckhart and Alexis de Tocqueville glimpsed the unlimited despotism toward which the modern political world was moving.

11. Emmet Kennedy, *A Philosophe in the Age of Revolution: Destutt de Tracy and the Origins of "Ideology"* (Philadelphia: American Philosophical Society, 1978).

12. Alexandre Koyré, *From the Closed World to an Infinite Universe* (Baltimore: Johns Hopkins University Press, 1957).

13. John Locke, *An Essay Concerning Human Understanding* (1690), bks. 1 and 2.

14. The first critique of the sources of revelation occurred at about the same time as Locke's attack on philosophy, in Richard Simon's *Critical History of the Old Testament* (1678), although the full-scale application of "historical" methods did not flower until the nineteenth century. Still useful as a survey is Albert Schweitzer, *The Quest for the Historical Jesus*, trans. W. Montgomery (1910; reprint, London: Macmillan, 1968).

15. A particularly revealing account, both of the dangers arising from the conflict between science and religion and of the necessity to recognize their ultimate compatibility, is to be found in John Henry Newman, *The Idea of a University*, ed. Martin J. Svaglic (Notre Dame: Notre Dame University Press, 1982; originally delivered 1852–58).

16. Hans Jonas, *Philosophical Essays: From Ancient Creed to Technological Man* (Englewood Cliffs, NJ: Prentice-Hall, 1974), Chaps. 1, 3, 7, 8; idem, *The Imperative of Responsibility* (Chicago: University of Chicago Press, 1978); and Leon Kass, *Toward a More Natural Science* (New York: Macmillan, 1984), especially "The New Biology: What Price 'Relieving Man's Estate'?"

17. St. Augustine, commentary on Psalm 49, *Ennarationes in Psalmos* (391–420).

18. Kass, *Natural Science*, 23.

19. C. S. Lewis, *The Abolition of Man* (New York: Macmillan, 1947), 69. See also Jacques Ellul, *The Technological Society*, trans. John Wilkinson (1954; reprint, New York: Vintage, 1964); Martin Heidegger, *The Question Concerning Technology and Other Essays*, trans. William Lovitt (New York: Harper & Row, 1977).

20. Lewis, *Abolition of Man*, 77.

21. Ibid., 80.

22. David Ehrenfeld, *The Arrogance of Humanism* (New York: Oxford University Press, 1978). Ehrenfeld provides an empirical description of "the wide and widening discrepancy between the world-pervasive faith in reason and human power and the living reality of the human condition" (xii).

23. Alexandre Kojève, *Introduction à la lecture de Hegel* (Paris: Gallimard, 1947); *Introduction to the Reading of Hegel*, trans. James H. Nichols, ed. Allan Bloom (New York: Basic Books, 1969). The translation does not cover all of the original, but it does include the intriguing footnote on what the supersession of our humanity must mean at the end of history. "If one accepts 'the disappearance of Man at the end of history,' if one asserts that 'Man remains alive *as animal*' with the specification that 'what *disappears* is Man *properly so called*,' one cannot say that 'all the rest can be preserved indefinitely: art, love, play, etc.' If Man becomes an animal again, his arts, his loves, his play must also become purely 'natural' again. . . . The definitive annihilation of Man properly so-called also means the definitive disappearance of Human Discourse (Logos) in the strict sense. Animals of the species Homo Sapiens would react by conditioned reflexes to vocal signs or sign 'language,' and thus their so-called 'discourses' would be like what is supposed to be the'Language' of bees. What would disappear, then, is not only Philosophy or the search for the discursive Wisdom, but also that Wisdom itself. For these post-historical animals, there would no longer be any (discursive) understanding of the World and of the self" (159-60).

24. Kojève expressed this fancy in an interview that took place in 1968. See the report in Barry Cooper, *The End of History: An Essay on Modern Hegelianism* (Toronto: University of Toronto Press, 1984), 303. Cooper's book is an excellent commentary on the significance of Kojève's interpretation of Hegel. See also the discussion in Tom Darby, *The Feast: Meditations on Politics and Time* (Toronto: University of Toronto Press, 1982), 170–91.

25. The notion that philosophy is an obscure, irrelevant enterprise of academic departments is, as Alasdair MacIntyre has pointed out, of fairly recent origin and is more reflective of the collapse of the foundational role of philosophy than anything else. For in general, ideas do not continue in a self-contained vacuum, apart from the concrete reality of society and history that have made them possible. They arise from the living exigence of articulating the order of existence, through which they consti-

tute the world of meaning that is the reality of our individual and social actions. "Every action is the bearer and expression of more or less theory-laden beliefs and concepts; every piece of theorizing and every expression of belief is a political and moral action." MacIntyre, *After Virtue*, 2nd ed. (Notre Dame, IN: Notre Dame University Press, 1984), 61.

26. Grotius (1583–1645) was the first to suggest that natural law could dispense with its theological foundation, but he did not provide a comprehensive elaboration of this project.

27. MacIntyre, *After Virtue*, 46.

28. Alan Gewirth, *Reason and Morality* (Chicago: University of Chicago Press, 1978), commits the first error. John Rawls, *A Theory of Justice* (Cambridge: Harvard University Press, 1971) and Ronald Dworkin, *Taking Rights Seriously* (Cambridge: Harvard University Press, 1977) are guilty of the second.

29. MacIntyre, *After Virtue*, 23.

30. Ibid., 71.

31. Ibid., 253. The "paradoxical" character of our moral experience sets us up for the betrayal of our best intentions. "For each of us is taught to see himself or herself as an autonomous moral agent; but each of us also becomes engaged by modes of practice, aesthetic or bureaucratic, which involves us in manipulative relationships with others. Seeking to protect the autonomy we have learned to prize, we aspire ourselves *not* to be manipulated by others; seeking to incarnate our own principles and stand-point in the world of practice, we find no way open to us except by directing towards others those very manipulative modes of relationships which each of us aspires to resist in our own case. The incoherence of our attitudes and our experience arises from the incoherent conceptual scheme we have inherited" (*After Virtue*, 68).

32. Our ideas of justice and punishment originate in the experience of revenge. Even the "categorical imperative smells of cruelty" (*GM*, 65; see also 63).

33. See *WP*, sec. 4 for Nietzsche's account of what humans derived from "the Christian moral hypothesis" and would now lose without it. "To love man *for God's sake*—that has so far been the noblest and most remote feeling attained among men. That the love of man is just one more stupidity and brutishness if there is no ulterior interest to sanctify it . . ." (*BGE*, sec. 60).

34. "Residues of Christian value judgments are found everywhere in socialistic and positivistic systems. A critique of Christian morality is still lacking"(*WP*, 7).

35. Not only does he include himself in "we immoralists" (*WP* sec. 749), but he sympathizes with the Dostoeveskian criminals who are really the "strong human beings" that society has made sick, and reserves his greatest admiration for "the man who proves stronger than society" in his crime, Napoleon (*TI*, sec. 45).

36. Karl Löwith, *Meaning in History* (Chicago: University of Chicago Press, 1949), 214–222; *From Hegel to Nietzsche*, trans. David E. Green (New York: Doubleday, 1967; German original, 1941). See also Mircea Eliade, *Cosmos and History: The Myth of the Eternal Return*, trans. Willard R. Trask (New York: Harper & Row, 1959; French original, 1949).

37. Eric Voegelin, *Science, Politics and Gnosticism*, 32. Stanley Rosen presents a similar conclusion at the end of his lucid study: "I have tried to carry through a critique of modern nihilism by showing how, on its own principles, it reduces to silence and slavery." *Nihilism: A Philosophical Essay* (New Haven: Yale University Press, 1969), 138.

38. "From the moment faith in the God of the ascetic ideal is denied, a *new problem arises*: that of the *value* of truth" (*GM*, sec. 24).

39. "The noble type of man experiences *itself* as determining values. . . . Everything it knows as part of itself it honors. . . . The noble human being, too, helps the unfortunate, but not, or almost not, from pity, but prompted by an urge begotten by excess of power" (*BGE*, sec. 260).

40. There have been no instances of an ideological regime being successfully liberated through internal resistance; recent changes are due more to the inner dissolution of the ideology over time than to the strength of opponents or reformers.

41. Löwith, *Meaning in History*, "Epilogue."

42. Paul Ricoeur, *History and Truth*, trans. Charles A. Kelly (Evanston: Northwestern University Press, 1965; French original, 1955), especially 287–304.

43. MacIntyre, *After Virtue*, 219.

44. MacIntyre has explicitly acknowledged this in his most recent book, *Whose Justice? Which Rationality?* (Notre Dame, IN: University of Notre Dame Press, 1988). At the end of his lengthy discussion of the different traditions of rationality and justice, he wonders how it might be possible for someone outside all traditions, without criteria or points of reference—that is, the autonomous liberal self—to arrive at a recognition of the embracing worldview that grounds one of the traditions of rationality and justice (396–97). "How then could such a transformation be possible? Only, it seems, by a change amounting to a *conversion*, since a condition of this alienated type of self even finding a language-in-use, which would enable it to enter into dialogue with some tradition of enquiry, is that it becomes something other than it now is, a self able to acknowledge by the way it expresses itself in language standards of rational enquiry as something other than expressions of will and preference" (emphasis added). The problem is that MacIntyre nowhere addresses this core philosophical problem, the Platonic *periagoge*, conversion (*Republic*, 518d). Yet we may take his acknowledgment as welcome encouragement for the focus of this book.

45. Leo Strauss, *Natural Right and History* (Chicago: University of Chicago Press, 1953), 31–32, also 100, 105; see also *What Is Political Philosophy?* (Glencoe, IL: Westview, 1959).

46. Leo Strauss, "Political Philosophy and the Crisis of Our Time," in *The Post-Behavioral Era*, ed. George J. Graham and George Carey (New York: McKay, 1972), 217–42.

47. Jacques Maritain, *Man and the State* (Chicago: University of Chicago Press, 1951), 159. See also his earlier *Integral Humanism: Temporal and Spiritual Problems of a New Christendom*, trans. Joseph W. Evans (Notre Dame, IN: University of Notre Dame Press, 1973; French original, 1936).

48. The term *postmodern* has been used with wide currency over the past two decades. Most recently, it has been applied to those who acknowledge the collapse of all attempts to provide a foundation to order and who insist that alternatives are no longer possible. The difficulty is that such luminaries as Jacques Derrida, Michel Foucault, Richard Rorty, et al. are really stuck at the end of modernity, its disintegration, without having gone beyond it toward anything genuinely postmodern. See for an overview *After Philosophy: End or Transformation?*, ed. K. Baynes, J. Bohman, and T. McCarthy (Cambridge: MIT Press, 1987).

49. Eric Voegelin, "The Gospel and Culture," in *Jesus and Man's Hope*, ed. D. Miller and D. G. Hadidian (Pittsburgh: Pittsburgh Theological Seminary Press, 1971), vol. 2, 59–101.

CHAPTER 2

Catharsis

Irony is a theme that must inevitably loom large before any sympathetic observer of the modern world. When one considers the bright shining optimism with which our age began and the dark destructive horror in which it threatens to end, we cannot help but be impressed by the sense of an order in reality beyond the plans and purposes of human control. Our dreams have been more than fulfilled in many respects, but the result turns out to be vastly other than we intended. What could be more ironic than the contrast between the great technological power at our disposal and the great spiritual helplessness of our attempts to guide its use? What could be more ironic than the difference between the ideal of universal freedom and the reality of universal manipulation? What greater twist of fate can be conceived than the evolution from humanitarianism into murder? The perspective of irony is indispensable if we are to place these events in their appropriate context. For it is within the widest horizon of history that we are most powerfully compelled to recognize our participation in a process of reality of which we are neither source nor master. Irony provides the balance in which the weighing of history must eventually take place. At the end of his lengthy study of Russian culture, James Billington devotes a chapter to the irony of Russian history, recognition of which he considers necessary to complete the picture. "The ironic view contends that history laughs at human pretensions without being hostile to human aspirations. It is capable of giving man hope without illusion."[1]

Such a perspective points the way toward a dissolution of the obsessive dream of power and the restoration of an order of hope more solidly grounded in the reality of human nature. The irony of modern history may well turn out at its deepest level to consist not in the unintended consequences of the exercise of power, but in the eventual reestablishment of those very convictions most emphatically rejected by the inauguration of the modern age. Surely no consequence could be more unintended than this, nor more astonishing to the protagonists. Yet such, we will attempt to argue, has been the case. The spirit of arrogant self-assertion has engendered a quite opposite sense of the limitation of power, of the finiteness of human nature, and of humility before the mystery of the cosmos. An age of extravagant ideological constructions has given way to a profoundly skeptical realism that is suspicious of all utopian suggestions. Most surprising of all, the resolute insistence on the death of God as the first principle of human freedom has engendered a persistent resurgence of faith in God as the bedrock of human dignity. It is the messianic secular ideologies that now cause us to wonder about "the future of an illusion." From whatever aspect one views it, the irony is that is has been the hostility of the modern world itself that has provoked the rediscovery of the moral and spiritual truth of these older traditions.

This is the outcome of Billington's reflections on Russian culture. He shows it to have been, perhaps because of the lack of its own philosophical tradition, prey to all the winds of revolutionary ideology from the West. In Russia the modern experiment could be carried to its most extreme manifestations, given the absence of a sufficiently critical opposition to the drive for innovation. This is a phenomenon that Russian thinkers themselves, from Berdyaev to Solzhenitsyn, have observed. Russia, Solzhenitsyn frequently warns, has passed through a compressed form of the crisis that in the West is distended over a much longer period of time. The result is that Russian society has in many respects emerged on what Herzen called "the other shore." "Through deep suffering, people in our country have now achieved a spiritual development of such intensity that the Western system in its present state of spiritual exhaustion does not look attractive," writes Solzhenitzyn (*WSA*, 33–35). Billington's work predates most of the publications of Solzhenitsyn and the other dissidents, but the "cleansing" and "purification" under Stalin could have readily been predicted by him. "It would be ironic, indeed," he speculates, "if God were in exile somewhere in the 'atheistic' East; and if the culture produced amidst its silence and suffering were to prove more remarkable than that of the talkative and well-fed West."[2]

The reasons for this development are not hard to see. If the modern age is truly revolutionary, in the original sense of the term, then we should not be too surprised if we find ourselves back at the point from which we began. (Of course, it goes without saying that such a return will never be quite the same as the initial position.) For the more we try to make reality conform to our ideological preconceptions, the more we are confronted with its intractability. The conflict makes us painfully aware of our participation in an order of things that is not wholly amenable to our control. We may attempt to deny the presence of a transcendent moral reality, but the more we struggle to reject it the more the awareness reasserts itself. Atheism can sustain its negation of God only by constantly focusing on what it seeks to reject. This is the phenomenon of bad faith that has been so well analyzed and illustrated in our time; the deliberate closure toward reality involves a continual effort to remember what it is we want to forget.[3] When the futility of this enterprise becomes inescapably plain, then it is only natural that the neglected dimensions of experience should reassert themselves among those who are sufficiently open to apprehend them. The attempt to suppress certain aspects is itself responsible for calling attention to what is missing. Persecution has often been likened to hammering a nail; the harder it is struck the deeper faith goes.

Biographical Experience

The modern world has reached the limiting point of its development when the attainment of absolute power has obliterated all constraints of purpose. Slowly but progressively the person has been stripped of all transcendence to become merely the agent or subject of power; essential humanity has been submerged within the totalitarian construction of an absolute future fulfillment. But it is at the point where the individual has been reduced to an "interchangeable zero" that something remarkable occurs. One finds within oneself a force of resistance. A power that enables a person to withstand the destructive terror that crushes him or her at the same time reveals the participation of the unique, irreplaceable, transcendent 'I' in the reality that endures beyond defeat. Having lost faith in all dogmas and systems, one is thrown back on the resources of one's own soul. There one discovers the immediacy of living truth that can again enable one to live and die as a human being. One recognizes this experiential source as the fount for all the ideas of truth, goodness and justice within the great spiritual traditions of human history, only now one has made them one's own by living them out. A new or a newly rediscovered force is unleashed into history and the possibility of a renewed civilizational order has at last erupted into the modern world. This is the nature of the catharsis that many of the profound individuals of our day have gone through. It can point the way for those who have ears to hear.

The proviso is essential because the achievement of liberation from the oppressive ideological climate is not to be obtained without cost. It is to be reached only by struggling toward it. Nothing could be further from this discovery than reverting to traditionalist formulas, without appropriating the living reality to which they refer. Mere opposition to the tendencies of the modern world will not be enough to provide us with a new foundation; the cup of contemporary misery must be drained of its bitterest dregs if we are to be sure of possessing the spiritual strength to overcome it. Above all, what characterizes thinkers who are postmodern is that they have entered fully into the spirit of modernity and emerged on the other side with a vision of reality that has proved itself superior. The catharsis is not an incidental biographical aside. It is the essential means by which the destructive abyss has been penetrated, and the concrete discovery of reality by which human beings can ascend from the maelstrom of chaos. The thinkers whom we will discuss all have in common their beginning in a sympathetic acceptance of the modern project.

Dostoevsky

This sympathy is probably most true of the first in the line of contemporary exemplars, Fyodor Dostoevsky. The extraordinary parallel between his work and the explorations of Nietzsche was acknowledged by the latter in his remark that Dostoevsky was "the only psychologist, incidentally, from whom I had anything to learn" (*TI*, 549).[4] Even more than Nietzsche, Dostoevsky entered into the spirit of the time, not only by sympathizing with the revolutionary movements, but also by actually participating in an underground socialist group in Petersburg during the 1840s.[5] Dostoevsky was fully part of the disaffected intelligentsia of Russian society and had moved from liberal philanthropy to Christian socialism and finally toward the atheistic Communism of Belinsky. He was a member of the socialistic discussion group around Petrashevsky, and subsequently withdrew into the more radical and activist core led by Durov. This group clearly intended to play a part in the instigation of popular unrest and in the armed struggle to follow; they conspired to operate a secret printing press as the first step. For this they were arrested along with other Petrashevists in 1849, and Dostoevsky was among them. A mock execution and last-minute reprieve was part of the punishment, followed by four years of penal servitude and then service in the ranks. Dostoevsky stood on the scaffold "without the slightest repentance" and would willingly have suffered martyrdom for his convictions. His revolutionary will was not to be broken by death, and he went on to confess that he could even have followed the path of terrorism pioneered by Nechaiev. "Probably I could never have become a Nechaiev, but a Nechaievetz—for this I wouldn't vouch, but maybe I could have become one . . . in the days of my youth" (DW, 147).

Dostoevsky had approached the abyss toward which revolutionary nihilism beckoned. This is why he could understand the true nihilists and iconoclasts of the 1860s and portray them with such unerring accuracy in *The Possessed*. He had plumbed the capacity of the human heart for evil, and knew it as a possibility that is never more present than when we have been given virtually unlimited power over other human beings. This awareness dates from his prison years, when Dostoevsky's work began to take up the problem of the titanic or demonically powerful personality. He recounts in *The House of the Dead* how even one of the good-natured lieutenants would frequently flog a man to the point where he cried for mercy.

Those who enjoy unlimited power over the flesh, blood and soul of their fellow creatures, of the brethren in Christ; those I say who enjoy that power and can so utterly degrade another being made in the image of God, are incapable of resisting their desires and their thirst for excitement. Tyranny is a habit which may be developed until at last it becomes a disease. I declare that the noblest creature can become so hardened and bestial that nothing distinguishes it from that of a wild animal. (194)

If this can be done by the "noblest creature," what of those truly Napoleonic or criminal types who regard themselves as being "beyond good and evil" (CP, 235–36)?

Yet this realization did not lead Dostoevsky to a simplistic rejection of his own revolutionary past. He continued to acknowledge the deeply persuasive reasons that can lead a person to take up even a murderous or terroristic course. The core revolt against the order of things is powerfully expressed by Ivan Karamazov's ringing condemnation of a universe in which innocent suffering is permitted. He cannot accept the justice of a God whose world contains the heartrending cries of children cruelly tortured by their parents. This objection is followed by the exposition of the Grand Inquisitor, who proclaims his own man-made creation to replace the God-given order that he no longer finds supportable. Dostoevsky is so effective in presenting the Inquisitor's arguments that they have often been mistaken for the author's own position. This is why he worried that he might be misunderstood, for not all of his readers would be used to apprehending the truth of life

that he had known by encountering it in extremis. Of the Grand Inquisitor chapter he wrote in his notebook: "Even in Europe there are
not and have not been atheistic expressions of such force; consequently,
it is not as a boy that I believe in Christ and confess Him, but *my
hosanna has passed through a great furnace of doubts*"[6]

Dostoevsky's faith had been reached by going through the crisis of
European nihilism, which only he and Nietzsche foresaw in all its starkness and horror. Without witnessing the totalitarian apocalypse of the
twentieth century, he had contemplated the depth of spiritual evil that
was its source. This was the cleansing furnace that burned away all
reliance on comforting illusions and conventional responses. It insured
that the faith he discovered at the center of his being would have endured the trial and emerged as the radiant truth of a new order. Toward
the end of his life he was beginning to have something of this kind of
impact in the public arena, as the magical moment of the Pushkin
Speech (1880) indicates. There Dostoevsky almost succeeded in reconciling the deep-felt enmities of Russian society, especially between the
Slavophiles and westerners. And even when Russia had begun its fateful descent into revolutionary darkness, the influence of Dostoevsky
could still be seen among the Octobrists and especially within the religious and political awakening of the Russian emigré culture of Berdyaev, Bulgakov, Struve, and others.[7] His influence in Russia has
continued as a steady trickle down to the present, when it bursts forth
in the great contemporary torrent that is the work of Solzhenitsyn and
his colleagues.

Solzhenitsyn

The story of Solzhenitsyn is, if anything, even more extraordinary
than that of Dostoevsky. For his is the catharsis of the victim who rises
to the spiritual height of victory over his oppressors.[8] He was a child
of the Russian Revolution, part of the first Soviet generation to come to
maturity under Communism, and he fully supported the ideology of
dialectical materialism on which it was based. But while serving as an
artillery officer in 1945 he was arrested and sentenced to eight years of
"corrective labor camp" and three years of internal exile, for making
derogatory remarks about Stalin in a personal letter to a friend. This
experience was to be the turning point in his life. He went in as a loyal
and convinced Communist, but came out a faithful, repentant
Christian. When he first entered the camps, he found himself arguing
with the loyalists; then he lapsed into silence, and finally he emerged
to argue against them (*GA* II, 338). His transformation came about pri-

marily as a result of the profound spiritual experiences he underwent, rather than any instruction in the dogmatic or intellectual content of the Christian faith. He left the camps a new man who could exclaim his gratitude. "I nourished my soul there, and I say without hesitation: 'Bless you, prison, for having been in my life!'" (*GA* II, 617). The illumination he received there became the ordering principle for his life's work of bearing witness to the fate of the millions whose lives had been submerged in the "Gulag Archipelago," as well as to the more comprehensive convulsion of the 1917 revolution that has become his magnum opus, *The Red Wheel*.

This was also the source of spiritual strength that made possible the other great miracle in his life: his successful contest with a powerful Soviet government. After the providential publication of Solzhenitsyn's *One Day in the Life of Ivan Denisovich*, the doors to further publication were essentially closed to him in the Soviet Union. Nothing more critical of the destructiveness of Communism could be permitted. Solzhenitsyn lived in daily expectation of fresh arrest and imprisonment, while he worked secretly on his most devastating works. The seizure of his "archives" in 1965, including the manuscript of *The First Circle*, he experienced as "the greatest misfortune in all my forty-seven years" (*OC*, 103). But it was also the great liberation that opened up his life as a free man. He could now speak out publicly on whatever he chose; he fully accepted the possibility of arrest and the termination of his work, now that it was no longer in his hands. By his willingness "to accept even death" he won his freedom to address the world, and now found himself to be "a man with extraterritorial rights and diplomatic immunity" (*OC*, 147). By the time the Soviet authorities awoke to what had happened, he was already too famous to be touched by them. The calf had butted the oak and the futility of the enterprise had not entirely redounded on the calf. "The oak has not fallen—but isn't it beginning to give just a little?" (*OC*, 439).

Solzhenitsyn's achievement is a most remarkable and concrete testament to the infinite spiritual mystery of the person. It points toward that spark of transcendence that raises the human being above all politics, all history, and even the whole universe. We have long been aware, Solzhenitsyn observes, that prison is capable of bringing about profound spiritual transformation in a human being (*GA* II, 604), but it took the absolute deprivation of the Stalinist camps to definitively establish it. This is not to assert that all the inhabitants of the gulag underwent a rebirth. A majority and perhaps the best of them were simply extinguished, and of those who survived the greater number did not ascend toward eternal truth. But enough decided for the higher way to demonstrate its paradigmatic force. They discovered that there is a limit beyond which one has nothing more to lose, and that it is there one encounters one's immortal soul. "Just understand one thing," the prisoner Bobynin declares to the minister of state security, Abakumov, "and pass it along to anyone at the top who still doesn't know that you are strong only as long as you don't deprive people of *everything*. For a person you've taken *everything* from is no longer in your power. He's free all over again" (*FC*, 96). This is the "awesome power" of the *zek* who is capable of living by the light of his own irreproachable conscience.

Philosophy has left the world of theory to become once again the constitutive reality of human life. A man who is thrown into prison, Solzhenitsyn recalls, is in an entirely new situation where nothing is clear; there are no rules and everything he learns has to be discovered by feeling his way toward it. In these circumstances he may find himself appealing to the thieves to toss a fellow political prisoner out of his bunk in order to make room for him. Only afterward is he pricked by the pangs of conscience that warn him of how much he has lost for the sake of a slight temporary improvement in comfort. "And thus it is that we have to keep getting banged on the flank and snout again and again so as to become, in time at least, human beings, yes, human beings" (*GA* I, 659). In this way ideas are sifted and tested by life until one arrives at the truths a human can live by. A new firmness and strength takes hold of one as one knows with unwavering certainty what it is that is more precious than life itself. This is why the suggestion is not so farfetched that in the community of prisoners assembled in the "ark" of *The First Circle*, Solzhenitsyn found "that bliss which all the philosophers of antiquity tried in vain to define and teach to others" (*FC*, 340).

However, this is not to be taken as implying that all prospective philosophers ought to be locked up in a totalitarian prison. It is only to maintain that such an experience does not present an insuperable obstacle, and it may be of positive benefit. The experiential recovery of truth is not confined to any one set of circumstances or conditions, as the cathartic revival of philosophy and Christianity in a wide variety of situations demonstrates. What is universal is the suffering search for truth. Without being physically incarcerated it is still possible for a man or a woman to endure the full brunt of the contemporary nihilistic crisis. By dint of the same courageous openness that first induced them to accept the challenge, it is possible for them to follow the experiential movement toward the ultimate eternal reality that enables them to live beyond emptiness. The disintegration of all ideological supports and the determination to live without resort to illusions, performs the same purificatory function as the material and psychological deprivation of the *zeks* in the archipelago. To the person who is capable of following it through, this experience can lead toward the same meditative ascent. Among several individuals who might be identified as exemplars of this process, the most clearly representative is probably the French Algerian writer Albert Camus.

Camus

What distinguishes Camus is the self-consciously deliberate character of his experiential search for truth. It formed the enduring commitment that he sought to pursue over the course of his entire life.[9] There was nothing fortuitous or accidental in the stages he passed through, for they were the landmarks of an inquiry that imperiously and progressively unfolded from its origins toward the goal implicitly contained within it. Camus understood his life in this way as a cumulative enterprise of working his way out from the darkness of European nihilism toward the light of a new civilizational order. He felt himself called to live out the tragedy of the modern world without surrendering to the "escapes" of Marxism or Christianity. The attainment of existential truth had become, in his view, the moral and political imperative of our day (*N* II, 120–21). Writing in *Combat* in September 1956 Camus declared: "We believe that the truth of this century cannot be reached except by going to the conclusion of its own inherent drama. If the epoch has suffered from nihilism, it is not by ignoring nihilism that we will reach the morality that we need" (*E*, 312). It is only to be obtained by going to the bottom, "aller jusqu'au bout," as he repeatedly phrased it. It was a task that came to define the structure of his life.

The *Carnets* or *Notebooks* published after his death reveal his perseverance in this vocation. There are certain writers, he observed, whose work must be taken as a whole if they are to be understood rightly, and he clearly intended to include himself in this category. Throughout the *Carnets* he makes repeated attempts to sum up the course of his work and to distinguish it as a succession of related stages of one meditation. *The Stranger*, his first novel, is point zero; *The Plague* is progress; and the final uncompleted stage was to be the emergence of the saint (*N* II, 20). A little later he identified five different stages, moving from the absurd, to revolt, judgment, heartbreak, to creation corrected (*N II*, 158). Finally he reached the most profound understanding of the unity of his works by linking them through a progression of myths:

> I.   The Myth of Sisyphus (absurd)
> II. The Myth of Prometheus (revolt)
> III. The Myth of Nemesis (N II 257)

In each phase he simultaneously wrote a novel, a philosophical essay, and a play: during phase 1, these were *The Stranger*, *The Myth of Sisyphus*, and *Caligula*; during phase 2, *The Plague*, *The Rebel*, and *The Misunderstanding*; the final phase remained incomplete but certainly included *The Exile and the Kingdom*, of which *The Fall* was originally a part, and also the unfinished autobiographical novel *Le Premier Homme*. His writings are to be seen, in other words, as the outpouring of one continuous reflection on the truth that is the measure of the modern chaos.

But they are not the reflections of a detached observer of the spectacle. Camus was an engaged participant who entered as fully into the events of history as circumstances would permit. Growing up in a poor working class district of Algiers, he inevitably gravitated toward socialism and the Communist party. This was the organization that appeared to hold the most promise of resolving the great social inequities he saw around him. Camus first joined a front organization and then the Communist party in 1935, but because of his refusal to accept their cynical reversal of support for Moslem nationalism, he was expelled from the party two years later. His political position until the outbreak of the war could be described as pacifist anarchism. Yet after the Nazi attack he volunteered for service, although he was rejected because of his tuberculosis. In the latter part of the war he was prevented from returning to Algeria and joined the underground resistance, editing the first issues of *Combat*. After liberation this became a key newspaper in shaping the founding public morality of the new political order. Camus's editorials were enormously popular and influential at the time, although his hopes for a more profound and enduring political change were disappointed.

The powerful social and political interests in France reasserted their customary prerogatives. Camus himself became less sanguine about revolutionary political change as he understood more clearly the intimate connection between totalitarianism and all ideological systems. His own political activities increasingly took the form of attempts at public persuasion, paralleled by private initiatives on behalf of specific

individuals. Even in the last major upheaval in his lifetime, the wrench-
ing protracted conflict in Algeria, he poured out his energies on behalf
of a reasonable and moral solution. Camus's public career in these later
years may indeed be regarded as a model of the kind of balance needed
if we are to apply moral principles to politics without veering into destructive extremes of moralizing.

What made this impressive equilibrium possible was the profound
spiritual catharsis he had lived through in his own life. Beginning from
a position not too much different from that of Meursault in *The Stranger*,
of passion for the truth wherever it may lead, even to the point of
incurring the condemnation of society, he found his way back to an
affirmation of the transcendent truth of morality and a profession of
the redemptive power of love in the human condition. By entering fully
into the disintegration of all values and ideas, Camus encountered the
meaning provided by life itself beyond all interpretations and constructions. This led him deeper into the sources of the crisis. Camus explored not only the collapse of traditional principles, but also the
metaphysical revolt that, as long as it persists, ensures that no easy
restoration of classical and Christian order is possible. *L' homme revolté*,
The Rebel, is his voyage into the stormiest waters of the modern convulsion. He dwells with the spirit of Nietzsche and of all the other great
rebels of our era, in order to unfold more faithfully the experiential
logic of their assertions. There he reaches the turning point that is of
such crucial significance for our age. Camus discovers that the principle
of their revolt does not invariably lead toward the epidemic of messianic
fantasies and the orgy of nihilistic destruction with which we are so
familiar. Revolt can more consistently generate a profound political
modesty, a "relative utopia," respectful of the limits within which justice can be realized. He finds the strength that can save humanity from
the plunge into the abyss. "Nihilism, carried to its extreme, consumes
and strangles itself within its contradictions. We hold fast to this point,
beyond which there will be either death or resurrection" (*E*, 738). The
untimeliness of Camus's own death cut short the further development
of this experience, but his indisputable movement toward resurrection
left no doubt concerning the direction its elaboration would have taken.

To the multitude of lost and disoriented individuals for whom faith
in all the gods, ancient or modern, is dead, Camus showed the way
toward the recovery of transcendent spiritual truth in human life. In
his own cathartic exploration, he fully shared the fate of his contemporaries. As a consequence, the conclusions he reached could claim the
authority of fidelity to the logic of their common underlying experience.

The necessity for a nondogmatic restoration of the foundation of order has so clearly become the imperative of the day, that it may be regarded as the unifying theme and the criterion of relevance for much of the philosophical striving of the twentieth century. Measured against this requirement, Camus surpasses almost all others, both in the depth of his existential vision and in the power of his articulation.

He is perhaps closely paralleled only by the work of his compatriot Simone Weil. She followed a clearly equivalent path in her refusal of all doctrinal and ecclesiastical entanglements lest they obscure her quest for the truth of experience. Simone Weil presents the extraordinary example of a mystic who would not even pray, for fear that the power of suggestion would interpose an illusion between her soul and God. There is almost an identity of vocation with Camus in her decision to "remain beside all those things that cannot enter the Church,"[10] in order to testify to the love of Christ revealed in all persons. The perceived exclusivity of Christianity was such an obstacle for her that she preferred to remain outside, exemplifying something very close to Camus's ideal of becoming "a saint without God" (P, 230). The intensely mystical nature of her conviction, however, tended to remove her too precipitously from the world of common experience and her own early death prevented the formulation of a more considered account of her illumination.

Voegelin

At the other end of the spectrum from the mystical there has been the more prosaic, but no less decisive, response from the world of scholarship. A remarkable generation of scholars has labored to remove the ideological *obscura* preventing the study of human life. Through their enlargement of the empirical horizon of investigation, the inexhaustible depth of experience has again come into view as the source of order and of all conceptualizations of order. We have already alluded to the revival of interest in classical political philosophy as an event of major importance. We should now also refer to the equally significant developments in the history of religion, the study of primitive or archaic cultures, the investigation of the non-European high civilizations, and the ever-increasing recognition of the spiritual sources of the Western symbolization of order. Noteworthy milestones in the opening of these horizons were the appearance of William James's *The Varieties of Religious Experience* (1902), Rudolph Otto's *The Idea of the Holy* (1917), as well as Henri Bergson's *Two Sources of Morality and Religion* (1932). All three provided empirical demonstration of the centrality of experiences of transcendent Being, as constitutive of the essence of religion and as foundational for the moral and political order. Since then the work of Mircea Eliade in comparative religion, Hans Urs von Balthasar in theology, Marie König in Paleolithic symbolism, D. T. Suzuki in Buddhism, and a host of others has established the experiential origin of all human efforts at articulating the order of existence throughout history. Few within this sizable scholarly community, however, have explicitly connected their work on fundamental experiences of truth with the cathartic recovery of existential order that has emerged in response to the totalitarian destruction of truth. One prominent exception is the political philosopher Eric Voegelin.

Voegelin himself ran the gauntlet of totalitarian danger when in the 1930s as a young political scientist at the University of Vienna he turned his attention to the impending political upheaval.[11] He wrote two major studies of the race idea, meticulously analyzing its defects, and had just published a devastating critique of the ideological mass movements as deformed political religions when the Nazi *Anschluss* occurred. Rather than accept clearly imminent arrest he fled with his wife to Switzerland, and from there to America. For Voegelin too the encounter with totalitarianism proved to be a determinative event. It launched him on a search for both the roots of the disorder and the principles of right order to overcome it, within the history of ideas from the Greek and Judaic origins until the present. At this point he was operating within a conventional political theory framework. He began a history of political ideas along the standard lines of Sabine and other texts, although careful readers of the manuscript can already discern the emergence of that much wider horizon of sentiments and motivations soon to preoccupy him. The break came, Voegelin recalled, when after working through the great revolutionary thinkers of the nineteenth century, "it dawned on me that the conception of a history of ideas was an ideological deformation of reality. There were no ideas unless there were [first] symbols of immediate experiences" (*AR*, 63). From writing a conventional history of political thought that was at this time substantially completed, he shifted to a study of the fundamental experiences of reality and their correlative symbolic forms. This became the subject of his monumental work *Order and History*.

Voegelin's work unites the world of dispassionate study and scholarship with the passionate search for moral and political order. They are kept perfectly in balance because he has reached such a profound understanding of their interrelationship. He has seen that there are no self-contained moral, political, or metaphysical theories floating freely in some generalized intellectual realm. There are only the ideas of specific individuals who developed them in the concrete situations of their lives; to these we must always return if we wish to apprehend their meaning as it originated or was significantly determined. Moreover, at that point of origin we discover that theories and symbols of order do not emerge in the form of detached speculation: they are the constitutive self-understanding of the order in which human beings live. "Human society is not merely a fact, or an event, in the external world to be studied by an observer like a natural phenomenon. Though it has externality as one of its important components, it is as a whole a little world, a cosmion, illuminated with meaning from within by the human beings who continuously create and bear it as the mode and condition of their self-realization." (*NSP*, 27). Theory is itself only one such event in the concretely emergent symbolizations of order, and while it is of far-reaching significance, it does not supplant the validity of the other forms. This is why Voegelin could regard his lifelong study of the millennial search for order in history not as a "vain and perishing curiosity,"[12] but as a fulfillment of his human obligation to understand both the roots of the present disorder and the source of that remediative order so badly needed by our time. *"Order and History should be read, not as an attempt to explore curiosities of a dead past, but as an inquiry into the structure of order in which we live presently"* (*OH* I, xiv).

Through his understanding of the constitutive nature of all symbolizations of order, Voegelin pursued the same cathartic resolution of the crisis as Camus, Solzhenitsyn, and Dostoevsky. He recognized that the ideological constructions are not simply the result of logical and empirical argumentation; they derive their appeal most fundamentally from the sense of participation in a higher reality obtained by their adherents. For this reason they cannot be revised or refuted by critique alone. It is necessary to delve beneath the intellectual surface to the experiential basis of their power, to acknowledge what is ethically and factually compelling in them, and to seek to dissolve the component of closure and revolt that is the source of their apocalyptic fanaticism. Voegelin understood that the will to power, the *libido dominandi*, must be broken, to reestablish the order of transcendent Truth in which all men and women live. This can only be done if the souls of ideologues, and of all of us who are more or less the products of their influence, can be touched by the revivifying reality of the original experiences of order. Voegelin saw this as his essential task.

The return from symbols which have lost their meaning to the experiences which constitute meaning is so generally recognizable as the problem of the present that specific references are unnecessary. The great obstacle to this return is the massive block of accumulated symbols, secondary and tertiary, which eclipses the reality of man's existence in the Metaxy [In-Between]. To raise this obstacle into consciousness, and by its removal help in the return to the truth of reality as it reveals itself in history, has become the purpose of *Order and History*. (*OH* IV, 58)

The cathartic experience is indispensable to this recovery, because only those who have contemplated the absolute abyss of disorder possess the requisite openness for the apprehension of existential truth. As long as one is convinced of having the answer, then the opening of the soul toward transcendent Being cannot take place. This condition is so fundamental that Voegelin has identified the Question as the one constant within the great variety of experiences of order (*OH* IV, 316–330). "Question and answer are held together, and related to one another, by the event of the search. . . . The answer will not help the man who has lost the question; and the predicament of the present age is characterized by the loss of the question rather than of the answer."[13] When the problems are traced to this level, it quickly becomes evident why doctrinal arguments will remain fundamentally inconclusive (although not without usefulness on their own terms), and why ultimate recourse must be to the living truth of experience. For as Voegelin explains; "There is no answer to the Question other than the Mystery as it becomes luminous in the acts of questioning" (*OH* IV, 330).

He has little time for responses to the crisis that do not go to the roots. Such well-intentioned contributions as liberalism, conservatism, traditionalism, humanism, Christian democracy, pluralist democracy, and natural law constructions are all firmly rejected as "secondary ideologies." They define themselves largely in terms of that to which they are opposed, and thereby unconsciously incorporate much of the worldview of the ideologies they seek to reject (*AN*, 189). Voegelin appreciates the difficulty of freeing oneself from an ideological climate of opinion. He has had to continually struggle toward the openness of his own questioning over the years. Yet it is only as a result of this effort that he has acquired the detachment to acknowledge what is compelling even in thinkers with whom he otherwise deals quite severely. Voegelin accuses Marx, for example, of being a "swindler," (*SPG*, 28) but at the same time he recognizes that "Marx has laid his finger on the sore spot of modern industrial society . . . that is the growth of economic institutions into a power of such overwhelming influence on the life of every single man, that in the face of such power all talk about human freedom becomes futile" (*ER*, 299). The Marxian diagnosis is "on the whole sound," and Voegelin is even willing to consider the necessity of revolution. He knows that history contains many instances in which "a destructive outbreak of evil supplies the force for breaking an unjust order and substituting an order of superior justice" (*ER*, 232). Although Voegelin had little sympathy with Marxism, apart from a student flirtation, he displayed an evenhandedness in dealing with it and the other political movements that was not always easy for readers to assimilate. He became a notoriousy difficult thinker to categorize.[14] No more than Solzhenitsyn, Dostoevsky, and Camus can he be neatly labeled as a reactionary a revolutionary or something in between. For they are representative of those courageous spirits who in every great historical crisis have not sought refuge in the tried and true, but have set forth on the ocean of mystery to discover terra firma anew. The same could of course be said of many in the line of modern thinkers from Descartes on. Self-confidence and daring have not been noticeably lacking among the many great thinkers who have set out to discover the foundations for a new order of existence. The difference is that this particular group has been among the very few to have successfully negotiated the voyage back to land.

The Descent into the Abyss

The fundamental problem for the individual who seeks to oppose the current of the day is the lack of a foundation from which to mount a resistance. Having been a part of the climate of opinion for so long before the first glimmerings of objection emerged, one no longer possesses the requisite independence of viewpoint from which to launch a critique. Our reality is so structured by the socially dominant interpretations that the individual requires considerable inner strength to assert his or her authority as a truth superior to that of society. Voegelin has carefully retraced the steps by which classical philosophy emerged against such odds in the oppressively corrupt atmosphere of the polis (*OH* III, chaps. 1–3). He thereby reminds us of the perennial nature of the difficulty. The uncertainties and doubts that universally afflict such individuals are not easily put aside. Like Socrates, we must be prepared to undertake the "longer and more arduous way," which leads up from the cave of darkness and ignorance to the light of the Good. For it is onl/ when the soul of the individual has grown to the point that he or she knows the superiority of the reality within that the prevailing social constructions can be dismissed as phantoms.

Beyond the Absurd

Before one reaches this transparence, a sojourn in the wilderness must take place. There one is assailed by confusion and an overwhelming sense of loneliness, in confronting the omnipotent social and historical forces ranged against one. How could it be that the whole world is wrong but I? Perhaps there really is no higher moral order to which humans are called. What if nihilism is true and nothing else exists? What if "everything is permitted" is the watchword by which reality operates? For the person who senses the compelling power of these suggestions, while at the same time everything within him or her cries out against them, the result can be an endless turmoil and anguish from which there really seems to be "no exit." This is the experience of the absurd so well documented by the existentialists. The more we struggle with the problem, the more its insolubility becomes apparent, the more it is seen to be an absurd situation, the more it leads us to the limits of nausea, despair, and death. "There is but one truly philosophical problem," Camus begins his meditation, "and that is suicide. Judging whether life is or is not worth living amounts to answering the fundamental question of philosophy" (*MS*, 3). It is no coincidence that the phenomenon of "logical suicide" was first described by Dostoevsky. His spiritual antennae had detected it as the counterpart of the contemporaneously emergent phenomenon of nihilism (*DW*, 538).

When the absurd has become the starting point for philosophical reflection and the question Why go on living? its focus, then it requires a courageous dedication to openness not to retreat into an illusory form of hope. Camus was extremely critical of the existentialists on this score. He always refused to consider himself one of them because of their persistent tendency to "escape" into substitute forms of transcendence, merely replacing one arbitrary construction for another. They regarded the encounter with the absurd as a demonstration of the limits of reason and, therefore, as a signal for a leap of faith that turned the absurd into an absolute or resulted in a reaffirmation of the traditional God. Camus preferred to remain with the tensional opposites of "my appetite for the absolute and for unity and the impossibility of reducing this world to a rational and reasonable principle" (*MS*, 38). That contradiction is the absurd. Instead of making a "leap" he sought to live without going beyond what is strictly revealed in experience. His was the more difficult experimental way of living solely with the truth, in order "to find out if it is possible to live without appeal" (*MS*, 39). This attitude was embodied in "the stranger," Meursault, whose unwillingness to pretend to feelings he does not possess brings about his condemnation, but who remains unshaken in his passionate commitment to truth.[15]

What happens to those who accept both reason and its limits, who acknowledge the absurdity of life without meaning and respect it as the first truth of reflection, is that the lucidity of this opposition becomes its own supreme value. In their defiance of absurd existence, which they do not seek to escape, they discover their own transcendent greatness. "That revolt gives life its value" (*MS*, 40). They experience this discovery as a liberating event that releases them "from everything outside that passionate attention crystallizing in [them]" (*MS*, 44). The meditation that began in the anguished feelings of alienation moves through revolt to liberation, and reaches a joyful commitment to a life that is all the more intense for not containing a definitive meaning. Such a person has found the value of life itself that lies deeper than all "values." "He can then decide to accept such a universe and draw from it his strength, his refusal to hope, and the unyielding evidence of a life without consolation" (*MS*, 44). In the *Notebooks* for the same period, Camus writes of reaching a turning point in his life, where he could say yes *and* no in absolute freedom, where he had regained his *patria* beyond happiness and unhappiness, and where he was "aware now of where my strength lies, scornful of my own vanities, and filled with that lucid fervor which impels me forward toward my fate" (*N* I, 60).

Because he had remained faithful to his original inspiration of persevering in openness to truth, his soul had grown to the point where its own transcendence of the absurd constituted his raison d'être. This growth is what gives rise to the "absurd man," the individual who lives life fully in the awareness of its futility and yet is not overcome by it. Camus identifies several types of this existence, such as Don Juan, the actor, and the conqueror. All three share a consuming passion for some particular goal, but its attainment is so ephemeral that the futility of the pursuit is kept constantly before their minds. Virtually any role we play can fulfill this function of living transparently in the absurd—"it is enough to know and to mask nothing" (*MS*, 67)—but the preeminent example is the work of artistic creation. The artist bears witness to a "dogged revolt" against the human condition, through his or her struggle to win meaning from a world in which he or she knows the effort is doomed in advance. The comprehensive symbol for all of these enduring, unending struggles of humanity is the myth of Sisyphus. In contemplating the fate of this "absurd hero," Camus focuses attention on the hour of return. Sisyphus is walking down the mountain to roll the stone back up, fully aware that it will only fall down again. This is the hour of reflection when the burden bears upon him all the more harshly because of the respite from physical exertion.

The lucidity that was to constitute his torture at the same time crowns his victory. There *is* no fate that cannot be surmounted by scorn. . . . I leave Sisyphus at the foot of the mountain! One always finds one's burden again. But

Sisyphus teaches the higher fidelity that negates the gods and raises rocks. He too concludes that all is well. This universe henceforth without a master seems to him neither sterile nor futile. Each atom of that stone, each mineral flake of that night-filled mountain, in itself forms a world. The struggle itself toward the heights is enough to fill a man's heart. One must imagine Sisyphus happy. (MS, 90–91)

An element of Nietzsche's *Übermensch* is clearly present in Camus's Sisyphean vision, with its defiant will to prove itself superior to fate; just as they have much in common in their trust in life itself as the self-sufficient guide to existence. But a difference in tonality is also discernible. Where Nietzsche asserts the *amor fati* as his ultimate affirmation of being, the very insistence with which he professes it betrays the lack of serenity and joy in his reconciliation. Camus appears closer to the Greek ideal of trust in the mysterious order that, nevertheless, remains impenetrable to humanity. A note of openness to life as a source of truth, rather than as a hostile force against which the human will must prevail, discloses itself to us. We will examine the more "Greek" complexion of Camus's experience at greater length later in this book. For the moment all that is necessary is to notice it in order to appreciate the difference as well as the similarity with Nietzsche. The same sense of life as a mysterious wellspring of truth is to be found most elaborately in the mystical naturalism of Dostoevsky, with whom Camus was intimately familiar.

To "love life more than the meaning of it" is the cry of all Dostoevsky's heros who are tempted by the nihilism of power and yet are saved from the abyss. Those who are not so fortunate, such as Stavrogin (*The Possessed*) and Svidrigailov (*Crime and Punishment*), are invariably the ones who have also closed themselves off from the appeal of life. Unlike Ivan Karamazov, they are incapable of being moved by "the sticky little leaves in spring" (K, 274). A radical openness to life can enable one to reach the heights of ecstatic vision, as testified to by the Elder Zossima. At the very least, it is a thread of life held out to all who are devoid of hope, as Dostoevsky himself experienced it. His first account of the grace of life is to be found in a letter he wrote to his brother hours after the reprieve from his mock execution.

Brother, I have not lost courage and I do not feel dispirited. Life is life everywhere, life is within ourselves and not in externals. There will be people around me [in penal servitude], and to be a *man* among men, to remain so forever and not to lose hope and give up, however hard things may be—that is what life is, that is its purpose. . . . Life is a gift, Life is happiness, each minute could be an eternity of bliss.[16]

The recognition that life is more important than the meaning assigned to it is the first step in the realization of a truth beyond ideology.

But it is no more than that. Solzhenitsyn recounts that one of the principal "national traits" of the *zek* is the "vital drive," that thirst for life that has honed their skills of survival to a high degree (*GA* II, 503, 516). This is the gist of the advice given him by the "cruel and determined" camp veteran on his arrival. "The main thing is: avoid general assignment work" (*GA* I, 564). It soon became apparent to Solzhenitsyn, however, that the love of life could not be the last word. Despite the advice he had received, general assignment work could not be avoided "at any price." When the imperative of surviving until the day of release is fully exposed before us, the turning point has been reached. It is "the great fork of camp life. From this point the roads go to the right and to the left. One of them will rise and the other will descend. If you go to the right—you lose your life, and if you go to the left—you lose your conscience" (*GA* II, 603). But what can induce a human being to lose one's life in order to save one's conscience? The words have a strangely familiar ring to them, yet are hollow without the underlying reality of a power that is stronger than life itself. Where is a person who has only just freed him or herself from the falsity of ideology to discover such strength?

The Revolt against Evil

The answer, of course, lies in a continuation of the same effort of resistance to all life-destroying constructions. In choosing life over its interpretations we choose not only for ourselves, but also as a universal value. "From the moment that life is recognized as good, it becomes good for all men. Murder cannot be made coherent when suicide is not considered coherent" (*R*, 6). This is the second phase of Camus's meditation, which arises from a non-Nietzschean opening toward the good revealed by life itself. In asserting that life is worth living, one asserts every human life as a value transcending any measure of its meaning or meaninglessness. The revolt against the absurd has expanded to include the revulsion against all social and political schemes proceeding from a nihilistic valuation of existence.

Nazism was the ideology against which Camus first took up the struggle in earnest. In his "Letters to a German Friend" we can see the beginnings of the position he adopted in *The Rebel*. He recognized the nihilistic core of national socialism, which placed love of country above love of justice. But as yet he had no means to argue against it except the inarticulate sense of its wrongness. Addressing himself to the Nazi foe he wrote:

You never believed in the meaning of this world, and you therefore deduced the idea that everything was equivalent and that good and evil could be defined according to one's wishes. . . . And, to tell the truth, I, believing I thought as you did, saw no valid argument to answer you except a fierce love of justice which, after all, seemed to me as unreasonable as the most sudden passion. Where lay the difference? Simply that you readily accepted despair and I never yielded to it. (*RRD*, 27)

By the time he came to write *The Rebel*, Camus had expanded his meditation into the arguments with which to oppose the murderous ideologies. His passionate resistance had crystallized as revolt, defining itself not only in relation to an opposite, but also in terms of the standard by which the judgment is made. The rebel is a person who not only says no, but who also says yes. He or she affirms that "there is a limit beyond which you shall not go," and that its defense constitutes the supreme good, surpassing even that of life itself. The rebel knows that the part of the self worth preserving, from which rebellion springs, is that without which life would not be worth living. Above all, the rebel has discovered an order of right and wrong that is grounded in the nature of things beyond the human will. "Analysis of rebellion leads at least to the suspicion that, contrary to the postulates of contemporary thought, human nature does exist, as the Greeks believed. Why rebel if there is nothing permanent in oneself worth preserving?" (*R*, 16). As such, rebellion illuminates what is common to all humans and what therefore constitutes the basis for community. The defense of oneself necessarily points toward what is worth defending in all others. "In absurdist experience, suffering is individual. But from the moment when a movement of rebellion begins, suffering is seen as a collective experience" (*R*, 22).

The only question is, What is it that makes this proclamation of a transcendent limit anything more than another subjective assertion? Camus's response is that he is neither adopting an arbitrary personal viewpoint nor attempting to impose another external dogma. He is rather beginning from the sense of absurdity and revolt that is the very source of the murderous ideological fantasies. He is not reintroducing "values" from the outside. He is simply reflecting on the question that our age poses for all of us who must ask "whether all rebellion must end in the justification of universal murder" or whether it can discover "the principle of reasonable culpability" (*R*, 11). In exploring this question we have no guidance other than the sense of revolt against evil that is the source of the question itself. Any principle of limitation that does not arise from this common experience lacks authoritative status. "Therefore it is absolutely necessary," Camus concludes, "that rebellion

find its reason within itself, since it cannot find them elsewhere"
(*R*, 10).

It is in the struggle against its own excesses that the sense of revolt
is articulated, to the point where the principle of self-limitation and its
rightness are capable of ordering human existence. Camus's exploration
returns to the beginning of the contemporary phase of the modern
revolutionary movement, in the French Revolution of 1789. There both
king and God were deposed to make way for the rule of autonomous
reason. When human beings were allowed to be guided by the law of
nature thus written in their hearts, the theory went, the general will
would reflect their true inner virtue. The Reign of Terror that followed
was no accident, in Camus's opinion, but a logical consequence of this
doctrine of humanity's self-sufficient natural goodness. The doctrine
lead to the conclusion that vice was not the result of moral failure, for
which men and women were responsible, but arose from natural weakness that could be cured through discipline. Later revolutions did not
make this mistake of naively idealistic expectations; they set about the
business of subduing the world before placing any reliance on the perfection of human nature. In part this was the effect of the contribution
of Hegel and the German philosophical tradition. They immanentized
virtue within the historical process and looked toward its final realization in the fulfillment of history within time. Subsequent revolutionary
movements assumed a variety of forms, all derivative from this radically
historical construction of order. They include schemes of anarchic universal destruction, the attempted deification of the state, the persistent
absolutization of matter, and the exaltation of terror as the supreme
weapon. All of them spring from "the equivocal conception of a world
that entrusts to history alone the task of producing both values and
truth" (*R*, 146). By loosing such ideas upon the world, the great modern
thinkers such as Hegel and Nietzsche have, in Camus's amazingly blunt
assessment (for someone from the circle of J. P. Sartre), provided "alibis
to the masters of Dachau and Karaganda." And while this does not
necessarily lead to a condemnation of their entire philosophical reflection, "it does lead to the suspicion that one aspect of their thought, or
of their logic, can lead to these appalling conclusions" (*R*, 137).[17]

Camus's most profound intuition is that "European intelligence" has
betrayed "its heritage and its vocation" (*E*, 362). We have arrived at a
"knot of history" in which we cannot escape our complicity except by
struggling "in order to diminish *from now on* the sad atrocity of mankind" (*E*, 363). This involves the rendering of harsh judgments against
a revolutionary tradition that ends in concentration camps. The tradi-

tion began to undermine its own principle the moment violence was legitimated by the overarching historical goal. No future attainments can outweigh, in Camus's view, the injustice committed in the present, nor, and just as important from his perspective, is an order founded on oppression likely to unfold into one of justice. The nihilistic emptiness of terrorists, the endless cynicism of Marx's proletarian dictatorship, just as much as the inflexible ruthlessness of fascism, are roads that all lead toward the same miserable end. Having stepped outside the bounds of common humanity, these movements cannot easily restore an order they no longer possess. The key for Camus is not to lose contact with the original sense of justice from which revolt has sprung. By confronting the full extent of the consequences of such a rupture, he has grown to the point where he can maintain that no other good, no matter how compelling, can ever justify the suppression of the primary sense of rightness that is the source of all subsequent goods. His soul has resolved to do all that is possible to oppose injustice, short of committing injustice in the process.

The great exponent of this insight, for Camus and for all who seek to free themselves from the horror of the modern world, is undoubtedly Dostoevsky. It is not surprising that Camus shows a continual involvement throughout his career with the work of the Russian novelist, and that analyses of *The Possessed* and *The Brothers Karamazov* figure so prominently in his philosophical essays.[18] As powerful penetrating critiques of the revolutionary ideologies, Dostoevsky's analyses can hardly be surpassed. Their secret is that they arise from within the heart of the revolutionary movement itself, applying its own principles of justice and freedom to itself and thereby giving birth to the most devastating exposition of its darkness. The critique is so faithful to the revolutionary inspiration that Dostoevsky runs the risk, as he acknowledges, of leaving his readers in doubt as to where his own position lies. Does he remain a defiant supporter or has he become a disenchanted idealist? What is clear is that the modern revolutionary movement emerges stripped of its essential ideological rationale. No appeal to the greater historical goal is permitted to dilute the harsh reality of the evil that has been adopted as the means of attaining it. The good that is pursued becomes the criterion by which all that is done in its name is to be measured. Even more than Nietzsche, Dostoevsky insists on holding the ideological activists up to the light of their own principles.

His own experience taught him the necessity of confronting this contradiction. During his years in the penal colony at Omsk, he first encountered at close hand the Russian people whom all his actions had ostensibly

been intended to benefit. The result was a shattering collapse of Dostoevsky's entire socialist worldview. He might have stood defiantly before the
execution squad, but he could not stand the realization that his great
humanitarian impulse had been founded on falsehood. Up close, the beloved "people" proved to be nauseating; he could not avoid an instinctive
withdrawal into the prisoners from his own class. He even preferred the
society of foreigners to his own countrymen. On the second day of Easter
week a horrible fight broke out and Dostoevsky retreated in disgust from
the barracks. On the way he met one of the Poles, who mirrored his
response with a scornful, "Je hais ces brigands." It brought him up short
and forced him to realize that all his love for the people had been nothing
better than the contempt borne by this upper-class foreigner for them. He
returned to the barracks utterly devastated. Throwing himself on his bed,
Dostoevsky abandoned himself to the flood of images and reminiscences
that came over him. One memory in particular stood out, as if called forth
for this occasion. It was the incident with the peasant Marey.

Dostoevsky was nine years old and had gone out alone to explore
the shrubbery and woods beyond the house. Suddenly the cry "A wolf's
running!" froze him in his tracks, terrified. He ran out into the field
where the peasant Marey was ploughing. Although the serf could find
no wolf, he took great pains to comfort the distraught little boy. He
promised to defend him from the wolf and gently reassured him that
all danger had passed. Eventually the boy calmed down sufficiently to
make his own way home under the watchful, protective gaze of Marey.
Dostoevsky told no one about the incident and had not recalled it until
then. "This means," he reflected,

that it had hidden in my soul imperceptibly, of its own accord, without any
effort of my will, and then it came to mind at the needed time: that tender,
motherly smile of a poor, peasant serf, his crosses, the shaking of his head:
"See, how thou art frightened, little kid!' I remembered particularly that thick
finger of his, soiled with earth, with which he so calmly, with such timid
tenderness, touched my trembling lips. No doubt, anyone would have cheered
up a child—but here, at this solitary meeting, something, as it were, altogether
different had happened; and if I had been his own son, he could not have
bestowed upon me a glance gleaming with more serene love. And yet, who
had prompted him?—He was our own peasant serf, while I was a nobleman's
son anyway. No one would find out how he had caressed me and no one would
reward him. Was he, perhaps, extremely fond of little children? —There are
such people. The meeting was a solitary one, in a vacant field, and only God,
maybe, perceived from above what a profound and enlightened human sentiment, what delicate, almost womanly, tenderness, may fill the heart of some
coarse, bestially ignorant Russian peasant serf, who, in those days, had even
had no forebodings about his freedom. (DW, 209–10)

What transpired within Dostoevsky as a result of this recollection cannot be assessed on the basis of the mere description alone, however moving it may be. Joseph Frank is, I believe, correct in regarding it as a genuine conversion experience.[19] It was the great turning point in Dostoevsky's life. From it light radiated over his own past and the whole historical movement of his world. To get some sense of the impact of the recollection on him we must take note of his own account of the penetrating change wrought within him.

> And when I climbed down off the boards and gazed around, I suddenly felt that I could behold these unfortunate men with a wholly different outlook, and suddenly, by some miracle, all the hatred and anger completely vanished from my heart. I went along, gazing attentively at the faces which I encountered. This intoxicated, shaven and branded peasant with marks on his face, bawling his hoarse drunken song—why, he may be the very same Marey; for I have no way of peering into his heart. (*DW*, 210)

The nature of this experience was meditatively unfolded by Dostoevsky throughout his works, and we will explore its meaning more fully later. At present we are interested in its significance as the basis for his critique of the modern revolutionary movement. He no longer floundered in the depression and confusion that had overwhelmed him on first entering the penal colony; nor was he still entangled in the welter of revolutionary abstractions and illusions that he had brought with him from the past. A far-reaching shift of perspective had occurred, once the undeniable reality of goodness had entered his soul in the memory of Marey. He now beheld a truth that exposed the falsity of his former humanitarianism and, at the same time, taught him the true nature of concrete human love. The incident with Marey had been an epiphany, of the depth of love within a human heart that pours itself out in care for another without consideration of return. From that point on Dostoevsky would measure love by this criterion and, by such a test, not surprisingly would find most forms wanting. But he found none were more defective than the claim of service to universal humanity, which barely concealed its real motivation in the megalomania of power. Dostoevsky reserved his most scathing critiques for the form of love to which he had himself been most attracted: humanitarian activism beyond the restraints of good and evil.

The Hollowness of Ideology

In their enlightened repudiation of traditional precepts of right and wrong, their nihilistic rejection of all conventional values as hypocritical, and their conviction of the absolute moral superiority of their own goal, the modern revolutionaries put themselves forward as the founders of a new ethical order. Nothing, Dostoevsky came to realize, could be further from the truth. Without a pure disinterested love from the start, we have no way of reaching it in the end; without a self-effacing modesty concerning our goal, we have no way to resist the most excessive self-aggrandizement; and without a firm recognition of the reality of good and evil, we inevitably succumb to the worst temptations of power. This is the substance of much of Dostoevsky's writing after *The House of the Dead*. It is the common theme of the five great novel-trage-dies, first announced in *Letters from the Underground*. There the young hero is a typical product of the liberal enlightened age, as he drifts along his "stream of consciousness" without any firm landmarks in reality. Dostoevsky's portrait of the underground man is both a damn-ing portrayal of the interminability of doctrinaire disputes, and a hope-ful demonstration of the irrepressible freedom of actual human nature. A human being ultimately escapes explanation or prediction within the limits of any finite system. The hero is torn between his aspiration toward goodness and beauty and the opposing tendencies toward de-bauchery and cruelty. He is unable to follow one path to the exclusion of the other. At the point where he is most inclined toward goodness, during the episode in which he tries to win Lisa back from a life of prostitution, his impulse is most grotesquely perverted. He heaps scorn and insult on her in crushing succession. When put to the test, his compassion is shown to be motivated by the lust for "power over some-one" (*LFU*, 139). Without a firm anchor in transcendent moral truth, love is doomed in its struggle with evil. "I could not love her," the underground hero explains, "for the reason that, to me, love always connotes tyrannisation and moral ascendancy" (*LFU*, 134–44).

By following out the consequences of a liberal or socialist inclination to compassion, Dostoevsky reveals the point at which it falls drastically short of its own principles. At the same time, he articulates the ethically grounded love that is the truest expression of this impulse. The last thing we encounter in his novels is a moral judgment. All of his char-acters are judged in the light of their own expressed principles. The author's part consists in placing them in situations in which all that is contained within them is called forth. As the enigma of their personal-ities is unfolded according to their own inner dynamic, we are provided with a paradigmatic exposition of the tensions and conflicts present in every human heart. This is what makes the interior struggle of Raskol-nikov, in *Crime and Punishment*, such a powerful means of exploring the humanitarian-utilitarian ideologies with which his reflections begin. When we follow his progress we discover that these justifications for murdering the old pawnbroker and her sister are paper-thin. They quickly give way to the real purpose of testing Raskolnikov's own resolve to become a "Napoleonic" individual, who is capable of living beyond good and evil.

The horror within the solitary soul of Raskolnikov is magnified many times in the depiction of a society given over to the forces of revolutionary destruction in *The Possessed*. At one level is the older generation of liberals, represented intellectually by Stepan Verkhovensky and his circle, and politically by Governor von Lembke, his wife, and his associates. They are the ones who give birth to the iconoclastic generation of nihilists. "It's our own idea," Stepan Verkhovensky complains, that "is so incredibly distorted and twisted around" (*P*, 288). This new generation is epitomized in his own son, Peter, whose fanatical revolutionary activism clearly arises from dissatisfaction with the comfortable idealistic illusions of his father's liberalism. He has pinned all his hopes on the expectation of reaching "the other side" through a great transformative convulsion. It all comes down to the question, he explains, of whether you want the "slow solution" of incremental criticism and piecemeal change or "a quick solution, whatever it may consist of, which will finally enable men to organize their society themselves, not just on paper but in reality" (*P*, 389–90). By focusing so exclusively on the result, allowing it to eclipse all other considerations, the soul of the revolutionary is forged. Nothing will be permitted to stand in the way of the success of the cause.[20] The nihilistic abyss of the revolutionary project is brilliantly satirized by Dostoevsky in the closed logic of Shigalov's ideological system. He describes the social order that will succeed the present as one in which one tenth will exercise unlimited control over the remaining nine-tenths. "I have become entangled in my own data and my conclusions directly contradict my original premises. I started out with the idea of unrestricted freedom and I have arrived at unrestricted despotism. I must add, however, that any solution of the social problem other than mine is impossible." (*P*, 384).

On this level his reasoning is sheer idiocy and even comic, but it becomes truly evil once we descend to the level of action. When Peter reveals what makes his revolutionary organization work he lists the invention of ranks and functions, sentimental claptrap ("socialism mostly propagates itself through sentimentality"), the membership of unmitigated crooks, and last, the shame of not being liberal enough (*P*, 367–68). He even admits, "I'm a crook and not a socialist" (*P*, 402), but it is his mentor, Stavrogin, who forces him to recognize he is also a murderer. The secret to the cohesiveness of a revolutionary cell, according to Stavrogin, is to "convince any four members of a cell to kill the fifth, assuring them that he's about to inform on them, and, lo and behold, they'll be linked to you forever by the blood spilled" (P, 368). This suggestion, taken from the real-life example of Nechaiev, is precisely the sum total of the actions eventually undertaken by the "historic" forces of revolution in the novel. The other disasters that befall—fires, riots, and murders—are the result of the activities of the criminal and "scum" elements unleashed by the process of social disintegration. At the center of this demonic madness is the man who stands for Russia as her husband, Nikolai Stavrogin, the gospel figure of the possessed man whose name is "legion."

In Stavrogin, Dostoevsky concentrated the core of the mystery evoked by this murderous humanitarianism. All of the other characters look toward him as the one who can resolve the contradictions of their existence in the ultimate meaning of his personality. Stavrogin has clearly planted the seeds of inspiration in Peter and the others; they continue to regard him as the essential foundation of their projects. Peter pleads with him to play a role in the revolutionary organization, beseeching him with the most extravagant language as "my idol," the "true aristocrat," the "fairy tale prince." "You think nothing of sacrificing your own or someone else's life. You're just what I need. I don't know anyone like that except you. You are the leader, the sun, and I'm your worm" (P, 400). This is the secret of the fascination and power that Stavrogin wields over almost everyone: that he "feared nothing" (P, 194, 404). And it is the awful truth revealed in the confession he presents to Bishop Tikhon.

The cross, which is synonymous with the name Stavrogin, is the suffering of a man cut off from all transcendent reality. His temptation is to imprison himself and the whole world within the closed indomitable power of his will. He is reminiscent of Nietzsche's *Übermensch*; we have in Stavrogin one of Dostoevsky's most profound explorations of such a soul. The "fairy tale prince" confesses to Tikhon that he could have hanged himself or blown up the whole world out of boredom (P, 418). Then he recounts the story of his mistreatment of twelve-year-old Matryosha, who ended by lewdly offering herself to him. As a result she became so overwhelmed with guilt that she killed herself. But worst of all was that Stavrogin was virtually an accomplice to her suicide, as he deliberately refrained from intervening to prevent it. He knew he had become "a low and loathsome coward" who would never again recover his self-respect. There was even a certain pleasure, he acknowledged, in the agreeable feeling of having become so evil. It was then "for the first time in my life, I formulated to myself in so many words the idea that I neither know nor feel what evil is. It wasn't simply that I had lost the feeling of good and evil, but that I felt there was no such thing as good and evil (I liked that); that it was all a convention; that I could be free of all convention; but that if I ever attained that freedom I'd be lost" (*P*, 426). Behind all the language of humanitarianism lies the abyss of evil within the soul of Stavrogin. The titanic striving of the overman has no other purpose than the testing of his own limitless strength. Tikhon correctly perceives that the confession too is not genuine but only one more mask, one more means of testing Stavrogin's will to power. Yet even Stavrogin cannot surmount the final obstacle of the futility of power without purpose, which is only exacerbated by its increasingly successful exercise. Having tried his strength in everything, he comes back to the question, "What was I supposed to *apply* my strength to? That I could never see and I still don't see it to this day" (*P*, 690). The closure of his soul can ultimately find its expression only in the hero's suicide.

The dark side of humanitarianism pursued beyond the bounds of morality has rarely been exposed so relentlessly, and we have only considered a fraction of Dostoevsky's analysis. Its other major component consists of an examination of the truth that Stavrogin is unable to accept, embodied in the collapse of faith within his two alter egos, Kirillov and Shatov. They are of course his disciples. Having reached their positions under Stavrogin's inspiration, they are ever unable to sustain them without his support. Their relationship is one of the most successful applications of Dostoevsky's technique of employing a "double" for the exploration of character and problems.[21]

Kirillov, for example, provides an opportunity for reflection on the full tragic dimension both of Stavrogin and of the spirit of revolt in the modern world. When we first meet him he is talking about becoming the new man who has conquered pain and fear; he has concluded that this ultimate power will be attained when he is prepared to kill himself. The next discussion with him reveals his project as a mystical quest for the moment of eternal harmony; when time stands still all human life will be transformed through the presence of goodness incarnate (*P*, 223–26). But all this talk about becoming a "man-god" suggests, Stavrogin warns, that "next time you'll be believing in God" (*P*, 225). This observation is not too far off the mark, as the final conversation with Kirillov before his suicide reveals. His problem is that "if there's no God, then I'm God" (*P*, 635), of unavoidable necessity. All men have previously invented God in order to go on living in meaning; now Kirillov will be the first man in history not to engage in this self-deception. To bring the salvation of absolute freedom to all humankind, the first to discover it must make "the supreme gesture of free will [which] is to kill oneself" (*P*, 635). The unendurability of a world without God has driven Kirillov to the desperation of killing himself to become God.

Equally struck by the longing for God is the printer Shatov, into whose mouth Dostoevsky puts his own vision of the messianic spiritual mission of the Russian people. Stavrogin has formulated the principle that "a Russian cannot be godless. As soon as he becomes godless, he ceases to be Russian" (*P*, 235). Now Shatov elaborates this idea of the search for God as the distinctive national trait of the Russians. All nations are founded on the religious ideal, not on the ideas of science and reason, which have "never yet managed to define good and evil or even distinguish between them" (*P*, 237). The nation has existence and stability only to the extent that it believes that "it alone to the exclusion of any other possesses the sole truth" (*P*, 238). Shatov has bought Stavrogin's argument that the assignment of primacy to power and not to inner spiritual regeneration has been the great perversion of Christianity, the third temptation, to which Catholicism and the West have fallen. Only in the Russian Orthodox nation has the truth been preserved; its defense and propagation has now become the great national purpose. Yet no more than Stavrogin can Shatov answer yes when the former presses him to know if he believes in God. Shatov responds that he believes in Russia, in the Russian Orthodox church, in the body of Christ, in the Second Coming. "'But in God? Do you believe in God?'" I—*shall* believe in God'" (*P*, 239). The divine reality that could have dissolved the closure of soul is glimpsed by Stavrogin and his epigones, but the demonism of power retains too strong a hold to permit a responsive opening to the invitation of grace.

Only in the celebrated figure of the Grand Inquisitor does Dostoevsky focus such a searching light on the abyss of evil within the schemes of humanist self-salvation. There the contrast between the contempt the Inquisitor bears for human nature and the ostensible concern he expresses for human happiness could not be greater. It is brought to the height of dramatic visibility through the confrontation with Christ. The Inquisitor accuses Christ of "acting as though thou didst not love them at all" (*K*, 302), in placing the burden of freedom on human beings and inviting them to make a free response of faith. It is only the elect who are capable of supporting this gift; so that, if one cares about the happiness of all, as the Inquisitor claims to do, then it is necessary to relieve humans of this awful responsibility. Then we will see how "all will be happy and will no more rebel and destroy one another as under Thy freedom" (*K*, 306). The third and final temptation of Christ, which embraces the other two, the surrender of spiritual truth in exchange for political power, is the final statement of the Inquisitor's position. "In the end they will lay their freedom at our feet, and say to us, 'Make us your slaves, but feed us'" (*K*, 306). For he who feeds them, the Inquisitor observes, also supplies "all that man seeks on earth—that is, some one to worship, some one to keep his conscience, and some means of uniting all in one unanimous and harmonious ant-heap" (*K*, 305–6). The surrender of their humanity, of the inner freedom of response that is the essence of all that constitutes the human person, is the only way that such "weak, vicious, worthless and rebellious" creatures can be made into the "happy children" of every utopian dreamer's fantasy.

Today, more than a century later, it is astonishing to discover the extent to which Dostoevsky is misunderstood. Of course, the author withdraws so much in allowing his characters to speak for themselves that the possibility of misinterpretation is always present. But how one can miss his intention of exposing the dehumanizing baseness of the Inquisitor's humanitarianism is difficult to understand. Yet it is not incomprehensible once one considers the degree to which the position of the old cardinal remains influential, in spite of the intervening wars, camps, and exterminations since Dostoevsky wrote. Camus highlights the abandonment of liberty as the great failure of the revolutionary movement in the twentieth century. This factor above all else explains the degeneration of revolutionaries into Caesarism and military socialism once they are in power. The debate moreover persists in the form of arguments for moderating the demands for liberty, especially in the Third World, as the price that must be paid for more rapid rates of development and redistribution. Proponents of such shortcuts have chosen bread in preference to liberty, not realizing that their bread depends on their liberty. "If someone takes away your bread, he suppresses your freedom at the same time. But if someone takes away your freedom, you may be sure that your bread is threatened, for it depends no longer on you and your struggle but on the whim of a master," wrote Camus (*RRD*, 94). Once humans have surrendered their freedom they have lost not only the foundation of all that makes them worthy of humanitarian concern, but also any means of voicing their objection to the potentially limitless abuses that may now be perpetrated upon them.

Evil Unmasked

The presence of widespread social attitudes of acquiescence and collusion ultimately explains the phenomenon of totalitarianism in our time. The Gulag Archipelago cannot be considered as an isolated or accidental phenomenon. As its victim, Solzhenitsyn gradually came to understand that the entire blame for the statewide apparatus of terror and destruction could not be laid at the feet of one man, Stalin (GA, III, 78f.). It was only possible because that one man had the active cooperation of other government leaders, party officials and members, the secret police, military forces and prison service, the major social and cultural institutions, and the ordinary Soviet citizens. All had become corrupted or had sunk into submission and all shared in the responsibility and guilt, including Solzhenitsyn himself, as he slowly came to realize. But what made the sheer scale of cruelty and destruction possible was that all these willing collaborators felt themselves justified in the actions they performed.[22] They were not committing evil deeds, but rather were taking steps that they perceived to be good in terms of the reigning ideological construction. Solzhenitsyn complains about the depiction of evildoers in earlier world literature, that they are invariably shown as black-souled individuals who know their own evilness. By contrast, his exposure to the inferno of twentieth-century evil has taught him that "to do evil a human being must first of all believe that what he's doing is good" (GA I, 173). Macbeth's self-justifications are feeble compared to what is available now through ideology. "Ideology—that is what gives evildoing its long-sought justification and gives the evildoer the necessary steadfastness and determination. Thanks to *ideology*, the twentieth century was fated to experience evildoing on a scale calculated in the millions" (GA I, 174).

This recognition is what has made Solzhenitsyn such an implacable anti-Communist or, more correctly, an anti-ideologist. For it is not the communitarian aspect to which he primarily objects, but the radical dissociation of Communism from all considerations of right and wrong. That is the feature it shares with all ideological systems. His is no knee-jerk reactionary position, but one reached through experiencing the endless tyranny that results when men and women are free to wield power without moral restraints. To the human being who is "unaware of any higher sphere, it is a deadly poison" (GA I, 147). Those who joined the organs of state security were almost all of this type; they were drawn to the work precisely for the intoxicating experience of power. "All without exception *were in his hands, and anyone, even the most important, could be brought before him as an accused*" (*GA* I, 147). The humanitarian rationale had slipped so far into the future that it was no more than a memory, and ideology had assumed the principal function of allowing those who possessed power to exercise their will in total freedom.

Given this perspective one can understand why Solzhenitsyn has until now been so generally dismissive of suggestions of improvement or reform within Communism. He has only been willing to concede that changing circumstances may bring forth a revision of tactics. Otherwise Communist parties are the same the world over, as long as they continue to believe in their ideology. "All of the Communist parties, upon achieving power, have become completely merciless."[23] Even the famous post-Stalin reforms did not constitute any change in principle; the reformers continued to jail whomever they wished, only without imprisoning the additional unnecessary ones also included by Stalin. Solzhenitsyn concludes *The Gulag Archipelago* with some reflections on the state of the Soviet legal system in the early seventies and observes that nothing fundamentally had changed. While fewer people were held within the gulag, the entire process remained in place. It was still the case that once an investigation had begun through denunciation it must end in a conviction. "We make no mistakes" remained the rule. Nothing guarantees, Solzhenitsyn warns grimly, that the mass purges of the Stalinist era could not begin again at any time: "The vessel of our Law is ready for the sharpest turn" (*GA* III, 524). It is not surprising, therefore, that he ends by agreeing with the analysis of socialism presented by his colleague Igor Shafarevich. The mathematician-dissident concludes his survey of *The Socialist Phenomenon* with the observation that in the drive to eliminate all that constitutes the individuality and preciousness of human beings, we must ultimately discern behind socialism an urge for the destruction of humanity and for self-destruction.[24]

The fact that Communist governments have continued to distance themselves from the worst efforts of ideology and that the ideological faith itself appears to have collapsed, does not substantially affect this analysis. It is difficult, if not impossible, to sustain a clearly suicidal course as a permanent condition of existence. We should not be surprised at such pragmatic adjustments or at the decline of ideology it implies. However, if we wish to understand the phenomenon in its essence, we must be prepared to confront it in its fullest manifestation, apart from the revisions and compromises that invariably modify it over time. This is, as Voegelin has remarked about the Gnostic revolutionaries, "a methodological necessity" (*NSP*, 152). The ideological project, the transfiguration of human nature on a mass scale, is an impossible task, and therefore can only be studied clearly in those extreme cases where the impossibility is ignored. Otherwise we run the risk of overlooking the core messianic impulse within the more modest pragmatic attempts at realization. "The compromise would be taken for the essence, and the essential unity of the variegated Gnostic phenomena would disappear" (*NSP*, 152). For Solzhenitsyn and his colleagues the key issue is, not the partial reforms that have been introduced, but the degree to which the principle of ideology has been abandoned. This is the pivotal question. And it is unlikely to be resolved until the full extent of the ideological darkness, the abyss of self-destruction contained within it, has been finally confronted. Perhaps at no time more than the present is the witness of those who have undergone the catharsis of greater significance.

Release

We might consider that for the individual, a prolonged confrontation with the dark destructive forces of revolution would obliterate any sense of hopefulness concerning our modern world. Desolation and despair may well have become the only response possible for many who have immersed themselves in the horror. But it is not for the thinkers whom we are considering. They experienced the death of the modern revolutionary impulse as a catharsis, a release from what has oppressed and an entry into what liberates. For to have steadfastly contemplated all that is lost through an inhuman humanitarianism and to have resisted it, is at the same time to have reached a very clear apprehension of what is most valuable in human life and how it may best be preserved. Diagnosis and therapy are correlative movements of the same struggle for truth.[25] The articulation of the nature and source of the descent into evil is, at the same time, the exposition of the criterion that can guide the ascent toward the good. Moreover, the resistance against evil would not have been possible, we have emphasized, without an opening toward the reality of goodness as an experientially superior force. Nothing can be assured in advance of the conflict, but once it has been concluded, the victory is evident.

It is a victory for the love of life over the urge for universal destruction. In place of the Bakunian love of death, expressed by the ringing Soviet acclamation, "all together we shall die" (*UR*, 63), is a recognition of life as the arena in which the struggle for meaning must occur. The attempt to gain significance through self-destruction is seen as an illusory escape. It pins everything on a future generation that, when it arrives, will also pass away without any more ultimacy than those now living. Revolutionary violence is revealed for what it is: the last gasp of a movement that no longer believes in itself and that vainly seeks to demonstrate its superiority over a life it no longer loves. The dream of humanity as the savior of its world stands exposed as the point at which modern civilization began its fatal descent toward death. Once the desire to dominate the conditions of existence has eclipsed all other considerations, the hollowness of the ideological schemes becomes fully apparent. "The secret of Europe," Camus concludes, "is that it no longer loves life" (*R*, 305). Freud conceived of the death instinct as a universal human inclination, but he may well have been describing only the peculiar state of his own late modern civilization. When humanity has separated itself from the order of which it knows itself to be a part, then there is nothing to restrain the fantasies of self-aggrandizement that lapse finally into collective suicide. Dostoevsky's image of Kirillov killing himself to become God has symbolized it perfectly.

By pursuing the revolutionary project to its logical conclusion, however, we have at the same time freed ourselves from its influence. Once the reality of life has reestablished itself as the only one in which the struggle for order can be carried on, then the illusory attempt to escape the human condition is recognized for what it is. The spell of "the magic of the extreme" has been broken. Participation in life is again accepted as the mysterious foundation for all other meaning in human existence. No order, it has been recognized, can be based on a rejection of life, which, while not the highest value, is the ineluctable condition for the realization of every other value. A blessed release has been obtained from the burden of creating an order to dominate the whole of reality. Even our noblest and most heroic actions, we have begun to see, merely contribute to the emergence of order; they can never achieve its definitive realization. Without an acceptance of participation in life as the condition that cannot be abolished, then every attempt to create order will be distorted into the *madness* of the extreme.

This is the position reached by Camus at the end of *The Rebel*, when he announces "a renaissance beyond the limits of nihilism." Having exhausted the deadly attraction of a future historical transformation,

with all its "inhuman excesses," we can again begin to live in the present with "that strange joy which helps one live and die, and which we
shall never again postpone to a later time" (R, 306). Camus's secret is
that he has accepted life itself, with its opportunities and limitations
for the realization of order, as the foundation that cannot be
superseded. He has discovered the principle of "reasonable culpability,"
the "meridian" point within rebellion. This principle is what enables
revolt to attain the good in opposition to the evil, without plunging
toward the extreme of the best that ends by destroying all. "Man can
master in himself everything that can be mastered. He should rectify
in creation everything that can be rectified. After he has done so, children will still die unjustly in a perfect society" (R, 303). But it is only
those who accept this condition who will relieve the suffering of even
a few. Those who reject it end by vastly increasing the misery of many
more.[26]

The experience of confronting the extremes has brought palpable
evidence of the moral order that we cannot transgress, even for the
sake of justice, without perverting our capacity to do good. Humanity
as the creator of its own ethical order is sheer illusion. Once we have
lost touch with the enduring landmarks of right and wrong, we have
nothing by which to guide our progress toward the good. And correlatively, we have opened ourselves up to the full influence of evil that
now invades our soul under the guise of the good. If we step outside
the *Tao*, to adopt C. S. Lewis's usage, we have no way of stepping back
in.[27] The project of creating an autonomous human morality has exposed the nihilism that Nietzsche discerned at its core; its large-scale
application has revealed the realities of truth, goodness and beauty that
it is in the process of destroying. The unmistakable clarity of the situation makes ambiguity no longer possible. Either one is truly motivated
by a love for human beings, and one abandons all subjectivist-historicist
views of morality as the worst enemy of humanity; or one openly admits that one does not truly care for human beings, and contemp-
tuously proceeds to manipulate them for no other reason than the
pleasure of depravity itself.

Either way, the independent reality of good and evil is plain. They
are not defined by our subjective preferences, but are the forces that
pull on a person's soul and make us what we are as we respond to
them. In the unfolding of the modern humanist impulse we have
reached the point where the starkness of the choices is this simple. That
is what accounts for the power of Solzhenitsyn as a writer and the
strength of the characters he portrays. He lives entirely in an ethical

world where the reality of good and evil has eliminated all the falsity of ideology. Nothing stands between individuals and the choice they are to make, which will draw them up toward spirit or drag them down toward animality. His heroes are faced with the most difficult circumstances of human life where "what men live by" is put to the test.[28] All that is fabrication slips away in this condition; human beings stand in naked judgment before themselves and others. The overwhelming reality of good and evil as the only things that matter, becomes clear.

Ideology may have provided a publicly acceptable cloak for wrong-doing, but when confronted with the realities of life and death it crumbles apart. The system is indeed incredibly strong, insofar as it is capable of carrying out whatever action is required with absolute ruthlessness. But it is at the same time enormously fearful of any criticism precisely because it knows its own precarious moral foundation. Solzhenitsyn and the dissident movement represented a worse threat to the Soviet Union than the military might of the West because they struck at the moral legitimacy of the Communist state. Their criticisms could not be permitted because the authorities knew the extent to which their regime is based on the prohibition of any questioning of its fundamental character or purpose. The ferocity of the response is testament to the self-awareness of the regime's radical flaws. Without the unremitting suppression of dissent the power of the Communist party would collapse, and the ruthlessness of the suppression is only made possible because of the absence of any questions concerning its justification. The power of an ideological state rests on just such a vicious circle, which a handful of individuals can jeopardize through their voluntary self-sacrifice.

The key to the dissidents' success was in freeing themselves from the blindness of ideology. They had become capable of seeing reality as it is. To individuals who have acquired a sense of the reality of good and evil as the true measure of human life, the world appears very different from the one apparent to those still enveloped by propaganda-clouded conventions. The transparent artificiality of the official Communist ideology is blithely dismissed by Solzhenitsyn as he enters into an exploration of the reality of Soviet society in *The First Circle*. Using the Dantean device of hell as a series of concentric circles, he shows, apart from the obvious reference to the technical prison, *sharashka*, as the least-tormenting first circle, that the successive layers of depravity in Soviet society effectively consign their inhabitants to deeper levels of hell. The prisoners, by contrast, even those departing for harsher regimens, are freeing themselves from this greatest evil.

Beyond the emptiness of the freedom of the "free" employees of the prison, there is the bureaucratic warfare of the prison administration, the personal misery of the head of the institute, Yakonov, and finally the subhuman brutality and dread-filled doom of the minister for state security, Abakumov. But in the central part of the book, and occupying the deepest circle of this spiritual hell, is the prime mover of the whole, Joseph Stalin. Solzhenitsyn devotes a lengthy series of chapters to his portrait of the ideological leader. As a study of the soul of such a nihilist it can worthily be compared to Dostoevsky's Grand Inquisitor. The major difference is that here the emphasis is on the self-knowledge of Stalin, drawing on the profound inner contradictions that are the essence of his private torture.[29]

The contrast is repeatedly built up between Stalin's public persona as the omniscient leader of the Communist Revolution, and the actual reality of his unflattering past. As a seminarian he turned to socialism only because he liked to have men follow him. When he was arrested by the Tsarist police, he caved in to pressure and became an informer. During the First World War he was saved from service because of a comfortable exile. And eventually, when the Revolution did come, he used it for personal gain and as a means of advancing in power. His strength derived from the secrecy with which he guarded his decisions, never taking anyone at their word or being held to his own, never forgiving anyone who had betrayed him, and never allowing himself to "worry about theories that have always been good for nothing" (FC, Chap. 20). With this outlook he purged all his former colleagues and successfully swindled his allies in the West, Roosevelt and Churchill. He consolidated his power at home, and then contemplated a third world war to complete the process on a global scale. But for what? He knew that Communism would not mean universal fulfillment, but a "strict submission" to discipline and "incomplete satiety" as the only way of ensuring that existence determines consciousness (FC, Chap. 22). Nor could it be for himself, since it was of no benefit in helping him to face the end of his existence as a sick, mistrustful, solitary old man. He was utterly alone, without a friend in the world, and the terror of death had begun to invade his being. Even his vaunted ability to derive strength from despair (FC, Chap. 18) could not rescue him from the desolation of a totally closed soul.

In complete contrast is the opening of the soul undergone by the prisoner Gleb Nerzhin, the mathematician whose biography resembles that of the author. Throughout the book we observe the noose of suppression tightening around his neck as at the same time his inner spiritual expansion carries him beyond the confines of despair. At the beginning Nerzhin is a skeptic who is testing the wisdom of various philosophical positions. He engages in conversation with those of the other prisoners who can cast some potential illumination on this inquiry. Finally his own position becomes clear. He abandons skepticism—"when you are in an iron vice one no longer cares for the skeptical smile of Pyrrho" (FC, Chap. 85)—as he asserts his conviction that "justice is the cornerstone, the foundation of the universe" (FC, Chap. 47). Nothing can outweigh the value of the growth of the soul into the reality of this transcendent justice; all else must be judged in its light. This is what enables him to remain faithful to his wife. He refuses the offer of love from one of the free employees, Simochka, despite all the pressures and deprivations he has experienced in prison, including the knowledge of his imminent return to the camps and death. Before, he explains, "I had no idea what good and evil were, and whatever was allowed seemed fine to me. But the lower I sink into this inhumanly cruel world, the more I respond to those who, even in such a world, speak to my conscience" (FC, 600). His soul has reached such a degree of inner strength that he can compel the prison security officer to return a confiscated book of poems, through the sheer threat to tear it from the major from the other side of the grave. The novel ends with Nerzhin and the others being carted off to the hell of the camps, "filled with the fearlessness of those who have lost *everything*" (FC, 673).

This is the transformation that Solzhenitsyn witnessed in those around him in prison. He records his astonishment at discovering a younger generation, represented by three youths in Butyrki prison, who "leaped that whole future chasm of indifference in one jump" to find themselves in the realm of enduring spiritual truth. Their inspiration was Lieutenant Shmidt's last speech at his trial:

> For thirty years I have nurtured
> My love for my native land,
> And I shall neither expect
> Nor miss your leniency.

They were not languishing in prison but were, on the contrary, proud of it. It was in their company that the first stirrings of a new vision began to arise in Solzhenitsyn's soul. "Was it not here, in these prison cells, that the great truth dawned? The cell was constricted, but wasn't *freedom* even more constricted?" (GA I, 614). The scales of ideology and conventionality began to drop from his eyes as he began to pierce the veil of illusions, self-deceptions, and indifference. He recognized that living for the day of his release was utterly without meaning since it would bring no true freedom. "As if there were any liberty in this country! Or as if it were possible to liberate anyone who has not first become liberated in his own soul" (*GA* II, 606). That is where reality lies. The only freedom worth having is the inner freedom of soul to pursue what is good without qualification. It is the life of the true self that becomes possible only when we recognize growth in virtue, not in possessions or comfort, as the ultimate purpose of our existence. Eventually Solzhenitsyn reached the firm conviction that it is in relation to this inner spiritual life that all else must be measured. "For a good person even a crust is healthy food, and to an evil person even meat brings no benefit" (*GA* II, 610).

By accepting this deprivation of all things, even life itself, Solzhenitsyn had attained that spiritual equilibrium that is the life of the true self. How can I stand my ground, he had asked himself, when confronted by the overwhelming might and merciless cruelty of the ideological Soviet state? In the beginning he was totally unprepared for the ordeal, but little by little the example of others began to illuminate the way for him. After a while he was able to formulate the needed wisdom:

From the moment you go to prison you must put your cozy past firmly behind you. At the very threshold, you must say to yourself: 'My life is over, a little early to be sure, but there's nothing to be done about it. I shall never return to freedom. I am condemned to die—now or a little later. But later on, in truth, it will be even harder, and so the sooner the better. I no longer have any property whatsoever. For me those I love have died, and for them I have died. From today on, my body is useless and alien to me. Only my spirit and my conscience remain precious and important to me. (*GA* I, 130)[30]

The extraordinary discovery he made was that this was enough, that the power of spirit and conscience is sufficient to overcome all the suffering that may be required of a human being. His responsive pursuit of the good was gradually lifting his soul up to a higher order of reality that made everything else endurable. On the other hand, if he rejected the voice of conscience within him, this could lead to the loss of that spiritual core whose preservation outweighs even life itself. For this reason, Solzhenitsyn concludes, "our torturers have been punished most horribly of all: they are turning into swine, they are departing downward from humanity" (*GA* II, 613).

However strong the totalitarian regime may be and however invincible its ideological system, reality has not been changed. Good and evil remain the parameters of human existence. And every individual knows this irrespective of how much he or she may seek to deny it—indeed, this truth is more often evinced by the very stridency of the attempted rejection. Nor can we disregard the imperative of following the good and avoiding the evil, without suffering the consequences of this self-betrayal. The illusion of an autonomous human morality made by men and women and designed with a view to their convenience, with all the attendant messianic exaggerations that are likely, turns out to be no more than the dream it always was. For even in the midst of the wildest utopian fantasies a flickering awareness of this truth is preserved in those who remain human beings. Key to Solzhenitsyn's success in mounting his resistance and, by implication, to all similar efforts to oppose the ideological deformation, was that the rightness of his position was recognized even by his opponents. At every stage it was only necessary to demonstrate firmness or to single out those individually responsible, and the seemingly impregnable bastion of ideology crumbled apart.

All men and women live in the common world of mutual moral responsibility. We all know about it or are brought to encounter it through the inescapable experiences of suffering, finiteness, and death. Sooner or later we are compelled to recognize that the only way for a human being to participate in what is lasting and real is through the surrendering of self that enables us to take up the obligations we owe to one another and to God. We know that it is only when we have ceased to demand a special exception for ourselves, to overstep the requirement of dying to self on the way to attaining virtue, that we again live in the world of common humanity. No shortcuts are possible for any individual or for any age. Belief in the magical transformation to be worked by external political or material activism are no more than that—private beliefs utterly without foundation. The cathartic trial through which we have passed has brought us to realize more clearly than ever what we have known all along. There is no other way but the suffering purification of self for a human being to acquire true goodness of soul. There is no other way "to become in time a human being."

We have now reached a "firm and unshakable" conviction as a result of our struggle with the disease or madness that has infected our civilization. But the inquiry cannot be concluded here. The insights we have gained into the nature of human existence raise all the more intensely the question of how these insights could have been lost. After all, we have not discovered anything new, only reacquainted ourselves with the wisdom of the ages. This understanding has not so much been lost as deliberately pushed into the background of modern secular consciousness. How could such a disorder have occurred? How could it have taken hold of a whole civilization? And once its consequences could be observed, how have we managed to persist in it, virtually to the point of our own self-destruction? We are clearly not describing some individual or occasional moments of weakness here. This madness is something that has absorbed many of the brightest minds of our day and exercised widespread social influence. It is imperative that we understand how our civilization could be overtaken by such insanity, if we wish to avoid a repetition in the future and if we wish to ensure that its spell has indeed been exorcised, at least for a time. For a blindness to the ordinary human sense of right and wrong, the willingness to inflict unlimited suffering and misery on others, and the inability to recognize the contradiction of inhuman humanitarianism, all presuppose an enormously powerful force as the sustaining passion behind the self-deception. This is why it is not enough to resist the symptomatic disorder, as we have described such a countermovement in this chapter. The struggle against disorder can only be successful if we are willing to descend to the level of causal motives.

NOTES

1. James H. Billington, *The Icon and the Axe: An Interpretive History of Russian Culture* (New York: Vintage, 1970), 590. For an interesting parallel see Reinhold Niebuhr, *The Irony of American History* (New York: Scribner's, 1952), who defines irony as the situation in which "virtue becomes vice through some hidden defect in the virtue" (vii).

2. Billington, *Icon and Axe*, 594.

3. The phenomenon is acutely analyzed by Sartre in *Being and Nothingness*, trans. Hazel E. Barnes (New York: Philosophical Library, 1956), pt. 1, chap. 2, "Bad Faith." The broader historical manifestations are explored by Nicolai Chiaromonte, *The Paradox of History* (Philadelphia: University of Pennsylvania Press, 1985), chap. 6, "An Age of Bad Faith."

4. For the comparison with Nietzsche see Henri de Lubac, *Drama of Atheist Humanism*, 167–87. Still useful is Lev Shestov, *Dostoevsky, Tolstoy and Nietzsche*, trans. Bernard Martin (Athens: Ohio University Press, 1969; Russian original, 1903).

5. The definitive literary biography of Dostoevsky is presently being produced by Joseph Frank. Three of the projected five volumes have so far appeared: *Dostoevsky: The Seeds of Revolt, 1821–1849*; *Dostoevsky: The Years of Ordeal, 1850–1859*; *Dostoevsky: The Stir of Liberation, 1860–1865* (Princeton: Princeton University Press, 1976, 1983, 1986). Konstantin Mochulsky, *Dostoevsky: His Life and Work*, trans. Michael A. Minihan (Princeton: Princeton University Press, 1967) remains a useful source. Other standard biographies include David Magarshack, *Dostoevsky* (Westport, CT: Greenwood, 1962); E. H. Carr, *Dostoevsky (1821–1881): A New Biography* (London: Unwin, 1931); Avrahim Yarmolinsky, *Dostoevsky: His Life and Art* (New York: Funk & Wagnalls, 1971); and most recently, Geir Kjetsaa, *Fydor Dostoevsky: A Writer's Life*, trans. S. Hustvedt and David McDuff (New York: Elisabeth Sifton/Viking, 1987).

6. *The Unpublished Dostoevsky: Diaries and Notebooks (1860–81)*, ed. Carl R. Proffer (Ann Arbor: Ardis, 1973), vol. 3, 175.

7. See, for example, Berdyaev, Bulgakov, et al., *Vekhi* (1909); trans. Marian Schwartz, *Landmarks* (New York: Karz Howard, 1977). This and a second volume of essays, *De Profundis* (1918), were the inspiration for Solzhenitsyn's own anthology of dissident authors, *From Under the Rubble*.

8. The most comprehensive biography of Solzhenitsyn is Michael Scammell, *Solzhenitsyn: A Biography* (New York: Norton, 1984). Considerable material is provided by Solzhenitsyn's own partial autobiography, *The Oak and the Calf*. Indispensable for the assembly of documents and responses to Solzhenitsyn, as well as bibliography, are: Leopold Labedz, ed., *Solzhenitsyn: A Documentary Record*, 2nd ed. (Harmondsworth: Penguin, 1974); John J. Dunlop, Richard Haugh, and Alexis Klimoff, *Aleksandr Solzhenitsyn: Critical Essays and Documentary Materials*, 2nd ed. (New York: Macmillan, 1975); and John J. Dunlop, Richard Haugh, and Michael Nicholson, *Solzhenitsyn in Exile: Critical Essays and Documentary Materials* (Stanford, CA: Hoover Institution, 1985).

9. The most recent biography by Herbert R. Lottman, *Albert Camus* (Garden City, NY: Doubleday, 1979), is also the most reliable on the details of his life. Also useful is Patrick McCarthy, *Camus: A Critical Study of His Life and Work* (London: Hamilton, 1982); Donald Lazere, *The Unique Creation of Albert Camus* (New Haven: Yale University Press, 1973); and the excellent collection of essays edited by Ramond Gay-Crosier, *Albert Camus* (Gainesville, FL: University Presses of Florida, 1980).

10. Simone Weil, *The Simone Weil Reader*, ed. George A. Panichas (New York: McKay, 1977), 22. See her "Spiritual Autobiography," 10–26.

11. For an account of Voegelin's biography see Ellis Sandoz, *The Voegelinian Revolution* (Baton Rouge: Louisiana State University Press, 1981), and Voegelin, *Autobiographical Reflections*. A good general discussion of Voegelin's work is provided by Eugene Webb, *Eric Voegelin: Philosopher of History* (Seattle: University of Washington Press, 1981).

12. Voegelin adopted as the motto of *Order and History* Augustine's principle that "in the study of creature one should not exercise a vain and perishing curiosity, but ascend toward what is immortal and everlasting" (*De Vera Religione*, XXIX, 52).

13. Voegelin, "Gospel and Culture," 62–63.

14. "I have in my files the documents labeling me a Communist, a Fascist, a National Socialist, an old Liberal, a new Liberal, a Jew, a Catholic, a Protestant, a Platonist, a neo-Augustinian, a Thomist, and of course a Hegelian—not to forget that I was supposedly strongly influenced by Huey Long. This list I consider of some importance, because the various characterizations of course always name the pet bête noire of the respective critic and give, therefore, a very good picture of the intellectual corruption and destruction that characterizes the contemporary academic world. Understandably, I have never answered such criticisms; critics of this type can become objects of inquiry, but they cannot be partners in a discussion" (*AR*, 46).

15. A similar experience is explored in *Caligula*, the play that is assigned to this first cycle of the absurd.

16. *Selected Letters of Fyodor Dostoyevsky*, ed. Joseph Frank and David I. Goldstein, trans. Andrew MacAndrew (New Brunswick, NJ: Rutgers University Press, 1987), 51–53. Dostoevsky's ordeal became the basis for an identical story recounted by Prince Myshkin in *The Idiot*, 80–81.

17. Camus reports in *Notebooks* II a remarkable conversation that took place between Koestler, Sartre, Malraux, Sperber, and himself on 29 October 1946. Camus insisted that we who have come from Nietzscheanism, nihilism, or historical realism ought to admit we have been deceived and that there are moral values. When Sartre refused to condemn the inhuman deportations in the U.S.S.R., Koestler replied: "It must be acknowledged that we as writers betray history if we do not denounce what must be denounced. The conspiracy of silence is our condemnation in the eyes of those who come after us" (*N* II, 145–46). See also Eric Werner, *De la violence au totalitarisme: Essai sur la pensée de Camus et Sartre* (Paris: Calmann-Levy, 1972).

18. Camus adapted both of these novels for the stage and performed in them himself. Lottman, *Camus*, 175, 528.

19. Frank, *Years of Ordeal*, chap. 9.

20. Solzhenitsyn is drawn toward a remarkably parallel analysis in his effort to understand the terroristic revolutionaries of Russia preceding the 1917 revolution. A conversation between two "revolutionary" aunts reveals the depth of this tradition in Russian society and exposes the nihilistic abyss at its core. Veronika, their niece, suggests that revolutionaries ought to draw the line at individual murder. But Aunt Agnessa insists that "revolutionaries are not to be judged by the yardstick of old-fashioned morality . . . terror, and only terror, leads revolution by the hand! Without terror to guide it revolution would simply get bogged down in the Russian mud and clay. Only the winged horse of terror can drag it out. You must not look at terror itself, but at its lofty aims. Terrorists do not kill this or that individual—in his person they are endeavoring to kill evil itself" (*AUG*, 435–36).

21. Dostoevsky was fascinated with the struggle between different selves within the one personality. He referred to this means of exploration as "my usual substance," and regarded the use of the double as his principle literary innovation. *The Double* is of course one of his earliest stories. In later years the device becomes one of the primary structural principles for organizing the novels. Nowhere is this more evident than in *The Possessed*, where everyone else revolves around the enigmatic figure of Stavrogin. "The Prince is everything," Dostoevsky remarked. See Mochulsky, *Dostoevsky*, 434.

22. The level of twentieth-century slaughter has only previously been approached during the wars of religion in the sixteenth and seventeenth centuries. There a parallel conviction of total and unassailable righteousness prevailed within the opposing sides.

23. Solzhenitsyn, "Communism: A Legacy of Terror", *Detente: Prospects for Democracy and Dictatorship*, 61; see also 59. This speech is included in *Sobranie Sochinenii*, vol. 9. We might note that the contemporary moderation of Communist ideology is occurring

within the exhausted older regimes and not within the more youthful variants, such as Vietnam, Cuba, or even China.

24. Igor Shafarevich, *The Socialist Phenomenon*, trans. William Tjalsma (New York: Harper & Row, 1980); see also his "Socialism in Our Past and Future," *From Under the Rubble*, 26–66.

25. "The truth of order has to be gained and regained in the perpetual struggle against the fall from it; and the movement toward truth starts from a man's awareness of his existence in untruth. The diagnostic and therapeutic functions are inseparable in philosophy as a form of existence," writes Eric Voegelin (*OH* I, xiv).

26. This point is well illustrated by the enormous contribution of trade unionism in improving the conditions of workers, in contrast to the virtual absence of tangible results under the influence of Communist governments. The opposition between evolutionary socialists and their revolutionary brethren is of course well known. Marx utterly derided any attempt to improve the wages and conditions for workers as a distracting postponement of the final revolutionary solution.

27. Lewis, *Abolition of Man*, 77; see also "The Poison of Subjectivism," *Christian Reflections*, ed. Walter Hooper (Grand Rapids: Eerdmanns, 1967).

28. See Chapter 8 of that title in *Cancer Ward*, which is in turn a discussion of Tolstoy's treatment of the same question.

29. The English eighty-seven-chapter edition of *The First Circle* is a deliberately "lightened" version of the original ninety-six-chapter manuscript. Among the many significant changes in this now complete edition is a considerable expansion of the chapters on Stalin. The linchpin of the plot is also changed, from a story about the betrayal of medical knowledge to one concerning the Soviet acquisition of the secrets of the atomic bomb.

30. In a similar vein is the response of the old lady who had hidden the metropolitan of the Orthodox church during his escape, but would not surrender the names of the others involved. "There is nothing you can do with me even if you cut me into pieces. After all, you are afraid of your bosses, and you are afraid of each other, and you are even afraid of killing me. . . . But I am not afraid of anything. I would be glad to be judged by God right this minute" (*GA* I, 131)

CHAPTER 3

Diagnosis

In seeking to understand the contradictions of modern civilization between ideal and reality, between the vaunted humanitarian ambitions and the pitiless cruelty of their application, it is essential to distinguish levels of responsibility. When one asks how such enormous dichotomies could be sustained, we must recognize that the falsity has not been equally visible to or clearly apprehended by all. Some of those involved in carrying forward the programs of dehumanization have simply been too stupid or too insensitive to take full cognizance of what was going on. Others have found it a convenient way of furthering the perennial human cravings for self-gratification and power. And present in every society is a sizeable contingent who simply go along because that is the thing to do, having never conceived of the possibility of going against the all-powerful force of social pressure. But there are always some, the most intelligent and independent-minded, without whose cooperation none of this would have been possible. They are the ones who have contemplated the nihilistic abyss of ideology and persisted nevertheless. To reach some insight into the process that occurs within such a soul, is to begin to understand how the spiritual disease of modernity can invade a whole civilization.

Ultimately the object of the analysis must be to shed some light on the historical movement that has culminated in the contemporary spiritual wasteland. All of those who have come through the experience of catharsis have understood this necessity. To a greater or lesser extent each of them has demonstrated that no explanation of our contemporary "time of troubles" is possible without reference to the historical perspective. They recognize that the totalitarian regimes of destruction are not bizarre, idiosyncratic interruptions in the otherwise rational progress of civilization. Such phenomena could not occur without a widespread disintegration of spiritual order within the affected societies, and a more widely dispersed paralysis of will within the nations of the world that permitted them to go on unabated. One man, one group, or one party cannot be held responsible for all; the guilt is more extensively shared both within and across the generations. "It is a serious misunderstanding of historical forces to believe that a handful of men can destroy a civilization before it has committed suicide, to use the phrase of Toynbee," writes Voegelin (ER, 79). For the definition of a civilizational crisis is not that a breakdown of order has occurred, but that when this has happened the "remedial forces" that ought to restore order prove to be ineffective (ER, 180). Spiritual disorder consists in the universal awareness of what ought to be done, combined with the universal refusal to do it and the pervasive flight toward rationalizations.[1] Without this inner process of psychic disintegration, the external process of uninhibited political destruction could never occur.

A historical approach is therefore a virtual necessity if we wish to understand how the erosion of spiritual truth has occurred. Even if one is primarily concerned with the problems of the present, one is eventually redirected to the historical background in order to make sense of what is going on and to frame an adequate response. It was in this way that Solzhenitsyn was led to write his great history of the gulag and then of the Russian Revolution of 1917, but he found that his exploration could not simply stop there. The larger context of modern history had to be at least sketched in outline; otherwise his work would lack a frame of reference. This he provided in a surprisingly incisive manner in the latter half of the Harvard Address. There he showed his awareness that the contemporary crisis must ultimately be traced back to the spiritual revolution of modernity that began with the Renaissance. The ideas that have become socially powerful today, "the autonomy of man from any higher force above him," the lack of any "intrinsic evil in man," and the refusal to admit "any higher task than the attainment of happiness on earth," are all to be found in the intellectual currents that emanate from that period. The devastation we witness around us is "the calamity of a despiritualized and irreligious humanistic consciousness," which is the common source of the political movements of East and West.[2]

In a similar manner Dostoevsky understood his analyses of the moral disintegration of the Russian family as a way of illuminating the larger collapse of Russian society. This in turn merely reflected the more extended disintegration of modern civilization within the historical process. He was acutely aware of living at a critical period, which most of his contemporaries barely perceived in their concern about a society that no longer existed. His own task, as he understood it, was to transcend obsolete "landowner literature" by focusing on the chaos around him. He sought to discover therein "the laws of both this decomposition and the new construction" (*DW*, 592). Unremitting scrutiny of the interior struggles of his characters was the means Dostoevsky chose in order to explore the broader historical convulsion within modern civilization. The central feature of this crisis he identified as the "Catholic" heresy, against which Orthodoxy had broken away, and which now had reached its culmination in the socialist revolutionary movement. This heresy is the error of making power rather than spiritual conversion the foundation of order. He considered it to be the "Catholic principle" because of his understanding of Catholicism as resting on the idea that "Christianity cannot survive on earth without the earthly power of the Pope" (*DW*, 225; also 728; *I*, 560). However, this principle was not confined to Catholicism. Its most consistent expression was to be found in atheistic socialism, which had dispensed with the need for a divine authorization. Socialism recognized that the assertion of the self-sufficiency of autonomous political power had made humanity its own highest reality and rendered religion obsolete. The history of the modern world represents a continuous unfolding from just such a point of origin.[3]

A parallel interpretation is provided by Albert Camus's return to the beginning of the modern revolutionary movement. He finds the same belief in the self-sufficiency of human nature, the autonomous virtue of individuals, and, when that fails, the power of human will to bring about the desired historical transformation. Camus records the dolorous decline into cruelty and compulsion as the inevitable consequences of these convictions. As we have seen, he links responsibility for the concentration camps of this century to the ideas and commitments of the previous two hundred years. A relentless logic is at work in the movement from enlightenment through revolution to terror as the innovators reveal their willingness to sacrifice concrete human beings for the sake of the future perfection of humanity. Camus's struggle with the disorder of the present is, first and foremost, a grappling with the historical roots of the problem. He sees it as the only way to ensure that the mistakes will not be repeated.

The same inspiration has guided the even more expansive historical inquiry of Eric Voegelin. He is one of several scholars who, like Christopher Dawson, Arnold Toynbee, and others, turned to history in order to understand the source of the horrendous events through which we have lived. Voegelin's study of the ideological movements and of their quasi-religious nature led him back not only to their intellectual origins, but also to the motivational roots in the various strands of the Western religious experience. In particular, he discovered their affinity with Gnosticism, a heretical movement in Judaism and Christianity that emerged around the time of Christ. That perspective necessitated an exploration of the symbolisms that had been deformed, Judaism and Christianity. But his inquiry could not stop there. It also had to include the symbolism in which the restoration of individual and political order is articulated, Greek philosophy. Finally the perspective could only be complete if it were extended to the earlier and parallel symbolizations of the order of existence as they have emerged within human history. Voegelin's work makes it clear that we can have no hope of understanding the contemporary world unless we are familiar with both the historic symbolizations of order and the historic deformations of order that have contributed to it. Arbitrary or conventional restrictions of the inquiry cannot, in his view, be tolerated if we are to lay hold of the ultimate roots of the disorder.

Common agreement exists, in other words, that the source of the contemporary chaos must be traced to the historical origins of our age and, even further, to the very structure of Western civilization itself. Clearly, such a multilevel and multistage perspective on the contemporary world is the only means of ensuring we have reached the most comprehensive framework. But it also enormously complicates the task of assessing the influence and responsibility of the various factors involved. To claim competence over the entire historical sweep from the ancient world to the present would be foolhardy or foolish. Even an investigation of the modern period as a whole is fraught with dangers, both theoretical and empirical. Fortunately from a philosophical point of view such mastery is not required. What is needed, as the thinkers we are concerned with realized, is the capacity to identify the crucial elements without which everything would have developed quite differently. It is essential to isolate the key spiritual level, the innermost existential response to reality, that determines how the influence of all subsequent events and experiences will be accommodated within the overall result.

The close of the previous chapter alluded to the importance of such a focus. For the spiritual catharsis achieved by those who have confronted the full consequences of the abyss, raises even more prominently the question of why a similar response was not forthcoming among so many others and at an earlier time. Why has the inhuman cruelty of a humanitarianism without moral restraints been recognized by so few? And of the many who have seen clearly the consequences of this train of thought, why have they persisted in it anyway? Why indeed have the great thinkers of the modern world led us down a road they knew to have such a disastrous end? When one considers how close we have come, and still are, to self-annihilation, one has to wonder at the spiritual force that can blind human beings for so long to the results of what they are doing. If we are to avoid a further unraveling of our precarious hold on order, it is imperative that we reach a clear comprehension of the passion that can so distort the normal responses of human beings toward life. One is reminded of Camus's remark that all he sought was "to live the life of a normal man." What is it that has prevented so many men and women from being normal?

The Revolt against God

Metaphysical Revolt

The factor that has consistently been singled out as the fundamental determining influence in the modern age is what Camus has referred to as "metaphysical rebellion." What has turned the various attempts to install a modern revolutionary order into orgies of unlimited blood-letting is this detachment from any finite political objective. Having arisen from a revolt against the comprehensive nature of existence, virtually no tangible result can satisfy the motivating impulse. Only a total transformation of human nature and of the conditions of existence, which is in principle beyond the power of human agency to achieve, can assuage the fierce fire of revolution. As a consequence, the movement toward transfiguration, once it has begun, has an inbuilt dynamic to rage to the point of its own exhaustion, unless it encounters the resistance of a superior physical force to prevent it. The enormous destructive force of modern political movements can only be understood by recognizing the source from which their energies spring. "Impatience with limits, the rejection of their double life, despair at being a man, have finally driven them to inhuman excess" (R, 305).

This is the factor that blinds human beings to the deathly consequences of their actions, to the blatant contradiction within their espoused ideals, and to the futility of the entire transfigurative project. None of these considerations are effective in restraining their actions. For this reason any attempt at a rational refutation of their convictions is equally unproductive. In their view, the sufferings inflicted by such revolutionaries on themselves and others are insignificant compared to the overwhelming rightness of their position. All that matters is their sense of the profound injustice of the present state of the world, which stands irrevocably condemned before the transcendent passion for justice burning within them. This irreconcilable difference between the evil external reality and the pure inner goodness is the chief source of satisfaction. It provides the participants with a sense of their own irreproachable superiority to a meaningless world, which outweighs or overrides all other considerations of a more rational, commonsense nature. Who can expect such a fire of unlimited revolt to be checked by a mere adumbration of the consequences?[4]

Camus begins his account of the emergence of this complex of sentiments with the Marquis de Sade, one of the earliest representatives of metaphysical revolt. His version is characterized by revulsion against the unjust order of creation, followed by the resolve to oppose it with all the force of his being. Aware of his own lack of importance before the totality of the universe, however, de Sade is reduced to the only means of protest available to insignificant humanity: the deliberate commission of evil. His dedication to reaching the limits of depravity and cruelty—an avocation that has since become synonymous with his name—is continued wherever "man's emancipation is consummated in these strongholds of debauchery where a kind of bureaucracy of vice rules over the life and death of the men and women who have committed themselves forever to the hell of their desires" (R, 42). But its transitional nature is indicated by de Sade's continued willingness to acknowledge his actions as evil and to abide by the consequences of the moral order. He is followed chronologically and psychologically by the romantics, whose dandyism and perpetual self-contemplation before a mirror is intended to keep constantly before their minds the harsh injustice of their fate. When their sense of anguish and revolt has reached a fever pitch, it bursts the bonds of convention and becomes explicitly what it always has been: the revolt against God.

This is the impulse that spreads forth over the nineteenth century and reaches into our own as the fount of the ideological excess. Moreover, when the motivating source has thus been laid bare, the correlative implication of the position becomes equally plain: the divinization of human nature. The two are intimately related. It is a connection that is even stronger on the level of experience than in the conceptualization. Revolt against the God of creation would not have occurred, or become so radical, if it had not been fueled in considerable measure by the rivalry of humanity. For our overreaching hubris has not infrequently tempted us to "become like God, knowing good and evil" (Gen. 3:5). Conversely, the revolt against God that annihilates Him in the human heart inexorably turns humanity into its own *realissimum*, which must henceforth provide the principle and end of its own existence. When God is dead, then the apocalypse of humanity has begun. Having convinced itself of its own superior sense of justice, the modern world has thrown off the shackles of divine authority to at last become its own highest reality.

To find an illustration of this process Camus turns to the analyses of Dostoevsky, especially to the famous "rebellion" pronounced by Ivan Karamazov. This scene is further evidence, if such were needed, of Dostoevsky's ability to comprehend the modern mind so thoroughly that he could produce better arguments for atheism than the atheists themselves.[5] The strength of the passage derives from the logical intensity of the position developed by Ivan. This position has such force that even the gentle spiritual faith of his brother, Alyosha, finds it impossible to resist. They have met in a "stinking tavern" after twenty years and are not likely to meet again for another twenty, so their conversation plunges immediately into the "eternal questions" that disclose who they really are. Ivan understands that Alyosha does not want to hear a discussion about the abstractions of God and immortality, socialism and anarchism, but about the concrete meaning of these ideas in human life. "You don't want to hear about God, but only to know what the brother you love lives by. And so I've told you" (K, 280).

It is because Ivan pours out his heart, his innermost feelings, that a real communication of souls occurs and the convictions of the rebel appear so compelling, both to Alyosha and the reader. But we must not forget the role they play within the overall construction of the novel. In many ways Ivan is the central character, because it is within him that the most fundamental issues struggle for a resolution. It is important therefore to relate all that he says to his essential nature as a "riddle," suffering from an "aching heart" and torn between belief and disbelief. The "peculiarity of his heart," as it is perceived by the Elder Zossima, is that his question of the existence of God and immortality, "if it cannot be answered in the affirmative, . . . will never be answered in the negative" (K, 79). The revolt against God that he proclaims so stridently to Alyosha is virtually refuted in his own following account of the Grand Inquisitor.

Such is the power of Dostoevsky's analysis that his formulation has come to supercede that of the thinkers he sought to represent. Ivan's exposition has acquired a familiarity precisely because of its fidelity to the conflicting tensions of experience. He forthrightly states his willingness to accept both God and the providential divine plan by which all things are guided toward their fulfillment in the final moment of perfect eternal harmony. "Yet would you believe it," he asks Alyosha, "in the final result I don't accept it at all. It's not that I don't accept God, you must understand, it's the world created by Him I don't and cannot concede" (*K*, 279). The existence of God is indispensable, in other words, for Ivan's attitude to be sustained. Without a transcendent creator to be held responsible, it would make no sense to revolt against the order of things or to derive the consequences for human freedom contained in such a position. This is extremely significant for the whole modern phenomenon of revolt against God, which is not so much atheistic as antitheistic or anti-Christian.

What Ivan finds intolerable above all else in creation is the suffering of innocent children. This is for him the litmus test of a truly ordered cosmos and, like Dostoevsky, he has made a habit of collecting anecdotes of cruelty toward children as they surface in newspaper accounts and trials. So it is likely that the examples provided have a basis in fact. He recounts how the parents of a five-year-old girl cruelly punished her for soiling her bed. She was beaten mercilessly, smeared in her own excrement, and left to cry all night in a freezing outdoor privy. "Can you understand why a little creature, who can't even understand what's done to her, should beat her little aching heart with her tiny fists in the dark and the cold, and weep her meek unresentful little tears to dear, kind God to protect her?" (*K*, 287). Or there is the even more harrowing example of the little serf boy who mistakenly injured a hound's paw. He was taken by the general who owned him, to be stripped naked and made to run before the hounds. When they caught him he was ripped to pieces by the whole pack before the eyes of his mother. What, Ivan asks Alyosha, did such a monster as the general deserve? "To be shot" was the murmured response.

The problem is not that Ivan cannot conceive of some future or eternal moment when all such wrongs have been redressed and order finally emerges triumphant. It is that no conceivable fulfillment or harmonization can adequately recompense the cruelty inflicted on such innocents. The whole of knowledge and of the eternal happiness of humanity would not outweigh the cruelty. "It's not worth the tears of that one tortured child who beat itself on the breast with its little fist and prayed in its stinking outhouse with its unexpiated tears to 'dear, kind God'! It's not worth it, because those tears are unatoned for" (*K*, 290). But Ivan goes even further than this expression of common human perplexity before the mystery of suffering. In a remarkably perceptive passage Dostoevsky reveals how the spirit of revolt can so pervade the human soul that it refuses to be assuaged even by the demonstration of its untruth.

I don't want harmony. From love for humanity I don't want it. I would rather be left with the unavenged suffering. I would rather be left with my unavenged suffering and unsatisfied indignation, *even if I were wrong [khota by ia byl i ne-prav]*. Besides too high a price is asked for harmony; it's beyond our means to pay so much to enter on it. And so I hasten to give back my entrance ticket, and if I am an honest man I am bound to give it back as soon as possible. And that I am doing. It's not God that I don't accept, Alyosha, only I most respect-fully return Him the ticket. (*K*, 291)

To this the believer, Alyosha, can only register the weak objection that "That's rebellion." His inability to provide a response is further exposed when Ivan asks if he could agree to a world where the happiness of all had made it necessary "to torture to death only one tiny creature." "'No, I wouldn't consent,' said Alyosha softly" (*K*, 291).

The only counterposition that Alyosha can suggest is the example of the One whose own innocent suffering incarnates the perfect for-giveness required. But Ivan is prepared for this defense and has his prose poem, "The Legend of the Grand Inquisitor," ready in response. Its ostensible purpose is to demonstrate the superiority of the Inquisi-tor's love of human beings in comparison to that of Christ, whom he accuses of "acting as though Thou didst not love them at all" (*K*, 302). Christ's redemptive sacrifice has only placed a greater burden of free-dom on human shoulders, which the vast majority are utterly incapable of supporting. Unable to live up to the demands of faith, they are doomed to perish. The Inquisitor, on the other hand, has taken the burden of responsibility for good and evil upon himself. By freeing the great mass of humanity from the unending struggle for spiritual per-fection, he has achieved their true salvation. Happiness has been con-cretely realized in this life, and not just for a few. The Inquisitor has "saved" all of them. This is the reason for the haughty self-righteous-ness with which he regards his divine visitor.

And we who have taken their sins upon us for their happiness will stand up before Thee and say: 'Judge us if Thou canst and darest.' Know that I fear thee not. Know that I too have been in the wilderness, I too have lived on roots and locusts, I too prized the freedom with which Thou hast blessed men, and I too was striving to stand among Thy elect, among the strong and powerful, thirst-ing 'to make up the number.' But I awakened and would not serve madness. I turned back and joined the ranks of those *who have corrected Thy work*. (*K*, 308)

Here we have the equivalent of Ivan's expression of revolt in the pre-ceding chapter in the novel, only now it is directed specifically at the person of Christ. Christ's self-sacrificing love of human beings presents the greatest threat of its dissolution. At the same time we can more clearly observe the note of all-consuming pride that begins to reveal itself as the Inquisitor's ultimate motivating source. We sense how readily his lust for unlimited self-aggrandizement surpasses the original humanitarian complaints.

The ironic consequence of elaborating the revolt against God to this point of self-disclosure is that it undermines its own claim to legitimacy. Ivan is aware of this, as he acknowledges by agreeing with Alyosha's perception that the poem "is in praise of Jesus, not in blame of Him— as you meant it to be" (K, 309). Jesus is the one who truly loves human beings, who cares enough about them to want to preserve their essential human freedom. The processes by which this love operates remain mysterious and the objections to the damnation of multitudes are not removed, but the reality of God's love in Christ cannot be doubted. The Inquisitor, by contrast, is exposed as a nihilist who harbors nothing but contempt for human beings and willingly sets about their spiritual destruction.[6] His revolt in the name of suffering humanity is exposed as false. For although it may contain a germ of truth, which even an Alyosha would have to concede, it has been far too extensively perverted by the drive for universal domination. We begin to understand the real source of intensity behind the revolt against God: the desire to become God. "Your inquisitor does not believe in God," Alyosha declares, "that's his secret." And Ivan replies: "What if it's so! At last you have guessed it" (K, 310). It is not so much that he has ceased to believe as that he has killed God in his heart in order to become God himself. The parallel with Zarathustra's secret "If there were gods, how could I endure not being a god?" is fully evident.[7]

For the psychological process by which this self-divinization is sustained, we are referred back to the creator of the legend. Ivan's revolt arises from his passionate determination "to stick to the fact" of innocent suffering. "With my pitiful, earthly, Euclidean understanding, all I know is that there is suffering and that there are none guilty" (K, 289). He has closed himself off to the possibility of faith, which could provide a glimpse of the reconciliation to come in eternity. No harmonization that does not provide a resolution of the injustice here and now is acceptable. "I must have justice [vozmezhdiye], or I will destroy myself. And not justice in some remote infinite time and space, but here on earth, and that I could see myself" (K, 289). The passionate sense of injustice becomes so overwhelming that it eclipses everything else in his consciousness, blinding Ivan even to the nature of justice itself. All that matters is that innocent suffering has occurred and that nothing conceivable can justify it. The relief of suffering, the promotion of justice as far as possible, and openness toward the mystery of an order not fully disclosed to us are all obliterated by the raging passion of his anger. Nothing is allowed to occupy the center of his consciousness but the sense of revulsion at cosmic injustice and the conviction of his own unassailable righteousness. At this point the source of the distortion in Ivan's revolt becomes clear. His consuming obsession with injustice ultimately arises from the will to place himself above the whole of reality and sit in judgment over the transcendent God. The drive for self-divinization finally becomes transparent in the conclusion he draws, that "everything is lawful." For this could not be reached from the judgment that innocent suffering is unjust. Instead, what Ivan reveals is that his burning indignation at divine injustice is the powerful means of sustaining his illusion of human moral supremacy.

The Gnostic Divinization of Human Nature

The process of self-justification is identical with Voegelin's analysis of modern Gnostic consciousness. In searching for theoretical categories to understand the fanatical revolutionary activism familiar to Dostoevsky and the others, Voegelin discovered the affinity between the motivating experience of the activists and that of ancient Gnosticism. A structural similarity between the two can be discerned in the intense feelings of alienation and revolt that inspired them. In Gnosticism, those feelings were extended to the God responsible for such an intolerable world, who must henceforth be regarded as an irrevocably evil or fallen divinity and the implacable enemy of humanity. The hostility is heightened by the contrast between the pure spiritual ideal present in the soul, and the unregenerately evil world in which it finds itself embodied. When this conflict is brought to a fever pitch of intensity, as it is in Gnosticism, then the imagination flows irresistibly toward the visionary beyond or future, in which the true homeland of humanity will be realized. Gnosis or knowledge is the crucial means of attaining it. By understanding how the evil forces of the cosmic divinity may be defeated, goes the Gnostic line of thought, we can regain the translucent divine nature that is our birthright. The revolt against God and the correlative divinization of humanity, Voegelin came to realize, are not purely modern phenomena.[8]

They are the end point of a process that has been unfolding in Western civilization since the collapse of the medieval synthesis of spiritual and temporal orders. When the mystery of the interpenetration of these orders was no longer sufficient, the search for new forms of assurance about the meaning of human existence became necessary. It gave rise to a multiplicity of movements promising to assuage this anxiety concerning the purpose and significance of human life. Something more was needed than traditional faith in the providential divine ordering of reality, the trust that "to those who love God all things work for the good" (Rom. 8:28). It became necessary for human beings to penetrate more deeply into the mystery of God's actions in history and to acquire a more substantive role in the overall process. Voegelin understood it as a collapse of faith in the sense of "the substance of things hoped for and the proof of things unseen" (Heb. 11:1). It was an attempt to gain a more tangible certainty about existence than that provided by the tenuous link of faith. Humans sought to step beyond the boundaries of the human condition, no longer participants in divine reality but now partners who approached identification with God. "The attempt at immanentizing the meaning of existence is fundamentally an attempt at bringing our knowledge of transcendence into a firmer grip than the *cognitio fidei*, the cognition of faith, will afford; and Gnostic experiences offer this firmer grip in so far as they are an expansion of the soul to the point where God is drawn into the existence of man" (*NSP*, 124).

To illustrate the nature of modern Gnosticism, Voegelin selects the example of the Puritan revolutionaries. There the Christian origins are still explicit and the essential nature of the phenomenon is "not obscured by compromises with the exigencies of political success" (*NSP*, 152). Radical Puritanism also had the advantage of having been closely analyzed by a brilliant contemporary observer, Richard Hooker, whom Voegelin quotes liberally in his own study of the movement. Puritan Gnosticism is characterized first by a practice of severe unrestrained criticism of the established order of things in society. This is an attitude we recognize today as "moralizing," "hypermoralism," or "moral absolutism." It establishes the impeccable bona fides of the Gnostics as individuals of extraordinary moral rectitude, and becomes the basis for their authority to attack the failings and abuses of the government in power. The Puritans, in addition, based their position on an appeal to sacred Scripture. For this it was necessary to impose their own canons of interpretation, without admitting any rivals. But the decisive step is what Hooker described as "the persuading of men credulous and overcapable of such pleasing errors, that it is the special illumination of the Holy Ghost, whereby they discern those things in the word, which others reading yet discern them not" (quoted in *NSP*, 136). Voegelin particularly admires Hooker's sensitivity to "the nihilistic component of gnosticism in the Puritan belief that their discipline, being 'the absolute command of Almighty God, it must be received although the world by receiving it should be clean turned upside down; herein lieth the greatest danger of all'" (NSP, 143–44). In their view, the conviction of their own absolute righteousness absolved them of responsibility for the consequences, no matter how destructive. This in turn reveals the extent to which their motivations cannot be regarded as either truly virtuous or truly Christian. "All this," Voegelin concludes, "has nothing to do with Christianity. The scriptural camouflage cannot veil the drawing of God into man. The saint is a Gnostic who will not leave the transfiguration of the world to the grace of God beyond history but will do the work of God himself, right here and now, in history" (NSP, 147).

It is a disorder that can occur whenever the tension that humanity experiences between good and evil, perfection and imperfection, truth and falsity, threatens to fall apart into two separate realities. Dualism in this sense has long been recognized as a characteristic of Gnostic systems; it arises from the Gnostic tendency to project responsibility for disorder onto a source outside the self.[9] Fundamental to the Gnostic attitude is "the belief that the drawbacks of the situation can be attributed to the fact that the world is intrinsically poorly organized. . . . Gnostics are not inclined to discover that human beings in general and they themselves in particular are inadequate. If in a given situation something is not as it should be, then the fault is to be found in the wickedness of the world" (SPG, 86–87). This is both the chief source of the Gnostic appeal and the principal cause of Gnosticism's enormously destructive consequences in human life. Reality is dissociated into two worlds of the elect and the reprobate, between whom neither communication, conciliation, nor compromise are possible. "The real danger of contemporary wars does not lie in the technologically determined global extent of the theater of war; their true fatality stems from their character as Gnostic wars, that is, wars between worlds that are bent on mutual destruction" (NSP, 151).

The experience of reality as radically split between good and evil, spiritual and material components, is a constant within Gnosticism as far back as its origins in the pre-Christian era. But its elaboration could assume a wide amplitude of variations, including the creation of non-Gnostic symbolizations such as apocalyptic and chiliastic expectations. In the ancient world, Gnosticism was speculatively unfolded into psychodramatic representations of liberation and escape from the conditions of earthly existence, and return to a transcendent divinity beyond the cosmos. In the modern world, the great Gnostic systematizers invariably project a world-immanent transfiguration of the cosmos, which performs the same liberating function from the oppressive conditions of existence. Voegelin does not regard the distinction between extra- and intracosmic varieties as connoting an essential difference in the experience. The same motivations of alienation, revolt, and divinization remain, while the differences in orientation can be explained by reference to the prevailing civilizational circumstances. The ancient Gnostics were responding to the disorder of the Ecumenic Age; its succession of senseless imperial expansions promised no likelihood of restoring a meaningful political order. The modern Gnostics arose from the uncertainties created by the burgeoning social, cultural, and political energies of the late medieval world; this age seemed to be pregnant with the possibility of realizing a new civilizational order within history. In a world that is evidently moving toward some form of progressive fulfillment, gnosis is naturally directed along the lines of historical speculation (*NSP*, 126).

Such a bold conception as Voegelin's assertion of the Gnostic character of modernity, is bound to appear startling to minds familiar with the secular self-understanding of the contemporary world. Indeed, when he first propounded his view it did attract brief public notoriety.[10] It has a ring of strangeness about it that might even suggest an idiosyncratic source, until one begins to count up the number of similar studies that after the Second World War began to reach similar conclusions. There was particularly the work of Karl Löwith, who, while not using the category of Gnosticism, revealed the extent to which the great modern philosophies of history have merely secularized the preceding religious constructions. The Judeo-Christian eschaton has been transformed into a historical culmination within time.[11] Second, there were the extensive scholarly investigations of ancient Gnosticism conducted by Gilles Quispel, Hans Jonas, and others, who could not help but notice the parallel with contemporary patterns of thought.[12] Third, there have been the profound reassessments of the great eighteenth- and nineteenth-century thinkers in light of the totalitarian convulsions of the twentieth, undertaken not only by Camus, but also by Henri de Lubac, Hans Urs von Balthasar, Jacob Talmon, and others.[13] Finally, students of the millenarian and mystical activism of the Middle Ages, such as Norman Cohn, Jacob Taubes, and others, began to point out the correspondences with our own revolutionary movements.[14] All of these studies in one way or another can be seen as grappling with what Voegelin has called "the murderous grotesque" of our time. In struggling to understand it, all of these thinkers have reached a remarkable degree of consensus in their conclusions. Modern civilization, especially as manifested in its most uncompromising form in the ideological mass movements, is not to be considered as either a purely secular phenomenon, a reversion to pre-Christian paganism, or a quest for wholly novel religious forms of its own. It is primarily a deformation of the Christian experience that redirects the eschatological transfiguration toward an innerworldly fulfillment within time.[15] Voegelin's achievement within this context is to have identified Gnosticism as the appropriate theoretical category.

The Empirical Evidence of History

The emerging scholarly perspective concerning the intramundane religiosity of the modern world runs directly contrary to the conventional secular conception. This is undoubtedly the reason why it has made such little progress in terms of public consciousness. It also explains why the revised understanding of modernity has eventually become the target of attack by its intellectual opponents. The normal response to such a radical critique of the prevailing cultural and political presuppositions is simply silence. Debate occurs within well-defined parameters; anyone straying outside to question fundamental assumptions is conveniently ignored. Camus's complaint that he could not find in all the hostile reviews of *The Rebel* any attempt to respond to his criticism of the destructiveness of socialism, is by now familiar.[16] However, the increasing consensus on the pseudoreligious character of modernity has clearly been building toward a critical point, where it can no longer be ignored. As a consequence, a number of quite interesting recent attempts have been made to argue against it. They provide us with an extremely useful test of its tenability.

The most prominent critic is certainly the German scholar Hans Blumenberg. His work *The Legitimacy of the Modern Age* openly declares its intention of defending the nonderivative status of modernity. Only when it is recognized as *sui generis*, asserts Blumenberg, will our modern world be understood correctly, as a legitimate civilizational form that requires interpretation in its own terms. Blumenberg takes exception to the way in which Löwith assimilated modern constructions of history to the pattern of Judeo-Christian *Heilesgeschichte*. He objects to the reduction of the self-understanding of the modern world to a variant of Christian eschatology, because it imposes a one-dimensional framework on the rich complexity of factors and influences at work. On its face this is certainly a criticism worthy of consideration, but on closer examination it turns out to be something of a straw man. For it would be hard to find among any of the scholars mentioned earlier—Löwith, Voegelin, Talmon, et al—any assertion that the salvation-history model was the only influence in shaping the secular philosophies of history. These scholars have simply been less concerned with enumerating all the other factors involved. It is enough, in their view, to focus on the most crucial element, the one that provides the overriding sense of direction to the enterprise. Despite the separation from Christian faith, this remained the eschatological expectation.

But that does not eliminate the substance of Blumenberg's reservations. It cannot be denied that he has pointed toward a problem with the "secularization" thesis. He has insisted that the proponents not only demonstrate the similarity between secular and religious constructions, but that they also account for the evident differences between them.

Regarding the dependence of the idea of progress on Christian eschatology, there are differences that would have had to block any transposition of the one into the other. It is a formal, but for that very reason, a manifest difference that an eschatology speaks of an event breaking into history, an event that transcends and is heterogeneous to it, while the idea of progress extrapolates from a structure present in every moment to a future that is immanent in history.[17]

This is undoubtedly a justifiable requirement. If indeed the modern schemes of ideological revolutionary transformation are dependent on the background of Christian expectations, then it should be possible to identify the process by which the redirection toward an intramundane eschaton occurred. It may be that Blumenberg is merely being disingenuous here. He may have allowed prejudice in favor of the modern age to obscure his judgment of some of the "transpositions" already identified. Yet the core of his objections would still remain. The crucial role of Joachim of Fiore in modifying the exclusively transcendent orientation of Christianity to include the anticipation of a new age of fulfillment within time, has been extensively noted by Voegelin and Löwith. But even granting that instance, it must still be acknowledged that this is not nearly enough. What is needed to confirm the secularization hypothesis is the identification of a broad spiritual shift of attention toward a world-immanent telos.

Blumenberg's own suggestion that the analogies between the earlier religious and the later secular constructions arise from the attempt at "reoccupying" outmoded "question positions" is not theoretically adequate. It involves him in a denial of the very element of progressivity that constitutes the self-understanding of modernity. The entire consciousness of epoch, which separates the modern world from the medieval orientation toward eternity, would be inconceivable without the sense of movement toward a historical fulfillment. Progress without a culminating transfiguration would carry none of the same intensity of expectation and energy. If no more is expected than the incremental accumulation of achievements in the arts and sciences, social and political reforms, and the gradual improvement of the conditions of existence, then there is hardly any basis for anticipating an ultimate qualitative transformation within history. We are deprived of our membership in the final age of light and perfection, the expectation of whose dawning has been one of the most enduring ingredients of modernity. Finite specific achievements in science, technology, and politics do not in themselves provide a basis for this extrapolation toward the definitive transfiguration of human nature. Without its halo of eschatological expectations the modern world is unintelligible.

This is illustrated well by a recent study that attempted to understand the modern world in purely secular terms. The author sought to do "without reference to religious categories, by turning to the questions and desires generated by philosophic perspectives introduced in the second half of the eighteenth century." This is certainly possible and often illuminating. But it does not finally help us to make sense of why such thinkers as Marx or Nietzsche persisted in their "longing for total revolution," especially when the project readily discloses itself to be "a self-contradictory goal."[18] A theoretically more satisfactory explanation is needed if we are to penetrate the real nature of such phenomena. Yet it must also, as Blumenberg's criticisms have shown, be more solidly grounded empirically than the secularization hypothesis has previously been.

The final court of appeal for any interpretation of the modern world must be the material evidence of history. If we are making an assertion about the civilizational course we have followed, then the only way of confirming or denying it must be through a confrontation with the facts. Analysis of the psychological processes by which individuals and societies commit evil on an unprecedented scale and manage to persuade themselves they are working for the supreme good of humanity, may point toward the most radical spiritual disorder. Nietzsche may be correct in denoting us as the murderers of God who have been driven by the desire to become God. But the question of whether this truly represents the movement of our civilization as a whole can only be settled by a return to history itself. Is it true that modernity, as

Voegelin has suggested, is fundamentally Gnostic in character, motivated by a revolt against God that aims at the divinization of humanity? Only an examination of what actually has happened can decide the issue.

Specifically, we must examine the self-interpretations of the leading figures within the past five hundred years. For we have only the evidence of what they have said they were doing, as a basis for forming our judgment about the nature of their enterprise. They may have been mistaken in their intentions, and we may well consider them deluded or worse in what they sought to do, but we have no other means of knowing what they proposed except their own self-disclosures on the subject. Whatever our own personal estimations of the value and validity of their project, we cannot deny that their project was what it was. By focusing thus on the self-explications of its principal exponents, we should be able to resolve the conflicting conceptions of our world. The modern thinkers themselves provide the best guide to an understanding of the civilization constituted by their thought. Whether modernity consists of a discontinuous assertion of rational secular principles or an intramundane distortion of traditional Christian eschatology can only be determined by examining the self-reflections of those most intimately involved.

When we turn to the data of history in search of an answer, we find to our surprise and relief that much of the work has already been done. Contemporary historiography, one of the sciences of the modern world, has increasingly directed its attention to the history of which it itself is a part. Extensive scholarly research during the past fifty years has made available an abundance of historical material concerning all dimensions of our past. Indeed, the flourishing of historical studies is one of the great overlooked intellectual achievements of the century. It has resulted in a profound revision of the received wisdom regarding many earlier periods and events, including some of the most crucial for the Western inheritance. Of particular significance, from our perspective, have been the studies of the genesis of our own civilization in the history of early modern Europe. They have contributed to the growing consensus among social and intellectual historians of the religious underpinnings of many of the most prominent secularizing movements. Such insights have still not expanded much beyond the scholarly community, for they run counter to the pervasive self-understanding of society. But they are destined to have a decisive long-term effect. They provide startling confirmation of the intramundane religiousness of modernity and verify what can only remain a suspicion to those observing the ideological excesses of our own day.

The Early Modern Transformation of Christianity: The Renaissance Magus

We have already seen how militant Puritanism prefigured the essential nature of the modern revolutionary movements. Historians have now brought to light the extent to which the "radical Reformation" reached almost as far as the mainline efforts at reform.[19] Luther was astonished at the speed and facility with which his principle of "justification through faith alone" became radicalized into the quest for an immediate total transfiguration of individual, society, and history. His onetime colleague and admirer Thomas Müntzer illustrates the process extremely well. Müntzer moved from the search for an inner assurance of salvation to the demand for an external assurance of God's providence. He required to see the operation of absolute divine justice within the political realm. This led him along the inexorable path, after the princes of Saxony had rejected his call to become the instruments of God's judgment, toward social revolution. He became the head of the avenging divine host of the poor and downtrodden. The tragedy unfolded predictably toward the final scene of Müntzer at the head of a ragtag band of peasants, whom he led to their slaughter before the overwhelming military forces of the nobility outside Mühlhausen. His blinding sense of identity with divine justice had eclipsed all other awareness of reality. It is even reported that he declared his ability to catch the bullets of his enemies in the outspread mantle of his cloak.[20] Luther was deeply shaken by the misuse of his ideas in the German peasants' revolt. Yet his continued efforts, and those of the other reformers, at restoring balance between faith and political expectations could not prevent the repetition of this pattern throughout the sixteenth and seventeenth centuries.

The problem was that the Reformation had erupted into a civilization already shaped by the expectations of a new age of the spirit that went back to Joachim of Fiore. He had been the first to definitively break with the Augustinian construction of history, which regarded the present age as the millennium or last times, a *saeculum senescens*, that looked forward to consummation in the Second Coming and eternity. The Calabrian abbot introduced the notion of a third age, the Age of the Spirit. It was to follow the present Age of the Son, as *it* had followed the previous Age of the Father. Now the third age was about to intervene before the final end of history. As a result of this construction, Joachim inaugurated the endless succession of tripartite divisions of history that continue, as de Lubac has shown, to the present.[21]

Joachim gave expression to the shift of spiritual focus from an eternal transcendent telos to a penultimate or intermediate fulfillment within history. The approaching Age of the Spirit constituted a new revelation of what had been contained in the Old and New Testaments. It was to be led by a new spiritual leader, proclaimed by a new prophet, and characterized by a new human nature based on the monastic model. All human beings would enter into the fellowship of autonomous spiritual persons capable of living without the support or restraint of any kind of institution. Despite the often conservative intention of Joachim's teaching, its implications led toward revolutionary change. The anticipation of a terrestrial paradise tended to eclipse the importance of the eternal one; the message of the Spirit implied that the message of Christ had been superseded; and the Church with its sacraments, as well as the institutions of the state, were to be rendered obsolete. An inexorable logic led from Joachim's prophetic redirection of human striving toward an innerworldly fulfillment, to the construction of a final earthly kingdom independent of the transcendent God. When the divine substance is progressively drawn into humanity, the process of secularization has begun. It is not surprising, therefore, that Joachim's speculations became a powerful influence on all the sectarian paracletic movements from the medieval period to our own.

The turning point came when such revolutionary experiences moved from the radical fringes to occupy a position of respectability and legitimacy in society. Generally speaking, this occurred during the Renaissance. This period is conventionally identified as the beginning of the modern world because of the intense consciousness of epoch established then. Petrarch was the first to give it the designation of Age of Light, following the dark age dominated by "the celebration of the name of Christ."[22] The term *Renaissance—la rinascita*—was coined by Vasari, in his *Lives of the Most Famous Painters, Sculptors and Architects* (1550), to further specify the nature of the new age as a rebirth of the glory and beauty of the classical world. Until recently, the nature of the profound and far-reaching changes contained in this new perspective were not fully understood. Renaissance humanism was all too readily assimilated into the preceding Christian patterns of thought; the Christian humanism of Erasmus and his associates tended to blunt the edge of the dramatic shift taking place. But the picture has begun to clarify considerably, as a result of the researches of contemporary historians of the period. They have begun to uncover the extent to which the first great manifestation of modernity was rooted in a widespread and fundamental revolution of the spirit.[23]

Contrary to the prevailing conception of the Renaissance as the revival of rational humanism and scholarship, it now appears to have been a time of unprecedented interest in all varieties of spiritual and religious innovation. At the very beginning of the most quintessentially rational and secular activities, and continuing as an undercurrent to the present, has been a profound involvement with occult, mystical, and magical practices and forces. The great scientific figures of the period, especially Copernicus, Bruno, Kepler, and Newton, understood themselves to be engaged in the search for the highest divine Wisdom hidden within nature.[24] Rulers and courtiers freely experimented with a new politicoreligious symbolism that depicted the magical transformation of existence in the new nation-states. Widespread interest in mysticism led to the belief in a *prisca theologia*, or ancient theology, that was the original and the unifying truth in all the world's religions. The anticipation of a religious reawakening, as a result of this experiential contact with occult spiritual forces, gave rise to an intense expectation of broad social and political reform. The preeminent expression of this expectation is to be found in the succession of utopian constructions that poured forth, beginning with Thomas More's *Utopia* (1516). Above all, a new conception of the human being as a Magus, possessing divine creative powers, became firmly established.

This is the true nature of the changes introduced by the Renaissance. The age went beyond commercial, political, or cultural innovations to inaugurate a new self-understanding of human nature and its relationship to the whole of reality and to the divine ordering source. Revolutionary changes were greeted with widespread public acceptance. A rival religious form had been introduced under the guise of providing experiential renewal for an excessively rigid and dogmatized Christianity. For the first time in the history of Christianity, practices that had been consistently condemned—such as demonology, conjuring, magical manipulation, and so on—were not only tolerated but even acquired a new level of respectability. They could be viewed as legitimate attempts to communicate with the occult divine forces that are the ruling powers of the cosmos. This "natural magic" was put forward as radically different from the "black magic" that had always been prohibited by the Church. No appeal to the spirits of the underworld was taking place. The Renaissance Magi (like those of the Gospels) sought only to understand and to benefit from the hidden spiritual powers that mediated the divine order of reality. What had previously been confined to an underground presence now erupted into public consciousness as the possibility of sympathetic magico-mystical operations. Popes and priests, kings and queens, philosophers and scientists, artists and writers, all openly experimented with the idea of a human being becoming a Magus.[25]

But how was such a far-reaching revision of Christianity accomplished? Scholars of the Renaissance emphasize the extent to which the new magico-mystical interests were looked upon as a means of restoring genuine Christian piety. In addition, the distinction from the more disreputable forms of magic was sufficiently reassuring to allay most anxieties. Beyond this was the influence of the newly discovered texts from the ancient world, especially the *Corpus Hermeticum*. This latter text was mistakenly dated as contemporaneous with the principal speakers in the work, notably the Egyptian priest Hermes Trismegistus, believed to have lived around the time of Moses or even earlier. Men of learning in the Renaissance were convinced that here they had found the *prisca theologia*. This was the original divine revelation to all humanity and, therefore, a source of such pristine truth that it was beyond reproach. In fact the *Corpus*, along with the *Orphica* and the *Chaldean Oracles*, was a collection of syncretistic texts from the first two centuries A.D. whose religious character was essentially Gnostic. The error, which was persisted in even after it was discovered, became a convenient cover for the real source of attraction: the novel assertion of humanity's transformative divine power. Like all Gnostic constructions, the Hermetic constructions made it possible for human beings to "divinize themselves by substituting more massive modes of participation in divinity for faith in the Christian sense" (*NSP*, 124).

This is very clear in the succession of thinkers who were associated with the Neoplatonic Academy of Florence between 1450 and 1550. The first is Marsilius Ficino, a Catholic priest and principal scholar to the Medicis. His project of translating Plato into Latin was interrupted by the arrival of the *Corpus Hermeticum*; it immediately absorbed his attention as the Egyptian original of Greek philosophy. Through Ficino's translation of the *Corpus*, the Gnostic understanding of human nature became widely available in the West for the first time. It portrayed humans as semidivine beings who had emanated from the Godhead and been drawn into the material world as its rulers; humanity was shown to possess the magical or creative divine powers capable of restoring all things to their original state of perfection. This view of our nature is celebrated in this oft-quoted passage from the *Asclepius*, one of the Hermetic texts:

Man is a marvel then, Asclepius; honor and reverence to such a being! Man takes on the attributes of a god, as though he were himself a god; he is familiar with the daemonkind, for he comes to know that he is sprung from the same source as they; and strong in the assurance of that in him which is divine, he scorns the merely human part of his own nature. How far more happily blended are the properties of man than those of other beings! He is linked to the gods, inasmuch as there is in him a divinity akin to theirs; he scorns that part of his own being which makes him a thing of earth; and all else with which he finds himself connected by heaven's ordering, he binds to himself by the ideas of his affection. He raises reverent eyes to heaven above; he tends the earth below. Blest in his intermediate station, he is so placed that he loves all below him, and is loved by all above him. He has access to all; he descends to the depths of the sea by the keenness of his thought; and heaven is not found too high for him, for he measures it by his sagacity, as though it were within his reach. With his quick wit he penetrates the elements; air cannot blind his mental vision with its thickest darkness; dense earth cannot impede his work; the deepest water cannot impede his downward gaze. Man is all things; man is everywhere.[26]

Ficino himself engaged in the kind of magic alluded to in this passage. By the use of music, talismans, and incantations he sought to sympathetically draw down the esoteric or hidden planetary influences that can create the physically, morally, and spiritually healthy personality. He was, however, careful to insist that he was only employing good or "natural" magic and not appealing to demons.[27]

Less reticent was his younger contemporary Pico della Mirandola, who willingly addressed himself to individual spiritual beings. He was supported in this by the authority of the Kaballah, the Jewish esoteric tradition that parallels Hermeticism. The Kaballah identifies the cosmic spiritual powers with the *sefiroth* or divine emanations, as well as with the intermediacy of angels that were easily compatible with Christian theology. A similar framework of occult or hidden divine influences and signatures existed within the Kaballah.[28] Human nature was similarly raised to a level just short of the divine emanations, and assumed the new messianic role of reintegrating the original unity of divine life flowing through all things. The concomitant revision of the nature of God, for whose self-actualization the self-unfolding through creation is now essential, completed the picture. The tendency toward a radical alteration of Judaism became evident in the antinomianism and nihilism implied by the symbolism. For evil had been transformed into a necessary cosmic moment and no longer represented the eruption of groundless spiritual revolt. Pico's combination of Hermeticism and the Kabbalah, in a "Christian Cabala," powerfully reinforced the theological respectability of the new forms of mystical experience throughout the sixteenth century.

Pico's famous *Oration on the Dignity of Man* provided what might be termed the manifesto for the conception of humanity as a divine Magus. The oration has long been familiar to readers of Renaissance literature, but only when it is placed within this background of Hermetic-Kabbalist mysticism does the precise nature of its references become clear—as, for instance, when he pictures God's address to Adam at creation:

> The nature of all other creatures is defined and restricted within laws which We have laid down; you, by contrast, impeded by no such restrictions, may, by your own free will, to whose custody We have assigned you, trace for yourself the lineaments of your own nature. I have placed you at the very center of the world, so that from that vantage point you may with greater ease glance round about you on all that the world contains. We have made you a creature neither of heaven nor of earth, neither mortal nor immortal, in order that you may, as the free and proud shaper of your own being, fashion yourself into the form you may prefer.[29]

What he has described is the experience of Hermetic-Kabbalist ascent through the spheres of the cosmos, which provides us with the knowledge of the sympathetic harmonies within all things. Human nature may ascend or descend, form itself into whatever it chooses, and thereby penetrate the secret of the divine signature or formation in all things. The gnosis of the occult influences, which provides the means of a Gnostic and Neoplatonic return to the One, is also the means for humanity's royal descent to become the god-ruler of the material world. "What has changed," according to Frances Yates, "is Man, now no longer only the pious spectator of God's wonders in creation, but Man the Operator, man who seeks to draw power from the divine and natural order."[30]

As the most extreme example of the Renaissance Magus stands the mercurial ex-Dominican Giordano Bruno. He carried the new experiences to their logical conclusion in dispensing altogether with Christianity and advocating a return to the Egyptian religion of Hermes Trismegistus. He proclaimed Hermeticism as the only authentic basis for spiritual and political order, for it was only through a Hermetic-Kabbalist mysticism that humans could acquire the transformative divine power to bring all things to perfection. Bruno created a magical memory system as the means of drawing the totality of divine-cosmic influences into himself. By manipulating the planetary images within, he believed he could attract the celestial powers into terrestrial reality and, at the same time, ascend through the levels of reality to become the "equal of God."

Unless you make yourself equal to God, you cannot understand God: for the like is not intelligible save to the like. Make yourself grow to a greatness beyond measure, by a bound free yourself from the body; raise yourself above all time, become Eternity; then you will understand God. Believe that nothing is impossible for you, think yourself immortal and capable of understanding all arts, all sciences, the nature of every living being. Mount higher than the highest height; descend lower than the lowest depth. Draw into yourself all sensations of everything created, fire and water, dry and moist, imagining that you are not yet born, in the maternal womb, adolescent, old, dead, beyond death. If you embrace in your thought all things at once, times, places, substances, qualities, quantities, you may understand God.[31]

Not surprisingly, Bruno was convinced of his own messianic mission to bring the light of Hermetic-Kabbalist reform to the whole known world. He tirelessly traversed the courts of Europe as first one, then another Renaissance ruler seemed ready to lend support to his program. The pattern continued until he eventually fell afoul of the Italian Inquisition while in Venice. There Bruno was burned at the stake for heresy in 1600.

This fate epitomized the decline of the Renaissance Magus, as the Hermetic-Kabbalist-alchemical doctrines lost their background of broad tolerance and support. The bitter conflicts unleashed by the wars of religion put an end to all religious novelty, and the growing realization of the incompatibility between the magico-mystical symbolisms and Christianity eliminated any possible ambiguity. Striking evidence of this change of attitude is the transformation of the Magus from a figure of veneration to one of ridicule in Jonson's *The Alchemist*, and eventually to one of detestation in Marlowe's *Doctor Faustus*. A brief renaissance of esoteric interest occurred in what Yates has called the "Rosicrucian Enlightenment," at the beginning of the seventeenth century. But already the integral components were beginning to dissociate into their separate directions.

One such component became the empirical and mathematical sciences promoted by Bacon, Marsenne, Descartes, and others. Even there, however, the new natural philosophy retained something of its occult background, as demonstrated by Bacon's *New Atlantis* and Newton's continued Hermetic interests. Another dimension continued into the secret mystical societies, of which the unidentified authors of the Rosicrucian manifestos founded the first. Their emphasis was on inner experience, cosmological speculation, and philanthropic service. Finally, there was the beginning of evangelical and pietist Christianity. It derived from the persistent desire within the Renaissance for a purer, simpler, and more immediate experience of biblical truth, but now came into its own with the work of Johann Arndt as well as that of the speculative mystics like Jacob Boehme. The first great wave of enthusiasm for the figure of the Magus had run its course, and, while leaving its mark on a variety of fields, dissipated its energies into the more definable objectives of scientific understanding and evangelical faith.

Yet this wave of enthusiasm did not ebb without first planting the seeds that would later come to flower in the grandiose visions of the secular messiahs. There is an unmistakable continuity of experience, as well as considerable continuity of influence, between this first eruption of the drive for self-salvation and its more explicitly antitheistic successor following the French Revolution. This continuity is illustrated well by the story of an experiment in Kabbalistic magic where two practitioners sought to create a *golem* or *homunculus*, a little man—a project we recognize today as the search for artificial intelligence, organic computers, or genetic engineering. The account indicates the clarity with which the implications of the enterprise were realized, and for that reason is worth quoting in full.

The prophet Jeremiah busied himself alone with the *Book Yetsirah*. Then a heavenly voice went forth and said: Take a companion. He went to his son Sira, and they studied the book for three years. Afterward they set about combining the alphabets in accordance with the Kabbalistic principles of combination, grouping, and word formation, and a man was created to them, on whose forehead stood the letters YHWH *Elohim Emeth*. But this newly created man had a knife in his hand, with which he erased the *aleph* from *emeth*; there remained: *meth*. Then Jeremiah rent his garments [because of the blasphemy: God is dead, now implied in the inscription] and said: Why have you erased the *aleph* from *emeth*? He replied: I will tell you a parable. An architect built many houses, cities, and squares, but no one could copy his art and compete with him in knowledge and skill until two men persuaded him. Then he taught them the secret of his art, and they knew how to do everything in the right way. When they had learned his secret and his abilities, they began to anger him with words. Finally, they broke with him and became architects like him, except that what he charged a thaler for, they did for six groats. When people noticed this, they ceased to honor the artist and came to them and honored them and gave them commissions when they required to have something built. So God has made you in His image and in His shape and form. But now that you have created a man like Him, people will say: There is no God in the world beside these two! Then Jeremiah said: What solution is there? He said: Write the alphabet backward on the earth you have strewn with intense concentration. Only do not meditate in the sense of building up, but the other way around. So they did, and the man became dust and ashes before their eyes. Then Jeremiah said: Truly, one should study these things only in order to know the power and omnipotence of the Creator of this world, but not in order really to practice them.[32]

The later arrogations of divine creative power to human nature are only different in not pulling back from the consequence of the death of God. When humanity absorbs all of the divine reality into itself, then no other God remains.

Viewed against this background, the process of secularization appears very different from the conventional notion of a separation from and diminishing of religious influences. It might even be regarded as the result of an increasing identification of the sacred and the profane, to the point that all awareness of difference has been eliminated. "Secularization could be defined," Voegelin suggests, "as a radicalization of the earlier forms of paracletic immanentism, because the experiential divinization of man is more radical in the secularist case" (*NSP*, 125). The variations that exist between the earlier and later forms, between the more or less extreme manifestations at any given point, are differences that can be related to one another along the continuum of humanity's progressive self-divinization. Puritans differ from Marxists primarily in the extent to which they continue to acknowledge a transcendent God beyond the paracletic agency of humanity. In Marxism there is no God because the divine substance has been wholly absorbed into the human. However much such bitter rivals as liberalism and Communism may wish to deny it, an underlying identity between them does remain. It emerges only when we have gone beneath the surface disputes to focus on their shared faith in the unlimited and irreversible achievements of human progress. This is the reason for Voegelin's insistence on the importance of "the principle that the substance of history is to be found on the level of experiences, not on the level of ideas" (*NSP*, 125).[33]

We begin to see, therefore, how the transcendent finality of Christianity was gradually redirected toward an innerworldly perfection. The process reached theoretical clarity when the transcendent being of God was absorbed into the unfolding historical movement. This is the achievement of the theosophical speculation of the Silesian mystic Jacob

Boehme. A self-taught visionary and a shoemaker, Boehme lived during
the "Rosicrucian Enlightenment" at the close of the great public period
of Hermetic-Kabbalist Christianity. He drew on all of the major spiritual
influences from the Renaissance and the Reformation, and through the
power of his own mystical vision as well as his speculative genius,
formed them into a new synthesis. It was thus that Boehme gave comprehensive expression to the new relationship between God, humanity,
and creation that had been emerging in fragments over the previous
century.[34]

God, in Boehme's construction, is first of all an *Ungrund*, a dark and
mysterious Groundless that is hardly aware of itself, since it lacks consciousness of its distinctness from any other reality. "No thing can be
revealed to itself without opposition. For if there is nothing that op-
poses it then it always goes out of itself and never returns to itself
again."[35] It is necessary for God to engender an opposition within and
eventually to project a reality outside. From this arises the whole unfolding of creation, fall, and redemption as the indispensable means for
the self-revelation of God to God. Boehme created this symbolism of a
dialectical process of opposition and reconciliation to express the new
worldview. The movement toward the innerworldly climax of divine
self-realization integrates the divine process within time, and makes of
humanity the crucial medium in which the totality is reflected back
toward the divine source. Boehme's construction perfectly expressed
the decline of divine transcendence, which is the essential condition for
its absorbtion into the intramundane process and the agency of human
nature. It answers the criticisms of Blumenberg and others, who ask
how the dynamic of a transcendent eschaton can be immanentized toward a historically progressive telos.

The Revolutionary Consummation: The Secular Messiah

Now we must consider the extent to which later explicitly secular
constructions of history were continuous or discontinuous with this
process of immanentization. The most identifiable starting point is undoubtedly the French Revolution. It is the beginning of the worldview
and the institutional structures that have come to form the self-understanding of modernity up to the present. The old world of monarchy
was definitively replaced by the new democratic ethos; the authority of
a divinely instituted law was superseded by the absolute claim to self-
determination. It was the beginning of the end of the ancien régime
and the birth of the world in which we continue to live. The impact of

this watershed event on its contemporaries can still be glimpsed in the ringing endorsement of Hegel's *Philosophy of History*.

The conception, the idea of Right asserted its authority *all at once*, and the old framework of injustice could offer no resistance to its onslaught. A constitution, therefore, was established in harmony with the conception of Right, and on this foundation all future legislation was to be based. Never since the sun stood in the firmament and the planets revolved around him had it been perceived that man's existence centers in his head, i.e. in Thought, inspired by which he builds up the world of reality. . . . This was a glorious mental dawn. All thinking beings shared in the jubilation of this epoch. Emotions of a lofty character stirred men's minds at that time; a spiritual enthusiasm thrilled through the world, as if the reconciliation between the Divine and the Secular was now first accomplished.[36]

This passage, which was delivered by Hegel more than twenty years after the French Revolution, still burns with the enthusiasm with which he and his student friends greeted the event. It was the realization of all their Enlightenment aspirations. But it quickly degenerated into the senseless Reign of Terror, in what was to become a familiar pattern of revolutionary success. The crisis precipitated by this debacle formed the preoccupation of an entire generation.

This preoccupation quickly led to the formation of a consensus concerning the reasons for the failure of the Revolution. Principally, the reasons coalesced around the recognition that the Revolution had only accomplished a political change, without including a deeper transformation of human nature. The expectation that the introduction of democratic forms would be sufficient to bring about a spirit of selfless service to the common good had proved to be illusory. Something more profound than a change of institutions was required. It was necessary to go beyond formal political structures and abstract appeals to rationality, in order to touch the very core of a person from which all his or her actions arise. We must feel ourselves infused with the force of a reality greater than ourselves if we are ever to be truly changed. Something must lift us far beyond our own petty interests and concerns into the realm of transcendent meaning, if we are to become capable of the kind of voluntary self-sacrifice that can alone ensure an order of *"liberté, egalité, et fraternité."* In short, something must take the place previously occupied by religion in order to bring about this most fundamental spiritual transformation.[37]

Even Kant, as we have seen, recognized that the moral order could not be realized practically without the postulates of God and immortality. But after the Revolution it became axiomatic that only a religious renewal or its equivalent could furnish what was needed. Another period of widespread spiritual experimentation followed. It spanned the political spectrum from Robespierre's Cult of the Supreme Being to de Maistre's assertion of papal-Catholic authority. Included were such widely diverse manifestations as the mystical intensification of Freemasonry, the expansion of evangelical and pietist Christianity, the turn toward nature mysticism among the romantics, the integration of revelation and philosophy within German Idealism, the invention of such new religious forms as the positivist Religion of Humanity and the Holy Alliance of Russia, Prussia, and Austria, together with a veritable explosion of interest in the mystical and esoteric giants of the past, especially Eckhart and Boehme.[38] All expressed the same conviction that mere political revolution was not enough. Order in society and history could finally be established only through the discovery of a new civil religion capable of exercising authority over autonomous human beings. This is the background from which the revolutionary ideological movements of the nineteenth century must be viewed. They begin with the attempt to supply the religious substance missing from a secular world.

The project is illustrated well by the most daring and brilliant thinker of the age, if not of the modern world, G. W. F. Hegel. When he first began to search for a new foundation to moral and political order in the 1790s, he conceived it as a form of *Volksreligion* or national religion on the ancient Greek model. Hegel experimented with the suggestion of Christianity as such a rejuvenated civil religion through the experience of mystical unity contained within it. By identifying God and humanity, it held out the possibility of the supersession of all opposition and alienation. Hegel looked toward the point when "spirit can venture to hallow itself as spirit in its own shape, and reestablish the original reconciliation with itself in a new religion, in which the infinite grief and the whole burden of its antithesis is taken up."[39] But Christianity still contained too much of a sense of the transcendence of God, of a separation between the human and the divine. It fell far short of the criterion he had set for himself: "Absolute freedom of all spirits who bear the intellectual world in themselves, and cannot seek either God or immortality outside themselves."[40] How could the absolute self-determination of individuals be maintained if there is a transcendent God who remains forever beyond their comprehension? This is the "unhappy consciousness" of the "I," which seeks to communicate with the divine but discovers that "it cannot be found, for it is supposed to be just a *beyond*, something that can *not* be found."[41]

In contrast, Hegel sought to elaborate "the Protestant principle" of contemplating all that was formerly beyond in one's own self-consciousness. This formidable task, of integrating divine and human reality without neglecting any of their respective differences, was accomplished only when Hegel shifted to the comprehensive perspective of Spirit, *Geist*, intermediate between them. Then it became no longer a matter of identifying God and humanity, but of seeing each of them as a moment in the dialectical unfolding of *Geist*. The transcendence of God becomes an abstract moment that contains its own negation or incompleteness within itself; it must be followed by the emergence of concrete human individuals through whom divine Being can become conscious of itself as Spirit. Unification can be achieved without either denying the reality of God or surrendering the freedom of humanity. For the finite consciousness of the thinker has not been surrendered to the mystery of the absolute. It has become the means by which the integration takes place. The finite consciousness of the author and the reader of *The Phenomenology of Spirit* is the instrument through which the universal self-consciousness of Spirit recognizes itself and becomes actual.[42] As a reconciliation between the human and the divine, Hegel's synthesis can hardly be surpassed. No wonder it exercised such a profound impact on his contemporaries and continues to influence the present.

Hegel had created the new form of religion. It was based on the autonomous freedom of human reason, while preserving and superseding all that had been contained within revelation. He understood it as the culmination of history. The "transfiguration" had been achieved and was no longer to be awaited in a world beyond; the work of "actual history" was over when the unfolding world-Spirit had reached "its consummation as self-conscious Spirit."[43] The divine substance had been more completely and more perfectly drawn into the historical process than ever before. Key to this success was Hegel's shift of perspective to the intermediate reality of Spirit. He could claim that the speculative transformation of his system was not a mere intellectual construction of his own mind. It was the actual reconciliation of universal Spirit with itself through the medium of Hegel's thought. Once that had taken place in actuality, it was only a matter of time before it penetrated the broad mass of social and political reality. Neither revolutionary action nor spiritual conversion was required; the conciliation had already taken place. The meaning of history could now be revealed from the perspective of its completion.

When Hegel turned his attention to the historical course, he identified the strand of meaning that had been fulfilled within himself. This is an invaluable source for recognizing the kind of experiences that lay behind his construction. Besides his inclusion of the main spiritual traditions of human history, he singled out for special attention the line of Neoplatonic mystical speculation from the ancient world to the present. He understood himself to be the successor of this tradition above all.[44] The reader will have already noted the similarity with the theosophic speculations of Boehme, the same conception of a dialectically unfolding Godhead through creation and history. This is no accident. Hegel was an avid reader of the mystics, especially Eckhart and Boehme, whom he saw as the real originators of his own work. In the *Lectures on the History of Philosophy* he identified the two fountainheads of the modern world: Francis Bacon for the empirical inductive principle that is the basis of modern science, and Jacob Boehme as "the first German philosopher" to apprehend the necessity for a negative within the absolute identity of God. Hegel was eager to acquire his own copy of Boehme's collected works, and there is strong prima facie evidence that the reading of the Silesian theosoph was instrumental in the formation of his conception of a dialectically unfolding *Geist*.[45] Whatever our judgment about the validity of the Hegelian enterprise, we can hardly deny that Hegel understood himself to be in the Magus tradition that reached back to the Renaissance and ultimately to Hellenistic gnosis.

But what of Marx? Surely here we have an avowedly secular understanding of human nature and its history? Certainly that is the essence of his famous rejection of Hegelian idealism, which he claimed to have finally stood on its feet. Marx directed unremitting attention to the material conditions of existence as the real foundation from which the intellectual superstructure arises. In his view, it is the dialectic between the changing means of production and the correlatively developing relations of production that is the true engine of history. That is what generates the succession of historical epochs, most recently bringing forth the bourgeois capitalist phase, and destined eventually to conclude in the emergence of global Communism. Religion, like the world of culture in general, is merely an expression of the dominant economic relationships and therefore not an independent variable within history. "It is not the consciousness of men that determines their being but, on the contrary, their social being that determines their consciousness."

That is why if one wishes to bring about a change in the order of society, one does not begin with an inner moral or spiritual conversion of its members, but with a radical political and economic revolution that transforms the "real" conditions of existence for human beings.[46] By following this course Marx expected to usher in the final age of universal human emancipation that would constitute the perfection and fulfillment of history.

Despite the resolutely materialist character of this conception, closer examination reveals that it is entirely constructed around the same faith in spiritual transformation as Christianity itself. Marx begins the *Communist Manifesto* with the assertion that "all previous history has been the history of class struggle," and concludes with the affirmation that the proletarian revolution will create a classless society, in which "the free development of each becomes the condition for the free development of all." Yet he has adduced no evidence in favor of his conviction. The fact that the proletariat is a class of such absolute impoverishment that it now stands for essential humanity, cannot be regarded as sufficient reason for expecting such a universal permanent change in human nature. Only a faith in transcendent divine intervention—or its equivalent—can support such a conviction. It becomes difficult, therefore, to resist the conclusion that the historical process, culminating in the world Communist revolution, performs this apocalyptic divine function for Marx.

The secular appearance of his thought is considerably diminished when one recalls his descent from Hegel. Marx's faith in the power of the titanic human spirit working through history, is no more than the contraction of Hegel's divine cosmic Spirit to its human carrier. The essence of his disagreement with Hegel is that there is no dimension of Spirit beyond the strictly human level. If one were looking for a textbook example of the process of secularization, this must surely be it. For everything else about Hegel's world-Spirit is simply carried over. This is most evident in Marx's conception of the dialectical unfolding of history, which must go through all its oppositions and reconciliations to reach its culminating fulfillment within time. Without participating in this creative divine process, it would be impossible for humanity to transform its own nature. Unless there is something more than human nature, we have no means of acting other than the old inadequate nature that we now possess.[47]

Moreover, this helps explain the intensity of Marx's rejection of religion. It is not that religion is illusory, hypocritical, or destructive, but that it constitutes a rival, perhaps the principal rival, to Marx's own

faith. The force of his rejection, which extends from his early Promethean declaration "In a word, I hate all the gods" to his insistence that
"the critique of religion is the presupposition of all critique," cannot be
mistaken.[48] A tone of invective arises from Marx's profound awareness
of the threat posed by transcendent faith. The presence of a divine
Creator jeopardizes the whole project of human self-salvation through
revolutionary action. Marx himself confirms this interpretation in a
unique passage where he notes the difficulty of dislodging the idea of
a creator from human consciousness.

Men have, he complains, the unfortunate habit of admitting that
they do not derive their existence from themselves. Marx is revolted by
this idea of creaturely dependence. "A man who lives by the grace of
another regards himself as a dependent being. But I live completely by
the grace of another if I owe him not only the sustenance of my life,
but if he has, moreover, *created* my *life*—if he is the *source* of my life."
He suggests that when we are confronted with the question "Who be-
got the first man, and nature as a whole?" we should inform the questioner that it is merely "a product of abstraction." Marx even envisages
that the questioner might persist nevertheless, and goes on to reveal
the real reason for not asking the question. "Since for socialist man the
entire so-called history of the world is nothing but the begetting of man
through human labor, nothing but the coming-to-be of nature for man,
he has the visible irrefutable proof of his *birth* through himself, of his
process of *coming-to-be*."[49] The question of God must be rejected because
it has "become impossible in practice." We are in the realm of the Nietzschean and Kabbalistic murder of God that accomplishes the apotheosis
of humanity.

Another comparable attempt is that of the contemporaneous French
positivist August Comte. He enacted the transition from rationalism to
messianism within his own life. Comte's biography is normally divided
into a positivist phase and a religious phase, although for him they
were a continuous unfolding of the same inspiration. He elaborated the
"law" of the three stages of history—theological, metaphysical, and
positivist—which was intended to establish the superiority of natural
science over all earlier forms of knowledge. Intellectual progress alone,
however, admitted Comte, would not by itself transform society. Comte
was spiritually profound enough to recognize the necessity of going
beyond a critique of traditional beliefs; what has become obsolete cannot be transcended until it is replaced. So under the inspiration of his
love for Clotilde de Vaux, he conceived a new religion devoted to the
service of Humanity. This was to become the "Great Being" in place of
the transcendent divinity of the traditional world religions. Comte de-

veloped extensively his conception of a Religion of Humanity, including the elaboration of rituals, a liturgical calender, and a sacramental and hierarchical structure modeled on Catholicism. Occupying the position of pope was of course Comte himself.[50] Yet despite such bizarre extremes it cannot be denied that his construction contains all the elements of our own abstract humanitarianism. Humanity is the intramundane absolute requiring our total submission in service; before it, individual human beings become utterly expendable. Even the language to describe this new conception of virtue, for example the term *altruism*, was coined by Comte. But what ultimately sustained the vision as a whole, enabling its supporters to overlook the destructive consequences, was the prospect of human beings finally becoming identical with the Supreme Being.

When one looks at the leading figures who shaped the modern world, in other words, there can be little doubt that they sought to draw the fullness of divine reality into the self. The reading of our civilizational history by Voegelin, Camus, Dostoevsky, and Solzhenitsyn as an expression of naked Promethean hubris, in which the creature sought to eclipse God the creator, is increasingly confirmed by the wealth of empirical studies cited in this chapter. This is no idiosyncratic or haphazard interpretation, however disturbing its implications may be. For it is not easy to admit that the fundamental thrust of our civilization, which has given birth to so many great and remarkable achievements, was radically misconceived. It is not easy for us, enjoying the benefits as well as the miseries, to acknowledge that the modern world originated in spiritual disorder. Yet such is the relentless logic of the experiences through which we have passed. Now it is confirmed by the researches of historical scholarship as well. Together they add even greater weight to our sense of having reached a historical turning point in which the madness has become universally transparent. The illusion, the masks of deception and self-deception—so agonizingly displayed in the meditations of Nietzsche—can no longer be sustained. Such dreams have lost their power of seduction for the moment, now that the work of critique has exposed their falsity to the light of day. This is all the more reason, therefore, for us to consider how they could have affected the greatest minds and most advanced societies, as the first step in the effort to develop a defense against their recurrence.

The Roots of the Crisis within Christianity

Inevitably the question of the ultimate conditions for the disorder of the modern age impressed itself more and more insistently on a man like Camus, who had to struggle with its effects around him. What was it in Western civilization that made it susceptible to messianic fantasies of destruction? Or we can observe Dostoevsky's earlier grappling with the deformations of Christianity that he felt had given rise to the modern spirit of revolt. But it is especially in the work of Eric Voegelin that we find the most prolonged exploration of the sources of the modern crisis. His investigations carry him through the maze of historical continuities and parallels stretching back to the Ecumenic Age and even earlier. He particularly singles out the advent of Christianity as the factor that greatly heightened the tension of existence, for better and worse. Voegelin has been roundly criticized for taking such a negative view of Christianity, or rather for permitting his empirical explorations to suggest such a conclusion. Yet he no more than follows the direction in which our questions spontaneously lead. Recently, as authentically Christian a voice as that of John Paul II has confirmed the necessity for such fundamental reflection.

The crises of European man are the crises of Christian man. The crises of European culture are the crises of the Christian culture. In this light, Christians can discover in the adventure of the European spirit, the temptations, infidelities and risks which belong to man in his essential relationship with God in Christ.

Even more deeply, we can affirm that these trials, these temptations and this result of the European drama, not only question the Church and Christianity from outside, as a difficulty or external obstacle in the work of evangelization which has to be overcome. Rather, in a certain sense, they are internal to Christianity and to the Church. So we will discover, perhaps not without surprise, that the crises of European man and of Europe are crises and temptations of Christianity and of the Church in Europe.[51]

The nub of the issue is identified by Camus when he remarks that metaphysical revolt is inconceivable without a transcendent creator God responsible for the whole world. For this reason he concludes that "in the Western World the history of rebellion is inseparable from the history of Christianity" (*R*, 28). Camus had a profound sensitivity to the world of Greek myth, with its experience of human beings and gods as part of the embracing mysterious order of the cosmos. He knew rebellion was inconceivable within such a world, since it lacked a single responsible cause. At the same time, Christianity abolishes the notion of a limit, as expressed by the Greek motto of "Nothing too much!" It is a "total religion" that demands of a person a total commitment, as it draws him or her toward an infinite eschaton beyond the world. Human beings are turned away from the cosmos to focus exclusively on this transfiguring movement of the self and history (*E*, 381; *N* II, 184). This is why, Camus asserts, "Communism is a logical outcome of Christianity. It is a history of Christianity" (*N* II, 128). He saw his own task as that of resisting the totalizing tendencies in each of them, to restore the Greek sense of equilibrium and of limit. His last project was to have centered on the myth of Nemesis, the divine force of punishment that humans draw on themselves by overstepping the order of the cosmos. The great challenge, as Camus understood it, had become that of articulating anew "the passage from Hellenism to Christianity, the true and only turning point of history" (*N* II, 267).

This is the direction pursued by Voegelin's exploration of Western responsibility for the contagion of totalistic revolt. What Camus only hinted at, Voegelin examined much more extensively, as he became increasingly aware of the degree to which the roots of the contemporary upheaval reach into the very nature of Christianity itself. We have already encountered his explanation for the eruption of sectarian activism within such movements as revolutionary Puritanism. He saw it as a collapse of or an inability to sustain the tension of transcendent faith. Christianity had become a victim of its own social success, by including great masses of individuals within it who did not have the spiritual maturity to support such a tenuous link. They sought "more massive" experiences of divinity to overcome their uncertainty about the meaning and significance of their lives within this world. The otherworldly character of Christianity did not provide such concrete reassurance. Indeed, uncertainty turned out to be "the very essence of Christianity." It asked men and women to surrender everything without asking for anything in return. Only in the experience of faith itself was reassurance given, and this was never quite the same as living in the midst of a cosmos filled with tangible, visible gods. It is a problem familiar to all world-transcendent faiths, as the prophets of Israel knew all too well.

What particularly exacerbated the tension within Christianity, according to Voegelin, was the extent to which the maximal differentiation of divine transcendence had taken place. God's presence was no longer tied to specific places or times or linked to any concretely existing people. Human fulfillment came to be defined almost exclusively by the movement toward this eternal divine reality beyond the cosmos. Everything that had tied us to life in the world seemed to have evaporated with the definitive revelation of our relationship with the God who is beyond it. Even the existence of the cosmos itself had become problematic. For what is the purpose in creating a world that is doomed in advance to annihilation? What is the point in struggling for achievements within it? The "dedivinization" of the cosmos was a process that had been completed by Christianity. From that point forward the problems of balance between life in the world and the movement beyond it have become a notorious source of difficulties. It is to this setting, Voegelin insists, we must return if we are to deal with the irrational ideological aspirations for transfiguration in our own time.

He has successively refined the categories of his analysis by distinguishing more clearly the two fundamental modes in which divine presence is experienced. There is the immediate revelatory experience within the soul, the interior pull toward what Plato called the Beyond, *epekeina* (*Republic* 509b). There is also the mediated experience of divine presence within the cosmos, as the ordering force sustaining and maintaining all the things from the Beginning (Gen. 1:1). These are the two permanent and irreducible ways in which human beings have experienced the presence of God. They must eventually be brought into harmony if life is to be lived in order. Neither the experiences nor their symbolizations, in the revelatory symbolisms and cosmogonic myths, can be reduced to a single encompassing dimension. Human knowledge of order is confined to the immediately apprehended movement of the soul; our comprehension of the cosmos is limited to what we extrapolate about the whole from the order within ourselves and visible around us. No privileged perspective is available for the participant to survey the meaning of the All (*OH* IV, 7–11).

The problem with Christianity, in Voegelin's view, is that it hinted at such a comprehensive perspective. When the eschatological direction of existence had been fully differentiated, then it seemed that the meaning of everything else could be determined. It was not long before the details began to be filled in in all kinds of ways, from the expectations about the imminence of the Second Coming to the elaborate divine cosmic speculations of the Gnostic systems. The absolute degree of divine self-revelation in Christ seemed to provide the key to a definitive understanding of the cosmos as well. Even within the New Testament itself, Voegelin discerns tendencies in this direction. St. John, for example, seems to confuse the two modes of divine presence, when he "lets the cosmogonic 'word' of creation blend into the revelatory 'word' spoken to man from the Beyond by the 'I am'" (*OH* IV, 18). The Word of Christ, which is identified with the Word of the Beginning, is also the divine presence that is "victorious over the cosmos." How are the two words related? Is the cosmos an evil to be overcome so that Christ can return to the glory he had "before there was a cosmos"? These are the questions Voegelin identifies in the gospel, and while he does not accuse St. John of Gnosticism, he points out that it is just this set of questions that ultimately gave rise to Gnosticism. In Christianity the impulse to extrapolate toward the whole course of reality is brought to the forefront. "The intensely experienced presence of the Beyond brings the problem of the Beginning to intense attention" (*OH* IV, 19).

What Voegelin means is elaborated more extensively in his chapter "The Pauline Vision of the Resurrected." He begins with a brilliant analysis of the nature of Paul's vision of the resurrected Christ, as the experience that convinced him "that man is destined to rise to immortality, if he opens himself to the divine *pneuma* as Jesus did" (*OH* IV, 242). This is the basis for the momentous consequences drawn by St. Paul. The key to the experience, Voegelin claims, is the sentence: "If we have no more than hope in Christ in this life, then we are of all men the most pitiful" (1 Cor. 15:19). He interprets this to indicate that for St. Paul hope in this life, in the Metaxy or In-Between state of our earthly existence, is not enough. It must be a hope that is already the beginning of the process of transfiguration itself, or it is almost worthless. The emphasis has shifted overwhelmingly toward the victorious end of the tale in which "we shall all be changed, in a moment, in the twinkling of an eye, at the last trumpet" (1 Cor. 15:51–52). The vision of Christ's triumph over the rebellious forces of the cosmos so dominated Paul's imagination that he could expect that those now living in Christ would not die, but would be transfigured in life at the Parousia. From this perspective, life in the Metaxy, in the tensional existence of hope, "recedes to comparative insignificance" (*OH* IV, 249). It is the tendency to let the movement toward the transfiguring end invade the whole of reality that Voegelin finds as the unbalancing component in the Pauline vision, and, as a consequence, in the Christian symbolization of order derived from him. The problem may be defined as "an inclination to abolish the tension between the eschatological *telos* of reality and the mystery of the transfiguration that is actually going on within historical reality. The Pauline myth of the struggle among the cosmic forces validly expresses the movement that is experienced in reality, but it becomes invalid when it is used to anticipate the concrete process of transfiguration within history" (*OH* IV, 270).

Once again it is essential to emphasize that Voegelin does not accuse Paul of spiritual imbalance. Rather he finds in the saint an inclination or tendency that in lesser minds could become virtually irresistible. For this is how Gnosticism, the great heresy of the early Church, first became a widespread phenomenon. It arose from an exaggeration of certain tendencies that were already present in Christianity. Most prominent is the devaluation of existence in the cosmos to the point that it becomes the principal obstacle to the transfiguring ascent toward union with the God beyond it. The essential fallacy of all Gnosticism is this illegitimate extrapolation from the glimpse of transfiguration in the present to its final definitive realization. "In the construction of all Gnostic systems, the immediate experience of divine presence in the mode of Beyond is speculatively expanded to comprehend a knowledge of the Beginning that is accessible only in the mode of mediated experience" (*OH* IV, 19). Such a powerful distortion of experience can only become acceptable if something more is at work than intense feelings of alienation and revolt at the miseries of the age. "The additional factor," Voegelin is convinced,

is a consciousness of the movement toward the Beyond of such strength and clarity that it becomes an obsessive illumination, blinding a man for the contextual structure of reality. For a Gnostic thinker must be able to forget that the cosmos does not emerge from his consciousness, but that man's consciousness emerges from the cosmos. He must, furthermore, be able to invert the relation of the Beginning and the Beyond without becoming aware that he destroys the mystery of reality by his speculative action; he must be insensitive to the fact that he is indulging his *libido dominandi*. I am stressing the magnitude of insensitivity required in the construction of a Gnostic system, in order to stress the strength and luminosity of eschatological consciousness necessary to make the Gnostic deformation intelligible. Considering the history of Gnosticism, with the great bulk of its manifestations belonging to, or deriving from the Christian orbit, I am inclined to recognize in the epiphany of Christ the great catalyst that made eschatological consciousness an historical force, both in forming and deforming humanity. (*OH* IV, 20)

This is a particularly strong expression of the responsibility that Christianity bears for the modern ideological madness, and as such leaves itself open to the charge of overstatement. For it is one thing to assert that Christianity provided the conditions for the subsequent deformations, and quite another to maintain that those distorting tendencies were already present in the New Testament itself. Voegelin's reading of St. Paul along these lines remains highly questionable. It is not at all evident, for example, that the Apostle to the Gentiles was "obsessed" or "dominated" (*OH* IV, 249) by the expectation of the Second Coming of Christ. Nor is it simply true that the New Testament as a whole is indifferent to the problems of order that arise from the requirement of continued existence in society and history. A much more tenable explanation is that the early Church was focused primarily on the core experience of the redemptive encounter with Christ. It would be surprising if this simplicity and centrality of emphasis were not the case. That this restriction to the core spiritual truth did not imply any real devaluation of existence in this world or any revolt against its order, is attested by the relative ease with which the early Church adjusted to the postponement of the Parousia. The powerfully heuristic indications of ethical and political order within the New Testament could then be elaborated through the rich tradition of Christian philosophical reflection. All of that must be borne in mind, I believe, if we are to place Voegelin's analysis in the proper perspective. Then it will become apparent that the connection he establishes with the modern revolutionary convulsion is not between it and Christianity in general, but only with Christianity's characteristic and long-standing distortions.

It is through the possibility for its distortion that the Christian differentiation of the transcendent *telos* of human existence ultimately stands behind the unquenchable "longing for total revolution." We have already seen that contrary to the self-understanding of the modern secular world and its erstwhile defenders, the prophets of universal human emancipation saw themselves as successors of the Renaissance Magi and the line of godded men and women reaching back to antiquity.[52] Now we have begun to penetrate their motivating roots. We discover that the passionate intensity of their quest for transfiguration is only intelligible as a variant, albeit a perversion, of the eschatological impulse of Christianity itself. Only someone steeped in a Judeo-Christian background could aspire, as Marx did, to such an unlimited goal. "Philosophers," he declared in one of his most famous aphorisms, "have only interpreted the world, the point however is to change it." How is human nature to change that of which it is a part? And Nietzsche was no more than reflecting the pervasive influence of Christian eschatology when he struggled so unsuccessfully to overcome the misery of living in a world of eternal return. These are not, as Camus understood, the feelings of a Greek soul, nor, as Mircea Eliade has shown, of any individual at home in a cosmological order.[53] For better or worse we live within the differentiated "eschatological myth" created by St. Paul; there is no going back to more compact experiences of one consubstantial cosmos. "The new Christs who appear in the first half of the nineteenth century and compete with the Resurrected of the Pauline vision, are the best proof, if proof were needed, for the constancy of the problem of transfiguration in historical consciousness" (*OH* IV, 254). After the divinization of human nature in Christ, no lesser form of transfiguration will do.

The long titanic struggle of the modern world may be seen as an attempt to achieve the self-divinization of our nature without going through Christ. Even where the attempt is explicitly made to draw the divine substance into humanity, as among the Renaissance Magi or the sectarian mystical activists, the operation is increasingly performed by human agency alone. The logic is inextricably moving toward the atheistic position of Marx or Comte. It is, as Nietzsche described it, the process by which humanity extends grace to itself. Pitiful and futile as this magical delusion may appear from the outside—How can we extend to ourselves what we do not yet possess?—it must not be allowed to obscure the tragic dimension of a Christianly formed inspiration become perverse. The spectacle of a civilization expending its energies in a self-destructive search for what cannot be found, what by definition cannot be achieved, the self-divinization of humanity, is enough to give pause to even the most hardened disciples of Prometheus. When all the possible avenues for creating the *Übermensch* have been exhausted and we are surrounded by the nightmare consequences of the effort, it may become the occasion for a realization of the profound self-contradiction that lies at the very root of the enterprise. At that point, we may even begin to recognize that the true path of divinization lies in the opening of the soul toward the God who poured himself out for human beings. The resistance to disorder leads us inexorably toward the ascent.

NOTES

1. Voegelin shows how Greek thought begins with just such an analysis of spiritual disorder, in Homer's *Iliad* (*OH* II, chap. 3). Toynbee adopted the term "Time of Troubles" to describe these periods of prolonged spiritual and political disintegration within civilizations. The term was originally coined in the context of the interregnum between Ivan the Terrible and Peter the Great, when Russia experienced great religious and political chaos. Solzhenitsyn has called attention to the internal nature of the process of social and political disintegration. He distinguishes between the different rates of corruption in the Baltic states and Russia itself; this was what determined the degree of ruthlessness with which the authorities could work their will (*GA* II, 640ff.).

2. See also Solzhenitsyn's Templeton Prize acceptance speech, "'Men Have Forgotten God,'" trans. A. Klimoff, *National Review*, 22 July 1983, 872–76.

3. Dostoevsky's understanding of the modern disorder is skillfully explored in Bruce K. Ward, *Dostoyevsky's Critique of the West* (Waterloo: Wilfrid Laurier University Press, 1986). Dostoevsky's own reflections on the West are contained in the account of his travels *Winter Notes on Summer Impressions*, trans. R. L. Renfield (New York: Criterion, 1955). For a clarificaiton of Dostoevsky's caricaturistic views on Catholicism see Denis Dirscherl, *Dostoevsky and the Catholic Church* (Chicago: Loyola University Press, 1988).

4. A fascinating overview of the modern revolutionary movements is provided by James Billington in *Fire in the Minds of Men*. Unfortunately, he only includes left-wing movements, thereby excluding such phenomena as national socialism and fascism, which are equally revolutionary in their own way. Indeed, political revolutions are themselves only a subset of the wider revolutionary transformation of Western civilization through the modern ideological movements. Many of the latter are movements of wide public appeal, such as positivism, Freudianism, progressivism, behaviorism, and feminism, with little in the way of political organization. The relationship between these ideological systems is frequently one of competition, but it can as often be one of mutual reinforcement.

5. Reflecting on what the critics had said about the *Brothers Karamazov*, he wrote: "The villains teased me for my uneducated and reactionary faith in God. These blockheads did not even dream of such a powerful negation of God as was put into the Inquisitor and in the preceding chapter, to which *the whole novel* serves as an answer." *The Unpublished Dostoevsky*, vol. 3, 175.

6. The Inquisitor's "mystery," as he admits, is that "we are not working with Thee, but with *him* . . . we took from him what Thou didst reject with scorn, that last gift he offered Thee,showing Thee all the kingdoms of the earth" (*K*, 305).

7. Sartre too defines the essence of humanity as the impossible quest of the "for itself" (*pour soi*) to become united with the "in itself" so as to become the *ens causa sui*, which is God. "Everything happens as if the world, man, and man-in-the-world succeed in realizing only a missing God." *Being and Nothingness*, trans. Hazel Barnes (New York: Philosophical Library), 623.

8. Voegelin first proclaimed this identification between modernity and Gnosticism in *The New Science of Politics* (1952) and later in *Wissenschaft, Politik und Gnosis [Science, Politics and Gnosticism]* (1959). He continued to elaborate and refine his understanding of the relationship right up to his final works, analyzing ever more carefully the inner spiritual process by which the Gnostic revolt is sustained. "Gnosticism, whether ancient or modern, is a dead end. That of course is its attraction. Magic pneumatism gives its addicts a sense of superiority over the reality which does not conform. Whether the addiction assumes the forms of libertarianism and asceticism preferred in antiquity, or the modern forms of constructing systems which contain the ultimate truth and must be imposed on recalcitrant reality by means of violence, concentration camps, and mass murder, the addict is dispensed from the responsibilities of existence in the cosmos. Since Gnosticism surrounds the *libido dominandi* in man with a halo of spiritualism or idealism, and can always nourish its righteousness by pointing to the evil in the world, no historical end to the attraction is predictable once magic pneumatism has entered history as a mode of existence" (*OH*, IV, 27–28).

9. St. Augustine understood well the appeal of Gnostic Manichaeanism, which had attracted him for a number of years before his conversion. "I still thought that it is not we who sin but some other nature that sins within us. It flattered my pride to think that I incurred no guilt and, when I did wrong, not to confess it so that you might bring healing to a soul that had sinned against you." *Confessions*, trans. R. S. Pine-Coffin (Harmondsworth: Penguin, 1961), V, 10.

10. A year after the publication of *The New Science of Politics*, Voegelin's argument became the basis for a reflection on the state of Western civilization in the special thirtieth anniversary issue of *Time* magazine. "Journalism and Joachim's Children," *Time*, 9 March 1953, 57–61.

11. Löwith, *Meaning in History*; see also his *Weltgeschichte und Heilesgeschehen, Sämtliche Schriften*, vol. 2 (Stuttgart: Metzler, 1981).

12. Hans Jonas, *The Gnostic Religion*, 3rd ed. (Boston: Beacon, 1978), especially the epilogue, "Gnosticism, Existentialism and Nihilism"; idem, *Gnosis und spätantiker Geist*, 2 vols. (Göttingen: Vandenhoeck & Ruprecht, 1934, 1954). Gilles Quispel, *Die Gnosis als Weltreligion* (Zurich: Origo, 1951). For the recently discovered Gnostic texts, see the collection in *The Nag Hammadi Library*, ed. James N. Robinson (SanFrancisco: Harper & Row, 1990).

13. Hans Urs von Balthasar, *Apokalypse der deutschen Seele*, 3 vols. (Salzburg/Leipzig: Pustet, 1937–39). Jacob Talmon, *The Origins of Totalitarian Democracy* (1951; reprint, New York: Praeger, 1961); idem, *The Origins of Ideological Polarization in the Twentieth Century* (New York: Praeger, 1980). Carl Becker, *The Heavenly City of the Eighteenth-Century Philosophers* (New Haven: Yale University Press, 1932). Ernst Lee Tuveson, *Millennium and Utopia: A Study in the Background of the Idea of Progress* (Berkeley: University of California Press, 1949).

14. Norman Cohn, *The Pursuit of the Millennium: Revolutionary Millenarians and Mystical Anarchists of the Middle Ages* (London: Secker & Warburg, 1957). Jacob Taubes, *Abendländische Eschatologie* (Bern: Francke, 1947).

15. A series of more specific recent studies has served to confirm this interpretation. In addition to those identified in the remainder of the notes for this chapter, mention should be made of the following: Jürgen Gebhardt, *Politik und Eschatologie* (Munich: Beck, 1963); Gerhart Niemeyer, *Between Nothingness and Paradise* (Baton Rouge: Louisiana State University Press, 1971); Tilo Schabert, *Gewalt und Humanität* (Freiburg/Munich: Carl Alber, 1978); Klaus Vondung, *Magie und Manipulation: Ideologischer Kült und politische Religionen des National-sozialismus* (Göttingen: Vandenhoeck & Ruprecht, 1971) and *Die Apokalypse in Deutschland* (Munich: DeutscherTaschenbuch, 1988); James M. Rhodes, *The Hitler Movement* (Stanford, CA: Hoover Institution, 1980).

16. Responding to the scathing review in Sartre's *Les temps modernes*, Camus pointed out that the reviewer "in effect energetically refused to discuss the central theses to be found in the work. . . . I have demonstrated, and continue to maintain, that there is within the revolutions of the twentieth century, among other elements, an evident enterprise to divinize man and I chose to clarify specifically this theme" (*E*, 759; also 761–68).

17. Hans Blumenberg, *The Legitimacy of the Modern Age*, trans. Robert M. Wallace (Cambridge: Massachusetts Institute of Technology Press, 1983; German original, 1966), 30.

18. Bernard Yack, *The Longing for Total Revolution* (Princeton: Princeton University Press, 1986), 17, 31.

19. For an overview see George H. Williams, *The Radical Reformation* (Philadelphia: Westminster, 1962). Cohn, *The Pursuit of the Millennium*; idem, *Europe's Inner Demons* (New York: Basic Books, 1975). Steven Ozment, *Mysticism and Dissent* (New Haven: Yale University Press, 1973).

20. Gunther Franz and Paul Kirn, eds., *Thomas Müntzer: Schriften und Briefe* (Gutersloh: Gerd Mohn, 1968). Walter Elliger, *Thomas Müntzer: Leben und Werke* (Göttingen: Van-

denhoeck & Ruprecht, 1975). Ernst Block, *Thomas Müntzer, als Theologe der revolution* (Frankfurt: Suhrkamp, 1960).

21. Henri de Lubac, *La posterité spirituelle de Joachim de Fiore*, vol. 1, *De Jochim à Schelling*, vol. 2, *De Saint-simon à nos jours* (Paris: Lethielleux, 1979, 1982). A slightly less expansive view of Joachim's influence is contained in Marjorie Reeves, *Joachim of Fiore and the Prophetic Future* (New York: Harper & Row, 1976). See also Bernard McGinn, *The Calabrian Abbot: Joachim in the History of Western Thought* (New York: Macmillan, 1985).

22. Theodore Mommsen, "Petrarch's Concept of the Dark Age," in Mommsen, *Medieval and Renaissance Studies*, ed. Eugene Rice (Ithaca: Cornell University Press, 1972).

23. I have tried to summarize the implications of the new historical studies in "Revising the Renaissance: New Light on the Origins of Modern Political Thought," *Political Science Reviewer* 11 (1981): 27–52. A more extensive overview is to be found in Stephen A. McKnight, *Sacralizing the Secular: The Renaissance Origins of Modernity* (Baton Rouge: Louisiana State University Press, 1989). Among the seminal historical studies the following are particularly noteworthy: Frances Yates, *Giordano Bruno and the Hermetic Tradition* (Chicago: University of Chicago Press, 1964); idem, *The Rosicrucian Enlightenment* (Boston: Routledge, Kegan & Paul, 1972); idem, *The Art of Memory* (Chicago: University of Chicago Press, 1966); D. P. Walker, *Spiritual and Demonic Magic from Ficino to Campanella* (London: Warburg, 1958); idem, *The Ancient Theology* (New York: Cornell University Press, 1972).

24. Frances Yates, "The Hermetic Tradition in Renaissance Science," in *Art, Science and History in the Renaissance*, ed. C. S. Singleton (Baltimore: Johns Hopkins University Press, 1967), 255–74. See also Betty J. T. Dobbs, *Foundations of Newton's Alchemy* (Cambridge: Cambridge University Press, 1975); Paolo Rossi, *Francis Bacon: From Magic to Science*, trans. S. Rabinovitch (Chicago: University of Chicago Press, 1968; Italian original, 1957); Allen G. Debus, *Man and Nature in the Renaissance* (Cambridge: Cambridge University Press, 1978).

25. Yates, *Giordano Bruno*; idem, *Astrea: The Imperial Theme in the Sixteenth Century* (Boston: Routledge & Kegan Paul, 1975); and *The Occult Philosophy in the Elizabethan Age* (Boston: Routledge & Kegan Paul, 1979).

26. Walter Scott, trans., *Hermetica: The Ancient Greek and Latin Writings Which Contain Religious or Philosophic Teachings Ascribed to Hermes Trismegistus*, 4 vols. (Oxford: Clarendon, 1924–36; reprinted 1968), vol. 1, "Asclepius," 295–97. For the original texts with a French translation see *Corpus Hermeticum*, 4 vols., ed. A. D. Nock, trans. A. J. Festugiére (Paris: Les Belles Lettres, 1954–60).

27. Ficino's dilemma concerning magic is explained by D. P. Walker as follows: "Natural, non-demonic magic is an obvious threat to religion, since it claims to produce the same effect without any supernatural agent; its logical consequent is atheism or deism. Demonic or angelic magic avoids this danger, but is more evidently unacceptable to a Christian because it is a rival religion." *Spiritual and Demonic Magic*, 83.

28. "All being in the lower realm of nature but also in the upper world of the angels and pure forms, of the 'Throne' of God, had in it something, a sefirotic index as it were, which connects it with one of the creative aspects of divine being, or, in other words, with a *sefirah*, or a configuration of *sefiroth*. It is the transcendence that shines into created nature and the symbolic relationship between the two that gives the world of the Kabbalists its meaning. 'What is below is above and what is inside is outside.'" Gershom Scholem, *On the Kaballah and Its Symbolism*, trans. Ralph Mannheim (New York: Schocken, 1965), 1922. See also his *Major Trends in Jewish Mysticism*, rev. ed. (New York: Schocken, 1946), and *Ursprung und Anfang der Kabbala* (Berlin: De Gruyter, 1962).

29. Pico della Mirandola, *Oration on the Dignity of Man*, trans. A. R. Caponigri (Chicago: Regnery, 1956), 7.

30. Yates, *Giordano Bruno*, 144–45.

31 Quoted in Yates, *Giordano Bruno*, 198.

32. Quoted in Scholem, *On the Kaballah*, 180.

33. This principle is not well appreciated even among otherwise astute observers of the modern world. As a result, phenomena that are essentially related, such as religious and political messiahs or millenarianism and revolution, are regarded as wholly dissimilar. For an interesting example of this type of misunderstanding see the exchange between Voegelin and Hannah Arendt in "The Origins of Totalitarianism," *Review of Politics* 15 (1953): 68–85.

34. See David Walsh, *The Mysticism of Innerworldly Fulfillment: A Study of Jacob Boehme* (Gainesville: University Presses of Florida, 1983).

35. Quoted in Walsh, *Mysticism of Innerworldly Fulfillment*, 54.

36. G. W. F. Hegel, *The Philosophy of History*, trans. J. Sibree (New York: Dover, 1956), 447.

37. The title of Franz von Baader's text, which was instrumental in the formation of the Holy Alliance, summarizes the requirements rather clearly: "On the Necessity for a New and more Intimate Connection between Religion and Politics Occasioned by the French Revolution" (1815). See F. Büchler, *Die geistige Wurzeln der Heiligen Allianz* (Freiburg: Inaugural Dissertation, 1929). Very similar is the sentiment of Novalis's essay "Christendom or Europe." "Let the true beholder contemplate calmly and dispassionately the new state-toppling era. Will not the state-toppler seem to him like Sisyphus? Now he has attained the summit of equilibrium, and already the mighty weight is rolling down the other side again. It will never remain on high unless an attraction toward heaven holds it poised on the crest. All your props are too week if your state retains its tendency toward earth. But link it by a higher yearning to the heights of heaven, give it a relevancy to the universe, and you will have it richly rewarded. I refer you to history. Search amid its instructive coherency for parallel points of time and learn to use the magic wand of analogy." *Hymns to the Night and Other Selected Writings*, trans. Charles E. Passage (Indianapolis: Bobbs-Merrill, 1960), 56.

38. Voegelin, *Enlightenment to Revolution*, chap. 7. Billington, *Fire in the Minds of Men*, especially chaps. 1–4; idem, *Icon and Axe*, chap. 4. Niemeyer, *Between Nothingness and Paradise*. On romanticism see M. H. Abrams, *Natural Supernaturalism* (New York: Norton, 1971); Renée Winegarten, *Writers and Revolution* (New York: Franklin Watts, 1974). For the influence of esoteric and mystical movements see August Viatte, *Les sources occultes du romantisme, 1770–1820*, 2 vols. (1929; reprint, Paris: Champion, 1965); Ernst Benz, *Les sources mystiques de la philosophie romantique allemande* (Paris: Vrin, 1968); Ernst Lee Tuveson, *The Avatars of Thrice-Great Hermes: An Approach to Romanticism* (Lewisburg, PA: Bucknell University Press, 1981); Antonie Faivre, *L'éso-terisme au XVIIIe siècle en France et en Allemagne* (Paris: Seghers, 1973).

39. G. W. F. Hegel, *System of Ethical Life*, trans. H. S. Harris (Albany: State University of New York Press, 1979), 185; idem, *Early Theological Writings*, trans. T. M. Knox (Philadelphia: University of Pennsylvania Press, 1971). On Hegel's relationship to the Enlightenment see the useful survey in Lewis Hinchman, *Hegel's Critique of the Enlightenment* (Gainesville: University Presses of Florida, 1984).

40. G. W. F. Hegel, "The 'earliest system-program of German idealism'" in H. S. Harris, *Hegel's Development toward the Sunlight, 1770–1801* (Oxford: Clarendon, 1972), 511.

41. G. W. F. Hegel, *Phenomenology of Spirit*, trans. A. V. Miller (Oxford: Oxford University Press, 1977), 131.

42. Charles Taylor, *Hegel* (New York: Cambridge University Press, 1975). For Voegelin's view of this procedure see, "On Hegel—A Study in Sorcery," *Studium Generale* 24 (1971): 335–68.

43. Hegel, *Phenomenology*, 478; also 487–88.

44. This is how his first biographer, Rosenkranz, viewed his development, as a rationalization of the theosophic speculation of the mystics. *Hegels Leben* (Berlin: Duncker & Humboldt, 1844). Hegel confirmed this interpretation in the preface to the 1824 edition of the *Enzyklopödie des philosophischen Wissenschaften*, where he expressed his fun-

damental agreement with the approach of Franz von Baader. The latter had undertaken to recover the mystical tradition, especially that of Boehme and the German mystics, as the basis for the rational idealist philosophy of the modern world. Moreover, one of Hegel's former students, Ferdinand Christian Bauer, published a work on Gnosticism in which he located Hegel within the Gnostic tradition going back to antiquity, *Die Christliche Gnosis* (Tübingen: Osiander, 1835). On Hegel's relationship to illuminism and Freemasonry see Jacques d'Hondt, *Hegel secret* (Paris: Presses Universitaires de France, 1968). The influence of speculative pietism isexplored in Reiner Heinze, *Bengel und Oetinger als Vorläufer des deutschen Idealismus* (Ph.D. dissertation, University of Munster, 1969).

45. For the chapter on Boehme see G. W. F. Hegel, *Vorlesungen: Ausgewahlte Nachschriften und Manuskripte* Bd. 9, *Vorlesungen über die Geschichte der Philosophie*, Teil 4, ed. Pierre Garniron and Walter Jaeschke (Hamburg: Meiner, 1986), 78–87. Hegel's letter of gratitude to his former student, van Ghert, for sending him an edition of Boehme's collected works is in *Hegel: The Letters*, trans. Clark Butler and Christiane Seiler (Bloomington: Indiana University Press, 1984), 573–74. On the general question of Boehme's influence on Hegel see Walsh, "The Historical Dialectic of Spirit: Jacob Boehme's Influence on Hegel," in *History and System: Hegel's Philosophy of History*, ed. Robert Perkins (Albany: State University of New York Press, 1984), 15–35.

46. Marx, "Preface to *A Contribution to the Critique of Political Economy* (1859)," in *The Marx-Engels Reader*, 2nd ed., ed. Robert Tucker (New York: Norton, 1978), 4.

47. How else can "the alteration of men on a mass scale" be achieved through human action? The transfiguring divine powers must somehow have become identified with human nature. *Marx-Engels Reader*, 193.

48. Marx's doctoral dissertation began with the following preface: "Philosophy does not make a secret of it. The confession of Prometheus: 'In one word, I hate all the gods',is its very own confession, its own sentence against all heavenly and earthly gods who refuse to recognize human self-consciousness as the supreme divinity. And none shall be held beside it." Karl Marx and Friedrich Engels, *Werke* Ergänzungsband, Teil I (Berlin: Dietz, 1973), 262. The dissertation dates from 1841. See also Marx's "Contribution to the Critique of Hegel's *Philosophy of Right*: Introduction," *Marx-Engels Reader*, 53–65.

49. *Marx-Engels Reader*, 91–92. The first, as far as I am aware, to interpret Marx as a secular messiah was Sergei Bulgakov, *Karl Marx as a Religious Type: His Relation to the Religion of Anthropotheism of L. Fuerback*, trans. Luba Barna (Belmont, MA: Nordland, 1979; Russian original, 1907). Solzhenitsyn refers frequently to this work, which he considers to be "one of the deepest analyses of the heart of Marxism and Marx himself." Bulgakov was one of the group who produced *Vekhi* or *Landmarks* in 1909, and his understanding of Marxism informs and is informed by their Orthodox perspective. For a contemporary example of the same kind of approach to Marx and Marxism see Leonard P. Wessell, Jr., *Prometheus Bound: The Mythic Structures of Karl Marx's Scientific Thinking* (Baton Rouge: Louisiana State University Press, 1985); and Alain Besançon, *The Intellectual Origins of Leninism*, trans. Sarah Matthews (Oxford: Oxford University Press, 1981).

50. The only significant omission from Comte's list of positivist saints, which also includes spiritual figures, is Christ. By the side of the human messiah there is no room for the divine one. Comte has assumed for himself or for humanity exclusive claim to the saving role. See Voegelin, *ER* chaps. 5–7; de Lubac, *Drama of Atheist Humanism*, 75–159.

51. Address to Fifth Symposium of European Bishops, *L'Osservatore Romano*, 7 October 1982.

52. For an overview see Ernst Benz, ed., *Der Übermensch: Eine Diskussion* (Zurich: Rhine, 1961).

53. Eliade, *Cosmos and History*.

CHAPTER 4

Ascent from the Depths

The leading figures of the modern world are spoiled mystics, *mystiques manqués*, who have sought to short-circuit the process of divinization. Instead of the patient and prayerful waiting in faith for the reception of God's grace, the opening toward the presence that "is able to do so much more than we can ever ask for or even think of by means of the power working within us" (Eph. 3:20), they exhibit the restless, over-reaching desire to bring this whole transformation under the control of human will. These individuals cannot endure the uncertainty of faith, and they seek perfection through the instrumentality of their own actions. Even where they pay obeisance to some superior reality, whether the divine cosmic forces of nature or the imperious exigencies of the dialectic of history, the underlying thrust remains the same. Humanity can only be assured of transfiguration if it brings this achievement about by itself. Humans can only be independent if they pull themselves up to the spiritual heights by their own bootstraps.

Yet despite the antitheistic character of this impulse, it cannot be described as unreligious. The revolt against God is still fundamentally concerned with God (*OH* V, 66–70). When Ivan and Alyosha meet to discuss the "eternal questions," it is not only about the existence of God and immortality. For as Ivan explains, "Those who do not believe in God talk of socialism or anarchism, of the transformation of all humanity on a new pattern, so that it all comes to the same, they're the same questions turned inside out" (*K*, 278). These questions arise from the profound longing for transcendence that remains even after the faith that evoked it has become impossible. The advent of Christianity has meant that within the societies penetrated by it, human beings have definitively discovered their movement toward eschatological transfiguration. Neither restriction to mundane existence alone nor return to a more compactly divine cosmos can any longer satisfy us. We have come to realize the truly imperfect and unsatisfactory nature of all finite existence, compared to the perfection of transcendent fulfillment offered to us in Christ. It is this transcendent hunger that is the real moving force behind the schemes of secular self-salvation within our world. At the same time, this hunger is also the most dramatic witness to the evident falsity and futility of such schemes. When Marx identified religion as "the sigh of the oppressed creature, the sentiment of a heartless world, and the soul of soulless conditions," he was more properly describing the desolation of his own post-Christian society.[1] Unfortunately, it could only be exacerbated through the collectivist absolute of Communism.

Marx was also describing, apart from the evident economic deprivation, the condition of religion that has lost its experiential substance. He was opposing the hollow shell of religion that appeared to serve no other function than that of "the opium of the people," undermining the desire to pursue their real economic self-interest. In a certain sense we might even say that Marx's revolt against the mendacity of Christianity, as he saw it, was motivated by a desire for genuine contact with the transcendent truth and goodness of Being. There is much in Marx himself, or in Comte or Hegel or Nietzsche, of "the sigh of the oppressed creature" that can no longer bear the weight of a senseless form of existence. It longs to ascend toward the world of meaning and reality that is truly divine. The spiritual aspiration is palpable in the "Economic and Philosophic Manuscripts," where Marx presents "true Communism" as the point where "the *other* person as a person has become for man a need," and where "what I make for myself I make for society, conscious of my nature as social." And as we have seen, the appeal of Marxism or of the other ideologies is not simply power. Of perhaps greater importance is the sense of participation in an order of higher reality, of transcending the self, that releases us from the senseless round of egotism. When the *Communist Manifesto* calls for the creation of a society "in which the free development of each is the condition for the free development of all," it is difficult to resist an inner movement of assent to the profoundly Christian expression of love for all human beings. Despite the patent self-deception going on in the secular messianic enthusiasms, it is not enough to accuse Marx or Comte of hypocrisy or insincerity. Mixed in with everything else is an element of genuine spiritual longing that can reach an almost mystical intensity. This longing is the real source of the appeal of secular mass movements for the most devoted and idealistic followers.

These idealists are appropriately identified as flawed Christians because that brings out the tragic self-destructiveness of their enterprise.

Their profound sensitivity to the pervasive spiritual crisis of the modern world has been perverted through the conceit that the crisis can be resolved by means of concerted political action within history. The ideologists are invariably correct in their identification of the problems. But the remedies they propose have merely served to intensify the original disease. Central to this failure has been the refusal to acknowledge the necessity for personal conversion as the only way of achieving the moral regeneration of society. While recognizing the disintegration of philosophic Christianity as the major source of the modern civilizational chaos, these ideologists have persistently rejected the call to repentance and submission to the transcendent order of rightness as the means of renewal.[2] They have understood the imperative of a spiritual foundation to order but they have utterly failed to provide it. A magical belief in the power of revolutionary or external action to perfect the inner person cannot alter this result.

All of the experience of attempting to implement this conception of social engineering has led toward one inescapable conclusion. The transfiguration of human nature that is its ultimate spiritual fulfillment is only possible through union with God after death, and movement toward that *telos* can only take place through the suffering surrender of self within and over a lifetime. Voluntary self-sacrifice is the only means of progress in the moral life. Destruction and coercion do not lead to any real moral achievement. In the target of such actions the results are deprived of any basis in free consent; in the practitioners any initial elements of goodness are progressively and completely eradicated. Everything in the ideological movements points toward both the profound longing for transcendent spiritual perfection within modern society and the absolute impossibility of reaching it through the coercive collectivist means so far employed. The most effective argument for the restoration of philosophy and Christianity today comes from their most vociferous opponents. Having recognized the necessity for a moral-religious foundation and failed to provide it, these individuals now point toward the restoration of that philosophic Christianity that has formed Western order since its beginning.[3]

The ideological movements reveal by their expectation of apocalyptic transfiguration that they are themselves variants of the Christian eschatological myth that they sought to replace. Now that the impossibility of such an endeavor has become clear, we are left with the suggestion that the longing can only be assuaged by returning to the source from which it sprang. If we are correct in seeing Hegel's demand for reconciliation with absolute Spirit, or Marx's quest for universal human emancipation, or Nietzsche's struggle to definitively overcome the spirit of *ressentiment*, as expressions of the Judeo-Christian expectation of an eschatological transformation of existence, then their respective aspirations can be fulfilled in no other way. For it was already evident before the attempt that the goal cannot be reached through the magic of violence. The results of the experiment have made that realization incontrovertibly clear. All that remains is the opening of faith toward the grace of God, as the only means available to draw us up to the highest actualization of our humanity. If the ideological movements arise from a false divinization of our nature, then they can only finally be overcome through the discovery of our true divinization. A quest that has originated in the Judeo-Christian experience of order, and nowhere else, can only be resolved by participation in that experience itself. That is where the movement toward eschatological divinization must lead.

The meditative unfolding of this insight is the subject of this chapter. We begin where the cathartic reflection left off in chapter 2, before the digression into diagnosis in chapter 3, although now with a fuller awareness of the context within which the struggle with the contemporary disorder must be carried on. Resistance to the forces of ideological destruction is more than opposition to specific individuals, regimes, or ideas. It is the front line of the conflict with the larger spiritual crisis of the revolt against God, which has convulsed Christian civilization in the modern period. Now we return to the concrete effort of resistance by Camus, Solzhenitsyn, Dostoevsky, and Vogelin, who did not necessarily begin as Christians. It was rather their search for a means of overcoming the demonic closure and violence of the world around them, that brought them back to Christianity as the only effective way to subdue the eschatological madness. In casting about for the spiritual resources to sustain them in their struggle with evil, they discovered the necessity for grace. They saw their own need of forgiveness as well as the forgiveness of others as the redemptive way toward the creation of order. As a consequence, they became experiential Christians who only later came to recognize themselves explicitly as Christian. These two phases form the two divisions of the chapter and within each of the parts we move from the least to the most articulately Christian formulation of their struggle.

The Redemptive Opening of Grace

Life without Bitterness

In the case of Camus the acknowledgment of the Christian dimension never came, and was even explicitly denied.[4] He was undoubtedly the least Christian of the four with whom we have been concerned. His reflections were dominated by the Greek character of his own Mediterranean experience, in continuity with the world of myth and in communion with the mystery of the cosmos. Camus's relationship to Christianity was always from the outside; he invariably viewed it in the most rigidly dogmatic terms. Yet there was no element of hostility in his attitude. He continued to look on Christianity in friendly terms and recognized a fundamental affinity with it. How Camus might have developed had he lived longer must remain a matter of speculation. What can be demonstrated, however, is that a further unfolding of the direction he had been pursuing would have arrived at a position virtually identical with Christianity. Beyond the Greek complexion of his thought there was also a profoundly and increasingly Christian dimension as well. It emerged as he entered more deeply into the struggle with evil. Indeed, it eventually became so pronounced that it is not too much of an exaggeration to say that Camus's experience became Christian in all but name.

In other words, even the most non-Christian of the postmodern thinkers was increasingly drawn in a Christian direction. At the beginning of his meditation he is what he was born, "a Greek heart" (*E*, 381) who tries to surmount the abyss of misery within the times. But from the point at which he begins the second stage of his inquiry, occupied with the problem of revolt against evil, his reflections turn more explicitly toward Christian themes. This is the period of *The Plague*. Camus confronts the problem of innocent suffering and is compelled to work out his attitude to the God of Christianity. The crisis of faith is lived through by the learned Jesuit Father Paneloux, and articulated in his relationship with the heroic doctor Rieux. At first Paneloux delivers a conventional sermon on the well-deserved nature of the calamity that has befallen Oran; he calls on his parishioners to regard the plague as an evil that can lead them toward spiritual goodness. Later he, Rieux, and Tarrou are compelled to watch the hour-by-hour agony of the young son of the magistrate as his little body is racked by the progressively more harrowing course of the disease. Finally they watch his death, his slight frame distorted into "a grotesque parody of the crucifixion" (*P*, 193). When Rieux protests that this child was innocent, Paneloux can only respond weakly that "perhaps we should love what we cannot understand" (*P*, 196).

The position of Camus is closest to that of Dr. Rieux, who asserts that he has "a very different idea of love. And until my dying day I shall refuse to love a scheme of things in which children are put to torture" (P, 196–97). He acknowledges that "grace" is something he does not possess, and seems to suggest that it might even be more of a hindrance than a help. What matters now is that doctor and priest are working "for something that unites us—beyond blasphemy and prayers," namely human health, the relief of concrete suffering. Paneloux uses his next sermon to elaborate the response he first uttered at the death of the child. It is no longer a matter of vague generalizations about good emerging from evil, but an existential struggle between the goodness of God and the horror of innocent suffering. He sketches out a position that may be broadly characterized as "Christian existentialism."

When we find ourselves with "our backs to the wall" then we must not seek to conceal the truth of the dilemma before us. We are faced with a choice in which "we must believe everything or deny everything. And who among you, I ask, would dare to deny everything?" (P, 202). There is no island of escape from the plague. It forces us to confront the dilemma of choosing All rather than Nothing. Only then will we be lifted up beyond ourselves to that higher vision, wherein we catch a glimpse of "truth flash[ing] forth from the seeming cloud of injustice" (P, 206). The unsatisfactory nature of this solution by way of a "leap" is brought out in the priest's decision to follow out its consequences in his own life. When he becomes ill he follows the advice of his own pamphlet, that it is "illogical" for a priest to call in the doctor. His choice to rely on God leads to the irrational conclusion that we should do nothing to cure the sick.

In contrast, the position represented by Rieux and articulated by Tarrou is the more sanely compassionate response. It is introduced by Tarrou with an explanation of how he came to realize that he has already had the plague. He joined a group that sought to destroy the society erected on the plague of execution, but in the process he became responsible for sentencing to death all those who stood in the way of the new world. The responsibility we all bear, direct and indirect, for the murder of others brings him finally to admit that "we all have plague" (P, 228).[5] All we can do is make every effort to cease being plague-stricken. "This, and only this, can bring relief to men and, if not save them, at least do them the least harm possible and even, sometimes, a little good" (P, 228). The best we can hope for is to become "innocent murderers," applying the principle of "calculated culpability" expounded in The Rebel. Tarrou can recognize but not attain the status of the "true healer." He wants, as he ultimately reveals, to learn "how to become a saint" in a secular world. Both he and Camus are confronted with the question, "Can one be a saint without God?" (P, 230).

Camus understood that the plague of "logical crime" can only be overcome by the sacrificial love of the saint (*N* II, 20).[6] He ends *The Rebel* with a similar call for an "insane generosity," a "strange form of love," that is willing to forego all for the sake of those who have nothing. But it does not get beyond this admission of a need. He is still too close to the perspective of Tarrou and Rieux, who cannot admit a God responsible for the injustice of the world. When Dr. Rieux looks out over Oran after the departure of the plague, he resolves to bear witness to the outrage inflicted upon them. And at the same time he acknowledges the good that is to be found in human beings in their "never ending fight against terror." They are the ones who "while unable to be saints but refusing to bow down to pestilences, strove their utmost to be healers" (*P*, 278). This may also be taken as representative of the limits of Camus's own spiritual expansion at this stage, because of the impossibility of his becoming an actual saint. A choice of Christianity would have separated him from all who remained beyond its consolations, and removed the urgency for concrete efforts to relieve the sufferings of human beings in the present.

Clearly, this was a rather rigid and formalistic interpretation that bore little resemblance to the lived experience of Christians. The exclusivist dimension of Christianity does not necessarily diminish respect for the ordering symbolisms of others; it can also heighten reverence for them as more compactly equivalent expressions of the same spiritual truth. But the inference that belief in God would cause us to cease caring for the sick in order to leave them to God, is a blatantly false dilemma. Why would not belief in God as easily lead to the conclusion that we are to be the instruments of God's providence to others? Indeed, Camus's inference is tantamount to a restatement of the devil's second temptation to Christ: to put God to the test in order to prove that Jesus can command the divine will. In a similar vein, Camus also interprets belief in immortality as a dangerous escape from our obligation to create an order of justice in this life (*R*, 21 n. 3). The reply might just as well be the more conventional one, that the prospect of eternal reward and punishment is an effective inducement for men and women to live up to their obligations toward one another. There is, in other words, nothing to be gained from trading such abstract charges apart from the concrete experience of the struggle to live in right order.

Camus understood this sterility, and when he abandoned his dogmatic objections to follow the logic of his unfolding experience of truth, we find him again moving in a Christian direction. This is especially the case in the novel written after *The Plague* and belonging really to the incomplete third phase of his development. *The Fall* deals not with theological discussion, but with the concrete problem of the demonically closed soul. Camus here tackles the nature of evil head-on. The hero, Jean Baptiste Clamence, who is also the sole character and narrator of this monologue, is presented as "a hero of our time." Like Lermontov's hero of the same title, he is "the aggregate of the vices of our whole generation in their fullest expression." Through the reflections of Clamence, an expatriate lawyer in gloomy cosmopolitan Amsterdam, Camus plumbs the spiritual depth of the contemporary civilizational crisis. Abstract philosophical speculation is brushed aside to explore the self-understanding of a man who knows what he does to be evil. It is the point where Camus's investigation moves decisively beyond the range of Greek meditation.

Even the title, *The Fall*, indicates the novel's affinity with a Christian world. In form it resembles the Christian tradition of writing confessions, and we should remember Camus's familiarity with St. Augustine in this regard.[7] But the central preoccupation of the narration with the problem of judgment most clearly establishes its Christian character. For this new John the Baptist does not announce the coming of clemency, as his name suggests, but declares his intention of definitively surmounting the need for it by escaping judgment. He reveals to an unidentified visitor that he has become a "judge-penitent," and goes on to explain this strange avocation by means of an autobiographical discourse. Before sinking into this nether world of seedy Amsterdam bars, the "last circle" of hell, Clamence was an admired and successful Parisian lawyer. His passion was the performance of noble acts. He would go out of his way to help people across the street, to defend the most hopeless criminal cases, to extend more and more the range of persons who fell under an obligation toward him. The former lawyer gives a lyrical depiction of how he "soared," felt himself to have become a "superman," supremely happy in the knowledge of his own rightness and superiority over all others. But then, at the height of his feeling of self-satisfaction, something cracked. An incident occurred that exposed the hollowness of his life.

He was walking home one night across the Pont Royal when he passed a slim young woman dressed in black. Shortly after, Clamence heard the sound of a body striking water, then a cry for help that moved downstream and ceased. He did nothing. Instead he walked slowly away and told no one. Other incidents followed that revealed the hypocrisy of his noble public persona. He found it impossible to stifle the desire for revenge against a motorcyclist who had beaten him up. Clamence discovered that his real aspiration was to become a "gangster." The thought of exercising unlimited control over others, especially a woman with whom he was having a relationship, took hold of him. Finally, while crossing another bridge at night, he was suddenly surprised by the sound of a big, hearty laugh, seemingly directed toward him. The whole world seemed to be laughing at him. That was the moment of his great discovery.

Clamence realized that he was placed under judgment. "In short, the moment I grasped that there was something to judge in me, I realized that there was in them an irresistible vocation for judgement. Yes, they were there as before, but they were laughing" (*F*, 78). He recognized the same process at work in all others, the awareness of judgment and the desire to escape it. "People hasten to judge in order not to be judged themselves" (*F*, 80). The ultimate motivating impulse behind this disposition is the desire to escape judgment, without undergoing the repentance and reform that would be needed to become free. Our deepest inclination is "to cease being guilty and yet not to make the effort of cleansing ourselves" (*F*, 83). The characteristically modern disease is the desire to live in this "limbo" state that refuses responsibility for both good and evil. It is very close to the condition of soul described by St. Paul in Romans 7:18–19: "I can will what is right, but I cannot do it. For I do not do the good I want, but the evil I do not want is what I do." It is the kind of differentiated turmoil of soul that could never have been identified by a Greek.

Camus's exploration of the spiritual crisis of contemporary humanity has been brought to a distinctly pre-Christian stage. Clamence continues to be haunted by the memory of the woman falling into the waters of the Seine. He recalls it as "the bitter water of my baptism" (*F*, 108). For it was not a baptism of forgiveness and regeneration, but of his determined closure to such a possibility. He now lives in the "little ease", painfully aware of his own guilt and the guilt of all humans, yet firmly convinced of the unavailability of grace. It is the Last Judgment without God recurring every day. In his view, the sole purpose of God in earlier times was merely to provide "a huge laundering venture," to guarantee the innocence of humanity by shifting the blame to a Creator. Now we have seen through this subterfuge. We know that not even Christ was without guilt; he was responsible for the slaughter of the innocents by Herod. Clamence lives in a hermetically sealed world.

The last step is the discovery of his new career of judge-penitent as the means of sustaining his world. He realizes that he can escape the only judgment left, the judgment of human beings, by regaining his superiority over them. But this cannot be done by surpassing them in virtue, since he has none. It can only be successful if he exceeds their condemnation through self-condemnation. "Inasmuch as one couldn't condemn others without immediately judging oneself, one had to over-whelm oneself to have the right to judge others" (F, 138). He has to practice being a penitent in order to be free to judge. This is precisely the art he is exercising in the course of the story itself. He now goes about repeating the account of his own depravity to any who will listen to him. This self-disclosure is then held up to his interlocutor as a mirror, a universal portrait of the age, in which everyone recognizes his own guilt. In this way Clamence has succeeded in extricating himself from the scrutiny of others. He can permit himself everything by being the first to confess his own infamy. Once again he knows the "intoxi-cating" feeling of being like God. "And as for me," he exults, "I pity without absolving, I understand without forgiving, and above all, I feel at last that I am being adored" (F, 143).

The abyss of pride is relentlessly exposed. Clamence makes clear that his discourse has the purpose of "silencing the laughter" (F, 131).[8] He seeks "to block the door of the closed little universe of which I am the king, the pope and the judge" (F, 128). Moreover, it is plain that this is the same motivation as he discerns in the moral philosophers of our world. They are still Christian in their hearts, even though they no longer admit it, because it is the one way for them to continue to judge others. The secular substitute is moralizing. What distinguishes this approach is that "they believe solely in sin, never in grace" (F, 135). What they most want, of course, is grace, and Clamence admits this was his own need too. In its absence the only alternative is the erection of a closed universe. Camus could not have brought the problem to a clearer state of development. There is nothing of the Nietzschean or Marxian perseverance in self-deception. Instead, the futility of the en-terprise is made transparent; it is heightened. This is why I use the phrase "pre-Christian" to describe it, because the meditation is poised for the opening toward grace that is needed.

For its further development we must turn to the more directly self-reflective writings. From the beginning there was in Camus a faith in the cosmos that saved him from the shrill excesses of revolt. He records his "Return to Tipasa" (MS, 139–51) as an anamnestic search for the "special grace" that he has always had and knows he needs to come alive. An unsatisfied thirst for "loving and admiring," he knows, has turned our world into a desert. "For violence and hatred dry up the heart itself; the long fight for justice exhausts the love that nevertheless gave rise to it. In the clamor in which we live, love is impossible and justice does not suffice" (*MS*, 144). The eternal beauty of the ancient ruins, the trees, rocks, woods and birds at Tipasa do not disappoint him. Camus recovers the wellspring of joy within himself, "the memory of that sky," that in the worst years of war kept him from despairing.

I had always known that the ruins of Tipasa were younger than our new constructions or our bomb damage. There the world began over again every day in an ever new light. O light! This is the cry of all the characters of ancient drama brought face to face with their fate. This last resort was ours, too, and I knew it now. In the middle of winter I at last discovered that there was in me an invincible summer. (*MS*, 144)[9]

This is the faith that assumes an increasingly Christian tonality as he struggles with the forces of evil within himself. His quest has been guided by the knowledge of the goal that is inchoately present within him. "I have put ten years into conquering what appears to me beyond price: a heart without bitterness" (*N* II, 95). The imperative for forgiveness, for redemptive self-sacrifice, progressively looms larger within him. He sees that the only means of overcoming totalitarianism is through surpassing it in its own goal of the divinization of human nature. Thus, he concludes, "we have but one way of creating God, which is to become him" (*N* II, 97). The difference is that now he is prepared to undergo the process of dying to self that alone leads toward transfiguration: "Not morality but fulfillment. And there is no fulfillment other than that of love, meaning the renunciation of self and dying to the world. To go to the end. *Disappear*. To dissolve oneself in love. It will be the power of love that creates, rather than myself. To lose oneself. To dismember oneself. To deny oneself in the fulfillment and passion of truth" (*N* II, 243).

The experience might best be described as proto-Christian because it lacks only the recognition of Christ, as the one in whom the kenotic process has been realized most completely. Or perhaps it is really Isaianic, in line with the redemptive truth of the Suffering Servant who prefigures Christ. At any rate, it is evident that Camus discovered in experience the grace of suffering, the power of redemptive love that is greater than the bitterness, violence, and destruction of a closed world. The reflections in his *Notebooks* from March 1950 on bear witness to the increasingly prominent role of love in his thought. Especially noticeable is that the emphasis turns more and more to the inability of merely human efforts to satisfy the longing for unconditional love. At the same time, we should not gloss over the fact that Camus continued to maintain his explicit rejection of Christianity throughout this period. Yet when he reverts to experiential reflection the inexorable movement of grace continues. "If I were to die ignored by the world, in the depths of a frozen prison, the sea, at the last moment, would fill up my cell, would lift me up above myself and enable me to die without hate" (*N* II, 270). The spirit of forgiveness finally surpasses the spirit of revolt.[10]

Repentance

An identical and more explicitly Christian movement is to be seen in the confessional dimension of *The Gulag Archipelago*. For while the book is a testamentary record of the millions who were imprisoned, tortured, and killed by the Soviet state, it is also the account of the unique meditative ascent of a single individual. In many ways it is Solzhenitsyn's most self-disclosing work. The first readers of the manuscript in the KGB did not realize that "in this book I have told the reader intimate truths about myself that are much worse than all the bad things their time servers can fabricate. That is the point of my book: it is a call to repentance, not a pamphlet" (*OC*, 536). Prison came to appear as a blessing to Solzhenitsyn because of this opportunity for self-reflection it forced upon him. He began to recognize his faults, his sinfulness, and his need for repentance and forgiveness. From that realization arose the enlargement of his soul to the point where he could offer forgiveness as the one indispensable means for the restoration of order. It was the result of his own unfolding experience, rather than theological or philosophical argumentation, that led him toward this position. For when Solzhenitsyn first entered the camps, he was no more of a Christian than Camus had been, although he had certainly been brought up in a more Christianity saturated environment than had the *pied noir* from Algeria.[11]

What he did bring to the gulag was an openness of soul that would not rest within any partial or restricted horizon. It was not enough for Solzhenitsyn to respond with compassion to the torment of his fellow prisoners, especially the returning generation of soldiers who had been dubbed ironically "traitors *of* the motherland" (since they were not traitors *to* the motherland). Their story seems to have been the first to seize hold of the young artillery officer. He resolved to bear witness to their plight, but did not stop at protest and complaint. He went on to explore the roots of this disaster in the devastating impact of ideology, as we have seen in his critique, and from there to the ultimate source of unbridled evil in the depths of the human heart. Moreover, it was not just any human heart, but the only one known to him firsthand— his own. He understood the abyss of evil within the Soviet regime because he had confronted its possibility within himself. The gulag experience was first and foremost a period of prolonged meditation on his own responsibility for evil.

He had discovered "a rewarding and inexhaustible direction" for his thoughts that would lead him on the upward path of ascent. "Remember everything you did that was bad and shameful and take thought— can't you possibly correct it now?" This was the advice of an old Jewish doctor Solzhenitsyn encountered, Dr. Boris Kornfeld, who had recounted the story of his own conversion to Christianity. He had become convinced that "there is no punishment that comes to us in this life on earth which is undeserved" (*GA* II, 611–12). If we ponder it deeply enough we will discover the transgression that has merited this blow. Solzhenitsyn took the words as prophetic, especially since the doctor was murdered that very night. By the end of his seventh year he had gone over his whole life and understood why it all had happened. Various incidents from these recollections are interspersed throughout the book as illustrations of the failings he knew were within him.

There was, for example, the sharp memory of an incident that had occurred while he was an artillery captain near the front. He was walking through the debris after a battle and he heard a cry for help in Russian. A prisoner was being whipped mercilessly forward by a security man on a horse. Any officer in any army, Solzhenitsyn observes, should have stepped in to prevent this pointless torture—but he was afraid. *"I said nothing and I did nothing. I passed him by as if I could not hear him* . . . so that I myself would not be infested by that universally recognized plague" (*GA* I, 256). Or there is the account of how close he came to becoming an officer of the secret police himself, one of the executioners, if some inner sense of revulsion had not held him back (*GA* I, 160). Yet this flash of nobility was not enough to prevent him from abusing the soldiers under him when he became an army officer. Even after he entered the camps, Solzhenitsyn had allowed himself to be enlisted as an informer, although he always managed to excuse himself from actually betraying anyone. That is why he made no claims to moral superiority over others. "What was I," he asked himself, "but a monstrosity?" (*GA* II, 286).

The experience of prolonged self-reflection worked a remarkable change within him. It is best recounted in his own words.

It was granted me to carry away from my prison years on my bent back, which nearly broke beneath its load, this essential experience: *how* a human bring becomes evil and *how* good. In the intoxication of youthful successes I had felt myself to be infallible, and I was therefore cruel. In the surfeit of power I was

a murderer, and an oppressor. In my most evil moments I was convinced that
I was doing good, and I was well supplied with systematic arguments. And it
was only when I lay there on rotting prison straw that I sensed within myself
the first stirrings of good. Gradually it was disclosed to me that the line separating good and evil passes not through states, nor between classes, nor between political parties either—but right through every human heart—and
through all human hearts. This line shifts. Inside us, it oscillates with the years.
And even within hearts overwhelmed by evil, one small bridgehead of good is
retained. And even in the best of all hearts, there remains . . . an unuprooted
small corner of evil.

Since then I have come to understand the truth of all the religions of the world:
They struggle with the *evil inside a human being* (inside every human being). It
is impossible to expel evil from the world in its entirety, but it is possible to
constrict it within each person. (*GA* II, 615)

From that perspective he could view the gulag archipelago in the most
spiritually expansive light. He had attained a stability of viewpoint that
enabled him to comprehend it without invective or complaint. For no
matter what level he was dealing with, whether the heartlessness of
the bureaucrats or the cruelty of the executioners, he had only to remember his own haughtiness as an officer and ask: "So were *we* any
better?" (*GA* II, 616).

   That is why he explains the "basic viewpoint" of the book is not one
of accusation or reproach. It is the acknowledgment that "all who suffered, all who were squeezed, all who were forced to make a cruel
choice ought rather to be vindicated than accused" (*GA* II, 265). There
is an aptness or readiness to forgive that includes not only our own
failings, but extends also to those "whose choice was even harder." And
beyond that, forgiveness must be extended to all whose genuine repentance makes them willing to receive it. Solzhenitsyn anticipates the
astonishment likely to arise from this suggestion that even murderers
and executioners be forgiven. "Must we forgive everyone?" He recognizes the need to draw the line between a forgiveness that amounts to
a condonation of their actions, and a forgiveness that brings about a
true reconciliation of human beings. The balance he strikes could be
regarded as a model for the mutual forgiveness required of a whole
century burdened with universal responsibility for evil.

No, I have no intention of forgiving everyone. Only those who have fallen.
While the idol towers over us on his commanding eminence, his brow creased
imperiously, smug and insensate, mutilating our lives—just let me have the
heaviest stone! Or let a dozen of us seize a battering ram and knock him off
his perch.

But once he is overthrown, once the first furrow of self-awareness runs over his face as he crashes to the ground—lay down your stones!

He is returning to humanity of himself.

Do not deny him this God-given way. (*GA* III, 436)

When we look for the experiential basis for this transformation, this softening, within the hardened soul of the *zek*, we encounter the usual difficulties. The softening was not reached as a result of discursive reasoning. Rather, this change within the soul of Solzhenitsyn was a penetration by transcendent reality that compelled him to see all things differently. The world about him had not changed; but the measure by which he judged it had. In light of the firm and unshakable divine reality within him, he saw all things in their true proportion. This is the difficulty in interpreting spiritual experience that has always caused such problems for commentators, including those commenting on Solzhenitsyn. It is why Plato insisted that he had never written anything really serious, because such things cannot be expressed. The most important part of philosophy is the transcendent reality within the soul of the philosopher—everything is measured in relation to that—and it cannot be communicated. It must be experienced.[12]

This is why we must be careful in interpreting spiritual experience not to classify it on the basis of phenomenal or external similarities. Solzhenitsyn's faith has been described by his biographer as a form of deism because, like the eighteenth-century *philosophes*, he usually speaks only of God without explicitly mentioning Christ and he usually draws from religion strongly moral consequences.[13] The categorization could not be more inadequate. When his experience is examined more closely we discover it is that of a man who is feeling his way toward Christianity, without imposing dogmatic constructions on the living truth emerging within his soul. While there may be a superficial resemblance to deism, the depth of the experience, the suffering from which it has arisen, the emphasis on repentance and forgiveness that it calls forth, all mark the profoundly Christian character of his faith. Most significant of all is the centrality of grace. For Solzhenitsyn's clear understanding of his transformation or ascent as the work of God within him is unlike the rational self-sufficiency of deism. The fullest account is in the poem he wrote while in camp as a way of remembering his thoughts at this stage.[14]

This poem too is reminiscent of Augustine's conversion in the *Confessions*, of course, the saint also was accused of being primarily Neoplatonic. Could we say that Augustine did not truly convert to Christianity, even though he had clearly understood the difference be-

tween Neoplatonism and Christianity for a long time before the crisis?
The same question could be asked of Solzhenitsyn.

> When was it that I completely
> Scattered the good seeds, one and all?
> For after all I spent my boyhood
> In the bright singing of Thy temples.
>
> Bookish subtleties sparkled brightly,
> Piercing my arrogant brain,
> The secrets of the world were . . . in my grasp,
> Life's destiny . . . as pliable as wax.
>
> Blood seethed—and every swirl
> Gleamed irridescently before me,
> Without a rumble the building of my faith
> Quietly crumbled within my heart.

Christianity had been a living reality for Solzhenitsyn in childhood, but
the secularizing pressure of ideology had gradually erased its influence.
Now he had time to reflect on the course of his whole life and on the
nature of human existence again. He could see more clearly without
the effect of distorting prejudice.

> But passing here between being and nothingness,
> Stumbling and clutching at the edge,
> I look behind me with a grateful tremor
> Upon the life that I have lived.
>
> Not with good judgement nor with desire
> Are its twists and turns illumined.
> But with the even glow of the Higher Meaning
> Which became apparent to me only later on.

Externally nothing had changed, but internally everything was completely different. The grace of God had seized his soul.

> And now with measuring cup returned to me,
> Scooping up the living water,
> God of the universe! I believe again!
> Though I renounced You, You were with me! (GA II, 614–15)[15]

The faith that had sustained him, that had invited him and to which
he had responded over the years, became suddenly transparent in that
momentary glimpse of eternal joy.

The Transforming Power of Love

The same transformative moment is the central theme of Dostoevsky's novels. It is the point toward which his characters move or fail to

move, as they respond to the pull of love or yield to the lust of domination. In *The Possessed* it is the old repentant liberal Stepan Verkhovensky who leads the way. Just as the denouement of the revolutionary disasters is about to occur, he declares that "the final word in this business must be general forgiveness" (*P*, 504). He has repented of his own part in fostering the liberal-revolutionary movement that now engulfs them, and he recognizes that it is only through a self-sacrificing love that a new order can be created. Nihilistic violence and terror must be utterly rejected. In a world in which all human beings are guilty, where all share in the responsibility for its collective evil, the word of universal reconciliation must be forgiveness. Verkhovensky wanders off with a woman who sells copies of the Gospels, to preach this word of truth. "First let's forgive everyone for everything . . . and let's hope they'll forgive us too, because we're all guilty toward one another, all of us. Everyone is guilty" (*P*, 661). He offers to become one of the herd of swine into whom the demons were transferred from the man called "Legion," and who were allowed to run off a cliff into the water to be drowned. Through such a sacrifice he hopes that the possessed man, Russia-Stavrogin, can be freed to end, like the man in the Gospel of Luke, sitting quietly at the feet of Jesus.[16]

The suffering through which he has passed has enabled him to see that there is no shortcut to moral regeneration. It can only come about through the humble abnegation of self that enlarges the soul to be filled with universal love. No human being can be exempted from this process, as the brothers Karamazov discover in their individual ways. "Unless a grain of wheat fall into the ground and die it abideth alone, but if it die it bringeth forth much fruit" (John 12:24). This is the motto of the book, and the refrain to which each of the characters returns as the rule of their lives. It is through repentance, the recognition of our own need for forgiveness and our willingness to accept the punishment imposed on us, that the way leads toward life. There are no exceptions to the "law of the planet." Any attempt to overstep this necessity will lead not to the growth of our humanity or of our inner self, but to its destruction and the downward fall to depravity. It is neither compassionate nor realistic to seek the transfiguration of human nature in any other way.

Dimitri Karamazov, the man who represents the vital passionate force of the earth, discovers that goodness cannot be seized by force. No more than Grushenka's love, is it to be attained by rudely taking possession of it. The pain of arrest and the false accusation of the murder of his father dissolves the obsessive power of his desires. He sees that everything else is empty but growth in goodness. When Alyosha comes to visit, Dimitri reveals the change that has occurred within him. "A new man has risen up in me. He was hidden in me, but would never have come to the surface, if it hadn't been for this blow from heaven" (*K*, 719). He no longer seeks the compulsive satisfaction of his desires. All of that has slipped away as he has come to realize the part he has been called to play in the great mystery of existence. Dimitri recounts the dream he had of passing by a burnt-out village in the cold steppes. People were standing around and a baby was crying from the cold and hunger (*K*, 615–16). "Why is the babe so poor?" he keeps asking himself afterward as he, like Ivan, is filled with a desire to help them. Now in prison he has finally understood that his own suffering is such a way. "It's for the babe I'm going. Because we are all responsible for all. . . . All are 'babes.' I go for all, because someone must go for all. I didn't kill father, but I've got to go. I accept it" (*K*, 720).

In a world in which none of us can detach our responsibility for the evil within it, the way toward regeneration does not lead through revolutionary violence. It begins with the purification of self that is accomplished by suffering. From there the voluntary acceptance of sacrifice may spread the truth of order to others, and when this is not evident, may nevertheless work its mysterious redemptive effect. Dimitri's willingness to sacrifice himself not for what he is accused of, but to atone for the evil he has actually done, makes little sense from a pragmatically rational point of view. Even less does the belief that his sacrifice will somehow make the world better for all the poor babes who are crying within it. But it has the ring of a profound truth about it. In a world where all things are connected, where the good or evil done in one part can have consequences elsewhere, it is not so irrational. The suffering willingly undergone by one person can have a wider effect on all others. Representative suffering begins to appear as the most definitive victory over disorder.[17]

In the case of Ivan the pride of revolt is stronger than the blinding passion of Dimitri. A more penetrating experience of the consequences is required to dissolve his hardness of heart. Not only the murder of his father, but also the arrest of his brother and his own physical and spiritual disintegration are all needed to erode the defensive rationalizations with which he has surrounded himself. He reaches rock bottom in the celebrated episode of his hallucination or vision of the devil. The latter mirrors back all the grandiose intellectual concepts that Ivan had developed. In this "poor paltry devil" he recognizes the reality of his own former conviction, that man must kill the idea of God within him in order to assume the role of God himself. Far from the creation of the man-god, what has resulted is nothing but the ingratiating self-interested creature, his double, that he beholds before him. Finally the bubble of Ivan's illusion, that "everything is permitted," is burst by the devil's question: "If you want to swindle why do you want a moral sanction for doing it?" (*K*, 789). The scene comes to a crashing conclusion when Alyosha bursts into the room to announce that Smerdyakov has hanged himself.

Smerdyakov is the direct and uncomplicated instrument of Ivan's philosophy. He has carried out the motto "everything is permitted" in the murder of their father. But unlike Ivan he has experienced none of the inner turmoil that lacerates the soul, yet can also prove the means for a purificatory release. The conflict between good and evil occurs most intensely in Ivan. His soul is the "battleground" recognized by Dimitri and Alyosha, and it is there that the contest will be decided. Crucial to an understanding of his personality is the recognition that he exists between belief and disbelief (*K*, 784), that his revolt has never cut off the possibility of faith. He has continued to respond, even in the midst of his closure, and this has meant, as Alyosha predicts, that "God will conquer" (*K*, 796). Ivan rushes into the courtroom to confess, "I am not mad. I am only a murderer" (*K*, 835).

Again the experience is recognizably Christian, although its articulation has stopped well short of making this connection explicit. Like Camus and Solzhenitsyn, Dostoevsky developed his Christian philosophy of existence principally by unfolding the implications of the struggle against evil. Nowhere is this more evident than in his own conversion experience. We have already discussed this episode of his recollection of the peasant Marey.[18] Its religious character remained so implicit that Joseph Frank is virtually the only commentator who has correctly identified it as a conversion experience, but the impact that the recollection had on Dostoevsky convincingly establishes its numinous character. A "miracle" had occurred, as "all hatred and anger completely vanished from my heart," and the transformation of Dostoevsky's whole former worldview began to take place. In the moment of his greatest despair, at the bottom of his suffering, the reality of transcendent Love in the example of Marey's utterly free expression of tenderness and care had flooded his soul. Yet the memory alone would not have been sufficient to accomplish this effect; rather, it was evoked by the reality that was overwhelmingly present within it. The closest analogue is probably to be found in the gospel accounts of the encounter various men and women had with Christ. They recognized a fullness of divine presence within him that transformed their lives.

It is paralleled by "The Dream of a Ridiculous Man" (*DW* , 672–90), which has been called the key to Dostoevsky's complex religious philosophy. Written shortly before *The Brothers Karamazov*, this is the story of a contemporary man who begins to feel that "everywhere in the world *nothing matters*." He returns home one evening resolved to commit suicide. Before he reaches his destination, however, he is interrupted by a young girl pleading for his help. The man brushes her away, but cannot remove her from his thoughts. Her suffering has touched him; he has discovered that something does matter. After a while he lapses into a dream. He dreams he has shot himself and is inside a coffin being buried. A heartfelt prayer for help burst forth within him. He is lifted up and travels through space until he reaches another earth, where he is eventually set down in the wonderfully idyllic setting of the Greek islands. This is paradise. It is filled with beautiful "children of the sun," living in perfect harmony with one another and with nature. "Innocent gladness sounded in the words and voices of these men" (*DW*, 682). After a while he becomes aware of a change in them. Their innocence has been lost and they become corrupt, given over to lies, cruelty, voluptuousness, jealousy, and anger. But what makes him see that this is a profound truth, and not a dream, is the realization that he has been responsible for their infection. "The point is that I have . . . debauched them all" (*DW*, 686).

When he awakes he no longer wants to kill himself. Instead, he thirsts for life. He wants to give himself over to the service of the Truth he beheld in the dream. "Ecstasy, immeasurable ecstasy lifted my whole being." He has had a profound and compelling vision of the path that human nature must follow in order to reach perfect unending happiness; it has penetrated his soul. The great Truth he beheld is that a person has only to turn away from evil in order to reach paradise. "I refuse and am unable to believe that evil is a normal condition in men. Yet they all laugh at this belief of mine. But how can I help but have faith: I saw Truth—my mind did not invent it, and I saw, saw it, and its live image filled my soul forever" (*DW*, 689). This is what escapes us when we view the account only from the outside; the hoary platitudes that made him appear strange or ridiculous have now become filled with meaning. They are the living truth of a reality that has impressed him as the most real reality there is. When the man asks how we can establish paradise on earth, it is this dimension of living concrete truth that he emphasizes. For it can be done in one day or in an hour. "The main thing is—love thy neighbors as thyself. This is the cardinal point; that's all, and nothing further is needed; it would at once be discovered how things should be arranged. . . . And I have found that little girl. And I will go! I will!" (*DW*, 690).

The love that is capable of overcoming the darkness within cannot be produced by us. It is a love that can be called forth only because we have first been loved; the grace of the living image of love must penetrate our souls. Before that has emerged we find evil irresistible and bear responsibility for our own share of augmenting it. But when the transcendent reality of love has made its entrance, then the obstacles shrink to the dimensions of their true insignificance. Compared to the reality within us they are now seen as derivative, lower levels of being. The supreme assurance of the triumph of good over evil in this experience is the source of the sense of the redemptive power of sacrifice. A recognition of loving self-sacrifice as the most effective means of conquering the evil of existence becomes the foundation for our whole worldview. It leads us on toward the transcendent consummation of the victory that can never be more than tentative in this life. The vision is completed in humanity's eschatological transfiguration.

Such is the movement in Dostoevsky and the others struggling with the chaos of the contemporary world. It is also the direction in which, as Voegelin has shown, the pre-Christian philosophy of Greece implicitly unfolded. The contest with evil and disorder is never final and often unsatisfactory in its outcome. Where or how is it to be completed? Plato and Aristotle struggled with a more compact symbolism to articulate the nature of this problem, especially with regard to the difficulty of incarnating the order of philosophy in the polis. They moved, Voegelin shows, in the direction of Christianity as the only means of resolving it. The necessity of a transcendent fulfillment is virtually recognized in Socrates's response to the improbability of achieving the "polis in speech," the best polis. "It makes no difference whether it exists concretely now or ever; that polis and none other is the one with which he is concerned" (*OH III*, 92; *Republic*, 592b). Aristotle brought the question of the relationship between the truth of the philosopher's soul and the lesser excellence achieved by all others to the point of maximum clarity. The distinction between spiritual and temporal orders was about to become transparent. All that was missing, Voegelin observes, was the *forma spiritualis*, "the heightening of the immanent nature of man through the supernaturally forming love of God" (*OH* III, 364). It is not that this was not present in Aristotle, but that its presence had not been differentiated.

Now that similar problems of the elimination of evil have compelled in our postmodern thinkers a similar pattern of development, it is noteworthy that the meditation has pointed toward the same culmination of Christianity. For no more than the Greek philosophers did the postmodern thinkers set out as Christians or with the intention of becoming such. It was simply that the exigencies of the conflict between good and evil pointed them inexorably in that direction. Of course, they undoubtedly benefited from the absorption of broadly Christian influences from the civilization formed by them. But it was only after they had made their own meditation explicit that they came to recognize its Christian character. We now turn to this acknowledgment phase of their unfolding experience.

The Recognition of Christ

The Need for Grace

The extent to which the Christian implications of their thought were recognized varies from one thinker to another. This is naturally a function of personal differences, as well as variations in their perception of the need or desirability of such explication. And it is not necessary for us to consider the degree of theological coincidence between them. Rather it is more useful to explore the variations in emphasis and the reasons behind them, as each of the four struggled with the consequences of their meditation. From this it should be possible to derive some insight into the problems with which they were concerned. Our purpose is not to sit in judgment on the consistency or lack of it in any individual's reflections, but to consider the direction in which their work has pointed and what further developments might be indicated by it. This is not an investigation of theology or even of political theory (in the conventional sense). It is primarily a study of the existential search for order in soul and society conducted by some of the most profound thinkers of the contemporary world.

In this sense Camus's strictures against Christianity must be taken as an expression of his own resolute opposition to all dehumanizing or deforming dogmas. They should not be regarded as a reflection of the deficiencies either in his own faith or in Christianity itself. He was reacting to what he perceived as a peculiarly doctrinaire form of Christianity that was indeed an obstacle to the full realization of order. If service to our fellow human beings is motivated only by the calculation of eternal rewards, it falls short of genuinely unselfish love. Or if the Christian love of human beings dictates a quietist surrender of all things to God's providence, then it is surely a poor response to the concrete need for relief of human suffering. But why Camus did not go beyond this straw man conception of Christianity to the reality of genuinely unconditional love is not of central significance. What is of interest is that this is the direction indicated by his meditation. We can take the limits of Camus's development as an *anima naturaliter Christiana*, as the sufficient demonstration of this finality. The lack of consistency with his negative judgment of Christianity is a secondary consideration.

A somewhat analogous aloofness toward Christianity, although from within the context of an explicit affirmation, is to be found in the work of Eric Voegelin. The reasons for his attitude arise from more crucial problems within Christianity and will be addressed more fully later. For the moment it is important to note Voegelin's declared assent to the message of the gospel.[19] The first three volumes of *Order and History* continually point toward the Christian revelation as the resolution of the experiential obstacles encountered in the struggle for order. We have already referred to Voegelin's assessment of the limitations of Greek philosophy. Its attachment to the "mortgage" of the polis precluded it from further differentiations. What the Greeks lacked was an understanding of the transcendent formation of the soul through grace. This is a formation that definitively lifts us beyond any concrete realization of order and points toward the eschatological transfiguration with God in eternity. But it is in Voegelin's investigation of the Hebrew prophets that the essentially Christian nature of his study becomes most apparent.

The prophets struggled with the recalcitrance and recidivism of the Chosen People. Eventually they were brought to admit the impossibility of incarnating the order of God within history, and had to face the question of how divine truth remains definitively victorious over the forces of untruth. They discovered that the only place where God's order approaches complete actualization is within the prophet himself. The suffering of the Servant points toward the universal order of humanity beyond any concrete society in history. At the same time, the prophet's willing submission to the consequences of evil is at one with the redemptive divine suffering that transforms evil into good. The mystery of representative suffering had been articulated by the Israelite prophets. In Deutero-Isaiah, Voegelin observes, "the order of being has revealed its mystery of redemption as the flower of suffering" (*OH* I, 501). However, it is not yet the reality of redemption in history. The manifestation of the fullness of divine presence in time has to await the appearance of Christ. Voegelin recognizes the preeminent nature of this event as the culmination of all human struggle for atonement to the transcendent order. "The participation of man in divine suffering has yet to encounter the participation of God in human suffering" (*OH* I, 501).

Christianity represents for Voegelin the maximal differentiation of divine and, correlatively, human being. He understands its specific character as the experience of "the bending of God in grace toward the soul," which is the fullest elaboration of the more compact experiences of philosophers and prophets. "The revelation of this grace in history, through the incarnation of the Logos in Christ, intelligibly fulfilled the adventitious movement of the spirit in the mystic philosophers" (*NSP*, 78). As a consequence, "the insight that man in his mere humanity, without the *fides caritate formata*, is demonic nothingness has been brought by Christianity to the ultimate border of clarity" (*NSP*, 79). Voegelin acknowledges that even conscientious thinkers today, such as Jaspers or Bergson, are inclined to pull back from this recognition of Christianity as the conclusion toward which their reflections point. But he flatly rejects such vacillations. He insists that this is not a matter of opting for a subjective or particularistic confessional allegiance; it is a necessity imposed on us by the unfolding dynamic of experience itself. We must remain faithful to the direction of fullest openness toward reality if we wish to reflect theoretically today. "Since the maximum of differentiation was achieved through Greek philosophy and Christianity, this means concretely that theory is bound to move within the historical horizon of classic and Christian experience" (*NSP*, 79).

Solzhenitsyn made a similar discovery through his own literary and existential investigation. Christianity or a Christianity-based worldview emerged almost of necessity as the only adequate means of coming to grips with the crisis in which we live. One of Solzhenitsyn's readers, Fr. Alexander Schmemann, pointed out the pervasively Christian nature of the author's perspective in *One Day in the Life of Ivan Denisovich*. Solzhenitsyn wrote back to thank him for pointing out something to which he had not really adverted himself.[20] In his writings a distinct progression is discernible toward the explication of a deeper, more Orthodox form of Christianity. Beginning with the discussion with Alyosha, the evangelical Baptist in *Ivan Denisovich*, he explores the most immediate experiential form of Christianity. Gradually a more expansive understanding of faith emerges through the recovery of the full amplitude of Orthodox Christianity in the succeeding works.[21] Finally we encounter the profoundly mystical experiences of Orthodox believers in *The Red Wheel*. It is difficult to avoid the suggestion that this also represents the pattern of intensification in Solzhenitsyn's own experience of faith.

The first indication of his attitude toward Christianity arises from his encounter with three young believers in Butyrki prison. Solzhenitsyn had scoffed at a prayer of Roosevelt's as hypocrisy. He was astonished when one of his young companions challenged this hackneyed dismissal of religion. It was right then, Solzhenitsyn reports, that "it dawned on me that I had not spoken out of conviction but because the idea had been implanted in me from outside" (*GA* I, 612). In addition, the young believers attacked Tolstoy not on conventionally Marxist grounds, but for being insufficiently Christian! His former prejudices were shaken and the gulag experience continued to impress Solzhenitsyn with the spiritual strength of Christianity. Of all the groups he describes, Christians were the ones who had achieved the inner balance of courage without bitterness or pride that was required to preserve one's humanity under such conditions. "They knew very well *for what* they were serving time, and they were unwavering in their convictions! They were the only ones, perhaps, to whom the camp philosophy and even the camp language did not stick" (*GA* II, 310). Such encounters were obviously the basis for the portrait of Alyosha the Baptist. In their conversation at the end of the day, Alyosha urges: "There you are, Ivan Denisovich, your soul is begging to pray to God. Why don't you give it its freedom?" (*ID*, 153). But Ivan resists on the grounds that prayers either "don't get through or they're returned with 'rejected' scrawled across them" (*ID*, 153). When he ponders it by himself, however, Ivan recognizes the rightness of Alyosha's assertion that we should only pray "about the things of the Spirit—that the Lord Jesus should remove the scum of anger from our hearts" (*ID*, 154). This is the only true freedom and the only genuinely human life worth living. "Alyosha did not lie. By his voice and his eyes one knew he was happy in prison" (*ID*, 156).

What is not elaborated in other works is Alyosha's attack on the Orthodox church. Rather, this attack is opposed by Solzhenitsyn. Although he seems to indicate that an evangelistic Christianity has the strengths of simplicity, directness, and spiritual power, with which it can appeal directly to secular men and women, he also recognizes its limitations. It is a narrow ahistorical experience with little to say about the great questions of history, the order of creation, and the eventual transfiguration of all things. Evangelism's tendency toward moralism and rationalism is particularly repugnant to Solzhenitsyn, as he makes clear in his polemic against Tolstoy. For although there are many Tolstoian influences in his writings, he rejects the deformation of Christianity that occurred in the great novelist's later didactic tracts. This is also the point at which Solzhenitsyn defines his opposition to all exclusively moral approaches to the regeneration of society. Without a grounding in Christianity, and preferably in the historically rich tradition of Christianity, such enlightened or moralistic liberalism will repeat the errors of its predecessors. Without the transcendent formation of grace, the collapse of autonomous morality is assured.

This is an aspect of Solzhenitsyn that bears careful examination. His struggle with the corrupting and deforming influences of ideology have led him to stress individual responsibility for evil and to appeal for an individual response as the beginning of the process of change. In many ways his own embrace of Christianity constitutes a second conversion, following on a moral conversion that awoke the voice of conscience within him. Moreover he was probably influenced by the recognition that his efforts at public persuasion were likely to be more effective if he confined himself to the most inclusive level of moral appeal. But none of this should be allowed to diminish the acknowledgment of the profoundly Christian source of his vision, which arose from the realization that moral goodness cannot be sustained unless it is anchored in the *mysterium tremendum* of God, the order of God's creation, and the mystery of God's redemptive action in Christ. The secular idea of a rational humanist morality is at best a pale ineffective substitute, and at worst the source of disastrous abstract moralizing. The dangers are for Solzhenitsyn best illustrated by the inflexible shrillness of the aged Tolstoy.

Solzhenitsyn explores the problem through the experiences of the young student volunteer in the Russian army of 1914, Isaaki (Sanya) Lazhenitsyn. Significantly, this character is modeled on his own father.[22] Through the eyes of this *narodnik*, one who "returns to the people," Solzhenitsyn seems to be defining his relationship with his literary-philosophical father, Lev Tolstoy, who was clearly a major influence on him. Sanya too has been enormously impressed with the legendary novelist and has sought to imitate his love for the simple life of the people. For this reason he has retained his unsophisticated name from the steppes, and has even gone so far in imitation as to reject the formal ritualism of church services. Sanya once met Tolstoy at his estate and heard from the prophet's own lips the recommendation "to serve the good. And so create the kingdom of God on earth" (*AUG*, 16). When Sanya pressed to know how this should be done, he received the reply: "Love is the only way. The only way. No one will ever find a better" (*AUG*, 17).

But the young student is incapable of holding his convictions so absolutely. He feels the pull of other obligations. This is why, contrary to the great man's advice, he continues to write poetry and why, despite his pacifism, he volunteers for the army. "I feel sorry for Russia" (*AUG*, 11) is the only explanation he can give. He is tossed about between the different authors he has read until when "he came to open *Vekhi* [*Landmarks*], he shuddered—it was the complete reverse of all he had read before, yet true, piercingly true" (*AUG*, 20). Faced with the impending disasters of the twentieth century, Berdyaev, Bulgakov, Struve, and others proclaimed in this anthology the revival of Orthodox Christianity as the only reliable bulwark of order in Russian society. Liberal or moral Christianity, stripped of the profound spiritual mysteries of redemption and resurrection, could not withstand the onslaught. This conviction is repeated, from the perspective of the declining stages of the catastrophe, by Solzhenitsyn and his dissident colleagues in their own anthology *From Under the Rubble*. The critique of Tolstoy's abstract moralizing is continued obliquely in *August 1914* through the conversation Sanya and his friend Kotya have with an eccentric Moscow scholar, Varsonofiev, whom they nickname "the Stargazer." Varsonofiev explains that history is not governed by reason. Unlike Tolstoy, he rejects the assumption that we possess the knowledge or means of realizing the ideal social order within time.

Varsonofiev's view is that history is an organic whole whose laws are unknowable. "The bonds between generations, bonds of institution, tradition, custom—these are the bonds that hold the flowing stream together" (*AUG*, 347). This is what makes the attainment of a perfect social order so difficult, because the laws for it are to be found "only within the total order of things" (*AUG*, 347). Varsonofiev represents, in other words, the Burkean respect for the mysterious wholeness of tradition, which should not be arrogantly swept aside in the name of whatever absolutes, no matter how exalted, lest we bring down upon ourselves calamitous consequences we have neither intended nor foreseen. Solzhenitsyn clearly has the experience of the Russian Revolution in mind here. But it is also a more general human problem of how to guide action in a world where the consequences can never be fully known. When the students ask Varsonofiev if their decision to join the army was after all good, he agrees that it was even though the reasons are inscrutable. "For some reason it is important that Russia's backbone not be broken" (*AUG*, 347). The entire episode seems to be directed against the simplistic absolutism of Tolstoy that can in reality lead to such disastrous effects. When asked about justice, the Stargazer replies that there is such a reality. "Yet not another of our own ones, which we have simply invented to fit our convenient earthly paradise. But that true justice, the spirit of which existed before us, without us, and for its own sake. And our task is to *divine* what it is" (*AUG*, 348).

The final demolition of Tolstoy's moralizing and, by implication, all purely moral approaches to order occurs in *October 1916*.[23] Sanya has been engaged for almost a year in the senseless slaughter of attrition that was to become the hallmark of "the Great War." One evening he returns from a particularly bad day in which his inadvertent carelessness has been responsible for the death of Tchverdin, a member of his own gunnery team. Alone and disconsolate he encounters the chaplain, Fr. Severin, and their conversation immediately plunges into the reasons for the war that has engulfed them. Divisions have come, the priest explains, because for the past four centuries humanity has been withdrawing from God. Even those who most vociferously proclaim their Christianity have not truly submitted themselves to God's guidance. Has it ever occurred to Sanya, Severin asks, that a man like Tolstoy was not really a Christian at all? "He is a pure product of our Voltairean nobility. And he did not have enough simplicity nor humility to go honestly to seek the faith alongside the peasants" (*OCT*, chap. 5; 64). Tolstoy's selection of bits and pieces from the Scriptures shows that, like the liberals, he thought he did not truly need faith. But what ultimately led him astray was his pride. He failed to acquire the most fundamental spiritual quality of humility. "Tolstoy himself is always in search of God but, if you like, at the same time God discomfits him. He wished to save man without the aid of God" (*OCT*, 65). Severin goes on to accuse the writer of forgetting all his literary sensitivity to "the world that escapes our spirit" yet exercises such enormous influence over us.[24] All is reduced to an impoverished abstraction. He wonders whether Tolstoy ever experienced the sense of his own finiteness, or ever knew that state "when the power to do what we will by our own will fails us and there is nothing left to do but pray. One desires to do only one thing—to pray, to give oneself over to the power infused by the Almighty. And if that is given to us, with what evidence is our heart illumined and the powers return to us. And we experience what can only be expressed: 'Preserve us and give us the gift of Thy Grace

[*Blagodatiiu*].' Do you know this experience?! . . . I was in the midst of just such an experience when I met you today" (*OCT*, 66).

What is missing in the liberal exhortation to simple moral goodness, even as heroically exemplified by the "Christianity" of Tolstoy, is an awareness of the depth of evil that tugs upon the human heart. This lack of awareness fails to recognize the extent to which the thinker's reasoning itself is infected with the disease. The absence of the requisite humility opens up an abyss of pride within the thinker. Before we know it we are back with schemes of universal emancipation that barely mask the libidinous self-aggrandizement of the activist. Solzhenitsyn seems to have identified this element of pride, which vitiated Tolstoy's efforts at the moral regeneration of society by blinding so many of his followers to the disastrous consequences of moralistic absolutism.[25] When this element is present, in the last analysis it is more important to feel one is right or superior or justified than to accomplish any concrete good. This is a temptation to which frail humanity is constantly prone. Even in our best moments, the possibility remains that we are "doing the right thing for the wrong reason." The innermost bastion of pride can only be finally dissolved through the acknowledgment that all the goodness we possess is not ours by nature or effort, but entirely by the gift of divine goodness itself. What frees us from the burden of self-perfection is the realization that it is not within our power to achieve. We must be brought to experience our own helplessness in the struggle against evil, in order to discover the reality of grace as the source of transforming goodness and love. It is the distinctly Christian experience of grace, of human helplessness and God's love, that is here identified by Solzhenitsyn as the foundation of order in existence.

A similar acceptance of divine mystery informs Solzhenitsyn's exploration of the great historical crises as well. The disaster of August 1914 and the debacle of 1916 sealed the fate of Russia for the succeeding century. Yet Solzhenitsyn's account is not a narrative of misery or complaint. It is a sympathetic exploration of the forces and causes at work. His meditation reaches up toward the most comprehensive understanding of the events, aware that their meaning can eventually be glimpsed only from the perspective of the mystery of God's providence.

The first historical turning point for Russia was the catastrophic loss of the Second Army under Samsonov. This was both symptomatic of and contributory to the larger defeat of Russia in the war; at the same time, as the entire force of Solzhenitsyn's narrative demonstrates, it was unnecessary. Russia was in no sense inferior to Germany in troops or material. All that it lacked was the wisdom to use them effectively, and this pattern of incompetence broadened and intensified up the chain of command. From the decision to move forward on the fifteenth day after mobilization (rather than the sixtieth), to the failure to build up adequate reserves of supplies along the border, to the slipshod manner of strategic planning and the feckless cowardice of the commanders in carrying plans out, the account is monotonously uncomplimentary. Everything conspired toward a defeat of the Russian army that was in no sense inevitable. Solzhenitsyn makes it clear that both in the opening encounters and in the subsequent campaign, "everything necessary had been done on the Russian side to ensure the enemy's triumph" (*AUG*, 332). It was a picture of "such unrelieved blackness" that no one could possibly have made it up (*AUG*, 324). There seemed to be a deliberate effort to ensure that "a Russian general's badges of rank [would] come to be seen as symbols of incompetence" (*AUG*, 324). The process of disintegration reached all the way up to the tsar, with his series of mediocre appointments and the final catastrophic decision to assume the military command himself.

Solzhenitsyn's exploration of the responsibility of individuals within this great historical dynamic profoundly illustrates his Christian worldview. Samsonov is the general on whom blame for loss of the Second Army has been laid, although Solzhenitsyn makes it clear that the fault was widely shared by others as well. Nevertheless, Samsonov does bear a crucial element of the responsibility. Distraught with uncertainties and anxieties, he longs for inner spiritual peace. He seeks prayer, the silent devotion in which "he could lay before God the totality of his life and his present suffering" (*AUG*, 275). He prays for divine aid in making his decisions and in the outcome of the battle on 15 August. And his prayer is answered. The burdens seem to be lifted from his shoulders and "his soul [became] less dark: all the weight and darkness soundlessly and invisibly fell away from him, evaporated, were drawn heavenward. God who could assume all burdens was taking this burden to himself" (*AUG*, 275). On the night before the Feast of the Assumption he hears the prophetic words, "Thou shalt be assumed" (*AUG*, 279).[26] The following day he decides to move toward the front to find out the situation for himself, thereby breaking off communication with army group headquarters and all of the separated corps of the Second Army. Even when one of the colonels points out that he is "neglecting the army commander's duty to control the *whole* army," Samsonov cannot be dissuaded.

Solzhenitsyn, however, does not pass any harsh judgment on the general, whose piety has led him astray.[27] Instead, while fully identifying Samsonov's culpability, he seeks to find in Samsonov's actions a deeper meaning of repentance and redemption that could eventually be the source of Russian regeneration. Samsonov has accepted his responsibility for the disaster and now offers himself as a sacrificial lamb in recompense. Vorotyntsev, the energetic staff colonel who by contrast is convinced of his own ability to turn things around, recognizes the change that has come over the Army Commander. "He was no longer surrounded by an earthly foe, no longer threatened; he had risen above all such perils. The cloud which darkened the army commander's brow was not, after all, one of guilt but one of ineffable greatness: perhaps outwardly he had done things which were contradictory by the worldly canons of strategy and tactics, but from his new point of view, all had been profoundly right" (*AUG*, 362–63). Samsonov has achieved a spiritual lucidity that enables him to see all that happened as part of God's plan. He has even had a premonition that defeat will lead to revolution within Russia (*AUG*, 384, 385). During the retreat Samsonov removes all his general's insignia and, thus stripped to his human essence, slips aside from his fellow travellers. His army has ceased to exist; now Samsonov ends his own life. He seems to stand, in Solzhenitsyn's mind, for the tragedy of Russia itself, a tragedy that, through the grace of repentance and the mystery of expiatory sacrifice, carries the promise of redemptive transfiguration.[28]

This perspective on the social descent into irresponsibility preceding the revolution is strongly confirmed by the conclusion of *October 1916*. There we meet a young woman who has only been mentioned once before in the book, but in such a way as to establish her symbolization of Russia itself (*OCT*, chap. 17). Zenaide or Zina (whose name suggests life) is an impetuous, headstrong young woman who prefers to follow the impulses of her heart rather than the conventional responsibilities of marriage and motherhood. That this is the problem for Russia as a whole is also indicated by the attention focused on the infidelity and martial breakdown of one of the central characters, Colonel George Vorotyntsev. In his case resolution of the crisis is not yet indicated in the two "knots" so far published. But for Zina a moment of realization does occur and is given the prominence of the final chapter of *October 1916*. It may be taken as representative of the way Solzhenitsyn sees the crisis of Russia herself being surmounted. The red wheel has been set rolling and it cannot be brought to rest until all who are responsible have acknowledged their guilt in repentance; then they may receive the grace of forgiveness and reconciliation. Solzhenitsyn's faith is sustained by his trust in the redemptive power of God's grace that works its mysterious transfigurative effect within the world.

When the second "knot" ends, Vorotyntsev and Zina have each come to realize the utterly illusory character of the freedom they have gained. Heavy with this burden, Zina enters a church where the evening office of Our Lady of Tambov is being sung. Above her is the icon of Christ the Pantocrator. It is an image that impresses the young woman with the harmonious order of creation we are obliged not to disrupt, while yet conveying the sadness of Christ who uttered no complaint against those who offended him. "All his pity went toward those who came to him, like her at this moment. His eyes absorbed all sorrow . . . and knew how to deliver us from all sorrow" (*OCT*, chap. 75, 570). She knows in that immaterial light that her dead baby son "existed somewhere somehow" (*OCT*, 570). Zina's thoughts turn toward her own condition. She has not intended to do harm and she has genuinely given her heart to the man she loves, but it has all turned out wrong. Now she had begun to see her own sinfulness and she follows the invitation of the priest to confess. Her faults, she acknowledges, were the seduction of a married man, the hurt she has gratuitously flung at his wife, the neglect of her own mother, who died without her, and the abandonment of her baby, which contributed to his death too. "Every stone withdrawn seemed to be forever freed from her" (*OCT*, 574). Confession is a release, a resurrection. But there still remains the fifth sin.

She has not yet been freed from the senseless passion to return to her lover. Whether the priest pardons her now or never no longer matters. "She saw with horror that she was condemned to *him*" (*OCT*, 575). It is all Zina can do to cry out: "My God, come to my aid! You see it, I want to tear myself away. But that is too much unhappiness. . . ." Exhausted and defeated, she has no more life left within her, when, as she listens to the words of absolution, "I pardon all your offenses," the breath of another life, "the Spirit floated above her and penetrated through her trembling." She looks at the priest and he understands her question. "In each of us there is a mystery greater than we suppose. And it is in communion with God that it is given to us to discern it. Learn to pray. In truth, you are capable of it" (*OCT*, 576–77). She still does not understand that *all* her sins are forgiven, until the word is spoken to her personally. Nothing in the world is more difficult than the sorrows of the family, the priest goes on, and it is seldom that we can decide to go one way and not another in this area. "How can you be ordered, 'do not love,' when Christ has said there is nothing higher than love. And he excepted no one from love" (*OCT*, 577).

The grace of forgiveness and reconciliation is the bedrock on which Solzhenitsyn's moral vision rests. Having recognized the inability of an autonomous humanist morality to overcome the bitterness and resentment of the struggle against oppression, the difficulty we experience in resisting the temptation toward pride and self-aggrandizement, and the virtual impossibility of accepting the mystery of reality without giving way to the destructive impulse of control, he arrives at an acknowledgment of the necessity for a supernatural foundation. Only when our hearts have been penetrated by divine love do we become capable of unconditional love ourselves. This is what enables us to reach to the limits of self-sacrifice, the giving of all without counting the cost that is the only effective means of subduing evil in existence. We become capable of doing all that we can do to change ourselves and others, while trusting the larger transformation of the historical process to God's providential care. Like the faith of Dostoevsky, this is an "ethic of resurrection," one that has emerged from the Good Friday of suffering as the one sure foundation of human life. But Solzhenitsyn's Christianity displays a serenity and equilibrium that is different from the turmoil within the soul of his predecessor.[29]

Humanity's True Divinization

The reason for the variation in the spirituality of Dostoevsky and Solzhenitsyn arises from their different positions within the cycle of the contemporary crisis. Solzhenitsyn has gone through the catharsis, but his work is primarily directed toward the restoration of order in its aftermath. As a consequence, his view of Christianity strongly emphasizes its moral component, the necessity for personal responsibility and struggle as well as the underlying role of divine grace in overcoming the impulsion toward evil and corruption in existence. Dostoevsky lived during the descending spiral and his work is primarily directed toward the struggle that occurs at the bottom of the abyss. Consequently, we can look to him for an articulation of the power of Christianity in confrontation with the forces of revolt. More than any other thinker but Nietzsche, he foresaw the maelstrom into which Western civilization was about to descend; but, unlike Nietzsche, he discovered within that confrontation the truth of Christ that overcomes the nihilistic lust for domination. This is why his worldview is more centered on the person of Christ than that of almost any other thinker of the past two hundred years.

Before exploring the Dostoevskian discovery, we should note that neither he nor Solzhenitsyn can be expected to provide a comprehensive account of Christianity. One frequently encounters even among the best commentators a tendency to focus on the dogmatic contents of a writer's faith. We have already mentioned the interpretation of Solzhenitsyn as a deist. Now we must deal with the characterization of Dostoevsky's Christocentrism as merely didactic or exemplary in nature.[30] What causes difficulty is the qualification "merely." For the inclination of a writer to focus on one aspect of the Christian revelation does not necessarily exclude an openness to the other dimensions as well. The fact that Dostoevsky does not elaborate on the themes of atonement or redemption should not be taken as an indication of their rejection. It should rather be regarded as signifying that the author did not apprehend a need to elaborate this or that aspect of the mystery. The difficulty is caused by our preoccupation with dogmas or ideas, to the neglect of an exploration of experiences and symbols. Spiritual experience is an inexhaustible living richness whose implications can be unfolded in a variety of directions depending on individual and social needs. Silence concerning certain consequences can only be taken as denoting an assignation of lesser importance within a particular historical context.

Such considerations are crucially important to a reading of Dostoevsky's religious philosophy, which is concentrated on the experiential truth of Christianity with a minimum of dogmatic articulation. His intention was not to restore Christianity, but to discover how the transformation of human nature and society that he had previously sought through revolution might be accomplished. Dostoevsky was aware of the Christian inspiration of this project; what he came through experience to learn was that it is only through Christianity that the project can be completed. All other routes are illusory and lead toward the destructive excesses of compulsion. Only the unreserved self-sacrifice of Christ embodies perfect love, as the ideal toward which human attainment must struggle and as the true perfection of our unhappy finite existence. The figure of Christ became for Dostoevsky both the fulfillment of and the response to the revolutionary madness. It had been by responding to the presence of Christ within the Russian peasant that the grace of unconditional Love had dissolved the will to power within Dostoevsky himself. On this basis he generalized its consequence for all human beings. If the transformation could only be realized though love, then it could only be begun by opening toward the One in whom love was most completely present.

His recollection of the incident with the peasant Marey had evoked such an epiphany of Christlike love for Dostoevsky. In his memory, the deep, gentle tenderness of the peasant had become transparent, revealing the unfathomable depth of divine love in Christ. It was at that moment that Dostoevsky came to know the Russian people and their ideal, who is Christ. No matter that they were ignorant of the dogmas or the explanations of their faith; they had a "heart-knowledge" of Christ which now became a living reality for him too.[31] They had acquired their faith not primarily from the Church or Scriptures, but from "those centuries of innumerable and interminable sufferings which they have endured in the course of their history, when, forsaken and oppressed by everybody, toiling for everybody, they remained with none but Christ—the Consoler Whom they then embraced forever in their soul, and Who, as a reward for this, has saved their soul from despair" (*DW*, 983). It was the kind of "living Truth" that had penetrated the soul of the Ridiculous Man and galvanized his whole existence in a new direction. Having seen the wisdom of the cross, that it is only through suffering that we can be cleansed to love with the simplicity and directness of Marey or Christ, Dostoevsky adopted this Truth as the focus of his life.

What this meant for him becomes clear in two passages of self-reflection from the later years. The first is the famous letter to N. D. Fonvizina shortly after his release from prison. She had given him the copy of the Gospels he had carried with him to prison, and he now wrote to comfort her on her own return home from exile.

I am not sure, but your letter gives me the impression that you felt sadness upon returning to your native land. I understand that. . . . I have heard from many, N. D., that you are a very religious woman. And not because you are religious, but because I myself have experienced and felt it, I shall tell you that at such a time one thirsts for faith as "the withered grass" thirsts for water, and one actually finds it, because in misfortune the truth shines through. I can tell you about myself that I am a child of this century, a child of doubt and disbelief, I have always been and shall ever be (that I know), until they close the lid of my coffin. What terrible torment this thirst to believe has cost me and is still costing me, and the stronger it becomes in my soul, the stronger are the arguments against it. And, despite all this, God sends me moments of great tranquility, moments during which I love and find I am loved by others; and it was during such a moment that I formed within myself a symbol of faith in which all is clear and sacred for me. This symbol is very simple, and here is what it is: to believe that there is nothing more beautiful, more profound, more sympathetic, more reasonable, more courageous, and more perfect than Christ; and there not only isn't, but I tell myself with a jealous love, there cannot be. More than that—if someone succeeded in proving to me that Christ was outside the truth, and if, *indeed*, the truth was outside Christ, I would sooner remain with Christ than with the truth.[32]

The doubt indicated in this passage is not between belief and disbelief, but the vacillation between states in which the truth is overwhelmingly clear and those times when it is not. It does not seem to be necessary to appeal to Kierkegaardian parallels and leaps of faith to explain this.[33] Such variations are a normal part of the human condition. The essential thing is that Dostoevsky's faith is founded on a certainty concerning Christ that, by comparison, leaves all other truths behind.

The other passage expands on the truth discovered in this experience. It is included in the reflections Dostoevsky jotted down on the day of his first wife's death.

Masha is lying on the table. Will I ever see Masha again? To Love man like *oneself*, according to the commandment of Christ is impossible. The law of personality on earth binds. The 'I' stands in the way. . . . Christ was able, but Christ was eternal, for all ages the ideal toward which man strives and according to the law of nature must strive. After Christ's appearance, it became clear that the highest development of personality must attain to that point where man annihilates his own 'I', surrenders it completely to all and everyone without division or reserve. . . . And this is the greatest happiness. . . . This is Christ's paradise. . . . And so, on earth man strives toward an ideal contrary to his nature. When man has not fulfilled the law of striving toward the ideal, i.e., has not *by love* offered his 'I' in sacrifice to people or to another being (Masha and I), he experiences suffering and has called this condition sin.[34]

Christ's total self-donation in love of all others, Dostoevsky had discovered, is the truth by which all other truths are to be measured. He recognized it as the point where "the law of the 'I' merges with the law of humanism" and, thus, the one way his former humanitarian ideals could attain their realization. At the same time, he drew from it the conclusion that we are immortal, because it would be "completely senseless to attain such a great goal if upon attaining it everything is extinguished and disappears, that is, if man will no longer have life when he attains the goal. Consequently there is a future paradisal life."[35]

It seems unnecessary to impose on these passages the narrow interpretation that Dostoevsky is asserting that humans are in need of no special grace in order to achieve this state, or that "the sole significance of Christ" is to serve as the divine exemplar of this morality of love. In the living richness of experience all of these dimensions are included without differentiating explication. The iconic presence of Christ drawing humanity toward an imitative self-transcendence is the operation of divine grace. Is this not the way in which Christ affected those whom he met, as described in the Gospels? Nor should we too readily conclude that Dostoevsky understood his experience as exclusively moral in nature. It also contained a strong element of the traditional Orthodox concept of *theosis*, divinization of human nature. Eternal life is not merely an inference drawn from the impossibility of frustrating the unlimited human aspiration for perfection, but an experience of the new life that wells up within those who open themselves to the Spirit of Christ. "Christ entered entirely into mankind, and man strives to transform himself into the 'I' of Christ as into his own ideal. Having achieved this, he clearly sees that everyone who has achieved this same goal on earth has entered into the condition of his final nature, that is, in Christ. (The synthetic nature of Christ is astonishing. It is, after all, the nature of God, which means that Christ is the reflection of God on earth.)" By means of this "true philosophy" Dostoevsky had acquired a profound sense of having pierced through to "the center and Synthesis of the universe and its outer form—matter: God, that is eternal life." Participation in the life of God was both the means and the end of his moral striving.[36]

From the time of this recognition Dostoevsky sought to evoke the iconic image of the "positively beautiful individual" in his novels. It was to be not only the criterion for a critique of liberal humanitarianism, but also a presentation of the living Truth of such overwhelming power that it would virtually compel our assent. The rebirth of Christ within his own soul would in this way be communicated to the soul of society. He drew heavily on the Orthodox tradition of holy fools and pious elders as the models for what he had in mind. *Don Quixote* had always deeply impressed him; he regarded it as the greatest book ever written (*DW*, 260, 836). But he found it difficult to create a believable parallel of his own. *The Idiot* was his first sustained attempt, and it is successful as a novel primarily because Dostoevsky did not impose his own preconceptions on the outcome. Prince Myshkin, the innocent saintly hero, is genuinely good, but in his impenetrable naiveté causes disaster everywhere he goes. He spurns and shames his fiancée, Aglaya, is responsible for the death of the other woman he loves, Nastasya Filippovna, and is powerless to lessen the turbulence of evil all around him. The explanation is to be found in all the repeated references to the prince as a "disembodied spirit." He has not attained his sanctity through the struggle with evil. His is not a love that has been reached through suffering, and so it is ineffective in the contest with the evil surrounding it. Myshkin exists as a glimpse of paradise, of what a human being might be, but he is incapable of showing us the way toward it.[37]

The verisimilitude of a novel requires that the hero engage in the struggle from which wisdom arises, not to have already received it as a gift. This is why Dostoevsky abandoned the attempt to make such a saintly figure the principal character. Saintly figures recede from being the center of action, to becoming the center of illumination in the stories. Thus the self-revelation or confession of Stavrogin emerges in his meeting with Bishop Tikhon Zadonsky in *The Possessed*. And in *The Adolescent* it is the pilgrim and legitimate father of the young hero, the wandering holy man Makar Dolgoruky, who reveals the innermost nature of the longing that drives all the other characters. He declares to the assembled company that he has never met "a truly godless man." They have all been restless men who have sought without finding the light they crave. "But they never think to face the only truth, although life without God is nothing but torture" (*A*, 373). Makar appeals to the other characters to recognize the voice of God, of Christ, within them and to surrender all in love for the well-being of others. He points the way toward the vision of paradise that he carries within him. It is a truth confirmed by the vision of Versilov, the actual father of the young hero, whose dream of universal brotherhood always ends with the reappearance of Christ "in the midst of the abandoned men" (*A*, 473).

The high point of this technique of representing spiritual truth was reached by Dostoevsky in *The Brothers Karamazov*. There he took his own advice, that "on earth there is only one positively beautiful person—Christ,"[38] by including Christ among the dramatis personae. The legend of the Grand Inquisitor and the testament of the Elder Zossima were intended to form a unity. It is Dostoevsky's most comprehensive attempt to transfigure the spirit of revolt, which he saw as the root of the emerging civilizational crisis. The appeal was made to his contemporaries to recognize that the paradise they sought was already present within them, if only they would open to the divine invitation to love as it was most fully embodied in Christ. Despite his own misgivings about the persuasiveness of the appeal, it is now recognized as one of the great works of Christian literature. The Grand Inquisitor chapter is possibly the most successful depiction of Christ outside of the Gospels.

Not without justification has it been suggested that it could form a suitable addition to the Christian canon.[39]

Dostoevsky had found the key to the convincing presentation of Christ within the agonistic framework of the novel. It was to portray Christ indirectly. The silent Savior who comes into the crowd in sixteenth-century Seville and then confronts the Inquisitor in the private dungeon interrogation is a powerful presence. He is made known to us precisely through the strength of the reactions he evokes in others, but especially in the wizened old cardinal. "'Is it Thou?' but receiving no answer, he adds at once, 'Don't answer, be silent. What canst Thou say, indeed? I know too well what Thou wouldst say . . .'" (K, 296). Nothing is said by Christ, nor is there any information to be conveyed. Everything is already known, for the Inquisitor reveals a self-knowledge that could not be improved upon by any critique. He knows that all his ostensible activities to benefit humanity are only a lie; they constitute an assault on the very core of human dignity. Nor can he claim to be moved to this extreme of desperation out of a pure impassioned concern for suffering humanity; nothing could be clearer than the contempt in which he holds human nature. The situation is fully transparent to each of them. "'And why dost Thou look silently and searchingly at me with Thy mild eyes? Be angry. I don't want Thy love, for I love Thee not. And what use is it for me to hide anything from Thee?'" Finally the Inquisitor reveals his true self: "We are not working with Thee, but with *him*—that is our mystery" (K, 305). The devil who had tempted Christ in the desert is the one with whom the Inquisitor now cooperates. His "secret," as Alyosha guesses, is that he no longer believes in God.

The contrast could not be greater, between the shifting, effusive rationalizations of the cardinal and the unspeaking, simple constancy of Christ. Jesus shows by his actions that he is the one who truly loves humanity. The infinite divine patience that is the foundation of human freedom extends even to the assault on God's creation by the ideologues. The love of individuals even in their sin is the way to evoke a properly human response; anything less would be an insult to God and an affront to human dignity. At the root of this defense of the innermost being of the person, human freedom, is the unconditional divine love that suffers all of the consequences of that freedom. Christ is the God become man who suffers at the hands of God's free creatures. The evil that arises from human freedom cannot be overcome by the coercive destruction of the human essence. It must be suffered through, in order to extract the response of repentance. At the same time, the triumph of love over hatred expressed in this sacrifice is the definitive redemption of human nature. Through the inner unity of all things, the mystery of representative suffering powerfully effects the transfiguration of the world. All of these consequences and more can be unpacked from the silent witness of Christ before the Inquisitor. But the power of Dostoevsky's portrayal derives from the concrete inherence of these consequences in this iconographic presence.

The unreproaching silence of Christ is a force more devastating than the Inquisitor can withstand. He is used to criticisms and complaints being hurled at him, and would welcome the opportunity to demonstrate his strength of will over all objections. But before this suffering Savior he is powerless. The truth about his demonic hatred and closure against reality comes from his own lips. In the presence of God's love incarnated in Christ, the condemnation of all false humanitarianism becomes irrefutable. The hell of his lust for domination could not become plainer. It reaches an unbearable intensity in the final gesture of Jesus when he "suddenly approached the old man in silence and softly kissed him on his bloodless aged lips. That was all his answer." Ivan reports that the old man "shuddered" and pointed the prisoner toward the door, commanding him to "come no more, never, never" (K, 311). He still holds to his idea because it is not to be expected that such hardness of heart would dissolve, but forever after "the kiss glows in his heart" (K, 312).

Strangely, the author himself was uncertain that readers would get his meaning. He felt the need to reply to the Inquisitor and Ivan with the long section "The Russian Monk."[40] It consists of the last discourse of the Elder Zossima taken down by Alyosha, and is Dostoevsky's own most extended attempt at depicting a "positively beautiful" individual. It is also the most sustained exposition of the profoundly Christian character of Dostoevsky's thought. For the elder is preoccupied with the problem of conveying the experiential essence of his own spiritual life. This is the response to Ivan's rebellion and the Inquisitor's rationalizations. There is no effort to refute them intellectually. Instead, the untruth, as Dostoevsky regarded it, is juxtaposed against the living reality of the elder's testament. Zossima seeks not so much to present a theological defense of Christianity, as to evoke a Christlike experience within the souls of his listeners. For this reason we should look to the discourse less for Dostoevsky's own explicit Christianity than for its experiential core. If we are prepared to read it in this way, then the seemingly loose and rambling meditation yields up its meaning. On the surface it appears sentimental and ineffective, especially compared to the compelling logic of the revolt preceding it, but its power lies in the capacity to evoke a similar experience within the reader. The ecstatic Christian nature mysticism at the heart of the elder's spirituality is presented as an experiment. He is constantly inviting us to participate in order to see that it is so. Its effect is demonstrated by the following episode with Alyosha, who understands only when he has undergone the same experience himself.

Zossima begins by recounting the two big experiences that revealed to him the true nature of reality. The first was the death of his younger brother, who, in the few weeks of his illness, reached an ecstatic visionary penetration of the paradise in which we live, if only we to begin to recognize it within ourselves. The second was Zossima's own conversion from a brutal and arrogant young officer into the gentle, unassuming monk he eventually became. He had provoked a duel with his rival for the affections of a young woman. Before the contest took place, Zossima flew into a rage against his orderly, whom he beat around the head so severely that it was covered with blood. Then he realized what he had done. He saw what he had become, and understood the request of his brother for forgiveness. "In truth, perhaps, I am more than all others responsible for all, a greater sinner than all men in the world" (K, 356). In the duel he allowed his opponent the first shot, then begged forgiveness; he resigned his commission and decided to enter a monastery. This is followed by the account of a third episode of conversion. A stranger came to the monk to confess a murder he had committed long ago but never admitted. Seeing the example of Zossima's duel had given him the strength to make a public confession of the dreadful secret he had kept in his heart all those years. "Heaven," he too had come to understand, "lies hidden within all of us—here it lies hidden in me, and if I will it, it will be revealed to me tomorrow and for all of my life" (K, 362). The way toward its discovery is the experience of the cross by which the old self is put to death and the new life reborn. "Except a corn of wheat fall into the ground and die," Zossima reminded him, "it abideth alone: but if it die it bringeth forth much fruit."

On the basis of such experiences Zossima concludes that it is "from these meek monks, who yearn for solitary prayer, the salvation of Russia will come perhaps once more" (K, 375). They are the ones who keep within themselves the pure image of Christ. "And when the time comes they will show it to the tottering creeds of the world" (K, 375). They will demonstrate that the brotherhood and justice so ardently sought by the modern world cannot be attained without Christ. In a passage that reminds us of the juxtaposition with the Grand Inquisitor, Zossima explains: "They aim at justice, but, denying Christ, they will end by flooding the earth with blood, for blood cries out for blood, and he that taketh up the sword shall perish by the sword" (*K*, 381). But the elder is more concerned with exemplifying the truth than with engaging in critique. He offers no arguments against the position of the Inquisitor. Rather, he tries to draw out of its aspiration to universal brotherhood and compassion an illumination of the true inner path toward the humanitarian goal.

Instead of giving way to the impulse of revolt at the sight of human wickedness, the elder counsels love. "At some thoughts one stands perplexed, especially at the sight of man's sins, and wonders whether one should use force or humble love. Always decide to use humble love. If you resolve on that once for all, you may subdue the whole world" (*K*, 383). In an appeal that seems to be directed toward Ivan, he implores: "Let not the sin of men confound you in your doings." Recognize that we are all responsible for all men's sins and stand equally in need of mutual forgiveness. In place of feelings of vengeance, seek to assume the burden of suffering since, even if we are sinless, we are guilty through not having been a light to withdraw the evildoers from their wickedness. Our pride can all too easily lead us into "murmuring against God" and imagining we are doing great deeds in sitting in judgment over all others. We must, above all, guard against this temptation. "On earth, indeed, we are as it were astray, and if it were not for the precious image of Christ before us, we should be undone and altogether lost, as was the human race before the flood" (*K*, 384). In begging forgiveness from all human beings and in extending our forgiveness toward them, we shall be imitating his redemptive sacrifice for humanity.

But the key to the elder's discourse is that we must do it in order to "see at once that it is really so." If we respond to the Christlike appeal of humble forgiveness, a new reality is born within us. A miracle of transformation occurs and we see in its light that we live in a world mysteriously linked to heavenly regions within it. The joy of suffering love radiates outward into an ecstatic nature mysticism, in which Zossima suggests we might even ask the birds for forgiveness. It may sound senseless but it is true on a deeper level. There, Zossima explains, we recognize that "all is like an ocean, all is flowing and blending; a touch in one place sets up movement at the other end of the earth" (*K*, 384). When we have once done a good action it never evaporates without effect, for the great truth is that its effect is added to the inexorable process of transfiguration going forward within all things.

But this is known only to those who have submitted themselves to the task. Only they will recognize the truth of Zossima's words, only they will have within them the living reality from which his teachings arise. They will understand his final appeal: "Love to throw yourself on the earth and kiss it. Kiss the earth and love it with an unceasing consuming love. Love all men, love everything. Seek that rapture and ecstasy. Water the earth with the tears of your joy and love those tears. Don't be ashamed of that ecstasy, prize it, for it is a gift of God and a great one; it is not given to many but only the elect" (*K*, 387).

This is the purpose that must be kept in mind in reading "The Russian Monk": to awaken the same experience in his listeners. In the language of evangelical piety used by the nineteenth-century *starets*, Zossima tries to draw Alyosha and the others into the same unreserved self-surrender of love.[41] Thus they will be opened to receive the rapture that discloses the mysterious oneness of all things, and their dedication to human service will in turn be brought to ever deeper levels. The discourse is not theological in nature or intent, but primarily a vehicle for conveying something of the ecstatic experience. In this sense it is similar to a Platonic dialogue or a gospel. The structure moves from the level of a common experience of evil, to the level of an uncommon experience of self-sacrifice as the only means of overcoming it. Behind the movement is the figure of the One, whose unconditional expression of love has already accomplished the redemption, as the guiding truth. There is relatively little elaboration of the meaning of Christ, in preference to the attempt to convey something of the experience of Christ. Zossima's discourse is a brilliant example of how the essentials of Christian experience can be communicated without Christian theology.

The same can be said of its continuation in the life of his pupil, Alyosha, whose development really only begins after the death of the elder. Alyosha undergoes his own crisis of the spirit as a result of the bitter disappointment he experiences when the remains of his beloved teacher begin to putrefy. A miraculous preservation has not been granted to the lifeless body of Zossima. The youngest Karamazov quits the monastery, outraged at the denial of this "higher justice" to the one he admired (*K*, 408). Only after wandering in the company of others does he return later that night to kneel in vigil beside the coffin. There while the account of the first miracle in Cana is being read he drifts into sleep. He dreams he is at the wedding feast, when he sees a familiar figure moving towards him. It is Father Zossima. The elder invites him to join the celebration, where all are drinking "the wine of new, great gladness." This was the purpose of the miracles, the reason why Christ has come among us. "He has made himself like unto us from love and rejoices with us. He is changing the water into wine that the gladness of the guests may not be cut short" (*K*, 435). Alyosha experiences the beginning of rapture within himself, but as he stretches out his hand to touch the elder he awakes to where he is.

Now he is on his feet and leaving the cell. He goes out into the open space, where he is comforted by the vault of heaven above, embraced by the slumbering beauty of nature, and heartened by the glimmering domes of the cathedral.

The silence of earth seemed to melt into the silence of the heavens. The mystery of earth was one with the mystery of the stars. . . . Alyosha stood, gazed, and suddenly threw himself down flat upon the earth. He did not know why he embraced it. He could not have told why he longed so irresistibly to kiss it, to kiss it all. But he kissed it weeping, sobbing and watering it with his tears, and vowed passionately to love it, to love it for ever and ever. "Water the earth with the tears of your joy and love those tears," echoed in his soul. (*K*, 436)

He experiences that mystic unity with other worlds of which the elder spoke, as he gives way to his longing "to forgive everyone and for everything, and to beg forgiveness." When reflecting afterward on what has transpired, he can only say, "Some one visited my soul in that hour." Something "firm and unshakable" has penetrated his soul and his life has been changed forever. Nothing more can be said. For the truth is that the transfiguration of a person is the work of impenetrable divine grace within.

When this discovery has concretely taken hold within a person, all other considerations pale into insignificance. It is the living truth that once "you have beheld it, you know that it is the Truth, and that there can be no other Truth whether you be sleeping or waking" (*DW*, 678). No further information or additional arguments are received, but now everything is viewed in an entirely different light. This is why the objections of Ivan in his rebellion or the criticisms of the Inquisitor are not answered anywhere directly by Dostoevsky. They cannot be. Innocent suffering and the misuse of human freedom remain what they are. The only difference is that now we are willing to accept the mystery of a reality in which such things occur. We recognize that they are not the only considerations, that it may not be for human beings to sit in judgment on the order of the whole, and that there is a truth even more profound than our feelings of injustice and rebellion. At that level is the assurance that even enormities such as these can be reconciled. We still do not possess the means of reconciling them, but we can trust in the order of a God whose love extends to assuming all the burdens of creaturely existence on himself. When we have recognized that it is only humble love that is capable of creating order, that railing against the injustice of creation only exacerbates the problem, then our complaints recede to more manageable dimensions. As with Alyosha, externally nothing has changed, but internally "something firm and unshakable as that vault of heaven" has entered into our soul.

In the confrontation between the "man-god" and the "God-man," the former has melted away. The figmentary character of humanity's grandiose posturing as its own messiah stands exposed for what it is. Such delusions are no more than the vain overheated evaporations of a fevered soul. The reality of God's love present in Christ offering himself up for us is so patently the redemptive victory over evil, that all other schemes fade away into unreality. Our efforts at autonomous self-transformation cannot stand comparison with the reality of divine love infused into our soul. The movement of human nature toward God could not take place unless God had previously inclined toward us. Even the stirring that urges us to seek God would not be there unless God had first moved us. The divinization of human nature is entirely the work of God, for the transcendent divine reality is unutterably beyond the reach of our power or the paltry determination of our will. What needs to be emphasized above all, however, is that these are no longer intellectual perceptions of truth. They have now become overwhelmingly real in experience.

The titanic striving for self-divinization and the ocean of human misery churned up by it have served only to show how far away humanity is from being a god. But for the souls who are not irreparably closed, this can bring about a new openness to grace. This is the meaning of the crisis and struggle through which Dostoevsky's characters pass. At the point of their greatest despair and emptiness, they are opened to receive the love of God within them. At the bottom of the abyss they can again hear the "still small voice" (1 Kings 19:12) that calls each one by name. It is the truth of life through death, the wisdom of the cross, that Dostoevsky fully experienced in his own life. For only in that state are we truly able to recognize the extent to which God has shared the human fate. "My God, my God, why hast thou forsaken me?" (Matt. 27:46) was the cry of Jesus on the cross. He had poured himself out so completely that as man he experienced the emptying of his divinity itself. Like modern men and women (and human beings in every age), he seemed to have lost irretrievably the feeling of the presence of God. God had betrayed him. The love of God is so complete that he has not only died for us, but suffered to the point of identity with our greatest sense of despair. When we reach that point we find the welcoming presence of Jesus forsaken, already there waiting to receive us. As the boundlessly forgiving pilgrim Makar Dolgoruky explains, "That's how it is in the world: every soul is tried and is consoled" (A, 411).

In the realization that no individual is exempt from this "law of the planet" of wisdom through suffering, spiritual growth through denial of self, the earlier overreaching hubris falls away. A new willingness to take up one's obligations replaces the previous arrogance and revolt. There is no longer the strident self-assertion that demanded a meaning and purpose from life. Now there is a humility that instead of demanding something from life, considers what life requires of us. Viktor Frankl records this crucial change that came about in some of his fellow prisoners in the Nazi concentration camp. They ceased complaining of the harshness of their fate and accepted it for what it was. In thus accepting it they discovered the grace of love that transfigures the darkness and sorrow of existence into joy. "Suffering had become a task on which we did not want to turn our backs."[42] Through grace they had discovered the participation of God in human suffering, without naming it as such. It is the reality of sharing, of friendship and love between God and humanity, that is most completely actualized in Jesus.

The realization of our unity with Jesus forsaken, as a living experiential reality, and not an intellectual abstraction, enables our unconditional assent to the mystery of the process in which we find ourselves. It was the desire for just such a total personal assurance of love that first awakened the revolt against the injustice of our human fate. The longing for union with the transcendent divine reality was differentiated within us by the appearance of Christ. All of the expectations that shape our attitudes and judgments toward reality have since been stamped with this eschatological impulse. However much we may regret the disappearance of the more compact equilibrium of trust in the order of the gods of the cosmos, that possibility is no longer available to us today. The disorder, the self-assertive extreme of defiance we see all around us, has no other source than the expectations generated by the epiphany of Christ. Now it is apparent that the unlimited aspiration for transfiguration into the life of the transcendent God can be satisfied in no other way. When this longing is not fulfilled in God, then it does not simply cease to exist. Its goal is pursued through the demonic energy of will, with all of the destructive consequences this implies. It is an impulse that, since it cannot be abandoned or abated, is doomed to frustration until it reaches the true fulfillment of its search. Only the unlimited divine love can satisfy the longing in our hearts called forth by the manifestation of God's presence in all its fullness in Jesus.

The rediscovery of this great and eternal truth does not, however, by itself create a postmodern order. It only provides the core illumination. The necessity still remains of showing how this foundation can support the order of human existence in society and history. And it must be acknowledged that Christians have not been overly successful at making this case in the modern period. The secular messianic revolt has not been the only factor behind the contemporary nightmare. A certain measure of responsibility must be assigned to the bearers of the philosophic-Christian tradition. Their inability to demonstrate how the fullness of God's self-revelation in Christ opens the way toward the fullness of human life, how Christ is the definitive realization of order, has been part of the problem. Moreover, this is related to a historic incompleteness in the Christian symbolism that became evident in Augustine's conception of the present age as a *saeculum senescens*. How is the transfiguration beyond history related to the process of transfiguration going on within history? How is the human struggle for civilizational progress related to our eternal progress? What is the Christian significance of the work of men and women within time?

Such are the problems that press upon any conscientious observer of our situation today. They can no longer be ignored. It is imperative that the existential rediscovery of philosophic-Christian truth be unfolded into the order of human existence within society and history. Having struggled and emerged victorious over its inverted opposite, Christianity can once again provide the authoritative public foundation of order. If the existential resolution we have followed is representative, then it must be capable of demonstrating this broader significance. The bearers of the philosophic-Christian illumination must be able to show how their experience provides the most profound realization of our humanity. Even further, they must be able to make transparent the philosophic-Christian significance of the movement of civilizational progress as well. Having passed from an earlier period that drew from the *contemptus mundi* an excessive devaluation of life within time, to the other extreme of exaggerated expectations of innerworldly fulfillment and transformation, we are back again at the center of the pendulum's swing. The prospects now are perhaps better than ever before for a balanced articulation of the order of human existence. The vitality and dynamism of civilizational progress is so palpably present that it cannot seriously be ignored. On the other hand, we have been cured of the dream of an intramundane apocalypse of humanity. More than at any other time in the past five centuries, there is a readiness to accept the eschatological mystery, with its tension between a transfigurative process going on within time and a fulfillment beyond all time. The tone of nonutopian hope is particularly apparent in the extrapolations of the postmodern thinkers. Like the Church, which defines itself by this pilgrim status between two worlds, these thinkers remain profoundly convinced that the order they have discovered within their own souls is determinative of human life in society and history, yet utterly incapable of final realization within it. To the elaboration of this existential vision of order we now turn.

NOTES

1. *Marx-Engels Reader*, 53–54.
2. It should also be acknowledged that the traditionalist carriers of philosophic-Christian wisdom have been equally deficient in addressing the problem of order. The scandal of corrupt Christianity bears some responsibility for the crisis of faith. But even more detrimental have been the repeated attempts to confront the challenge by means of an increasingly dogmatic assertiveness. The renewal of spiritual order cannot be expected without regaining contact with the life-giving reality of Spirit. The philosopher, Voegelin has observed, is called to find a way between doctrinaire defenders of the faith and equally doctrinaire objectors, without condemning either one. For "the tension between faith and reason, their conspiracy and conflict in time, is a mystery. Whether the traditionalist believer who professes truth in doctrinal form is not perhaps farther removed from truth than the intellectual objector who denies it because of its doctrinal form, he does not know. God alone knows who is nearer to the end that is the beginning. Nor must the philosopher remain undecided because he cannot penetrate the mystery—for as far as he can see within the limitations of his human understanding, the objector who cannot sense an unbroken reality behind the broken images moves on the same level of deficient existence as the traditionalist who, perhaps desperately, believes his broken image to be whole." Eric Voegelin, "Immortality: Experience and Symbol," *Harvard Theological Review* 60 (1967)3:249.
3. One of the most interesting phenomena of our time is surely the appearance of various postideological intellectuals glumly admitting that even if we can no longer believe in God, something equivalent to the transcendent faith of Christianity is alone capable of providing the foundation for order today. Heidegger's expectation of a parousia of Being, to whose intimations he himself remains peculiarly closed, is perhaps the most profound expression of this position. See his *An Introduction to Metaphysics*, trans. Ralph Mannheim (New York: Anchor, 1961). Other recent examples include Michael Harrington, *The Politics at God's Funeral* (New York: Holt, Rinehart & Winston, 1983), who insists that "there is no way back—or forward—to a religious integration of society on the model of Judeo-Christianity in any of its manifestations. But there is a need for the transcendental" (202). A similar perspective is evoked by Bernard-Henri Lévy, *The Testament of God*, trans. George Holoch (New York: Harper & Row, 1980).
4. From the many works on Camus's complex relationship with Christianity the following are among the most significant: Ingrid di Meglio, *Antireligiosität und Kryptotheologie bei Albert Camus* (Bonn: Bouvier, 1975); Jean Onimus, *Albert Camus and Christianity* (Tuscaloosa, AL: University of Alabama Press, 1970); Joseph Hermet, *Albert Camus et le christianisme* (Paris: Beauchesne, 1976); Bruce Pratt, *L'Évangile selon Albert Camus* (Paris: Corti, 1980); Anna Maria Hennon, *Die Frage nach Gott und dem Sinn des lebens bei Albert Camus and die Antwort der christlichen Philosophie* (Roetgen/Aachen: V. T. Berning, 1983).
5. This is closest to Camus's own interior commentary on the novel, as reflected in his *Notebook* for 1942. "I wish to express by means of the plague the suffocation we have all suffered and the atmosphere of menace and exile in which we have lived. At the same time I wish to extend this interpretation to the notion of existence in general. The plague provides the image of those who in this war have had the part of reflection, of silence—and that of moral suffering" (*N* II, 53–54). In *The State of Siege* Camus gives the totalitarian leader the allegorical title of "The Plague."
6. Mauriac was probably fairest when he described Camus, in the phrase of St. Augustine, as an "*anima naturaliter christiana*". Lottman, *Camus*, 452.
7. Camus's unsubmitted doctoral dissertation consisted of a comparison between Plotinus and St. Augustine, "Métaphysique chrétienne et neoplatonisme." It is included among the supplemental texts in *Essais*, 1224–1313.
8. Camus's reflections on the problem of execution are pertinent to this context. His objection to capital punishment is that it renders definitive judgment on an individual

whom we are only entitled to view in terms of relative guilt. Execution can only be permissible, in Camus's view, in a society grounded in religious faith; there it is not an ultimate judgment of the character or worth of the person. But in the contemporary situation the state assumes the role of God in rendering this final judgment. "And religions devoid of transcendence kill great numbers of condemned men devoid of hope" (*RRD*, 228). By prohibiting the practice of capital punishment, Camus argues, we can maintain the sense that the state is not absolute. We can recover the awareness of the transcendence of the individual and prevent the impulse to silence all further judgment.

9. Camus's affinity with the Mediterranean world, his closeness to the light of Greek civilization, comes through in passages such as this. It is what sustained him in the blackest moments of the contemporary devastation and distinguished him from the "existentialists" of Paris. It is not a groundless optimism, but a faith or trust that, despite all, humans still live in a cosmos and not a chaos. Camus constantly reminds us of how close he stands to the world of the classical myth. For a critical assessment of his Greek influences see Paul Archambault, *Camus's Hellenic Sources* (Chapel Hill: University of North Carolina Press, 1972).

10. During the latter part of World War II Camus was convinced that those who had collaborated with the Nazis should be punished without mercy, but later he came to agree with Mauriac that there was room for forgiveness, and began actively seeking pardons for the collaborators condemned to be executed. Compare *Essais* 287 and 372; Lottman, *Camus*, 408f.

11. See, for example, the recollections contained in Scammell, *Solzhenitsyn*, chap. 2, "Childhood."

12. "I certainly have composed no work in regard to [knowledge of philosophy], nor shall I ever do so in future, for there is no way of putting it in words like other studies. Acquaintance with it must come rather after a long period of attendance on instruction in the subject itself and of close companionship, when, suddenly, like a blaze kindled by a leaping spark, it is generated in the soul and at once becomes self-sustaining." Plato, *Seventh Letter* 341c–d. Trans. L. A. Post, *Plato, The Collected Dialogues*, Trans. L. A. Post, ed. Hamilton and Cairns (Princeton: Bollingen, Princeton University Press, 1961).

13. "Religion for him, it seems, is not an essential part of his being, but a contingent tool and even a weapon. The sentimental picture of him as a pious man of God is false. Solzhenitsyn certainly believes in God, though it is not always clear whether it is a Christian God, but he experiences insuperable difficulties in humbling himself. He is a deist and does not understand mysticism or the life of the church." Scammell, *Solzhenitsyn*, 992. Against this compare Olivier Clement, *The Spirit of Solzhenitsyn*, trans. Sarah Fawcett and Paul Burns (New York: Barnes & Noble, 1977); and Niels C. Nielsen, Jr., *Solzhenitsyn's Religion* (Nashville: Nelson, 1975).

14. No doubt his spiritual ascent is also contained in the much longer autobiographical poem entitled "The Way" written and memorized while he was in the camps. Apart from the few fragments quoted in Scammell's biography, only one early chapter of the poem, dealing with his war experiences, has been published: *Prussian Nights*, trans. Robert Conquest (New York: Farrar, Strauss & Giroux, 1974).

15. Compare Augustine: "You were within me, and I was in the world outside myself." *Confessions* X, 27.

16. Dostoevsky's original intention was that Stavrogin would end up like the man in the Gospel by sitting at the feet of Jesus after the devils had been expelled from him. See Mochulsky, *Dostoevsky*, 411.

17. This is surely the meaning of the story of Illusha, the unhappy young boy around whom a community of children is formed by Alyosha. Illusha's death is the occasion for the realization that in loving him, they have become "better perhaps than we are." It provokes the leader of the boys, Kolya, to ask if it is true "that we shall rise again from the dead" (*K* 940)?

18. See chapter 2. For Dostoevsky's Christian philosophy of existence see Vyacheslav Ivanov, *Freedom and the Tragic Life*, trans. N. Cameron (New York: Noonday, 1952); A. Boyce Gibson, *The Religion of Dostoevsky* (Philadelphia: Westminster, 1973); George Panichas, *The Burden of Vision: Dostoevsky's Spiritual Art* (Grand Rapids: Eerdmans, 1977); Jean Drouilly, *La pensée politique et religieuse de F. M. Dostoevsky* (Paris: Libraire des Cinq Continentes, 1971); I. Dolenc, *Dostoevsky and Christ: A Study of Dostoevsky's Rebellion against Belinsky* (Toronto: York Publishing, 1978). Indispensable for Dostoevsky's background in Orthodox mystical theology is V. Lossky, *The Mystical Theology of the Eastern Church* (London: James Clarke, 1957).

19. When asked if he was a Christian Voegelin would often respond, "I try to be."

20. Alexander Schmemann, "On Solzhenitsyn," in Dunlop, Haugh, and Klimoff, *Aleksandr Solzhenitsyn*, 28–44. Solzhenitsyn's reply is included on p. 44.

21. See Olivier Clement, *The Spirit of Solzhenitsyn*, chap. 11, "From Evangelism to Orthodoxy."

22. Scammell, *Solzhenitsyn*, 478.

23. This critique is itself the most convincing refutation of the charge that Solzhenitsyn himself is a deist. A good recent discussion of the literary relationship between Solzhenitsyn and Tolstoy is contained in James M. Curtis, *Solzhenitsyn's Traditional Imagination* (Athens, GA: University of Georgia Press, 1984).

24. "Having once given himself to preaching one might say that something happened to him; everything in this world that is inaccessible to our spirit, which governs us and provides us with strength, and which he knew about when he wrote his novels, it was as if he suddenly no longer perceived it. With what terrestrial impoverishment he treated the Sermon on the Mount! It is as if he lost all intuition. Such a great artist—and hardly the least reference to the incomprehensible plan of God for the World, to the intense attention he has for all of us and for each one in particular! What do I say, hardly an allusion! He refutes it rationally! Our personal immortality, our personal participation [*sobstvennuiu prechastnost*] in the divine essence—he refutes it all" (*OCT*, 65).

25. It is not without significance that two of the biggest villains of *August 1914*, the cowardly General Blagoveschensky and the self-important Roman Tomchak, are both admirers of Tolstoy and draw a good deal of the justification for their own self-serving actions from the teachings of the great man. See *AUG*, chaps. 6 and 53.

26. Solzhenitsyn conveys Samsonov's half-waking awareness through a wonderful play on words that is entirely lost in the translation. The voice declares, "Thou shalt be assumed [*uspish*]. . . . I shall succeed [*uspeiu*]? . . . No, thou shalt be assumed [*uspish*']. . . . I shall sleep [*usnu*]? . . . No, thou shalt be assumed [*uspish*']. . . . Thou shalt be assumed—this was from the Assumption [*Uspeniia*], this meant: you shall die [*umresh'*]" (*AUG*, 277–78).

27. Contrast this with the scathing depiction of the grand duke Nikolai, the commander-in-chief, and even of the tsar, whose piety had become a means of evading responsibility for the consequences of their actions (*AUG*, chap. 80).

28. A similar treatment is accorded the other central and very different character of *August 1914*, Stolypin. The prime minister embodied all that Russia so badly needed. His combination of firmness and reformism was just what was required to bring about the necessary political changes without provoking a revolutionary explosion. Solzhenitsyn regards him as Russia's "best head of government in a century, in two hundred years" (*AUG*, 655) and views his assassination in 1911 as the removal of the last defense against the revolutionary cataclysm. Yet at the same time, Solzhenitsyn never presumes to sit in judgment over history or to substitute his own wisdom for that of God. Through Stolypin's dying reflections he acknowledges, "It is as Thou hast ordered it, O lord, Thou whose designs are beyond our understanding" (*AUG*, 646). No hint of rebellion is permitted, even as Stolypin contemplates the weakness of the tsar (who went on to pardon the accomplices in the prime minister's murder). "It was God's will to send us such an Emperor at such a time. It is not for us, O

Lord, to weigh Thy purposes" (*AUG*, 651). Finally, Solzhenitsyn concludes the chapter with a quotation in all capitals that removes any doubt about the nature of Stolypin's sacrifice: it is in continuity with the redemptive suffering and death of Christ. "HE BROUGHT LIGHT TO THE WORLD AND THE WORLD REJECTED HIM."

29. Olivier Clement has clarified the relationship thus: "For Solzhenitsyn, the hurricane foreseen by Dostoevsky has been unleashed, the abyss has become history. It is no longer a question of looking for the forces of destruction beneath a surface stability, but of hunting among the ruins for the foundations of a possible way of life. Dostoevsky's approach was designed to combat the morality of his time; Solzhenitsyn is looking for an ethical base in his. One denounced false securities, shook foundations; the other denounces hell in history, builds on foundations. Both find Christ in hell, but one at the end of a process of destruction, the other at the beginning of a period of construction: Solzhenitsyn's work is 'edifying' in the full sense of the word; it triumphs over the nihilism that Russia produces in her history, not in her literature. But his ethic is forged in hell, on the edge of death; it is an *ethic of resurrection*, and this is the spiritual bond between him and Dostoevsky." *Spirit of Solzhenitsyn*, 138.

30. Commenting on the famous Christian confession Dostoevsky wrote on the day of his first wife's death ("Masha is lying on the table. Will I ever see Masha again? . . ."— quoted later in this chapter), Joseph Frank observes that "Dostoevsky makes clear that he does not consider any special gift of grace to be necessary: the incarnation of Christ has been sufficient to spur mankind into eternal struggle against its own limitations. . . . Indeed, the sole significance of Christ, as Dostoevsky speaks of him here, is to serve as the divine enunciator of this morality; he fulfills no other purpose, not even the traditional one of redeeming mankind from the wages of sin and death." *Stir of Liberation*, 298–99.

31. "It is said that the Russian people know the Gospel poorly, that they are ignorant of the fundamental principles of faith. Of course, this is true, but they do know Christ, and they have been carrying Him in their hearts from time immemorial. Of this there can be no doubt. How is the true conception of Christ possible without religious teaching? This is a different question. But the heart-knowledge of Christ, a true conception of Him, does fully exist. It is being passed from generation to generation, and it has merged with the heart of the people. Perhaps, Christ is the only love of the Russian people, and they love His image in their own way, to the limit of sufferance." *DW*, 38–39.

32. Dostoevsky, *Selected Letters*, 68.

33. Frank, *Years of Ordeal*, 162. Kierkegaard seems to have been concerned with heightening the uncertainty of faith in order to emphasize the radical nature of the leap or choice involved. Dostoevsky's focus is more on calling forth the full experiential truth on which faith is based, rather than remaining with a mere assertion or decision to believe.

34. *The Unpublished Dostoevsky: Diaries and Notebooks (1860–81)*, ed. Carl R. Proffer (Ann Arbor: Ardis, 1973), vol. 1, 39–41.

35. Ibid., 40; see also the continuation of this argument on p. 41.

36. Ibid., 41.

37. Mochulsky, *Dostoevsky*, chap. 15.

38. Dostoevsky, *Selected Letters*, 269–70.

39. "Never before in all world literature has Christianity been advanced with such striking force as the religion of spiritual freedom. The Christ of Dostoevsky is not only the Savior and Redeemer, but also the Sole Emancipator of man." Mochulsky, *Dostoevsky*, 622. See also Ellis Sandoz: "The Legend is, thus, many things at once: an analysis, a blasphemy, a warning, a curse, a prayer, a confession, a plea, a thanksgiving, a benediction. But above all it is an iconographic vision of God's grace infusing man's existence in this world to bind every wound, heal every heart, and fulfill every man whose soul opens to Him." *Political Apocalypse: A Study of Dostoevsky's Grand Inquisitor* (Baton Rouge: Louisiana State University Press, 1971), 218. An excellent

analysis of the truth of Christ's silence is contained in Ward, *Dostoyevsky's Critique of the West*, chap. 5. For a more ambivalent interpretation see Vasily Rozanov, *Dostoevsky and the Legend of the Grand Inquisitor*, trans. Spencer E. Roberts (Ithaca: Cornell University Press, 1972). The opposing view, which favors the Inquisitor's side of the argument, is summarized by Edward Wasiolek, *Dostoevsky: The Major Fiction* (Cambridge: Massachusetts Institute of Technology Press, 1964), 164–71.

40. Responding to Pobedonostsev's criticism that he had not yet refuted the atheistic arguments of Ivan and the Inquisitor, Dostoevsky wrote: "Yes, you have something there, and this is now my worry and concern. For I attempt, as a matter of fact, to give the answer to this whole *negative side* in Book Six, 'A Russian Monk,' which will be coming out on August 31. And that's why I am trembling over it, wondering whether it will be an *adequate* answer. What makes it even more difficult is that the answer itself is not a direct one, not really a point-by-point refutation of the ideas formulated earlier (by the Grand Inquisitor and earlier), but only an indirect one. What is offered here is a world view that stands in direct opposition to the one that was previously presented, but again the opposition is not made point by point but, so to speak, in the form of an artistic picture. And that is just what worries me—i.e. will I be understood and will I even come close to my goal. . . . Then, there are also some of the monk's teachings, which people will inveigh against as being absurd because they are too exalted. I know very well that they are absurd in the everyday sense, but, in another, deeper sense, they seem quite appropriate." *Selected Letters*, 486–87.

41. An interesting study along these lines is contained in Sven Linner, *Starets Zossima in The Brothers Karamazov: A Study in the Mimesis of Virtue* (Stockholm: Almqvist & Wiksell, 1975).

42. Frankl, *Man's Search for Meaning*, 124

CHAPTER 5

Restoration of Order

Christianity, as we have seen, is both the great source for the eschatological expectations of our day, and the great means of resolving them. Just as the longing for revolutionary transfiguration would not have been possible without the appearance of Christ, neither can the longing for transcendent perfection be satisfied except by opening toward the fullness of divinity in Christ. The aspiration cannot be denied, nor can its impetus be suppressed through appeals to reason. Having once experienced the movement toward eschatological divinization, contemporary men and women cannot be contented with existence within the limits of a finite cosmos. Life under such conditions is unbearable, and much of the bitterness of modern revolt derives from this heartbreaking realization. The pain and absurdity of modern life in a dedivinized world arises from this situation. Contemporary nihilistic despair is that of the Christian soul without God. Modern humans cannot recover the compact mystery of a "world full of gods."

Only the recognition of the infinite love of God fully participating in the burdens of human existence can restore our trust in the mysterious order of things. It is not that the comprehensive meaning of the whole is suddenly disclosed to us—we continue to see through a glass darkly—but that we are assured more profoundly than ever of its ultimate goodness. If the ground of being itself, God fully incarnate in Christ, has entered existence, then this event must be suffused with meaning for all other human beings as well. The iniquities and vicissitudes of our life on this earth do not have the final word. They reveal their unreality in the redemptive victory won by transcendent, suffering Love over them. By freely submitting, therefore, to the sufferings that fall to us, we allow our trials to be united with the final sacrificial triumph of Christ on the cross. We experience life as the movement toward full participation in the divinity of the God who empties himself to participate fully in our humanity.

In thus rejecting the counsels of those who would merely see in Christianity the root of political messianism, I am not in any sense discounting the cautionary value of their critique. Indeed, I am presupposing it. The difference is that I draw a different conclusion, and I base my argument on the Christian direction indicated by such critics themselves. Camus, we have seen, explicitly disavowed support for Christianity, but came closer and closer to it within the structure of his own experience. In a parallel fashion, Leo Strauss has hinted that revealed religion is a dangerous quantity that ought to be moderated through a return to the principles of classical political philosophy. He sees a "fundamental opposition" between the Platonic science of truth, with its unfolding into the conception of the best regime, and the prophetic belief that "men's conduct toward one another can undergo a change more radical than any change ever dreamed of by Plato."[1] Strauss moreover makes it clear that his sympathies lie with the Greeks. In true Averroistic fashion he glosses over the "usefulness" of religion— it is necessary for the masses who are incapable of philosophy—as if he were in danger of persecution from a zealous intolerant world. His emphasis is entirely on the negative consequences of religion, with virtually no acknowledgment of its potential as a force for order in society. Nowhere does it seem to occur to Strauss that the "catastrophes and horrors of a magnitude hitherto unknown" with which we have to deal today may not be tractable by the methods of a Greek philosophic wisdom that never conceived of the possibility of such radical revolt.

Even a thinker like Eric Voegelin, who explicitly affirms the Christian differentiation, does not always make it central to the struggle with contemporary disorder. He too finds within Greek, especially Platonic, philosophy the element of balance, of limit, of wholeness that is missing from the Christian involvement with the eschatological movement. It would be easy to conclude from the amount of discussion he devotes to the destabilizing influence of Christianity that he is uniformly negative in his evaluation of the symbolism. But when we add to this the general absence of positive assessments of Christianity in recent years, the conclusion becomes almost inescapable that Voegelin did not envisage a formative political role for revelation in the contemporary world. Yet this conclusion would be going too far. A more correct reading would be that Voegelin left the Christian dimension of his thought in a relatively undeveloped stage. He did not claim or aspire to be a system builder, and was content to leave the problems in the state of incompleteness they had reached in his own reflections. What is important is that Voegelin's thought, like that of Camus and Strauss, points strongly toward the Christian truth as the culmination of its own directional logic.[2]

Before that can be demonstrated, however, the validity of the reservations against Christianity must be acknowledged. It is not merely a collapse of the Judeo-Christian order that has occasioned the modern crisis. There was something problematic about Christianity from the start that made it peculiarly susceptible to the deformation into the search for an innerworldly transfiguration of existence. That element was its incompleteness as an eschatological symbolism. It had relatively little to say about the problems of order under the conditions of continued existence in the world. Even when the Church did adjust to the nonoccurrence of the Parousia, and accepted the Augustinian conception of the millennium as the intermediate time of the present, relatively little attention was paid to the civilizational achievements of human beings within time. In short, there has always existed a problem of balance within Christianity. This is well reflected in the profusion of radical heretical movements it has generated, of which the modern ideological movements may be regarded as only the most recent. Christianity must be supplemented by the symbolism that articulates the order of individual and social existence within time, if it is to attain the spiritual equilibrium of order. That symbolism is philosophy.

But if the conclusion we have so far reached is valid, that Christianity offers the best hope of restoring personal, political, and historical order in the present, then it must also be the case that it deepens the foundation of philosophic order as well. Christianity is not only compatible with the classical articulation of order; it also reinforces and energizes the pursuit of virtue in a way that philosophy itself could never do. Such a suggestion is bound to evoke hoary memories of the long-standing tensions between reason and revelation. From the high point of Aquinas's formulation of grace perfecting nature, to the low of Hegel's subsumption of revelation within reason, the issue has been well explored in the intellectual history of the West. It is not our purpose here to rehearse this extensive background; that can safely be assigned to another study. Our focus is on the experiential catharsis within contemporary civilization. Our discussion will be confined to the movement of experience within the postmodern thinkers. We will find as this chapter unfolds that the truth of Christ's revelation is the most adequate foundation for a renewal of ethical and political order in contemporary civilization. We begin with a discussion of the essential relationship and then examine the structure of order that emerges.

The Transcendent Foundation

The Experiential Movement toward Transcendent Reality

The most difficult element to convey in articulating the foundation of morality is, as we have seen in chapter 1, the sense of ultimate rightness that underpins it. No matter how persuasive we may be in framing arguments, whether based on teleology, irreducible axioms, or natural law, they remain ineffective until we can respond to the Nietzschean question: *Why* should I regard such principles as right? Arguments beg the question, for they always bring us back to the problem of justifying the choice of starting point. The ideological mass movements may in a certain respect be regarded as an expression of desperation, the pathetic inclination to latch on to something, anything, greater than ourselves, in order to infuse our actions with a sense of reality and purpose. As Nietzsche understood, human beings would rather will nothing than not will. When no ultimate foundation to existence can be found, then we will throw ourselves into false absolutes rather than admit the vacuum within ourselves. Even the futility of an illusory foundation is preferable to living without a sense of ultimate rightness. Although Nietzsche was unsuccessful in his search for this more authentic reality, he nevertheless pointed the way. Unless we recover a sense of what is transcendentally right, then our actions will be neither moral nor effective.

It is not enough to assert the rightness of one's principles. Their rightness must be grasped as an overwhelming truth within the experiential movement toward transcendent reality. This is why Voegelin abandoned his work on the history of political ideas, and sought to penetrate to the underlying experiences behind the symbolic forms. He did not regard a restoration of natural law or of the classical right by nature to be sufficient, because in such dogmatic formulations the link with the engendering experience is no longer present. Instead he emphasized the recovery of that original experience. By reconstructing the infrastructure of classical philosophy he discovered that the science of ethics and politics, which the Greeks invented, was not based on propositions about order. It was rooted in the living experience of the soul making its ascent toward the divine Good, which is "beyond being, exceeding it in dignity and power" (*Republic*, 509b). When Socrates was pressed for his definition of justice, one that would provide his young listeners with a reason for following it apart from any calculation of rewards, for its own sake, he invited them to follow "a longer and more arduous way" than the preceding discourse on the parts of the polis. This was the beginning of the parable of the cave that culminates in the vision of the Good. What is significant, Voegelin observes, is that nothing further is said about its content. No definition of the Good is possible because it is a transcendent reality. "The vision of the Agathon does not render a material rule of conduct, but forms the soul through an experience of transcendence" (*OH* III, 112).

The criterion of right order and the formation of the will that enables us to carry it out, is not the result of a train of discursive reasoning. Rather it is the concrete movement of the soul toward the ineffable divine reality that sheds its light over the whole of our existence. Aristotle refers to it in the *Nicomachean Ethics* as the process of "immortalizing," *athanatizein* (1177b33). Voegelin stresses the centrality of this "ontological" conception of ethics, if we wish to understand the classic understanding of "right by nature." For classical ethics is never about general propositions or formulas. Whenever there is a question of the rightness or wrongness of action, the appeal is always made to the experience of the *spoudaios*, the mature man, who contains the authoritative measure within his divinely informed soul. "The criterion of rightly ordered human existence . . . is the permeability for the movement of being, i.e. the openness of man for the divine; the openness in its turn is not a proposition about something given but an event, and ethics is, therefore, not a body of propositions but an event of being that provides the word for a statement about itself" (*AN*, 65). It is the experience of touching or participating in divine reality that is the self-justifying end of all existence. In that movement we are lifted up beyond ourselves, to share in that higher reality in comparison with which everything else occupies a less real mode of existence. It is the experiential affirmation of Plato's "God is the measure," and the wellspring of Greek ethical and political theory.

No further reasons are required when we experience the truth that contains its own proof within itself. Nietzsche's question, which seemed so insuperable before, now fades away in light of the overwhelming goodness toward which we are drawn. This is the folly of the attempt to provide morality with an autonomous rational foundation. In the rush to dispense with theological presuppositions and in the conviction that reason alone would be sufficient to justify right action, the modern philosophers from Descartes on have failed to recognize that any such formulation can never be self-compelling. A right formation of the will is necessary before we have the requisite disposition to regard the inferences as right. The predisposition cannot come from the arguments themselves, since they are dependent on it for their recognition and implementation. Only the movement toward greater participation in transcendent Being can bring the infinite regress of justifications to a conclusion. The incommensurable and interminable nature of contemporary moral debate cries out for the experience of higher truth that is its own foundation and that can, therefore, conclude the process of questioning. Reasoning toward end purposes continues indefinitely until it encounters the ineffable end-in-itself, and not as an abstraction but as its own concrete origin and goal.[3]

Such a knowledge through experience is not to be attained by reasoning our way toward it. It is the encounter with a reality that is not a ready-made or predictably accessible dimension of our everyday world. Unlike objects materially located in space and time, the experience of transcendent Being cannot be summoned at will. It is a reality that becomes present to us only through our existential opening toward its ordering influence. The insight that emerges from Voegelin's entire study of experiences and symbols of order is that the knowledge of order is rooted in participation. Only the person who has already consented to be formed by the transcendent pull of Spirit, will be able to discern its movements within him or her. The more willing we are to attune our lives to the voice of God, the more clearly and more forcefully will its presence be disclosed within us.

This structure is particularly evident in Voegelin's analysis of Moses and the thornbush theophany. Through the course of his life Moses has grown into the kind of person who will respond to the divine call. When he is pulled aside from tending his flocks by the appearance of a burning bush, he is already prepared to follow the experience into the ineffable depth of divine Being. Initially the presence makes itself known as one addressed to him personally, for it calls Moses by name. Then it makes itself known as divine, thereby establishing the proper distance between man and God. Only at that point does the revelation begin. The disclosure of God's knowledge, "I have seen the oppression of my people who are in Egypt" (Exod. 3:7), is identical with God's action in eternity. Now the action of God has begun in history with the revelation to Moses.

When Moses can hear the voice of God appoint him the servant of Yahweh, he has grown spiritually into the servant of Yahweh. The command could be rejected only by a man who could never hear it; the man who can hear cannot reject, because he has ontologically entered the will of God, as the will of God has entered him. When the consciousness of the divine will has reached the clarity of revelation, the historical action has begun. (*OH* I 407; see also IV, 229f.)

By opening his soul to receive the divine command, Moses is made ready to receive the ultimate revelation of the God who assures the people, "I will be with you." The name of God, which Moses is to bring back to the people, is "I AM WHO I AM." Beyond the aspects of God revealed within the experience is the impenetrable divine depth that can only be symbolized by the "I AM." It is the limiting point of the revelation reached by Moses when his soul has grown to the point of participating in and being formed by the abyss of transcendent Being.

This is the experience in which the Chosen People were constituted. From its beginning in the soul of Moses the illumination spread to the Hebrew tribes, who experienced it as a liberation from the spiritual bondage of Egypt. Through their communion with the transcendent "I AM," the Chosen People experienced their salvation from the senseless imperial world they left behind. At every stage of their historical struggle this was the reality to which they could return to measure the truth or falsity of the direction in which they were being pressed to go. It was the spirit that was embodied in the Decalogue and the Deuteronomic Code, but it was never merely reducible to the legal requirements in which it was expressed.[4] The obligation of following the Lord, of giving themselves entirely to the transcendent God who had been revealed to them, was never simply a matter of obeying the divine commands. It was above all a matter of attunement to the spirit of the Lord, which enabled them to participate in the preeminent divine reality. This was the experience elaborated by the prophets. They opposed the legalistic ritual observance with fidelity to the law of God written in the heart. The creation of order in individuals and society, they emphasized, is the fruit of the knowledge and fear of the Lord within us. It was their intimation of transcendent divine reality that led them to insist on caring for the widows and orphans, irrespective of whether we are explicitly directed to do so or not.

It is the same experience as can be identified, Voegelin contends, in the mystic philosophers who are the source of the Greek symbolization of order. When Parmenides came to describe the reality encountered in his illuminative experience, he simply applied the exclamatory "Is!" What he had experienced is the most real reality, the *realissimum*, in comparison with which everything else is unreal or nonbeing. The parallel with the Mosaic "I AM" is evident. A revelatory event of comparable significance had occurred, and it too became the foundation on which the order of a new society was erected. The orientation toward and participation in this highest reality became the indisputable measure of right action; everything that led toward it was good while all that detracted from it was bad. A life spent in pursuit or love of this wisdom was the only one that counted. This wisdom was a light that radiated over the whole of human existence. The search for attunement to "the unseen measure" became the task of the mystic philosophers, the lawgivers, the tragedians, and finally the classic philosophers. From the latter, Socrates, Plato, and Aristotle, we have received the language of ethical and political order. This was the means by which they articulated the truth that drew them from within, in opposition to the disorder that pulled on them in the world outside. Not only can order not be divorced from its ontological underpinnings, but without the experiential movement toward divine being there also would never have emerged a science of ethical and political order.

This structure is confirmed by the cathartic experiences of our own day. Having lived through the nihilistic disintegration of all principles, individuals like Camus and Solzhenitsyn discovered the reality of good and evil in their own experience. By responding to the attraction of the one and resisting the pull of the other, they recognized that an order of good and evil exists independent of our wishes. It becomes real as we seek to live out the concrete obligations placed upon us. We discover that there is more than the absurdity of existence, that there is a direction or an order that draws us toward its transcendent truth. "Awareness, no matter how confused it may be, develops from every act of rebellion: the sudden, dazzling perception that there is something in man with which he can identify himself, even if only for a moment" (R, 14). Solzhenitsyn describes it in the key symbol of "ascent." Withdrawal from the contagion of evil through the purificatory experience of suffering freed him from all feelings of malice, hatred, and irritability that used to drag him down. "The stones rustle beneath our feet. We are ascending . . ." (GA II, 611). This is the only way to describe the movement upward toward a higher order of reality. It is the faith that sustained him over the years of unending and seemingly futile effort. Solzhenitsyn gave expression to it in the proverb on which he based his Nobel Prize speech: "One word of truth outweighs the whole world." Clearly, the word of truth of an obscure, helpless zek is nothing compared to the material might of the Soviet Union. But for the person who has fully opened himself or herself to this truth in life, it is a reality of such overwhelming power that the physical strength of the state shrinks into comparative insignificance.

Voegelin's achievement is to have revealed the universal nature of this theological foundation of order. In contrast to the solidity of all previous symbolizations of order, the modern belief that order can be established on the basis of our reason alone appears as a superficial and frivolous conceit. No matter how far back the investigation is carried, the results are the same. All premodern civilizations, including cosmological and even so-called primitive societies, based the order of their existence on participation in the more enduring order of being.

We experience our own lasting in existence, passing as it is, as well as the hierarchy of lasting; and in these experiences existence becomes transparent, revealing something of the mystery of being, of the mystery in which it participates though it does not know what it is. Attunement, therefore, will be the state of existence when it hearkens to that which is lasting in being. . . . We are thrown into and out of existence without knowing the Why or the How, but while in it we know that we are of the being to which we return. From this knowledge flows the experience of obligation, for though this being, entrusted to our partial management in existence while it lasts and passes, may be gained by attunement, it may also be lost by default. (OH I, 4–5)

The desire for existence in truth is not an optional or incidental "value" that we may decide to choose but, as Mircea Eliade has shown, the constitutive characteristic of human beings in every society but our own.[5] All humans desire to participate in what is ultimately meaningful and enduring, rather than to lose or dissipate themselves in what is passing and senseless. Even our own ideological movements are a perverse testament to the inadequacy of formalistic or instrumental reason to satisfy this longing. When we have lost contact with an eternal divine reality, then we seek to base our existence on something that gives us a counterfeit fulfillment.[6]

This is an understanding of order that Voegelin probably first came across in the work of William James and Henri Bergson. James had complained about the "thinness" of the conceptual approach to philosophy, which consistently overlooked the "thickness" of actual experiential reality. "The only way to apprehend reality's thickness," he wrote, "is either to experience it directly by being a part of reality oneself, or to evoke it in imagination by sympathetically divining someone else's inner life."[7] Bergson had distinguished between the two sources of morality and religion. Morality that is statically based on social instinct, the internalization of behavior necessary for social cohesion and the common good, does not really take hold until it is united with a morality that utterly transcends any principle of self-interest. This is the source of dynamic morality or religion, which, in Bergson's conception, is radically directed toward that which is beyond all finite goals. Sustaining the order of a particular society is not enough. The individual is drawn up in love and service of all human beings and without limit. The culmination is reached in the love of God that flows over into action. "For the love which consumes him is no longer simply the love of man for God, it is the love of God for all men. Through God, in the strength of God, he loves all mankind with a divine love. This is not the fraternity enjoined on us by the philosophers in the name of reason."[8] Bergson understood morality as reaching its confirmation in this mystical climax. Whatever sense of rightness our actions have on the lower static level is ultimately derived from the residual awareness of this consummation.

By undertaking a global historical investigation of the search for order, Voegelin has provided empirical confirmation of the insights of Bergson and James. Humanity is everywhere constituted by the quest for fuller participation in the more real and more lasting reality of divine being, not by the prescriptions of abstract morality. What gives compelling force to any of our moral formulations is that they are apprehended as right within the experiential movement toward more eminent reality. This is the meaning of Voegelin's famous shift in 1943, from the history of political ideas to the study of the experiences and symbolizations of order within history.[9] He recognized that the ideas or conceptualizations of order are not self-contained entities. They acquire their meaning from the concrete apprehension of enduring higher reality, which they then seek to embody in principles and institutions. If we wish to recover the right order of existence for the individual and society, then we must not stop at the maxims and arguments with which they are conventionally clothed. We must return to what provides these expressions with their inner sense of rightness: the movement toward greater participation in the reality of transcendent Being.

The Definitive Realization in Christ

The only surprising element in Voegelin's recovery of the experiential reality of order is that he stops short of the one case of full mutual participation of man in God and God in man. He holds back from an acknowledgment of the ultimate ordering center of Christ. It is not, as we have seen, that Voegelin remains outside of the Christian horizon. Many quotations have been adduced to support the fundamentally

Christian thrust of his enterprise. He fully recognizes the ultimacy of differentiation achieved in the revelation of God in Christ. There is no doubt that Voegelin regards the Incarnation as the axis of history. "History is Christ written in larger letters," he has affirmed, thereby indicating the Christian amplification of Plato's anthropological principle that the polis is man written large.[10] But there is something missing, and many commentators have sensed its absence. There is a distinct coolness toward Christianity, as if Voegelin continued to view it from the outside. This coolness becomes noticeable in the contrast between the amount of attention he devotes to the negative, unbalancing elements of the Christian dispensation, and the paucity of consideration directed toward the role of Christianity as the "great formative force" for the attainment of order.[11]

If, after all, it is the experience of participation in the ultimate goodness of God that creates order in the soul, then surely the incarnation of God in human history is the definitive realization of order. No longer is the experience of divine being an esoteric or elite affair. Now it is concretely visible in history. The transcendent God fully present in Christ is both the most profound reality of our participation in the divine, and the most universally accessible revelation of its truth. For all who open themselves up to the spirit of God concretely manifest in Jesus, the same movement toward communion with divine reality is possible. It is certainly possible for a person to undergo this ascent in a more wholly inward way and without benefit of an incarnated witness. But there is no more perfect way of embodying the truth of the interpenetration of divine and human reality. The concrete historical presence of Jesus is a powerful focus for the human longing to ascend toward what is lasting and real. Jesus is so clearly the consummation and completion of the movement toward order within the soul that he must be regarded as the great center, radiating order into history.

When to this is added the recognition that in Christ the fullness of divine reality, the transcendent God, creates order in existence, we realize that he is more than an exemplar. Voegelin acknowledges the differentiation of grace as the key Christian experience. Yet he does not seem to follow through to the consequences of this recognition. Henceforth the emergence of order must be understood as the divine activity within the soul. The primary source of this saving grace is the Spirit of God that is present in Christ and, through him, is communicated to all who open to Jesus in faith. Christ is the mediator between God and humanity who surpasses all other forms of mediation, whether cosmological or philosophical. Now it has become utterly transparent that what draws us toward order, toward participation in Being, is the divine presence that is uniquely and completely present in Christ. By opening toward Christ we are being drawn by the divine reality that has fully absorbed humanity into itself in Jesus.

Beyond this core attunement to transcendent order is the extrapolation toward the order of the whole. The victory of Christ over evil, through his loving self-sacrifice on the cross, is experienced as the effective means of creating order in history. Voegelin has referred to the mystery of representative suffering that accomplishes the task of redeeming creation from evil and death. Now clearly, a danger always exists that this realization could split apart into the Gnostic dualism of a conflict between good and evil divinities. But that is only one possibility. As we have tried to emphasize in the preceding chapter, there is an equal, if not greater, possibility that the redemptive self-sacrifice of God on behalf of human beings could lead to a total rejection of Gnostic revolt. One finds no hint of revolt in the New Testament; there is rather a contrasting acceptance of mystery. The God who so loved the world as to surrender his own Son for it may still remain inscrutable, with much that is hidden and incomprehensible about him. Yet God has provided incontrovertible assurance about the only truth that matters: his love for humanity. No hint of resentment or rebellion can remain in the face of the God who has poured himself out for us.

At the same time, we behold in Christ the *telos* toward which our attunement to divine Being is directed. By surrendering himself to death, Christ is victorious not only over sin, but also over all of the limitations of finite existence. His love has been revealed as a force that is stronger than the power of death; physical death on the cross is the attainment of the spiritual life of the Resurrection. The process of immortalizing, of dying to oneself in order to live more in accord with the everlasting, is here shown forth in its perfect realization. The truth of the movement toward higher reality, the ascent from the ephemeral to the eternal, is concretely apprehended in the One who participates fully in divine being. In the resurrected Lord we behold the destiny of all those who open themselves fully to the divine *pneuma* of Christ. All who are united with Christ will likewise be transfigured and ascend with him to the Father in heaven. It goes without saying that this is not merely reducible to a discussion of beliefs about an afterlife. The focus is entirely directed toward the truth that is known as the only one that matters here and now; from there it moves toward the recognition of the perfect realization of this truth in the divinization of human nature.

This sense of Christ as confirming and deepening the philosophic truth of the soul is the source of both Dostoevsky's and Solzhenitsyn's faith. They arrive at Christ as people do in the Gospels, in search of spiritual truth. Nothing escapist or reactionary is involved in their turn to Christianity to discover the means of bringing about the moral regeneration of society. It is simply that they recognize Christ as the most profound mediator of the order all are seeking, even through the distortions of ideology. Having experienced not only the perversity, but also the hollowness of the liberal alternative, they can conceive of no other power capable of renewing the spiritual order of Russian society. The message of Christ is at once simple, profound, and effective in a way that surpasses all others as the means of leading human beings toward the good. It is this insight that makes the Russian articulation of the Christian foundation of order worthy of wider attention.

For Solzhenitsyn, Christianity is the primary means by which we can regain contact with the divine source of order. All that has happened to Russia since the fateful year of 1917, and within the larger process of modern civilization of which it is a part, can be succinctly attributed to one cause. "Men have forgotten God; that's why all this has happened." Solzhenitsyn used this remark, which he recalled from his childhood in the thirties, as the basis for his acceptance speech for the Templeton Prize for Progress in Religion. He recalled the gradual separation of Russia from religion, beginning with the seventeenth-century schism and ending with the advent of Communism, and pointed toward a parallel process in the West extending to the present day. The only difference is that in the East religion has been expressed through the atheistic hatred of the state, whereas in the West it has assumed the form of a voluntary degradation and destruction of the spiritual self. At the root of it all is the progressively modern disease of forgetting God.[12]

This is why we have lost the sense of the unconditional value of the person, and have come to regard ourselves as free to dispose of human life as we wish. Without a foundation in God, human morality becomes relativized. It was the "atheistic humanism" of the intelligentsia that "supplied an easy justification both for the hastily constituted revolutionary tribunals and the rough justice meted out in the cellars of the Cheka," writes Solzhenitsyn (UR, 271). Solzhenitsyn recognizes that resistance to evil must begin with the concrete effort to follow the dictates of one's own conscience. "Do not lie," he counsels his countrymen. There is no other, more absolute starting point. But it must not end there if the effort is to be successful. All of modern history has taught us that human resources are insufficient in the contest with evil. Our impulse to good must reach out toward its transcendent source if it is to have any hope of attaining its goal. This means an opening toward the form in which the divine being is most fully manifest in our society. That is Christianity.

Submission to the Fullness of Revelation

Solzhenitsyn does not look on Christianity as a crutch for his program of moral regeneration. This was the option pursued by Tolstoy and, to a lesser extent, Enlightenment liberalism. No, he and his colleagues in *From Under the Rubble* insist on a "sanctified" return to religion, accepting the full mystery of Christianity and embracing its institutional vessel in the Church. The time and effort that Solzhenitsyn has expended on ecclesiastical issues is extremely significant.[13] He and the other Christian dissidents regard the Orthodox church as the principal means of access to the transcendent ground of order. The experience of "the tragic absurdity of existence without God" (*UR*, 189) has brought them back to Christianity to find the answer to the spiritual crisis. But when the church of Christ to which they return is "deaf to these queries," they do not turn away in disillusionment from the flawed institution. In a spirit of openness, developed in the arduous spiritual trial through which they have passed, they strive to pierce the mystery of divine truth that lies behind the dross of human failure. If one is serious about the reform of society arising from a religious foundation, they insist, then one must accept that the process of regeneration must begin with a renewal of the Church itself (*UR*, 192).

The cornerstone of this rejuvenation is the recognition of the divine mystery of the Church. Because of the divine presence within it, the Church remains the vessel of eternal truth, no matter what the inadequacies of its earthly ministers. Solzhenitsyn and his colleagues display a characteristically Orthodox loyalty and love for the Church, which, one should recall, accomplished the conversion of Russia principally through the compelling beauty of its liturgy.[14] No objections can be raised against the Church, they contend, that have not been raised before. Yet the Church continues as the icon of divine reality outshining the corrupt entanglements of the world. "She stands immutably in place where she arose, God's witness and God's design—for nothing can distort her sacraments or corrupt her teachings," writes Korsakov (*UR*, 165). Korsakov and the others were led by the work of Fr. Pavel Florensky, an early victim of the gulag, toward the spiritual transformation worked within those who humbly submit to the divine authority of the Church.[15] "You fall on your knees, and are not alone . . . you are already in the Truth, and every spiritual effort you make, every sigh falling from your lips, brings to your aid the entire reserve of beneficial strength stored here" (*UR*, 167). By leaving aside all pretensions to human wisdom, we open ourselves in repentance to the mystery of divine wisdom present in the Church. From that luminous center, order is radiated over the whole of our existence.

Those who pick and choose what they will accept about Christianity remain forever outside of it. Like Tolstoy they may share a sense of the Christian moral imperatives, but they fail to penetrate the spiritual mysteries behind them. Korsakov explains that without this understanding of the Incarnation and the Resurrection, original sin and the Atonement, even an individual as saintly as Tolstoy could display "that same old tendency to deify Man, with his inability to resist temptation, that same alluring path of unswerving cast-iron logic, leading ultimately to the Antichrist and the Grand Inquisitor" (*UR*, 160).[16] Only when the submission is total, without reservation or condition, do we begin to see the path of Christian repentance as the way toward the creation of order. This is the most profound insight of Solzhenitsyn's experience. After the unprecedented human destruction of the twentieth century, the first step in the restoration of order is the recognition of our shared responsibility for the evil. "We are all guilty," he insists. All stand in need of forgiveness and must begin with our own willingness to forgive. Repentance thereby provides the means of overcoming the disordering effects of evil; recriminations and hatreds must be brought to a close for a new beginning to occur. The principle on which this new order will be created is neither the Western idea of unlimited freedom nor the Marxist "freedom" of historical necessity, but "the true Christian definition of freedom. Freedom is *self-restriction*! Restriction of the self for the sake of others" (*UR*, 136).

The importance Solzhenitsyn gives the role of the historic Orthodox church in forming this spirit can be seen in his refusal to admit any split between it and a purer underground replacement. Whatever the failings of the Church's leadership and however subservient to the state it may have become, none of this affects the divine truth within it. The whole history of Christianity bears witness to this. "If the sins of the Church hierarchy were transferred to the Christian people, then there would be no eternal and invisible Church of Christ. Instead, the Church would be constituted totally by fortuity and the will of individuals."[17] Religious services held without church buildings or without benefit of clergy are only a matter of necessity; they disappear as soon as churches and clergy become established again. It is because of this faith in the role of the Church that Solzhenitsyn directs his efforts at a reform of its present political direction. He elaborates an alternative between the extremes of total subservience to the state and the withdrawal into an underground existence. The third way would be the open assertion of its rights, without becoming either excessively provocative or excessively quietist. This would be tantamount to the recovery of its historic role of being part of history yet pointing toward a fulfillment beyond it. It represents a profound rearticulation of the political rights of the Church, which could be a source of guidance for the Christian churches of the West as well.[18]

Solzhenitsyn and his colleagues recognize that they are dealing with the broader problem of the relationship of the Church to the secular world. It is a continuation of the centuries-long tension between the twin directions in which Christianity has pointed. "These two aspects of the Christian attitude to the world," Evgeny Barbanov notes, "active participation in its transformation and renunciation of its temptations, turned out to be extremely difficult to reconcile" (*UR*, 182). There is both the desire to remain on Mount Tabor with the transfigured Lord and the compulsion to return to the world with the good news. Yet on the attainment of a resolution of this tension, the acquisition of an appropriate equilibrium, depends the spiritual mission of the Church and the transcendent order it imparts to a forlorn world. The position identified by Solzhenitsyn is one of active assertion of the rights of the Church in the name of the spiritual truth it represents. This is in contrast to the policy of accommodation and compromise previously followed by the Church. "We in Russia were the first to learn that one may not make the slightest spiritual obeisance to a force harmful to the people. The ultimate result of such a policy is self-destruction,"[19] writes Solzhenitsyn. He insists on refusing all concessions to the Communist state and the spirit of the age, as the only effective means of preserving the spiritual health of the Church and injecting the influence of transcendent truth into the secular wasteland.

This is the position he most forcefully outlined in his Lenten Letter to Patriarch Pimen. He severely criticized the leadership of the Church for agreeing so much to the demands of the state, ostensibly in order to ensure the survival of the Church, that it has virtually reduced its spiritual message to an irrelevance. If the Church speaks out only on the injustices that are remote and utterly ignores the greater evils that lie closer to home, then it becomes a travesty of itself. "By what reason-

ing," he asks the Patriarch, "could one convince oneself that the calculated *destruction*—one directed by atheists—of the body and spirit of the
Church is the best method of preserving it?" Instead, Solzhenitsyn calls
for a commitment to the policy of "predominantly public sacrifice" as
the only course for the Church to follow. When one is without power
and at the mercy of one's opponent, there always remains the power of
sacrifice. "He who is deprived of all material strength always achieves
victory in *sacrifice*."[20] This is the wisdom of the cross on which the
Church is founded. The Church is the ideal institutional leader for the
"sacrificial elite" who can draw order out of destruction.

The process must begin with the Church itself. Solzhenitsyn calls
on the Orthodox hierarchies to put aside jurisdictional and canonical
disputes as of only secondary importance compared to the task before
them. He asks them to adopt an ecumenical outlook that will embrace
the cooperation of all Christians. A united front, since reunification he
judges to be an unlikely short-term possibility, must be presented by
all Christians toward the evil of the world. But even deeper still is the
process of repentant purification that must go on within the Church
itself. Solzhenitsyn calls on his fellow believers to acknowledge that
"the condition of the Russian Church at the beginning of the twentieth
century *is one of the principal causes for the inevitability of the Revolutionary
events*."[21] Beyond that is the more general responsibility of the Church
for the modern world it helped set in motion. The sin for which "the
entire Orthodox people *have never repented*" is the seventeenth-century
schism and persecution of the Old Believers, which was the beginning
of the whole process of modern Russian history. Only by thus cleansing
itself of its own entanglements with evil will the Church acquire the
spiritual strength to lead the world along the same path. When the
Church has undergone this inner regeneration, then it will again become the principal witness for the transcendent truth of our earthly
existence. Solzhenitsyn looks forward to the condition of this postre-
volutionary Church "that is of such stature and is so suffused with an
unfading sense of searching, that even the Western world, now languishing in an unquenchable spiritual agony, will be drawn to us."[22]

To obtain as emphatic an endorsement of Christianity—and specifically of the Orthodox tradition—as the foundation of order, one would
have to go back to Dostoevsky. He is certainly one of the great exponents of the spiritual mission of the Russian Orthodox church. Solzhenitsyn has evidently drawn on Dostoevsky and the thinkers of the
twentieth-century Russian religious revival in arriving at his own conclusions. The unconventionality of Solzhenitsyn's avowal of the political

role of Orthodoxy is in marked contrast to the more liberal secular position adopted by the majority of Soviet dissidents. Sakharov is the most famous representative of this Western parliamentary tradition. More will be said about their disagreements later. For the moment it is essential to understand this tradition of missionary (not messianic as is often incorrectly suggested) Russian Orthodoxy, of which Solzhenitsyn is only one of the most recent examples. To elucidate it more thoroughly we must turn to the meditations of Dostoevsky. It was he who had to demonstrate the necessity for a Christian foundation in opposition to the arguments of a militant liberal-revolutionary ethos.

The Fulfillment of the Modern Humanist Impulse

After his conversion, Dostoevsky regarded his work as an effort to demonstrate the impossibility of moral and political order based on humanism alone. If there is no God, then humanity is the master of reality and everything is lawful for the ruler of the earth. "Magnificent!" Dimitri Karamazov exclaims. "Only how is he going to be good without God? That's the question. I always come back to that" (K, 721). Versilov, the father of The Adolescent, refers to it as "the Geneva ideas" or "virtue without Christ, which is the contemporary concept or, we may even say, the idea underlying today's civilization" (A, 212). The nightmare that was to follow from this anti-Christian philanthropy was so overwhelmingly clear that it became the theme of all Dostoevsky's writing (see DW, 151). He foresaw the darkness, coarseness, destruction, and inhumanity that would result from the attempt to build up a new order without a foundation in transcendent Love. It was a vision of such power that the fictional characters he created, Stavrogin, Svidrigailov, Ivan Karamazov, the Grand Inquisitor, almost seem to merge with the reality of history over the next one hundred years. By plumbing the depths of the modern revolt, as we have seen, Dostoevsky rediscovered the truth of Christ it so strenuously sought to deny.

This is the basis from which he moved toward the positive articulation of the Christian foundation of order. In contrast to the humanist assertion of the absolute freedom to create order, Dostoevsky insisted that the genuine love of order leads to the recognition of its divine source. The ordering of human existence toward goodness and truth and beauty is ultimately the work of the God who is the perfection and totality of these realities. But above all it is the work of the incarnate God, Jesus Christ, who is the radiant center of true humanitarian love within history. It is not that an explicit confession of faith is required before we can love one another. Rather, Dostoevsky maintained, the brotherly impulse, if it is to unfold into a genuine universal love, must be willing to acknowledge that it is not its own self-sufficient source. By humbly recognizing our limitations, our inability and failure to love, we are already moving toward a more profoundly loving reality. At that point the mystery of God's gift in Christ manifests itself to those who are ready to receive it.

This is the experience recounted by Versilov in *The Adolescent*. He is a typical Enlightenment liberal, one of the detached land-owning class from whom the nineteenth-century intelligentsia emerged. Versilov espouses the moral autonomy of human nature as the means of bringing about the liberal utopia of progress. In this sense he is similar to Stepan Verkhovensky, the father of a revolutionary, just as Versilov is the father of an underground man, the adolescent Arkady Dolgoruky. But unlike Stepan, Versilov has a depth and strength that enable him to follow out the implications contained within his idea, which leads him right back to Christ as the only adequate realization. Versilov explains a dream he has had to his son, in which he is drawn back to pre-Christian times and the golden age of the Aegean. Lorraine's painting "Acis and Galatea" is the setting for this true age of universal brotherhood; all the dogmas and doctrines that are such a source of strife among human beings have fallen away. Now they are free to give themselves over without restriction to the innocent expression of love. Bereft of any divine consolation, they lavish all their attention on one another. At that point of its virtual culmination, the dream of a humanist paradise on earth is transfigured within the heart of a man who is not unalterably closed to transcendent reality. "Well, strangely enough," Versilov explains, "my fantasy almost never stopped there. It mostly ended with Heine's vision of 'Christ on the Baltic Sea.' I realized I couldn't manage without Him altogether and so, in the end, He appears in the midst of the abandoned men. He comes to them, holds out His hands to them, and says:'How could you forget!' And at once, it's as if scales fall from their eyes and they break out in a stirring hymn of their new and final resurrection" (*A*, 473).

This is why, despite the profound changes that he had undergone, Dostoevsky could also point to the continuity with his earlier utopian socialist convictions. The ideal of universal brotherhood remained what it had been from the days of his association with Belinsky. He had always recognized the Christian source and character of this aspiration. Now he had come around to the admission that it is only through Christ that the ideal can be realized, even within the hearts of individuals. It is from there that it can be communicated, if there is to be any hope of dispersion, to the order of society and modern civilization as a whole. All who are truly motivated by love for human beings carry the implicit truth of Christianity within them, and sooner or later will reach the same recognition as Dostoevsky did. His admiration for George Sand remained unbroken from those earliest days, precisely because of her insistence on the inner transformation of human beings as the only true way toward a society founded on brotherhood. He saw her as, although a deist, "perhaps the most Christian among all persons of her age" (DW, 349). Without explicitly acknowledging it she had followed out the implications of her position to the point where it demonstrated, irrefutably, the Christian understanding of the person as its ultimate foundation.

She based her socialism, her convictions, her hopes and ideals upon the moral feeling of man, upon the spiritual thirst of mankind and its longing for perfection and purity, and not upon "ant-necessity." All her life she believed absolutely in human personality (to the point of immortality), elevating and broadening this concept in each one of her works; and thereby she concurred in thought and feeling with one of the basic ideas of Christianity, i.e. the recognition of human personality and its freedom (consequently also of its responsibility). (DW, 349)

Unlike the secular determinist ideologies, Christianity does not deprive individuals of responsibility for evil. Their guilt is not sloughed off onto objective or social causes. But at the same time the burden of guilt is lifted through the forgiveness offered to all by Christ and, by extension, through the mutual forgiveness that all must extend to one another. Responsibility remains, but the guilt associated with it is removed through the grace of repentance and forgiveness. In this way a human being's inner spiritual self, his or her unlimited stature as a person, is affirmed and deepened. Dostoevsky understood the pressure to ascribe blame for wrongdoing to environmental influences, but he also recognized the abyss of dehumanization opened up by explanations of this type. In Christianity alone could he find such an unyielding insistence on responsibility and such a profound means of reconciliation (DW, 13). Through his suffering forgiveness of evil, Christ most completely affirmed the value of the inner person and provided the condition for the great spiritual miracle to occur: the answering response of love. The creation of order within soul and society is the work of love, which is the core of the Christian commitment. The efficacy of its appeal is never guaranteed, but there is no other way to attain the fulfillment of our humanity.

Christianity as the true fulfillment of the humanist impulse is, in many ways, the heart of Dostoevsky's experience of order. It is the central idea of his "return to the people," who are the principal carriers of this truth in the modern world. The "people," the simple Russian peasants (whose generic name, *Krestianstvo*, is identical with "Christian," *Christianstvo*), hold the answer to the humanism of the intelligentsia. They may not realize it, and clearly need the more articulate classes to expound the significance of their truth in relation to the modern world. But the Russian people as the carriers of Orthodoxy are the embodiment of the Christian faith. It was through them, Dostoevsky reported, that "I again received into my soul Christ who had been revealed to me in my parents' home and Whom I was about to lose when, on my own part, I transformed myself into a 'European liberal'" (*DW*, 984). There was nothing sentimental or romanticized about this attachment to the people. Dostoevsky had had firsthand acquaintance with all their weaknesses, debauches, and cruelties; they were not a race of peasant saints, by any stretch of the imagination. What counted, however, was the firmness of their grasp of the truth. While conceding that "bestiality" and "sin" were to be found among the Russian peasants as well as anywhere, Dostoevsky insisted that "the people do not accept—never will—their sins for truth" (*DW*, 985). They measure reality in the light of their eternal ideal—Christ. "With Christ there comes, of course, enlightenment, and in their superior, critical moments our people always settle national matters—always have been settling them—in a Christian spirit" (*DW*, 985).

It is through the people that the mission of Orthodoxy, which is identical with the mission of Russia, is to be fulfilled. The people are the ones who show forth in actual living the elevation of Christ's truth. They are the ones who carry the future of the modern world, the fulfillment of all its aspirations, within themselves. Dostoevsky had a burning vision of the transfigured age that would emerge once this recognition became universal. It is no longer a matter of religion or of churches, but more "precisely human progress, universal humanization of man—specifically thus conceived by the Russian people, who, deriving everything from Christ and incarnating their whole future in Christ and in His truth, are even unable to imagine themselves without Christ" (*DW*, 424). Dostoevsky has often been accused of messianism and even militarism in the elaboration of this vision. Nothing could be farther from his intentions, although some of his more enthusiastic expressions might encourage such a view. His suggestions for a pan-Slavic union and his belief in the necessity of Russian conquest of Constantinople should be discounted, as resulting from his concern over the sufferings of the Slavs at the hands of the Turks as well as his assessments of the requirements for the balance of power. They did not affect the fundamental principle of his position. That remained balanced on the knife-edge of possibility, the recognition that nothing stood in the way of a universal transformation of Russian and Western civilization. This was what constituted the dramatic excitement of Dostoevsky's appeal, as in the magical moment of the Pushkin Speech. But he never slipped from the balance into the assertion that the transformation could be brought about in any other way except through a free response, or that it justified a more coercive approach.

Dostoevsky remained firmly convinced that the means must be consistent with the end. If the Russian destiny is to bear witness to the Christian truth about human life, then it is a "universality acquired not by the sword but by the force of brotherhood" (*DW*, 979). This was his great hope of reconciling Slavophile and westerner, intelligentsia and peasantry within one Russian community. Through their unification, the truth of order emanating from Christ could be made the universal truth of the modern world. To become a genuine Russian meant for Dostoevsky to undertake this mission of universal service to humanity. He sought "to show the solution of European anguish in our all-humanitarian and all-unifying Russian soul, to embrace in it with brotherly love all our brethren, and finally, perhaps, to utter the ultimate word of great universal harmony, of the brotherly accord of all nations abiding by the law of Christ's Gospel" (*DW*, 980). Dostoevsky's appeal was not successful; it did not prevent the descent of tsarist Russia into chaos and revolution. Yet it continues to stand and to be taken up again as the great truth of our spiritual salvation, now that the false messianism of power has virtually exhausted itself.

The Nature of Postmodern Order

Beyond the core recognition of the transcendent order of Christ remains the necessity of translating the insight into the structures of order within human life. The most pressing need during an age of spiritual crisis is to recover the sense of contact with an ordering reality, but then we must also reflect on how that experience can become constitutive of order within individuals, society, and history. We have concentrated on the pneumatic center, the point of our participation in ineffable divine Being, which becomes the measure of a whole life. Now we must turn toward the noetic unfolding of the experience into ethical and political and historical order. This is a distinction that is particularly clear when Christianity performs the foundational role. In its essence, the Christian faith is about the movement toward⁻ the divinization of human nature with and through God in eternity. How that is to affect the order of existence within time is continually in need of elaboration, since it has not been the primary thrust of the experience. This is why the conjunction of Christianity with philosophy, which *is* focused on the creation of order in existence, has been of such historic importance. Each symbolism reinforces and complements the other. Philosophy acquires a more explicitly transcendent authorization for its truth, and revelation obtains the means of imprinting its ordering influence within history.

Authoritative Spiritual Truth

No aspect of the relationship between philosophy and revelation is more fundamental than the philosophic defense of the experience of revelation itself. Especially during an era when faith has collapsed, when the source of its authority is under attack, and when philosophizing itself has become "critical" or self-conscious, this has become a first necessity. In this book I did not begin with the philosophy of consciousness that would provide a rationale or justification for the assumptions on which the book is based. Thus I may have given the impression that I was merely proposing a "Christian" perspective on the world. Now I hope to make it clear that this strategy is consistent with the philosophy of consciousness behind it. The basic principle is that spiritual truth cannot be apprehended except through participation in it. One cannot know the realities to which truth refers until one has made them present to oneself, through a submission to their ordering influence. At a minimum one must be capable of engaging in a sympathetic reenactment. A theoretical analysis of these requirements would have relatively little impact on someone who was not already disposed toward openness. Much more persuasive is a direct and forceful presentation of the experience itself. In that way not only the converted but the waverers, and even some of the naysayers, can be expected to be drawn along with it.

Now, however, it is essential to fill in the larger context; otherwise there is a great danger that the light of transcendent truth could become isolated from the world it is here to save. Probably no one else has devoted as much attention to this aspect of the problem of order as Eric Voegelin. Having been educated in the post-Kantian tradition of philosophy, he understood well the nature of the objections against all forms

of metaphysical knowledge. Kant had demonstrated that our intellectual categories are applicable to the objects within our space-time experience, and that we can have no reliable knowledge of divine or
spiritual entities that transcend this world. Voegelin's modernness is
evidenced by his full acceptance of this critique, although he denies
that this represents a complete understanding of human knowledge.
He has sought to remedy the deficiency through his own philosophy of
consciousness. It is directed not only against the philosophical assault
on faith, but also against the more diffuse objections of subjectivism.
Religion, subjectivists assert, is a wholly private affair, and a liberal
society is founded on the conviction that nothing certain can be known
about God.[23] These are the formidable obstacles, constituting "a publicly accepted state of unconsciousness" (*OH* V, 44), that must be faced
by any conception of order rooted in the experience of transcendent
Being.

Voegelin's theory of consciousness did not emerge ready-made or all
at once, or even in any final completed form.[24] It was the product of a
lifetime of struggle with the problems of order thrown up by the ideological convulsions of the age. This is particularly evident in the last
unfinished volume of *Order and History*, appropriately titled *In Search of
Order*. There the elaboration of the philosophy of consciousness has
almost entirely eclipsed the historical character of the project. The analysis of consciousness has acquired this prominence because of Voegelin's increasing conviction that it is only through such clarification that
the experiences and symbols of order can be adequately recovered. To
overcome the distorting effects of ideology, it is essential to trace the
problems back to their source within consciousness. Then it can be
shown that the symbolisms of order arise from authoritative experiences of truth and that the ideological opposition is merely a willful
attempt to deny this awareness. Voegelin's task has become that of rais-
ing the "public unconscious" into consciousness; his weapon has become the analysis of the structures of consciousness in which truth
becomes known. By establishing the validity of the experiences of order
within an understanding of consciousness, he makes possible their recovery as authoritative experiences of truth within human existence.

If we want to break out of the public unconscious, we must analyze it and
thereby raise it into consciousness: We must remember the historical acts of
oblivion; in order to identify them as acts of oblivion, then, we must remember
the paradoxic complex of consciousness-reality-language as the criterion of remembrance and oblivion; and in order to recognize the paradoxic complex as

the criterion of truth and untruth, we must differentiate the dimension of reflective distance which stands, compactly implied in the Platonic *anamnesis*, at
the beginning of all noetic philosophizing. *(OH V, 44–45)*

Reflective distance or reflective awareness of the tensions within consciousness has become the means of retrieving from oblivion the remembrance of the transcendent reality. Correlatively, it is also the
means of ensuring that the experiences of existential truth do not fall
victim again to the deformation into dogmas or doctrines within competing ideological systems.

The breakthrough in Voegelin's elaboration of the philosophy of consciousness came when he abandoned his study of the history of political ideas. He realized, as we have seen, that this endeavor was one
more "ideological deformation" of reality. "There were no ideas about
order unless there were [first] symbols of immediate experience." Ideas
about order are derivative; they do not carry the evidence for holding
them within themselves. When they are examined to uncover their justification they appear to be based on nothing more than the arbitrary
assertion of will, until we recognize that this is not the real source of
their appeal. There would be no ideas, or their reference would indeed
be empty, if there were not concrete experiences of attunement to the
order of reality. By following the intimations of our spirit, we participate more fully in the order we already know. Far from constituting an
arbitrary choice of direction, this grounds human life in the most reliable criterion available: reality experienced. Ideas about order are
merely secondary refractions of the symbols that articulate this experiential illumination of reality. Order is differentiated not as a result of
abstract reflection, but through the efforts of exceptional individuals
who seek to unfold and reveal it within their own lives. No other perspective is available, apart from the struggle to realize existential truth.
We continue to live in this order, as long as we have not advanced
beyond it to a more differentiated experience of truth. There is no order
other than what has concretely emerged within the human history of
the search.

The participatory nature of spiritual truth is its central epistemolog-
ical trait. Kant was correct in stating that we cannot have knowledge of
that which we do not experience, but he was wrong in asserting that
divine Being or the immortality of the soul are irrevocably beyond the
range of experience.[25] Simply because they are not objects within the
external world does not mean that they cannot be experienced. For
besides the intentional activity of consciousness directed toward exter-

nal objects, there is also the reality in which consciousness participates
and which it knows precisely through participation.

There is a consciousness with two structural meanings, to be distinguished as
intentionality and luminosity. There is a reality with two structural meanings,
to be distinguished as the thing-reality and the It-reality. Consciousness, then,
is a subject intending reality as its object, but at the same time a something in
a comprehending reality; and reality is the object of consciousness, but at the
same time the subject of which consciousness is to be predicated. (*OH* V, 16)

Intentionality and luminosity are the two irreducible dimensions of consciousness, with reflective distance as the third that holds them together through awareness of their difference. Problems arise only when
the latter gives way to reflective oblivion and the difference between
the two modes is forgotten. Then the dimension of intentionality assumes exclusive authority and its model of objective or "thing-reality"
becomes the dominant understanding of human knowledge.

It becomes necessary to remind ourselves that a person not only
confronts objects within reality, but is himself or herself a part of reality.
This comprehending "It-reality" cannot become an object for us since
we are included within it; it can only be known through the expanding
luminosity of our participation in it. We know that we are part of a
whole, of which we are neither the origin nor the end, but whose
ground must be utterly other than the things in tangible visible existence. We do not understand the full concatenation of influences from
which our own actions arise, nor the full series of consequences they
will ultimately produce. But we do know the obligation or pull within
us that draws us upward toward the lasting, the true, and the good.
By responsively following this attraction toward higher reality we participate more fully in it and we acquire the knowledge and capacity to
follow its direction ever more faithfully. We never overstep the bounds
of the human perspective to acquire a comprehensive divine understanding of the order of things. Our knowledge remains tied to our
"essential ignorance." Nor, on the other hand, are we ever capable of
closing ourselves so completely to the awareness of the higher reality
that we sink below the human level. We continue to "know" that from
which we are fleeing.

Above all, our nature remains that of a questioner. This is the constant
Voegelin extracts as definitive of human consciousness throughout the
movement of history (*OH* IV, 316–35). The knowledge we possess is the
knowledge of the questioner. It cannot be radically transcended or radi-

cally suppressed, but it can be increased to the point of revelatory openness through a responsive unfolding. Within the question is the
knowledge of which we are in search. We know our own finiteness and
that of everything around us, and we know the divine ground that is
present as the force that moves our search in openness toward itself. The
structure of a quest is the common motivating impulse, Voegelin finds,
within a Babylonian myth, a Jewish apocalypse, or a Hindu Upanishad.
But it is within the Greek philosophical articulation that Voegelin finds its
most transparent expression. Summarizing the classic experience of reason, he observes: "The consciousness of questioning unrest in a state of
ignorance becomes luminous to itself as a movement in the psyche toward
the ground that is present in the psyche as its mover" (*AN*, 96). In every
instance it is only through a meditative unfolding of the question that
divine illumination of the order of existence is vouchsafed to us. "There is
no answer to the Question other than the Mystery as it becomes luminous
in the acts of questioning" (*OH* IV, 330).

It is, moreover, this questioning openness that provides the principle of verification within spiritual experience. The criterion in every
case is whether a particular expression is an advance or a decline from
the openness of our questioning. Insofar as we are moving toward the
reality glimpsed as the object of our question, we are moving toward
truth. Insofar as we are refusing to accept the question and turning
away from reality, we are rejecting truth and opting for falsehood. What
makes this a universal criterion is that it lies beyond all definitions of
first premises. Deeper than and prior to all ideological preconceptions
is the "questioning unrest"; the existential tension that is the motivating
source of all searching, reflection, and articulation cannot itself be denied. So that the truth brought up by any particular individual from
the meditative unfolding of his or her quest will be recognized by all
human beings as true insofar as it accords with the directional elaboration of their own questions. This is how Voegelin responds to the
perennial objections of subjectivism.

If the story is to evoke authoritatively the order of a social field, the word must
be spoken with an authority recognizable as such by the men to whom the
appeal is addressed; the appeal will have no authority of truth unless it speaks
with an authority commonly present in everybody's consciousness, however
inarticulate, deformed or suppressed the consciousness in the concrete case
may be. Using the Heraclitean distinction between private and public, we may
say, the appeal will be no more than a private (*idios*) opinion unless the questioner finds in the course of his quest the word (*logos*) that indeed speaks what

is common (*xynon*) to the order of man's existence as a partner in the comprehending reality; only if the questioner speaks the common *logos* of reality can
he evoke a truly public order. (*OH* V, 26)

The crucial element is the recollection that the truth emerges from
the unfolding of the quest; it cannot be known in any other way. This
is why Voegelin devotes almost all of his last volume to the thinkers in
whom this dimension of reflective distance is most fully elaborated.
Among the moderns, Hegel performs this service. Besides representing
the most profound deformation of order, Hegel is also the one who, in
Voegelin's view, most thoroughly analyzed the conditions for the restoration of order. He understood that the language of dogma is bank-
rupt and that the only way its truth can be recovered is by returning to
the movement of the quest from which it has emerged. "The truth is in
motion; even more, as we have seen, the motion is the truth" (*OH* V,
57). Hegel went on to turn the movement of the quest into an object
for consciousness that could be solved through his "science of the experience of consciousness," but this did not diminish the definitive
character of his achievement. "His rediscovery of the experiential
source of symbolization, as well as his identification of the fundamental
problems in the structure of consciousness, is irreversible" (*OH* V, 70).
For a more faithful rendering of that structure, however, Voegelin returns to the Greeks, especially Hesiod and Plato.

With Hesiod the transcendent character of the ground has not yet
been fully differentiated. As a result, he has to struggle with the symbolization of a movement from an unidentified source toward the creation of order within reality. This makes his meditation a perfect
illustration of how the tension toward non-thing reality must be han-
dled. Hesiod dealt with it through the symbol of Mnemosyne, Remembrance. "For there is no participation in the story of the It-reality
to be told unless it is 'remembered'; and how can it be 'remembered'
unless the participatory character of the story is really experienced in
the present experience of existential reality?" (*OH* V, 73–74). Even the
gods do not escape this participatory tension between the divine Beyond and the temporal Parousia. For the poet sings to remind them of
their own origination through the struggle to incarnate the order of a
divine reality that is itself beyond all struggle for incarnation. It is "a
story that presupposes the experience of the Beyond without symbolizing it" (*OH* V, 75).

At a later stage, Plato shows how the experience of the Beyond can
be symbolized without turning it into an "intentionalist entity." His
reflective distance is revealed in the care he takes to preserve his para-

dox of consciousness-language-reality. The Beyond and the order emanating from it can only be symbolized in the language of thingness, but
such concessions must not be allowed to obscure the truly non-thing-
like character of the reality depicted. Like Hesiod, Plato too insists on
recourse to the experience itself. "Only the process comprehending the
steps, when moved into reflective distance, will let the truth of existence become luminous by letting the symbols illuminate one another"
(OH V, 100). When this is done, then the poles of the tension between
creator and creation, divine and human, order and disorder themselves
partake of the tensional nature of existence. For example, the creative
force of the Demiurge is represented by Plato as an intermediate reality,
which is impossible to define apart from its role of struggling to impose
order on the chaos. Nowhere does Plato attempt to symbolize what is
ultimately beyond all tension. As a consequence, he arrives at a philosophy of consciousness that becomes transparent "for the paradoxic tension in formative reality . . . between the divine reality experienced as
formatively present at the ordering pole of the tensions and the divine
reality experienced as a Beyond of its concrete manifestations in the
process, between the God who reveals himself in his presence in time
and the God who remains the experienced but unknown reality beyond
time" (OH V, 107).

A parallel emphasis on the existential movement toward knowledge
distinguishes the philosophy of consciousness intuitively applied by Camus, Solzhenitsyn, and Dostoevsky. Their common conviction has been
that the only criterion of truth we can rely on is that which is provided
by life itself. When all doctrines and principles have become opaque,
then it becomes a matter of necessity to return to the sources in experience on which all truth ultimately rests. Dostoevsky understood that
the degraded immanentist view of human nature in modern science
and ideology "cannot be refuted by logic." It can only be overcome "by
faith, by the deduction of the necessity of faith in the immortality of
man's soul, by the inference of the conviction that this faith is the only
source of 'live life' on earth" (DW, 545). It should be noted that this has
little to do with the "idea" of immortality, because what Dostoevsky is
referring to has much more to do with this life than the next. It is the
fuller experiential reality signified by the term immortality that he is
really pursuing. For he observes the paradox that faith in immortality
"ties man all the more strongly to earth" (DW, 541). This truth about
human nature is confirmed by the only test available: the litmus of
experience. By opening toward the immortal dimension of existence,
we are led into a fuller life in the present. Under its inspiration we are

brought to a deeper, more genuine love for all humanity, since each individual is perceived as a unique irreplaceable depth in himself or herself. For Dostoevsky that is all the proof that is required.

This is why the thinkers who have worked through the crisis of modernity prefer to communicate their insights through novels. In contrast to discursive arguments, the medium of fictional literature allows a more immediate presentation of the experience. This is also the orientation that has guided their approach to the medium. All three novelists whom we have examined, Dostoevsky, Solzhenitsyn, and Camus, regard the novel as a means of exploring the directional tensions of reality, rather than as a vehicle for expounding the author's own monological point of view. After explaining that the novel does not attempt to impose a judgment on others, Camus goes on to describe it as a genre without a style. "In fact it requires the most difficult style, one that submits itself entirely to the object" (N II, 67). In a similar fashion, Solzhenitsyn revealed in a letter that "the literary form that attracted me most is that of the 'polyphonic' novel (with no main hero, the most important character in any chapter being the one whom the narrative 'catches up with' at that point), which accurately portrays the time and place of the action" (OC, 458). And of course the creator of the polyphonic novel is Dostoevsky.[26] We have already seen the extent to which he carries the process of the juxtaposition of positions, whereby the truth is embodied forth but not imposed by the author. He greatly admired Herzen's use of this technique of allowing the weaknesses of his own position to become fully exposed, rather than risk the impression of a contrived outcome. That, Dostoevsky remarked, is "the whole trick" of his art (DW, 4). One of the closest parallels, as Bakhtin has pointed out, is to be found in the Gospels. There Jesus simply proclaims, "He who has ears to hear let him hear." Living truth can be communicated in no other way; by encapsulation in a definition it becomes a dead letter.

The secret of these novelists' recovery of the Christian and philosophic symbolization of order has been this capacity to draw it forth from the depths of the contemporary disorder. The necessity of a Christianity-based philosophy of order is demonstrated in the existential logic of modernity itself. Nothing remotely resembling an imposed solution or the arbitrary assertion of values is involved here. Rather there is a sympathetic unfolding of the modern humanist aspiration for a new civilizational order centered on the moral perfection of the person. That becomes the basis for the critique of the project of constructing an autonomous morality, in which reason or human choice becomes the

self-sufficient ground of order. Analysis of the meaning and consequences of this enterprise has led, as we have seen in chapter 2, to the
recognition of the nihilistic abyss it has opened up. Now we are
brought to conclude that a faithful elaboration of the original moral
intent would lead toward the acknowledgment that what is right is
grounded in an order of reality beyond human existence. It is not a
matter of choice or of consistency or even of first principles. There *is* a
reality of good and evil in which we participate, and we are obliged to
follow the pull of the former and resist the attraction of the latter. For
all who are serious about the moral progress of human life, their own
and that of everyone else, the implication is inescapably clear. We must
open ourselves to the reality of goodness in order to be transformed
through its preeminent power.

At that point we are prepared to recognize the complete revelation
of incarnate divine goodness in history: Jesus Christ. Having admitted
the necessity of a transcendent foundation to morality, we can hardly
hold back from the acknowledgment of the most visible, tangible, and
perfect realization of that order. Contrary to the entire historical drift
of our epoch, we are led to confess that faith in Jesus remains the
preeminent way toward spiritual transformation. This is not a subjective
"leap of faith," but a recognition of the same moral reality in Christ as
we experience within ourselves. The movement toward goodness is recognized as the reality that is wholly present within Jesus; it is disclosed
in his actions and manifested as the fullness of divine love. Confirmation of this is contained in the knowledge within every human heart
that is willing to admit it. The ability to evoke an authoritative truth,
which even those opposed to it are compelled to acknowledge, is the
best indication of the nonsubjective status of this rediscovered Christian
foundation.

There is, in other words, a philosophy of consciousness that can
articulate the truth of this existential insight. It consists in showing how
the assertion of a transcendent moral order is an elaboration of the
structure of consciousness that is more or less transparent to all human
beings. This is not a particular or idiosyncratic point of view; it is an
explication of what everyone knows, and can be everywhere verified.
Nor does it require special efforts of introspection to identify it, since
it can be confirmed in the overt expressions of our world. Even those
who deny the reality of good and evil or reject the reality of divine
order nevertheless reveal the extent to which "they know that reality
moves not only into a future of things but toward their Beyond" (*OH* V,
35). Even while insisting on the self-created nature of such concepts,

they demonstrate the degree to which humanity lives in relation to an ultimately self-justifying ground of goodness. We continue to participate in a divinely ordered world, and even while denying it continue to affirm our tension toward a transcendent *telos*. Critique consists in the confrontation between these intimations of order and the substitute constructions that have been brought forward to replace them. Restoration of order consists in a faithful unfolding of the direction already implicitly known.

Acceptance of the Mystery of the Whole

The first step in the elaboration of order is to adumbrate the relationship between the transcendent movement of the soul beyond existence and its role in the formation of order within it. This, as we have seen, has been the great source of aberrations within Christianity. Once the transfiguring eschatological end has been differentiated there is a danger it will have a distorting effect on the search for an immanent order of existence. Eventually the achievement of an equilibrium between these tensions, of remaining in the world while not remaining of it, must become the focus of attention. Voegelin is the one in the contemporary context who has taken up such issues as are at the heart of the Christian tradition. Whatever we may feel about his restrained enthusiasm for Christianity, we cannot deny that he has performed a major service for it by grappling with the whole set of problems involved in its relationship to the modern world. In later years the problem of balance assumed on overriding importance for him, as he traced the modern convulsions to an immanentization of the Christian eschatological expectations, thus identifying the core of the contemporary crisis.

Christianity can only be the great force for order that it is, if the intensity of the experiential movement toward the Beyond does not eclipse the necessity for adjustment to the conditions of continued existence within the world. Transcendence and immanence, once they have been differentiated, are the poles of human existence. But the attainment of order is dependent on the discovery of a balance between them. By neglecting the problems of pragmatic existence in our longing for union with the resurrected Lord, we fail in our responsibilities toward one another and toward our world. For want of necessary action to prevent them, great evils may be done. Yet we cannot afford to devote our entire commitment to the achievement of order within temporal existence. If we do, we run the risk of separating ourselves from the ultimate source of order. Balance is a problem for all transcendent

symbolisms (Judaism and Islam face similar tensions), but it is especially acute for Christianity because of its maximal degree of
differentiation.

Voegelin's approach is to distinguish clearly between the different
modes of spiritual experience. The revelatory encounter with the fullness of divine reality (*theotes*, Col. 2:9) in Christ, or within a theophanic
event in general, is only an advance within one narrow segment of
reality. However much it may affect everything else, the opening toward the self-revelation of God is primarily a fuller apprehension of our
participation in divine being. "The new truth pertains to man's consciousness of his humanity in participatory tension toward the divine
ground, and to no reality beyond this restricted area" (*OH* IV, 8). Voegelin goes on to distinguish this immediate knowledge of divine reality
in the experiential movement toward the Beyond (*epekeina, Republic,*
509b) from the mediated knowledge of the divine ordering presence
within the cosmos from its Beginning (Gen. 1:1). The new awareness
of mutual participation of divine in human and human in divine reality
provides us with no further direct knowledge beyond the experience
itself. Both the order of the whole in which it occurs and the significance of the illuminative experience within it remain inscrutably mysterious. We must continue to symbolize the comprehensive order
whence we have come and whither we are going, and how we are to
get there, by means of a myth or "likely story," as Plato called it. Only
a cosmogonic myth can express this mediated knowledge of the divine
providential care from the Beginning. The newly differentiated order
reveals the kind of divine presence it is and therefore the truth with
which the myth must be harmonized. But it does no more than that.[27]

Such is the nature of the "eschatological myth" whereby Christianity articulates the movement toward its transfigurative fulfillment in the
Beyond. It is not knowledge, but only a vision or imaginative construction of how the process must conclude consistent with the divine movement within it. This is the symbolization of events that lie strictly
beyond the range of experience, yet not beyond the range of consciousness. The eschatological myth is an extrapolation from the transfigurative experience within the soul; it expresses the awareness that reality
is "aetiologically and directionally structured" (*OH* IV, 216). But it is no
more than an extrapolation. The exodus movement is still a movement
that takes place within the cosmos; it is not itself tantamount to a transfiguration of the cosmos. Voegelin emphasized the necessity for anchoring the theophanic experience within this larger mystery of the
whole. This can be done if we recognize that it is "reality as a whole"

that is "engaged in a movement in the direction of eminent reality," and that the experiential movement of the soul is an enterprise of "participation in the directional flux of reality" (*OH* IV, 216). Under no circumstances does the spiritual exodus bring the process as a whole within the grasp or control of the participant.[28]

Plato is the great exemplar of balance for Voegelin. Plato's cautious exploration of the world-historic significance of the spiritual outburst of philosophy provides the model for imitation. History is located by Plato within the larger cosmic rhythms of catastrophe and recovery, where memory only extends back to the beginning of the last cataclysm.[29] He could accept that even when philosophy had been realized in the form of the best polis, that it would eventually decline into the darkness of the deteriorating political forms. Yet no anxiety concerning the meaning of the process is evident, because the philosophers were closer to the original trust in the divinely pervasive order of the cosmos.

It can even be shown, Voegelin contends, that Plato was careful to ensure that his own theophanic experience did nothing to disturb that embracing faith. For although he was aware that beyond the divinity who noetically orders the cosmos is the divine reality that is free from the struggle with cosmic necessity, he preferred to leave its identity clouded in uncertainty. Thus it is never clear whether the "beyond the heavens" (*hyperouranion*) of *Phaedrus* 247 is the same or different from the Demiurge, or whether beyond the Nous and the Demiurge is a still further abyss of divine substance. Plato, according to Voegelin, was aware of the destablizing tendencies of the theophanic experience, "because it confronts the movement with a 'Beyond' that threatens to invalidate the theophanic events together with the process in which they occur" (*OH* IV, 233). The temptation toward a libidinous Gnostic domination of reality on the basis of such experiences could become intense, if the necessary precautions were not taken. Voegelin identifies this imperative as "the postulate of balance." It is what eventually comes to define the philosopher's task: to preserve the awareness of "the paradox of a recognizably structured process that is recognizably moving beyond its structure . . . as the very structure of existence itself" (*OH* IV, 227–28).

Now that the eschatological movement has been fully differentiated in Christianity, Voegelin advocates not a return to the compactness of the Platonic cosmos, but an extension of the philosophic postulate of balance. This involves the recognition of history as the most embracing horizon of mystery. Once the transfigurative exodus is discovered as the structure of reality, then the historical process is recognized as its boundary and manifestation. The balance between the movement and its consummation can be maintained only if we acknowledge that the meaning of history is impenetrable. There is no meaning to history apart from the process becoming luminous to itself. "What happens 'in' history is the very process of differentiating consciousness that constitutes history" (*OH* IV, 332). There is no length of time that once elapsed is sufficient to permit an answer to the question of the meaning of history. The reason is that any length of time is only a measure of the lasting of realities in existence. Even if we take the lasting of the astrophysical universe itself we cannot identify it with the lasting of the Whole, because it is simply "the time-dimension of a thing within the Whole that also comprises the divine reality whose mode of lastingness we express by such symbols as 'eternity'" (*OH* IV, 334). The mystery of history is inseparable from the mystery of the Whole in which it occurs; now it is recognized as the mode in which the process becomes luminous to itself. "History, thus, reveals itself as the horizon of divine mystery when the process of differentiation is discovered to be the process of transfiguration" (*OH* IV, 314).[30]

By opening toward the divine Beyond that draws us toward itself, while recognizing that the mystery of the process from the Beginning can only be glimpsed through myth, order is created in the soul of a human being. A responsive opening toward the reality present in the theophanic event requires an acceptance of the larger historical and cosmic process within which it occurs. There would be no spiritual illumination without this larger process; and the God who is revealed within human beings is also the God who is the source of all reality. We have already emphasized the extent to which Christianity is both a source of potential deformations of order and the most profound means of the restoration of order. This bears repeating within this context. In Christ, not only is the eschatological Beyond fully differentiated, but the full participation of God in the mysterious conditions of existence is also definitively revealed. The mystery of the process of reality becomes more than bearable through the assurance of God's presence in human history. Through the openness toward mystery, human beings become ready to follow the promptings of divine grace that are the source of the ethical order of existence.

The Creation of Ethical Order

Good and evil, virtue and vice, interests and obligations, are not possibilities to be pursued in a vacuum. They make sense only in relation to the entire direction of life, not in isolation from this overarching context. The norms of right action, we have emphasized, can only be grounded in the experiential movement toward preeminent divine reality. It is in the process of "immortalizing" that their rightness becomes transparent with an experiential reality that renders their truth beyond question. The theological virtues of faith, hope, and charity, which St. Thomas regarded as the foundation of morality, are not originally Christian. They were identified by Heraclitus and are no more than specifications of the existential tension toward the divine ground that Plato termed the Metaxy or Between (*OH* II. chap. 9). The love of the divine within this Between state provides both the moving force behind right action and the illuminative principle of guidance. In every instance, right action is measured by the advance toward or decline from attunement with the unseen transcendent measure. This is the classical understanding of ethics that, as Voegelin has shown, provides the ordering foundation for existence.

This understanding is in marked contrast to the modern conception, which is preoccupied with the lack of a foundation. The collapse of a consensus concerning the criteria by which good and evil are to be distinguished exercises a pervasive effect. The objection posed from a modern perspective to any suggestion of a science of order is: How can you prove it is true? How can we know what is right amidst the multiple shifting circumstances of life? How can we possibly assert a particular course of action as right? The modern obsession with psuedo-objective formulas is itself the great obstacle to the understanding of the philosophical position. Classical ethics has almost nothing to say in terms of definitions of virtues or universal rules of morality. Socrates went so far as to demonstrate to his fellow citizens that no universal definition of justice was possible. The entire thrust of classical ethics is toward the formation of a particular type of person. Once the soul is rightly ordered toward transcendent divine goodness, then it will choose rightly in light of that supreme truth. Aristotle and Plato recognized that the infinitely varied circumstances of life make universal rules impossible. But they insisted nevertheless on an independent measure of right and wrong. That criterion is the soul of the philosopher or the mature human (*spoudaios*).

What is right in any given context is what the mature person would do under those circumstances. This insight is, according to Voegelin, "perhaps the most important contribution to an epistemology of ethics and politics that has ever been made" (*OH* III, 300). Aristotle acknowledged that while everyone chooses what appears to him to be good, only for the "man of high moral standards" (*spoudaios*) do appearance and truth coincide. Since his soul is ordered toward what is ultimately good, he is already predisposed to do what is right in every concrete situation. Virtue is illuminated within his actions. "Thus," Aristotle concluded, "what is good and pleasant differs with different characteristics or conditions, and perhaps the chief distinction of a man of high moral standards is his ability to see the truth in each particular moral question, since he is, as it were, the standard and measure for such questions" (*Nicomachean Ethics*, 113a30). There is no other criterion of good action than what the person wholly devoted to doing what is right would do in the particular situation.

Like much else in classical philosophy this conception of ethics is very close to the commonsense viewpoint. It is the conclusion individuals sincerely searching for right order are likely to reach. If one is not preoccupied with the distractions of modern philosophy, Solzhenitsyn has shown, one will similarly conclude that the ethical truth of life is concretely objective. In response to the question of what we should do in the contemporary nihilistic environment, he replies that we must resolve not to lie. The lie is what covers up all kinds of violence and wrongdoing, and is the rationalization by which evil invades individuals and society. But he knows people will object, what *is* a lie? "The answer could not be simpler: decide for *yourself*, as *your* conscience dictates" (*UR*, 275). Once we have begun to participate in the truth, its nature will be revealed more and more fully as we open ourselves toward it. "Whoever steels his heart and opens his eyes to the tentacles of the lie will in each situation, every day and hour, realize what he must do" (*UR*, 276). The entire problem of the objectivity of values or moral judgments turns out to be a pseudo-problem once we adopt the concrete decision to follow out the intimations of truth already clearly known to us.[31]

The nature of ethics in a postmodern philosophy is that it has overcome the modern fixation on the subject-object dichotomy. It has returned to the Aristotelian understanding of practical wisdom as its foundation. "For him," Voegelin observes, "this knowledge merges into concrete action, and action is the truth of the knowledge; what separates the two is not the distance of subject and object but a noetic tension in the movement of being"(*AN*, 69). What Voegelin does not do is relate this classical emphasis on the concrete realization of virtue to its Christian consummation. With Christ, "the permeability for the movement of being," the sense of our participation in the ordering pull of the divine source, becomes fully transparent. He is the definitive revelation of "the truth of action" (*AN*, 64); now there can be no other paradigm of the mature person but Jesus. He is the One in whom the identity with divine goodness is so complete that he becomes the perfect illumination of human existence. This is the meaning of Dostoevsky's remark that "there is nothing more beautiful, more profound, more sympathetic, more reasonable, more courageous, and more perfect that Christ." Ethical action becomes, therefore, a matter of following the example of this concrete embodiment of transcendent divine goodness. Right action will be discerned and practiced ever more completely as we succeed in that opening up that St. Paul referred to as "putting on the mind of Christ."

The Principles of Political Order: Liberalism Transformed

Further specificity about ethics is always possible, both in terms of concrete actions and of intermediate explications of principle, but the essential thing is the originating spirit behind them. Once the fundamental orientation has been established, then the performance of right action becomes a matter of increasing moral sensitivity and growing empirical understanding. No insuperable obstacles remain. This is also the situation with regard to political order in a postmodern perspective. No more than the infinite variety of circumstances in individual life, does the endless complexity of communal life permit the application of a single political formula. The institutional organization of society is a secondary consideration compared to that of the spirit and the leadership that animates it. Having witnessed enough of the ideological attempts to change human nature through political and institutional transformation, the postmodern thinkers display an abiding determination to resist any assignment of priority to the political level. Social and political order must proceed from order within the souls of the individual citizens. This is why as a group the postmoderns are characterized by a remarkable flexibility with regard to political structures. It is one of the most distinctive features of a viewpoint purged of virtually all ideological inclinations.

This has made them notoriously difficult to categorize politically, and has been a source of continuing consternation to more conventionally acclimated readers. The most recent example is the shock of Western intellectual and public opinion at the discovery that Solzhenitsyn did not share their unquestioning faith in modern liberal democracy. Automatically it had been assumed that if one opposed totalitarianism then one must be a liberal democrat.[32] And while many of the Soviet dissidents are inclined toward a Western parliamentary form of government, Solzhenitsyn and his colleagues are not among them. Yet he is not opposed to liberal democratic institutions in principle. He simply does not regard such a form as the universal panacea it appears to be to those who cannot visualize an alternative. That is why, although he accepts that liberal democracy is a viable form of government in the West and expects that it will continue to function tolerably well, he is reluctant to import it into the vastly different historical setting of the Soviet Union. He unabashedly endorses the practicality of an authoritarian form of government for his own country. A nonideological form of absolute government is more likely to be effective, he believes, because of its greater capacity to maintain order within a society largely unacquainted with the mores of self-government. The crucial element for Solzhenitsyn is the lack of ideology. He is aware of the dangers of absolute rule, but concludes that "authoritarian regimes as such are not frightening—only those which are answerable to no one and nothing" (*UR*, 24).[33]

At the same time Solzhenitsyn is intensely aware of the inherent weaknesses of a liberal democratic order. He reminds us that it was during the brief period of democratic rule from February to October 1917 that Russia succumbed to the radical Communist revolution, thereby giving rise to the most enduring totalitarian regime of the century. The same might be said of other totalitarian revolutions; they emerged not from the metamorphosis of authoritarian governments, but from the collapse of weak democratic ones. A similar process of internal erosion and disintegration can be discerned, Solzhenitsyn informed the Harvard Commencement audience in 1978, within the historically long-standing and apparently solid democracies of the West. This sense of impending collapse of the liberal democracies is something he brought with him into his involuntary exile. The Russian experience with democracy had struck him as "a compressed resumé of the later and present history of the West" (*UR*, 128).

What Solzhenitsyn particularly objects to in liberalism is the element it has in common with Communism and all ideological forms: the lack of a moral and spiritual foundation. Where Communism explicitly disavows the reality of any objective moral order, liberalism merely disregards it by reducing it to the level of private subjective opinion. In the end it comes to the same thing. That is why Communism and liberalism are in effect "brothers under the skin," and why liberal societies have had such difficulty in mounting a principled opposition to Communist oppression. (The much touted triumph of liberal democracy in recent years has had more to do with the internal exhaustion of Communism than with any intellectual or political victories of the West.) Liberal democracy was ostensibly founded on the appeal to self-interest, "the pursuit of happiness," as a more reliable foundation than agreement concerning the spiritual fulfillment of human nature. For a long time an underlying consensus about the obligations that should govern human relationships coexisted alongside this minimalist public symbolism. But now, in the view of Solzhenitsyn and many others, that consensus has broken down. Under the repeated and persistent demands for an expansion of liberty, utterly free choice becoming the only authoritative guide to public policy, the notion of an independent moral order has almost entirely disappeared. Without that fundamental moral agreement the mutual self-restraint so essential to the process of self-government ceases to exist. Problems of "irresponsible freedom" proliferate as a prelude to the collapse of order.

It is because they are convinced that political order must be reestablished on this fundamental level first that the postmodern thinkers have focused their efforts on the restoration of moral and spiritual substance within society.[34] The object of this book has been to draw attention to this consistent commonality of direction. One can point to the efforts of Dostoevsky from the 1860s to the 1880s when he sought through literature and journalism to revitalize the spiritual substance of Russia in the face of the impending catastrophe. Camus performed an analogous role, especially in the political vacuum after the French liberation, through his efforts at renovating the moral and spiritual foundations of order. In our own time Solzhenitsyn is engaged in the same task. His aim is to bring about the kind of repentance and regeneration that can form the basis of order when the weight of ideology has finally been lifted within Russia. On the most expansive scale, Voegelin's historical work has been directed toward the recovery of the full range of experiences and symbolisms that have created order in human existence.[35]

Little has been said about the institutional arrangements that best reflect this renewed foundation. All that is clear is that they will not follow the pattern of either doctrinaire socialism or doctrinaire capitalism. Solzhenitsyn has occasionally allowed his characters to argue for "ethical socialism." Shulubin, in *Cancer Ward*, argues for a social and political order in which "ethical demands must determine all considerations" (*CW*, 442). Dostoevsky's vision unfolded toward what he termed "Russian socialism" and defined as "an ecumenical Church on earth." Russia carried within itself, he was convinced, the seeds of this global reawakening that would be characterized by "a universal communion in the name of Christ" (*DW*, 1029). In the same way, Camus continued to incline toward socialism, as long as it remained faithful to its original moral inspiration. The relief of suffering and the rectification of injustice remain essential public goals, but they must not become an excuse for committing even greater crimes in the process. One can even find in Voegelin, probably the most politically conservative of the four, an endorsement of the pragmatic necessity of governmental intervention in defense of the most vulnerable members of society.

What seems to be largely absent from all four is a recognition that a spiritually grounded liberalism is the most appropriate expression of what they have in mind. While they do not explicitly embrace liberal democracy, I believe it can be shown that a rejuvenated liberalism is in fact what their prescriptions imply. The reason is their common conviction that "the moral doctrine of the value of the individual [is] the key to the solution of social problems" (*UR*, 271). To the objection that individual virtue is never sufficient to guarantee the best society or state—for that institutional change is necessary as well—Dostoevsky replied that the spiritual condition of individuals *is* the very substance of social and political order. "Individual self-betterment is not only 'the *beginning* of everything,' but also its continuation and outcome. It—and it alone—embraces, creates and preserves the national organism" (*DW*, 1001). The moral or spiritual ideal comes first and then its institutional expression, whereas any attempt to impose a more perfect social or political order without first bringing about an inner change of heart within individuals will result in vacuous hypocrisy or the even worse perversions we have seen. Structural reforms and improvements are always of lesser importance than individual moral growth. Moreover, the end point of all institutional change is the promotion of inner personal growth in community. Social and political order serves no other purpose than the human good.

When one follows this line of reflection one eventually arrives at a position equivalent to that of classical liberalism: government is there to serve the individual and not the other way around. The only difference is that this service toward the individual is meant in a more profound sense than the conventional restriction to the pursuit of pleasure and self-interest. It is service based on an understanding of the individual human good that includes as its highest realization service toward others and the common good. This is the only true exercise of liberty. This understanding is the source of the conviction that the priority of the individual and of individual freedom is the sine qua non for all other social and political goods. This defense of individual liberty and dignity is, in many respects, the central idea of Dostoevsky and of all who followed his struggle with the totalitarian spirit. For even if society were to become materially abundant for all, Camus observes, "if liberty does not reign there, it will still remain a barbarity" (*E*, 794). Camus goes on then to define his position in traditionally liberal terms. "The word of order for today, for all of us, can be none other than this: without ceding anything on the plane of justice, to abandon nothing on that of liberty" (*E*, 796).

Solzhenitsyn too displays a surprising degree of insight into the conditions for liberal democracy. This becomes apparent in the most extensive political discussion in his works, in the long historical chapter on Stolypin (*AUG* chap. 65). It was Stolypin, Solzhenitsyn argues, rather than any of the erstwhile reformers and revolutionaries, who had the most profound understanding of Russia's needs. As prime minister he sought not to block the movement to reform the autocracy, but to guide it toward a constitutional monarchy. His only purpose was to prevent the call for self-government from becoming a demand for unlimited revolution. The epitome of the constitutional statesman, he favored reform but understood the correlative necessity of firmness. He recognized that the introduction of popular self-government could lead only to disaster, unless the people and their leaders had first undergone the intellectual, economic, and political developments that were its prerequisites.

To this end Stolypin labored to free the Russian peasant from the oppression and irresponsibility of communal farming. "Stolypin's central idea was that it is impossible to introduce the rule of law until you have independent citizens, and in Russia those citizens would be peasants. 'Citizens first, then civil rights'" (*AUG*, 552). In the same way he understood the necessity of building mediating institutions between the people and the government, and the absolute necessity of building a tradition of self-government from the bottom up. This became his plan for regional and local *zemstvos* or assemblies. Stolypin even initiated many of the welfare-state protections for individuals who were unable to provide adequately for themselves. Without abandoning the monarchy, which had proved of such historic importance to Russia, he sought to create an ethos of constitutional self-government. The core of his program was the formation of free, independent citizens equipped with sufficient virtue to take responsibility for their common actions. In connection with this task Stolypin understood, as few modern leaders have, the indispensable role of the older spiritual traditions such as the Russian Orthodox church. "'To reform our way of life, without damage to the vital foundation of our state—the soul of the people'" (*AUG*, 582) was his abiding aim. The conclusion that is hard to resist after coming to the end of this long sympathetic account is that he embodies Solzhenitsyn's ideal of the true modern statesman. However much he may have been maligned as an enemy of liberalism, Stolypin was, in Solzhenitsyn's view, the one true friend of liberal constitutional reform in prerevolutionary Russia.

Something similar may be said of all the postmodern thinkers. However much they may reject the label of "liberal," these thinkers are contributing to the renovation of this earliest and most enduring modern political form. They are part of what Voegelin has referred to as "the transformation of liberalism under the pressure of historical events." The two aspects Voegelin singles out in this phenomenon are clearly the central thrust of the thinkers who have worked through the crisis of the modern world. The first is "the absorption of social-ethical demands into classical liberalism." Voegelin identifies the welfare-state sense of responsibility as an example of this, but it is surely also applicable to the recognition of the wider moral foundations of political order. The second phenomenon is "liberalism's becoming filled with Christian substance."[36] The anchoring of individual and political order in the movement toward transcendent reality is the most profound and most remarkable feature of postmodern political thought. These thinkers have advanced the process of moral and spiritual renewal so far that it does not seem to be an exaggeration to maintain that they have done more to rejuvenate liberalism than most of its ostensible defenders.

Under their inspiration, liberation can rediscover its own philosophic and Christian foundations. Historically, the determining factor in the success or failure of liberal democratic regimes has had little to do with the nature of the symbolism itself; instead, it has had to do with the persistence of moral and religious traditions within the society, outside of and often ignored by the public political order. To bring about a genuine revitalization, a more profound understanding of this relationship is required. The postmodern movement must in some sense recognize that liberalism is not only derivative, as a secularization of philosophic-Christian order, but is an authentic expression of the latter in its own right. Liberalism must be recognized as the most faithful reflection of an experience of order that arises from the primacy of personal spiritual growth. Freedom is the indispensable condition for this process of "individual self-betterment," and a political order based on persuasion and consent is the only means of promoting this goal. Liberalism is, in other words, not only a practical necessity in a pluralist society, but is fully consonant with a philosophic-Christian understanding of human nature and its destiny.[37]

At the same time, liberal political order is the form most likely to be cured of the modern preoccupation with a world-immanent salvation. For while classical liberal thinkers do contain strong overtones of a utopian perfection within history, their symbolism is not necessarily wedded to that perspective. They are close enough to the classical and Christian foundation in the individual soul, with its movement ultimately toward an eschatological transfiguration in eternity, to be readily able to recover this more open understanding of history. If, for example, each individual is an end-in-himself or -herself, infinitely worthwhile and incommensurate with every other individual, then it follows that no social goal outweighs the value of this concrete human life. For this reason no world-historic future can be regarded as taking precedence over the existence of the individual. When the person is thus recognized as the source from which order emanates into society and history, then the hold of all utopian collectivist constructions has been dissolved. But to ensure that this insight will not subsequently be overwhelmed by the fascination with a new ideological fulfillment of history, it must be strengthened through the elaboration of the philosophy of history implicitly contained within it.

The Order of History from the History of Order

Voegelin is almost alone in the concentration and effort he has devoted to the development of a philosophy of history. It may well be his single most important contribution to the restoration of order within our time, for it arises from his concern with tracing the nature of the disturbance to its roots. The other postmodern thinkers have been aware of the historical dimension of the problems. But they have not focused on the extent to which the modern disorder arises from an unbalancing historical perspective that reaches back beyond the advent of Christianity. Voegelin has understood the necessity of articulating the order of history, if the experience of the transcendent foundation of order is not to derail into dangerous apocalyptic expectations. As a consequence, he has identified the outlines of what is possibly the first global postmodern philosophy of history.

"The order of history emerges from the history of order" is the opening sentence of his inquiry, *Order and History*. It provides the basic principle of his study: that there is no order or meaning to history apart from the direction illuminated through the human struggle to realize order in existence. We are participants and cannot apprehend what lies outside of this partial perspective. We cannot grasp the meaning of reality as a whole because we do not stand outside of it; we do not possess the capacity to view the total process as a unity from beginning to end. For this reason our existence is always surrounded by mystery. Even when the eschatological direction of existence has been fully differentiated, and history is revealed as the dimension in which the attainment of or decline from order takes place, that remains the limiting horizon for finite human nature. No penetration beyond it as to how the final transfiguration will occur, or as to whether particular events do or do not signal the end, or as to how the multiple uncertainties of our lives will ultimately be answered, is possible. We can know neither the day nor the hour of our final deliverance. Our part is only to follow the pull of divine truth that reveals itself in the Between state of existence.

There is no meaning of history other than the process of differentiation that constitutes history itself. No privileged position is allotted to those who come later, because all alike are participants in the order of being and thereby aware of their responsibility to unfold the meaning of this truth. Human nature and the conditions of existence remain a constant (*OH* I, 60f.). All that changes is the degree of differentiation achieved concerning the truth of participation in divine order. Moreover, the attainment of differentiation does not render the earlier symbolizations obsolete. For the later formulations are more narrowly focused on the mutual participation of divine in human and human in divine reality, rather than on the embracing wholeness of all things in which this theophanic event occurs. The most comprehensive symbolizations continue to be the earliest. We never dispense with the primary experience of the cosmos as a Whole, the consubstantiality of the different partners in the community of being. It is simply that this must now be adjusted in accordance with the truth revealed in more differentiated experience.

They are equivalent experiences that can be related to one another on a scale of compactness and differentiation, without implying the definitive inferiority or superiority of either. For although the more differentiated experiences do represent an authorative advance in attunement to the order of divine being, they also include a heightening of tension that makes the fall from attunement more likely. At the same time, the more differentiated experiences can only be understood in relation to the compact horizon from which they have been elaborated. And for every advance there is the necessity of symbolizing the comprehensive process depicted in the earliest cosmological symbolisms. The essential feature of a philosophy of history, according to Voegelin, is the recognition that the various spiritual symbolisms represent the variety of human perspectives on the ineffable truth of being. Like the tolerance of the early symbolic profusion by the cosmological civilizations, the appropriate attitude is one of comprehensive openness to all. "Every concrete symbol is true in so far as it envisages the truth, but none is completely true in so far as the truth about being is essentially beyond human reach" (*OH* I, 7).

Even the most differentiated experience of Christianity represents no more than one perspective on reality. The opening toward being requires the inclusion of the full range of experiences and symbolizations that have constituted order in human history. Once we have recognized that there is no truth about reality apart from the truth becoming luminous through history, then we begin to realize the necessity of exploring the global extent of the human relationship with the divine (*OH* IV, 331–33). The search for order today requires a willingness to include the variety of ways in which God has revealed himself to us, beyond the strictly defined limits of the Judeo-Christian revelation. They are all unique and irreplaceable perspectives on "the depth of the riches and wisdom and knowledge of God" (Rom. 12:33). This is why Voegelin's recovery of order has extended to this universal empirical openness. Without reducing the various symbolic forms to a monistic uniformity or ignoring their integral differences, he has pursued the one divine truth manifested over the entire range from the Paleolithic cave drawings to our own literature of the absurd.[38] The theoretical basis for this inclusiveness is his conception of equivalences of experiences and symbols. They are all equivalent experiences of reality that can be related along a continuum of compactness and differentiation, the earlier being understood from the perspective of the later and the later deriving their context from the earlier. "In practice this means that one has to recognize, and make intelligible, the presence of Christ in a babylonian hymn, or a Taoist speculation,or a Platonic dialogue, just as much as in the Gospel."[39] It is in this sense that Voegelin was able to expand Plato's anthropological principle to declare: "History is Christ writ large."[40]

NOTES

1. Leo Strauss, "Jerusalem and Athens," *Studies in Platonic Political Philosophy*, ed. Thomas Pangle (Chicago: University of Chicago Press, 1983), 167. In "The Mutual Influence of Theology and Philosophy," *Independent Journal of Philosophy* 3 (1979):111–118, Strauss makes it clear that he regards philosophy and revelation as mutually exclusive and as equally grounded in a faith that cannot be rationally justified. He also dismisses a caricature of the argument of the present study, "that we need today, in order to compete with communism, revelation as a myth" (114). What Strauss does not seem to consider is the possibility that the very depth of the contemporary crisis may lead to a rediscovery of the truth of redemption. This is part of the larger problem alluded to in chapter 1, of Strauss's refusal to go beyond the level of doctrines to the experiences underlying them. For that reason he cannot transcend a largely formalist reading of the Bible as, at best, "a human interpretation of God's action" (114). He does not consider the possibility that Scripture may be *both* a human interpretation and an expression of divine presence. The human interpretation cannot, for example, extend to the construction of what has never been experienced, such as the Mosaic 'I AM.' For an interesting comparison between Strauss and Voegelin see James Rhodes, "Philosophy, Revelation and Political Theory: Leo Strauss and Eric Voegelin," *Journal of Politics* 49 (1987):1034–60.

2. To obtain a fuller appreciation of Voegelin's Christian orientation one should consult not only *The New Science of Politics*, but also the letter to Alfred Shutz written at about the same time. See "On Christianity," *The Philosophy of Order*, ed. Peter J. Opitz and Gregor Sebba (Stuttgart: Klett-Cotta, 1981), 449–57. Important for the later period of his writings is Voegelin's essay "The Gospel and Culture."

3. Voegelin provides an interesting discussion of this whole problem in "On Debate and Existence," *Intercollegiate Review* 3 (1967):143–52. A parallel approach is developed by Claes Ryn, *Will, Imagination and Reason* (Chicago: Regnery, 1986).

4. "The commands are not general rules of conduct but the substance of divine order to be absorbed by the souls of those who listen to the call. . . . It is framed by the first and tenth commandments with their injunctions against the antitheistic rebellion of pride and the antihuman rebellion of envy. Between the two protective dams, in the middle, can move the order of the people through the rhythm of time. Through the articulation of the divine will into the commandments of the Decalogue Moses, indeed, has given Israel its constitution as the people under God in historical existence" (*OH* I, 426, 427).

5. "The man of the archaic societies tends to live as much as possible *in* the sacred or in close proximity to consecrated objects. The tendency is perfectly understandable, because, for primitives as for the man of all pre-modern societies, the *sacred* is equivalent to a *power*, and, in the last analysis, to *reality*. The sacred is saturated with *being*. Sacred power means reality and at the same time enduringness and efficacy. The polarity sacred-profane is often expressed as an opposition between *real* and *unreal* or *psuedoreal*." Mircea Eliade, *The Sacred and the Profane*, trans. Willard R. Trask (New York: Harcourt, Brace, 1959), 12–13. See also Eliade, *Myths, Dreams and Mysteries: The Encounter between Contemporary Faiths and Archaic Reality*, trans. P. Mairet (New York: Harper & Row, 1961).

6. Henri Bergson, *The Two Sources of Morality and Religion*, trans. R. Ashley Audra and Cloudesley Brereton (New York: Doubleday, 1932), especially 310–11, on "counterfeit mysticism."

7. Quoted in Sandoz, *Voegelinian Revolution*, 172.

8. Bergson, *Two Sources*, 233.

9. See chapter 2.

10. Voegelin, "Immortality: Experience and Symbol," 267.

11. Voegelin's relationship to Christianity has been an increasingly controversial issue ever since the publication of *The Ecumenic Age* (vol. 4 of *Order and History*). For some

representative samples of this debate see F. D. Wilhelmsen, "Review: The Ecumenic Age," *Triumph* (January, 1975):32–35; Gerhart Niemeyer, "Eric Voegelin's Philosophy and the Drama of Mankind," *Modern Age* 20 (1976):28–39; Bruce Douglass, "A Diminished Gospel: A Critique of Voegelin's Interpretation of Christianity," in *Eric Voegelin's Search for Order in History*, ed. Stephen A. McKnight (Baton Rouge: Louisiana State University Press, 1978); 139–54. My own contribution to this continuing debate is to be found in "Voegelin's Response to the Disorder of the Age," *Review of Politics* 46 (1984):266–87.

12. Solzhenitsyn, "'Men Have Forgotten God'."

13. See for example his "Lenten Letter" to Patriarch Pimen (1972) in Dunlop, Haugh, and Klimoff, *Aleksandr Solzhenitsyn*; 550–56; or his "Letter to the Third Council of the Russian Church Abroad" (1974) in Nielsen, *Solzhenitsyn's Religion*, 142–58.

14. Billington, *Icon and Axe*, chaps. 1–2.

15. Robert Slesinski, *Pavel Florensky: A Metaphysics of Love* (Crestwood, NY: St. Vladimir's Seminary Press, 1984).

16. Korsakov even went as far as suggesting that "there are grounds for regarding Tolstoy's worldly moralism, so pure and unselfish compared to my own, as one of the sources of Russian revolutionary philosophy, with its demand for the immediate establishment of goodness on earth" (*UR*, 161).

17. Solzhenitsyn, "Letter to Third Council," 147.

18. See Evgeny Barbanov's "The Schism between the Church and the World," *Under the Rubble*, 172–93. Solzhenitsyn understands well the dangers of a wholly spiritualized religion. It plays exactly into the hands of a state that insists, "You can pray *freely* / but just so God alone can hear" (*GA* I, 37).

19. Solzhenitsyn, "Letter to Third Council," 148.

20. Solzhenitsyn, "Lenten Letter," 554–55.

21. Solzhenitsyn, "Letter to Third Council," 151.

22. Ibid., 152, 157.

23. Even Locke, who tries to base his argument for toleration on the futility of compelling religious conviction, cannot avoid suggesting that the real reason is because no one can know which doctrines are true and which are false. "There is only one of these which is the true way to eternal happiness; but in this great variety of ways that men follow, it is still doubted which is the right one." *A Letter Concerning Toleration* (Indianapolis: Bobbs-Merrill, 1955), 31.

24. Voegelin's philosophy of consciousness is to be found scattered throughout his work. Among the most significant landmarks are the 1943 essay "On the Theory of Consciousness" and the later "Remembrance of Things Past," both in *Anamnesis*; much of *The Ecumenic Age* and virtually all of *In Search of Order* are concerned with problems of the philosophy of consciousness. A helpful informal guide is O'Conner, *Conversations with Eric Voegelin*.

25. "Reality, it is true, can move into the position of an object-of-thought intended by a subject-of-cognition, but before this can happen there must be a reality in which human beings with a consciousness occur. . . . In brief, man's conscious existence is an event within reality, and man's consciousness is quite conscious of being constituted by the reality of which it is conscious. The intentionality is a substructure within the comprehensive consciousness of a reality that becomes luminous for its truth in the consciousness of man," writes Voegelin, (*AN*, 10–11).

26. Mikhail Bakhtin explains the polyphonic nature of Dostoevsky's writing as "the principle of seeing and understanding the world and its formulation from the viewpoint of a given idea only for the characters, not for the author himself, not for Dostoevsky. . . . It is not a world of objects, illuminated and ordered by his monological thinking, that unrolls before Dostoevsky, but a world of mutually illuminating consciousness. . . . He searches among them for the highest, most authoritative orientation, and he thinks of it not as his own true thought, but as another person and his world. The image of the ideal man or the image of Christ represents for him the

solution of ideological quests. This image or this highest of voices must crown the world of voices." Bakhtin, *Problems of Dostoevsky's Poetics*, trans. R. W. Rotsel (Ann Arbor: Ardis, 1973), 20, 90. See also Robert Louis Jackson, *Dostoevsky's Quest for Form: A Study of His Philosophy of Art* (New Haven: Yale University Press, 1966); idem, *The Art of Dostoevsky* (Princeton: Princeton University Press, 1981). For a comparison between Dostoevsky and Solzhenitsyn along these lines see V. Krasnov, *Solzhenitsyn and Dostoevsky: A Study in the Polyphonic Novel* (Athens: University of Georgia Press, 1980).

27. Voegelin has occasionally acknowledged that speculative metaphysics performs the same role in a more abstract or conceptual fashion, although his preference is for the more concrete symbolism of myth. "Plato deliberately resorts to myths where another philosopher would use the instruments of speculation. One may well assume that he did this knowing that fundamentally it makes no difference in which system of symbols experiences of transcendence are expressed; possibly also because he felt that the myth is a more precise instrument for communicating the psychic excitement of the experience of transcendence, more precise than speculation, even though it is an instrument which not everybody can handle safely" (*AN*, 22). It has often been observed, however, that in following this Platonic preference Voegelin himself sacrifices some of the conceptual rigor that has been achieved in the history of philosophy. His own distinction between transcendent and immanent being, for example, might be made more precise through reference to Aquinas's distinction between essence and existence. Then it could be made clear that God is the only reality whose essence is identical with its being (*Summa Theologiae* I, Q.3, art. 4).

28. It need scarcely be emphasized that Voegelin has not said the last word on these issues. There are many other dimensions omitted entirely from his discussion. The Church in its entire sacramental life is, for example, an indispensable means of representing the redemptive transfiguration of reality within the Metaxy or Between state of existence.

29. For example, in the *Laws*, *Critias*, and *Statesman*.

30. The necessity of symbolizing this process of transfiguration within the world of human activity is clearly being increasingly recognized in Christian theology today. A recent significant example is the effort of John Paul II to develop a "creation theology" to articulate the co-creative character of human labor as it operates on the world in which it finds itself. See his encyclicals *Redemptor Hominis* (1979), *Dives in Misericordia* (1980), *Laborem Exercens* (1981), and *Solicitudo Rei Socialis* (1987), and the *Pastoral Constitution on the Church in the Modern World* (1965) from the Second Vatican Council.

31. As we have seen in chapter 1, the difficulty lies less in knowing what is concretely right or virtuous, than in apprehending the rightness of such universal inner intimations.

32. Liberal democracy is certainly the favorite alternative of many Soviet dissidents, including Andrei Sakharov. See his *Progress, Coexistence and Intellectual Freedom* (New York: Norton, 1968), and Solzhenitsyn's critique, "As Breathing and Consciousness Return," in *Under the Rubble*, 3–25. On their whole relationship see Donald R. Kelley, *The Solzhenitsyn-Sakharov Dialogue* (Westport, CT: Greenwood Press, 1982).

33. See also Solzhenitsyn, *Letter to the Soviet Leaders*, trans. Hilary Sternberg (New York: Harper & Row, 1974).

34. "How many dozens of years—five? six? seven?—must one have lived," Varsonofiev asks, reflecting on the Russian liberal revolutionaries, "in order to understand that the life of a society cannot be reduced to the political and not exhausted by institutions? The time in which we live is a well without a bottom. The contemporary is no more than a piece of fluff on the surface of time" (*OCT*, chap. 73; 551). A similar perspective is masterfully developed in the short story "Matryona's House" in Solzhenitsyn, *Stories and Prose Poems*, trans. Michael Glenny (Harmondsworth: Penguin, 1973).

35. Other studies that have focused on the foundational political role of these thinkers include: Ellis Sandoz, *Political Apocalypse* (Baton Rouge: Louisiana State University

Press, 1971) and the same author's "Philosophical Dimensions of Dostoevsky's Politics," *Journal of Politics* 40 (1978):648–74; Edward E. Ericson, Jr., *Solzhenitsyn's Moral Vision* (Grand Rapids: Eerdmans, 1980); Fred H. Willhoite, Jr., *Beyond Nihilism: Albert Camus's Contribution to Political Thought* (Baton Rouge: Louisiana State University Press, 1968); Barry Cooper, *The Political Theory of Eric Voegelin* (Lewiston/NY: Edwin Mellen Press, 1986); Dante Germino, "Eric Voegelin's Framework for Political Evaluation in His Recently Published Work," *American Political Science Review* 72 (1978):110–21; Brendan Purcell, "Solzhenitsyn's Struggle for Personal, Social and Historic Anamnesis," *Philosophical Studies* 28 (1981):62–88; and my own "Dostoevsky's Discovery of the Christian Foundation of Politics," *Religion and Literature* 19 (1987):49–72.

36. Voegelin, "Liberalism and Its History," *Review of Politics* 36 (1972):520.

37. A reevaluation of liberal democracy along these lines has, for example, occurred within the Catholic church. From an earlier era in which liberalism was regarded as the archetypical enemy of Christianity, the church moved to embrace liberal democracy as politically (if not economically) closest to its own understanding of true human freedom. The change was clearly marked in *Mater et Magistra* (1961) which asserted "that individual men are necessarily the foundation, cause and end of all social institutions" (par. 219). Equally decisive was the Second Vatican Council's *Declaration on Religious Liberty* (1965). Behind this shift of attitude by the church lay the writings of such political theorists as Jacques Maritain and John Courtney Murray.

38. A similar openness to the diversity of spiritual forms is expressed by Fr. Severin in *October 1916*: "Divine truth, it is like the Mother-Truth of popular legend. When seven brothers went to see it, they saw it from seven different sides, under seven different aspects and, on returning, everyone gave a different account" (chap. 6, 74).

39. Voegelin, "Response to Professor Altizer's 'A New History and a New But Ancient God,'" in *Eric Voegelin's Thought: A Critical Appraisal*, ed. Ellis Sandoz (Durham, NC: Duke University Press, 1982), 191.

40. Voegelin, "Immortality: Experience and Symbol," 267. Voegelin provides an excellent illustration of how the Christian differentiation provides the viewpoint that radiates its light over the entire history of the human struggle for order. He uses the Christian symbolism to illuminate the meaning of the Platonic, as he explains Plato's treatment of the movements beyond the Between state of existence. "The movements, then, are not indifferently equal but distinguished in their meaning as (a) a movement toward a state of existence from which 'as it were, God is absent' (*Timaeus* 53B) or (b) an immortalizing movement toward likeness (*homoiosis*) with God" (*OH* V, 106). This is a clarification of the Platonic text that could only be made from the perspective of the Christian differentiations of the utter transcendence of God and the eschatological fulfillment of human existence.

CHAPTER 6

Beyond the Crisis of Modernity

The question with which our study leaves us is whether this rediscovery of the transcendent foundation of order can extend beyond the experience of a few remarkable individuals. Does it contain implications for the larger order of Western civilization? Can it form the basis for a renewal of the spiritual traditions within our contemporary secular world? Is there a possibility of the wider rediscovery of the roots of moral and political order in the nihilistic wasteland of our age? Has the crisis of modernity been surmounted? Or are we merely witnessing the resurgence of a private experience of faith? The question of the representative significance of such experiences is not only the one on which the conclusion of this book turns. It is also the question on which the fate of the modern world depends. From the beginning our study has operated on the premise that the experience of individuals who have undergone the catharsis of the modern world entails this wider significance. Now we must consider the likelihood of this suggestion's becoming more concretely effective.

The basis for the expectation of relevance is that the postmodern thinkers have discovered the truth of philosophy and Christianity *within* the modern world. They have not been antiquarians or devotees of a long forgotten past. Instead they have been thoroughly modern human beings who have participated fully in the events and movements of their time. The crises and sufferings that their age has undergone have been the very ones lived out in their personal lives. Their rediscovery of traditional spiritual wisdom has not come through abstract argument or scholarly erudition, although such instruments can later be put to good use in its elaboration. It has first been a truth discovered in the furnace of experience. What makes their recovery of philosophy and

Christianity an act of originality is that they have rediscovered these ancient symbolisms not only as a historical tradition, but also as a living answer to the problems of order in the modern world. What distinguishes the postmodern thinkers as a group is their capacity to comprehend the meaning of philosophic Christianity as the truth of the modern world. They have made this discovery in the depth of the abyss. But whether their insight will be recognized by the world as its own truth is the question that remains open.

The ultimate determination of the answer to this question lies not in the realm of discussion but of action. The question of whether we have moved into a postmodern era can finally only be decided by the response that we as a civilization make to what has happened. This is what will decide whether the thinkers we have examined represent the beginning of a renewed civilizational order or are merely an epiphenomenal blip within the long protracted process of spiritual exhaustion. All that can be explored at this point are the conditions for a spiritual and political restoration of order along the lines indicated by the postmodern experience. That is the subject of this chapter, which is divided into two sections, as suggested by the two phases involved in such a reorientation. First is the line of meditative reflection that must be followed in order to bring about this type of profound redirection of perspective within modern civilization. Second is the fundamental change of public or political forms that would arise from the implementation of a postmodern *Weltanschauung*. What would it mean to live in a social and political order that had contemplated the abyss and freed itself from the horrible fascination, yet had not simply turned its back on the essential features and real achievements of the modern world? A brief concluding section offers some final reflections on the prospects for such a transformation.

Repentance

The Cathartic Release from Ideology

The logic of the postmodern experience suggests the necessity of undergoing some form of cathartic release. Modernity is a spirit or a frame of mind so deeply embedded within us that we can break free from its influence only with great difficulty. An event or process of shattering impact seems to be virtually required if we are to get a glimpse of reality beyond our restricted contemporary horizon. Having been enveloped by the climate of opinion for such a long unthinking time, we need to be roughly shaken into an awareness of reality. If the nightmare of the twentieth century has been the result of this dreamlike condition, then a powerful shock is required to rouse us into a state of wakefulness. Like Koestler's sleepwalkers, we need a penetrating experience to pierce our somnambulance. It is not so much a question of knowing about an alternative to the closed rationality of modernity, but of apprehending the truth of that alternative so profoundly that it makes all our previous sense of reality appear ephemeral.

The necessity of such a profound reawakening seems all the greater when one realizes the extent to which history is littered with attempts to overcome the crisis of modernity. Tragically, the vast majority of these attempts succeeded only in deepening that very crisis. From Descartes to Kant to Hegel to Marx and Nietzsche, the story has been the same. A real sensitivity to the impossibility of sustaining an order based on a rational critique has given rise to well-intentioned efforts to provide what is missing. But the results have turned out to be quite other than expected. The attempt to restore spiritual substance to a civilization that has lost it, has more often than not been eclipsed by the libidinous desire to dominate reality as a whole. Instead of the intended rediscovery of spiritual truth on a new foundation, there is the vain and empty contrivance of comprehending reality within a system. We have not succeeded in breaking free of the conceit that order can be erected on the basis of our autonomous reason. The infection of modernity, the dream of living within the parameters of the closed self, has overpowered the longing to live in contact with reality beyond it.

A cathartic experience is needed, therefore, not only to shake us from our complacent ignorance, but also to ensure that we finally break free from the prevailing worldview. For this purpose it is essential to confront all the implications of the modern impulse. All of the possibilities contained within the humanist experiment of an autonomous rational order must be unfolded and recognized for what they are. Nothing can be left unexplicated or unexamined if we wish to reach a clear understanding of the problems. Only by drawing out all that is contained in the modern experience can we have any real possibility of going beyond it. Not to make too much of the Hegelian dialectic, there is nevertheless a certain sense to his insistence that an era of history can never be completed until it has brought forth all that is contained within its idea. Only in this way can we be sure that we are not embracing one more form of the tired rationalist dream in our own restorative efforts. The criterion that must guide our search is a profound awareness of the abyss opened up by the modern crisis. For it is only by firmly contemplating the full extent of the problem that we can have any hope of attaining the spiritual truth that overcomes it, and not merely add one more symptom to the monotonous course of the disease. This has been the guiding principle of this book.

But now the question will inevitably be raised whether everyone is required to go through the experiences of a Solzhenitsyn or a Camus. Is there no other way than through suffering the hardships of totalitarian imprisonment? The answer, of course, is yes. There are many other ways toward the same discovery. What is important about each of them is that they share the sense of undergoing a catharsis, of dissolving the true inner imprisonment that affects all of us in whatever society we happen to be. That requires our acknowledgment of the full extent of the modern catastrophe: we have dreamed a dream and created a nightmare. Now the connection between them must be admitted. Mere senseless suffering is never sufficient to bring about this change; many who were imprisoned in the camps did not respond to the invitation to ascend. What is required is the suffering of repentance that leads toward self-illumination and the recognition of our own responsibility for the dehumanization of our world. The evil we witness within our century is not the result of some individual or incidental failings along the way. It is the integral consequence of the kind of modern civilization we have all had a hand in making. And with the decline of this century's worst ideological excesses, the great danger is that we will too easily overlook the extent to which we have all been affected by the disease. Already the sound of self-congratulation is in the air.

That is the great significance of the postmodern thinkers. For they are the ones who have most completely resisted the temptation to regard themselves as superior to the spirit of the age. Solzhenitsyn has made a call for repentance the central theme of his struggle to create a new order. Without a full and open acknowledgment of what has happened and an honest expression of sorrow for our own responsibility within it, we have not succeeded in getting beyond the present destructive condition. He points out that the only regret among the post-Stalin generation of leaders in the Soviet Union was that the great purges had also included the imprisonment of Communists. No expression of repentance for the gulag archipelago as a whole, nor any attempt to prosecute those most directly responsible for its horror, has yet taken place. There has not even been any repentance for collaboration with the long-defamed Nazi regime. "When did so much generally recognized villainy escape judgment and punishment?" Even in the West with its Nuremberg Trials, repentance has been incomplete. It has not extended to the

West's own responsibility for the emergence of the totalitarian foe, or the acknowledgment of its own guilt in consigning the two million repatriated Soviet citizens to almost certain death at the end of the war. "Why should we expect anything good to come of it?" Solzhenitsyn asks. "What can grow out of this stinking corruption?" (*GA* III, 468).[1]

That is the question that forces itself upon us today. If we are serious about overcoming the impasse at which we have arrived, then we must be prepared to take the full measure of the disaster we have reaped. Totalitarianism and liberalism are not two utterly different worlds. They are twin dimensions of the one modern civilization. The catharsis that Camus and Solzhenitsyn have gone through in their own lives is not a purely personal affair. It is a microcosm of the cathartic evolution of modern Western history since the Renaissance. To reach the same realization as they have it is merely necessary to contemplate fully the course of that history as the unfolding of a constant and intensifying anthropocentrism. This does not require any unusual degree of historical imagination, since we are living at a time when the course of the modern world has reached its denouement. All that is demanded of us is an open recognition of the horrors that have taken place and of their integral relationship to the history that has produced them. The catharsis consists in acknowledging the connection between the ideas and their dehumanizing consequences. It is interesting to note that the postmodern thinkers surmounted their own personal crises only through the elaboration of its wider civilizational significance.

The process that is occurring in reality must be brought to its conclusion, through the exposure of the moral bankruptcy of all ideological forms of thought. No shred of an excuse must be left to disguise their responsibility for the enormity of evil they have wrought within our time. We owe it at least to the millions of victims of Communism, Nazism, and fascism to resolve that their murderers will not have the last word on their deaths. They did not die as a result of historical necessity or because of the requirements of one or another version of humanitarian perfection. They must not be allowed to sink into forgetful oblivion. Rather they must be recognized as a sacrificial holocaust on the altar of human self-aggrandizement. Their deaths must become the symbol of or testament to the impossibility of achieving human happiness through the exercise of absolute power.[2] If such disasters have been necessary to cure us finally of the dreams of unlimited power in the service of humanity, as seems to be the case, then let the lesson not be lost. We must not shrink from the recollection of our recent horrendous past. It must be confronted and contemplated, and allowed to work its inescapable effect on souls not entirely closed to the suffering inflicted on our own.

Yet we cannot afford to languish in guilt or self-pity or even in exchanging recriminations. That in itself can become an escape or diversion from our true responsibilities. If we do indeed wish to repent and reform, then we must continue to reflect on how such unlimited cruelty and misery could have happened. We must not seek to excuse the appalling inhumanity on the basis of individual or national characteristics. Responsibility must be firmly allocated to the ideas that gave rise to such movements. For it must be admitted that the abrogation of all moral restraints occurred first in the realm of thought; the wholesale extermination of historically retrograde peoples was no more than an application of the accepted intellectual principles. No collapse or incomprehension of the original inspiration was involved. Through absorption of the world-transformative messianic role, humanity had attained a position of such dominance that good and evil were henceforth to be determined by it alone. The staggering political arrogance we have seen was preceded by an equally astonishing spiritual megalomania. One has only to think of Hegel's incorporation of God within his system of science, Marx's Promethean hatred of all gods that deny human "self-creation," Comte's apocalypse of humanity within his Religion of Humanity, and Nietzsche's titanic overman who proceeds from the murder of God.

The fruit of this "egophanic revolt" (*OH* IV, 260) is fully recognized when one realizes that the scale of twentieth-century destruction would not have been possible without this grandiose rationalization. No matter how much human beings may assert that we are the beginning and end of our own existence, that we are capable of giving a law unto ourselves (*Z*, 63), we know that the ground of our existence remains beyond ourselves. The deception can only be sustained with the aid of an elaborate system of concealment. We can still not flagrantly engage in evil. It must be couched within the language of idealism, and the more awful the evil the more intense is the concern with its legitimation. Few more telling demonstrations of the universality of the knowledge of good and evil can be conceived than this "compliment" of hypocrisy on a grand scale that vice pays to virtue. Nor can one imagine a more profound illustration of the impact of ideas on our world. But therein too lies one of the most potent weapons of resistance, as Solzhenitsyn discovered, in the struggle against the deformation of existence. The elaborate systematic framework that is apparently the great strength of an ideological regime is at the same time the location of its greatest weakness.

The very elaborateness of a regime's intellectual camouflage reveals the awareness of its deepest insecurity. Violence, Solzhenitsyn discovered, soon "loses confidence in itself, and in order to maintain a respectable face it summons falsehood as its ally" (DOC, 376). We are incapable of doing evil without finding some excuse by which to comfort and reassure ourselves of its rightness. That is why the most effective means of opposition to violence is to resist and undermine the lies that are its foundation. "Live not by lies" is the core of Solzhenitsyn's appeal to all of us, if we wish to break the vicious circle in which "violence can conceal itself with nothing except lies, and the lies can be maintained only by violence" (DOC, 376). Even those who are powerless in every other way still have the capacity to refuse to participate in lies, and few courses of action have a more devastating effect on the perpetrators of evil. We can all refuse to collaborate in violence at least to this extent. That is the point at which our personal ascent from the gulag of ideology begins. By starting with the lies of which we are aware, we distinguish truth from falsehood, and gradually the realm of reality expands at the expense of the realm of delusion. When the two are juxtaposed against one another, the Grand Inquisitor and Christ, the power of violence and false humanitarianism melts away.

The thinkers we have examined have shown how a successful resistance to the ideological extreme of modernity can be mounted. They have succeeded through their willingness to pursue problems to their final conclusion. All of them have shared Solzhenitsyn's conviction that "there are no loopholes for anybody who wants to be honest" (DOC, 378). By refusing to stop halfway, they have succeeded in reaching the reality of humanity's true participation in divine being, the reality so grotesquely distorted within the eschatological activism of revolution. Men and women of faith have always been anathema to the founders and dispensers of ideology; they call into question the premise of human omnipotence on which the messianic project is based. But what of individuals who have also established the connection between religion and the political order? They have shown that it is the love of Christ that ultimately provides the resource by which evil is overcome, and that the ideological professions of humanitarianism are but a false substitute for this reality. Not only is Marxism "the opiate of the intellectuals," but even worse—it is their religion! Through their own passage from ideology to philosophy and Christianity, the postmodern thinkers have condemned the totalitarians out of their own mouths. They have shown that for anyone who cares about the welfare of human beings, and who no longer wishes to compromise with deception and violence, the path leads infallibly toward the care for the inner person most fully manifested in Christ.

The Responsibility of Liberalism Acknowledged

This response is in marked contrast to what has generally emerged from within the liberal camp, with its ostensible commitment to the defense of human rights. The West, curiously, had to await Solzhenitsyn's *Gulag Archipelago* before it began to treat Stalin's regime with the same disdain reserved for the Nazi Holocaust. Even after the West had briefly roused itself to indignation at this exposition of the scale of Communist cruelty, it soon slipped back into its previous state of comfortable somnolence. And the mood turned distinctly sour when Solzhenitsyn suggested that the same spiritual problems might presently afflict the West as well.[3] In this pattern of fitfulness, indifference, and hostility we can discern the uneasy awareness of Western co-responsibility for the disasters that have overtaken our world. We have become so acclimated to the language of two worlds, from the demands for "unconditional surrender" to the rigidities of the Cold War, that we fail to recognize that liberalism and totalitarianism are aspects of the same world. The one modern world is manifested within each of them. One could not be without the other. They needed their mutual opposition not only for self-identification, but also and more important, for self-affirmation. For it was through their opposition that they mutually affirmed the criteria by which their achievements were to be measured, and therefore the ultimate source from which they derived their legitimacy. In each case this turned out to be little more than the satisfaction of material wants and desires.

In the West there is not only the guilt arising from the failure to resist the military advances of totalitarianism, whether fascist, national socialist, or Communist, but also the deeper historical responsibility of liberalism that spawned the revolutionary movements. A Western susceptibility toward short-term compromises, even a willingness to sacrifice the lives of millions of others rather than disturb one's own tranquillity, and the persistent refusal to respond to the call for national self-sacrifice required by our international responsibilities, are all familiar components of the pattern. They do not arise by accident. Rather they are a consistent reflection of the underlying spiritual uncertainty at the root of modern liberalism. We have found it difficult to mount a principled critique of or opposition to the secular messianic movements because liberalism itself is based on just such an aspiration toward utopian abundance and fulfillment.[4] Only liberalism does not pursue this end through revolution, but through the infinitely more successful means of capitalism and technological innovation. Indeed, we are no longer sure if we even have any moral principles from which to reproach the abuses of totalitarian regimes. The impetus of liberalism toward the privatization of all moral principles has effectively removed them from the arena of rational public debate. As private subjective opinions they are all equally valuable, and equally valueless.

We earlier observed the capacity of liberalism to recover and deepen its genuinely spiritual roots, but here we should dwell on the ever-present contrary tendency toward spiritual vacuity. Something of the shock that the eruption of totalitarian regimes caused for liberalism can be detected in the responses that began in the 1930s. It was the point when liberal democracies first realized they were without moral or spiritual defenses against this demonically powerful foe. T. S. Eliot's *The Idea of a Christian Society* is a fairly representative expression of the need to restore the spiritual foundations of liberalism. He speaks for "the many persons who, like myself, were deeply shaken by the events of September 1938, in a way from which one does not recover; perhaps to whom that month brought a profounder realization of a general plight." Eliot goes on to reveal the feeling of humiliation, of a need for contrition, and of a failure beyond any errors of government. It cast "a doubt about the validity of a civilization."

We could not match conviction with conviction, we had no ideas with which we could meet or oppose the ideas opposed to us. Was our society, which had always been so assured of its superiority and rectitude, so confident of its unexamined premises, assembled around anything more permanent than a congeries of banks, insurance companies and industries, and had it any beliefs more essential than a belief in compound interest and the maintenance of dividends?[5]

Almost for the first time, liberal thinkers began to become aware of the inherent weakness of their symbolism. Nowadays the necessity of providing a defense of liberal democracy has become commonplace. We are inclined to forget that the recognition of the need to shore up its foundations is of very recent vintage. John Stuart Mill, in his famous *Essay on Liberty*, was concerned mainly with the dangers to individual freedom, especially freedom of expression, arising from the conformist social pressures within a mass democracy. His celebrated "principle of liberty," that we are justified in interfering with the liberty of an individual only to prevent harm to others, strikes us in retrospect as amazingly one-sided even for an essay. Some critics have charged that Mill's formulation of liberty is even compatible with a despotic form of government. Certainly there is no shared conception of the highest human good as the unifying basis for Mill's society; the highest values are a commitment to the undefined goal of progress conceived as the product of unfettered freedom of exploration. The core conception of human dignity and rights is anchored not in the spiritual nature of human beings, but in an appeal to utilitarianism and individual whim. Freedom of expression is justified as instrumentally necessary to the achievement of progress and as integral to human self-realization. It is not because human beings are ends-in-themselves. We have had our sensitivity to the consequences of dehumanizing ideas heightened by the events of this century, but it does not lessen the obtuseness of liberal political thought. With Mill we observe how the most respected exponent of liberalism in its contemporary form could provide the ammunition with which to wipe out the conception of the infinite dignity and worth of the person. Since Mill there has been no consensus as to why liberals should be defenders of human rights.[6]

What has become clear, however, is the continuity between liberalism and the revolutionary ideological movements. Solzhenitsyn alluded to this in his identification of their common derivation from Renaissance humanism, the ideologies being only a more consistent unfolding of the principle of humanity's absolute autonomy. Others, including Voegelin, have traced the lines of influence that emanate from the Enlightenment and find their terminus in the era of revolutions.[7] Radical Enlightenment liberals, disciples of Locke such as Helvétius, D'Alembert, Condorcet, and Turgot, display a remarkable insensitivity to the loss of the inner spiritual worth of the person. Helvétius cheerfully reduces human nature to a pleasure-pain mechanism that can be reliably manipulated by a skillful legislator. By this means he predicts the emergence of an harmonious utilitarian utopia. Turgot formulates the concept of our membership in the *masse totale* as determinative of our individual significance, while D'Alembert and Condorcet conceive the purpose of human existence wholly in terms of functional goals. Rousseau provides the capstone to this generation of hollow men by most thoroughly evacuating all moral constraints on human action. His identification of good with the objects desired by the "general will" leaves no independent measure of right and wrong.[8] Voegelin shows that the contents of the nineteenth-century ideological systems had all emerged in the Enlightenment; all that needed to be added was the will to work a revolutionary transformation through their resolute imposition on reality.

Even the more moderate strand of liberalism in the English-speaking world, which had remained open to the classical and Christian mediation of order, has progressively followed the same reductionistic decline. Human beings are treated less and less as free moral agents, capable of guiding their own actions in the light of eternal truth within them and deriving their dignity from this ultimate responsibility for self-determination. Instead, each is seen as a conglomeration of disorderly impulses without a ruling principle. He or she is incapable of relating to others except through the assertion of subjective claims against them or on the haphazard basis of his or her own private whims. Government then serves no other role than the maintenance of external order among such chaotic, atomistic individuals. Among the many ways this deterioration can be documented, perhaps none is more startling than the strange concatenation of opinions within the writings of the most influential American jurist of the century, Justice Oliver Wendell Holmes.

Despite the wisdom he displayed in upholding New Deal legislation aimed at the worst abuses of industrialization, he could furnish no adequate explanation as to why human beings should be thus defended or accorded such rights. For Holmes there was "no meaning in the rights of men except what the crowd will fight for," in much the same way as "a dog will fight for his bone." He freely admitted that he could find "no reason for attributing to man a significance different in kind from that which belongs to a baboon or to a grain of sand."[9] Under such a conception, government reduces to the raw exercise of power by which it bows to the will of the strongest segment, as the only means of ensuring the emergence of order. "What proximate test of excellence can be found except correspondence to the actual equilibrium of force in the community—that is, conformity to the wishes of the dominant power? Of course, such conformity may lead to destruction, and it is desirable that the dominant power should be wise. But wise or not, the proximate test of a good government is that the dominant power has its way."[10] There is neither the possibility nor the necessity for an appeal to the higher justice present within the human soul as the principle of order.

It is not surprising therefore that the succeeding history of constitutional interpretation in the United States—and in the other liberal democracies—has progressively stripped away all connection with the inner spiritual order of the soul. Virtually no hint of awareness survives that government has a positive duty to promote the kind of virtuous development that is its own foundation. Only out of this lack of awareness could American jurists reach the conclusion that the anti-establishment clause of the First Amendment required an attitude of militant neutrality toward all public expressions of religion. Jefferson's unfortunate metaphor of a "wall of separation" between church and state was magnified into an absolute barrier against government aid to religion in any form, no matter how nondiscriminatory the basis. By also relying heavily on Madison's even more idiosyncratic attitude toward religion, the Supreme Court has adopted a separationist position directly contrary to what almost all the other authors of the First Amendment sought to produce. It is now, for example, not only impossible to provide aid to religiously affiliated schools, but also no concessions can be made to the cause of religion through setting aside time for instruction, prayer, or even silence. This situation has generated the even more ludicrous attempts by textbook publishers to sanitize all references to religious faith in their recounting of the American experience! The drive toward a "secular state" is indeed so irresistible that the fundamentalist objections against the establishment of "secular humanism" as a religion seem to have some merit.[11]

The situation is, however, even more curious still. At the same time that the Court has been working to block all official encouragement of religion, it has been exalting the rights of private conscience under the free-exercise clause to new heights. As long as religious belief steps forward in the name of pure subjective self-assertion, then it can be permitted wide latitude. The Court has even been prepared to occasionally suspend the normal operation of the laws, rather than find itself accused of stymieing such expressions of liberty (as in the case of exceptions to compulsory school attendance laws). The outcome for religion has, as might be expected, not been the most favorable. An inevitable consequence is the reaffirmation of the utterly private status of religion within a liberal democracy, which makes it absolutely clear that faith has no authoritative foundation and thus no basis for exercising public influence. This impression is dramatized by the kind of "free exercise" that is invariably permitted. "Belief will be left to the private conscience," Walter Berns observes, "and one effect of this will be to exalt the belief that is idiosyncratic, resting solely on the individual will, which in turn rests on the passions, not, as orthodox Christianity or Judaism would have it, on the will of a providential God."[12]

In one area after another we see the same pressures at work. The right to individual liberty has become the club with which to bludgeon not only all possible limitations on freedom, but every principle on which such restraints might be based as well. Individuals have become pure claimants in their relationship to the public authority and to all others; they are to be viewed wholly through the role of asserting their subjectively perceived rights. Such rights themselves have no other foundation than private will. They are not essentially related to the order inherent in human nature and therefore required by what is consonant with the attainment of true humanity. Nor are they integrally connected with the responsibilities of the citizen and therefore in some way essential to the process of self-government. Ultimately, rights in this scheme are rooted in subjective impulse and in the equally inconstant dispensations of public policy. An earlier liberal tradition that saw men and women as the bearers of obligations as well as rights, and understood the concomitant nature of the two, is replaced by a radically atomistic pluralism in which rights no longer have any independent validity.[13]

This transition is most visible in the way freedom of speech has been transformed into "freedom of expression." Freedom of speech has traditionally been derived from the recognition of what is necessary for individual and political self-government. As such, protection was extended only to what could be conceived as speech, argumentation, and persuasion in this sense. It did not include every form of utterance that may proceed from a human being. But now the right has been limitlessly expanded to such an extent that the law has become incapable of making any distinction between forms of speech. Since all are accorded equal protection, they are regarded as equally valuable and therefore as equally true. Liberal governments have put themselves in the impossible position of not being able to declare as false those very doctrines that are unalterably opposed to their most cherished principles of individual liberty and dignity. By refusing to distinguish between forms of speech and the levels of protection they deserve, liberal courts, Berns has argued, have placed themselves in the impossible position of being unable to defend their own constitutional system against its opponents. If the ideas are not wrong per se, then what is illegitimate about them when they acquire organizational backing? This is of a piece with the difficulties that arise in the area of public morality. By relentlessly focusing on the rights of private self-expression as the only substantive ones, the courts have progressively removed the justification for intervention in the name of protecting public morality. They have thereby made it "impossible to distinguish between virtue and vice."[14] Without such a distinction there ceased to be a basis for morality, public or private.

Most revealing of all is the direction in which liberalism has evolved in dealing with human life itself. There the concept of human nature that is increasingly dominant becomes utterly clear. Included within this context are the emerging liberalization of euthanasia, the ever-expanding access to all kinds of new procreative techniques, and the burgeoning possibilities of control over life and death, human potential and human achievement, presented by the field of biomedical technology. It might be observed that the amazing new powers available to us, when humans can become the object of manipulations directed toward their own convenience, could not have happened at a worse time. We have probably never been less endowed with the moral or spiritual wisdom needed to guide their use. This is evident from the most significant and widespread instance of the abuse of this technology in the ubiquitous availability of medically induced abortions. *Roe v. Wade* is the most crucial case in this area. It not only provided the legal carte blanche for the practice of abortion, but it also constitutes one of the few explicit statements of principle demonstrating the contemporary liberal understanding of human life. The basis for the decision is sufficiently revolutionary that it calls into question the entire preceding tradition of respect for the inalienable rights of human beings. At the same time, it has made possible a level of destruction of human life (over one million per year in the United States since 1973) on the scale of exterminations in the totalitarian states.[15]

What is most disturbing about the Court's opinion in *Roe v. Wade* is not the errant usurpation of legislative powers in this area, nor the idiosyncratic choice of viability as the determinant of personhood, nor even the needlessly unlimited access to abortion that the ruling permits. Most appalling is the attack on the foundation of human rights that it represents. For the first time since the infamous *Dred Scott* decision, the Court decided that an entire category of individuals could be excluded from humanity, and therefore deprived of even the most minimal right to life. By means of such euphemisms as "biological life" and "potential life," it concluded that the fetus does not qualify as a person and can be denied all legal protections. Simple membership in the human species is not sufficient; one has to reach certain levels of human attainment. The great problem with this approach is, as George Grant has pointed out, the doubt that it casts over the notion that human beings anywhere possess rights by virtue of their nature. "Because such a distinction between members of the same species has been made, the decision unavoidably opens up the whole question of what our species is. What is it about any member of our species which makes the liberal rights of justice their due?"[16] The answer, of course, is that we have no basis, that rights are now assigned through the shifting ad hoc determinations of what we consider essential to an adequate "quality of life."

It is not necessary to take sides in the debate in order to recognize this more profound level of problems that ultimately lies behind it. For it is evident that a woman does have a presumptive right to privacy, to self-determination, and to choice over the disposition of her own body. It is equally true that those choices can often be hard and the consequences difficult to endure. But in *Roe v. Wade* and its aftermath the tragic dimension of such choices is completely overlooked. Abortion is more than an exercise of free choice. It does involve the destruction of life that over the course of pregnancy is increasingly recognizable as human. All who are involved sense that abortion is more than a simple medical procedure to remove an unwanted growth. What is to be eliminated is identifiably and separately human, of the same species as the mother, and therefore the bearer of a presumptive right to life and choice too. If the decision is made wholly in favor of the mother, then it suggests that the choice is arbitrary. It might be decided in other ways, and, who knows, if the political forces shift far enough perhaps it will be. At any rate, nothing is inherently sacrosanct about membership in the human species that endows us with imprescriptible rights. All assignation of rights is a matter of policy, without any further foundation than the temporary coalitions of interests.

Humanity has been sacrificed on the altar of its own convenience or utility. No longer an end-in-himself or -herself, the sine qua non for the possession of any other rights, the individual has been subordinated to those qualities and achievements now considered indispensable to acceptable human functioning. The transition within liberalism has been astonishing, from the firm self-evidence of the equal and inalienable "rights of man" to the admission that some human beings are not "men" at all and can therefore be deprived of all rights. Instead of inhering in nature, rights must now derive their basis from legal decrees. This is what has prompted some commentators to reflect that while we may not yet have arrived at full-fledged totalitarian practices, *"in our ways of thinking* we are closer to the totalitarian conclusion than we may wish to think."[17] When our truncated notion of rights was finally put to the test in the comparison between the rights of members of the same species, we discovered that we had no ultimate basis for deciding between them. Without a foundation in principle, the rights of the most defenseless can safely be ignored in the interest of the strongest. *Roe v. Wade* is the case that lays bare the philosophical bankruptcy of liberalism.

For this collapse has not simply resulted from the impact of new technological pressures. The disintegration of liberalism has largely been the consequence of its own internal forces. It has progressively undermined itself. But what is it within liberalism that has given rise to this process of self-dissolution? In searching for an answer we can point to the difficulty that liberal governments have in forming the spiritual order of their citizens. It is difficult to exercise a moral influence while insisting that all such teaching must be confined to the private realm. Or we can bemoan the ambiguity of the liberal symbolism at its inception. It sought to create a consensus on the basis of self-interest while relying on the continued existence of the older virtues of self-restraint and self-sacrifice. Or we could blame the tendency to focus exclusively on the rights of citizens, without adverting to the correlative duties that are the ultimate justification for respecting such rights. But perhaps the most fundamental of all these interrelated causes is the persistently escapist utopianism of successive generations of liberal thinkers. They imagined that the order of society could be sustained indefinitely without devoting any attention to the order within the souls of its members, that a liberal institutional order could be preserved without retaining the understanding of human nature and dignity that is its source.

The contemporary formulation of this inclination is that "right is prior to good," that there is no necessity to affirm the moral principles on which liberalism is based.[18] Whenever difficult questions arise involving profoundly conflicting conceptions of human nature and the human good, liberalism generally takes the easy way out. It removes them from the public realm and assigns them to the determination of private conscience. Whether the differences have been over religion, abortion, "lifestyles," euthanasia, or obscenity, the pattern has remained the same. Divisive public issues are resolved by expanding the range of private rights. Only when direct tangible harm to others can be demonstrated is political intervention justified. The problem is, as we have seen, that withdrawal into official indifference or neutrality has not prevented the communication of an authoritative public teaching. By relegating the decision over euthanasia, for example, to the private wishes of individuals, government is declaring that the life of the sick and dying is of no inherent value. It is worth only whatever their own subjective assessment assigns to it. In the same way, the state teaches that prenatal life has no intrinsic value apart from the subjective valuation of the mother. The state proclaims that lifelong marriage is in no way inherently better, when it provides the same contractual protections for "alternative lifestyles." The fatal mistake is the utopian conceit that liberal democratic regimes can escape responsibility for the consequences through the veil of neutrality.

This is why these regimes are so astonished at the most profound consequence of their actions: the disappearance of the classical-Christian conception of individual dignity and worth. Worse than the damage caused to any particular aspect of human life has been the destruction that has been worked on the idea of humanity itself. The accumulated series of unremarkable specific concessions has accomplished a profound effect: nothing less than "the abolition of man." There is nothing either exalted or noble about a humanity composed of a mass of atomistic individuals, each claiming the prerogative of unfettered self-expression and the limitless gratification of desire. No longer a moral or spiritual being who possesses freedom and dignity, the human person reduces to a chaotic aggregate of passions no more deserving of respect "than a baboon or a grain of sand." The state is thus obliged to follow no more ultimate principles in determining the boundaries between individuals than utility and convenience. It is not without reason that liberal pluralism has been called "a sort of confidence game in which, in the guise of showing respect for individual rights, we are in reality asked to consent to a new kind of society based on a new set of beliefs and values."[19] Because of its relentless pressure to relegate more and more questions to the exercise of private self-determination, liberalism has experienced great difficulty in resisting the tendency toward extremes. This is so even when such extremism undermines the very foundation of individual rights. Liberalism hardly presents a barrier to the emergence of totalitarianism. It has in fact provided the schemes of dehumanizing self-destruction with an important component of their legitimation.

Regeneration

The Truth of Existential Order

The spiritual crisis of the modern world affects all sides. It even reaches into the symbolism that sought through an ambiguous compromise to avoid confronting the full nature of the problem. Liberalism in our own time has finally revealed its loss of inner spiritual direction and, as a consequence, its responsibility for the progressive destruction of human nature. In light of the bankruptcy now exposed at its core, it is difficult to claim that liberalism stands for any higher idea of the dignity and worth of the person. We recognize that the uneasy compromise at its inception, which has indeed been a source of stability for three centuries, is now on the verge of falling apart. Possessive individualism, the rights of an acquisitive self-interested liberty, and the pull of our true self, fidelity to the obligations of the natural moral order, could only be held together for so long. Their conjunction was probably doomed to collapse from the start. The former was legally enshrined in the social contract, while the latter was implicitly expected to continue as the effect of other social institutions. Without a public defense of the foundations they could hardly be prevented from crumbling.

Yet the result, as I have tried to suggest, has not been uniformly negative. The collapse of the liberal moral consensus and the recognition of its dehumanizing consequences has rendered the nature of the modern crisis with a clarity unrivaled since the Renaissance. Our problem is the loss of contact with the ordering spiritual traditions of Western civilization, and the resulting necessity of reestablishing the connection or discovering new spiritual sources of order. Philosophy and Christianity have come increasingly under attack since the sixteenth century, because they are no longer regarded as representing the authoritative truth of reality. Whether the fault lies in the ossification of the traditional symbolisms or in the rigidity of minds unable to get below surface appearances, is irrelevant. There is enough blame on both sides. The point is that the modern world begins in this crisis of the spiritual disintegration of established forms. It defines itself through the continuing search for the truth that can perform the same compelling foundational role as the philosophic-Christian synthesis did in the medieval world. Liberalism sought to create order without a thorough recognition of this problem. The ideological thinkers were more profound in their recognition of the need for a new authoritative reality; they were more deceptive in their espousal of humanity's capacity to provide its own absolute reality.

The only difference now is that the experiment has run its course. We are less likely to be taken in by either the liberal or the ideological approaches, to found order on either false compromises or on illusory absolutes. Each of them leads toward coercion and destruction, because no truly humanizing reality is present within them. This is the meaning of the catharsis through which we have passed—if we are willing to maintain our steadfast meditation upon it. It is the reason why we can be somewhat more sanguine about the future. When the old errors have finally been removed and their attractions have dissipated, we have the opportunity to grapple again with the real problem of order within the contemporary pluralistic world. For virtually the first time since the Renaissance, we can openly confront the problem of creating individual and political order in a social context where the traditional ordering symbolisms are no longer effective. How do we sustain order in a modern society when we can no longer rely on the influence of classical philosophy and traditional Christianity? How else can we be persuasive, if it is not through what is right by natural teleology or what is required of a follower of Christ?

When the symbols have become opaque, then it is fruitless to erect them as dogmatic absolutes or secondary ideologies. A purely conservationist approach that seeks to maintain the imprescriptible authority of the traditional forms is doomed to irrelevancy and inefficacy. In some ways the liberal preservation of residual meaning in a new compromise or the ideological longing for infused transcendent purpose are almost preferable. At least one is addressing, however inadequately, the real needs of the day. But the most appropriate response to the meaninglessness of earlier symbolic forms is to recover the living experiences of truth that engendered them. That, however, is easier said than done. It requires a predisposition of faith or trust that the earlier symbolisms embody reality, before we can begin to open toward a reenactment or recovery of the experiences behind them. For most modern men and women it is in this prior disposition of faith that the real difficulty lies. We can no longer trust that we live in a cosmos and not a chaos, that there is a divine order that will disclose itself to us if we are open to it, or that we are personally addressed by the reality of transcendent Love.

This is where the experience of catharsis plays its indispensable role. The dissolution of the earlier attempts, through liberal individualism and the substitute absolutes of ideology, to provide the foundation of order is a first step toward the real alternative. It opens us up to search for the ground beyond finite existence. The failure of self-interest or of illusory absolutes to create order within soul and society points us in the direction in which truth lies—the trust that order is created to the extent that a human being responds to the pull of transcendent goodness within him or her. We know that moral growth cannot be produced through an external manipulation of interests, nor can it be accomplished through self-absorption within the mass identity of the collective. Inner spiritual progress is the fruit of self-discipline, through which one acquires the virtues. We know that we do not possess this spiritual order ready-made or as a gift. Only through struggle is it to be obtained, and most fundamentally through the painful opening of our selves to the point of participating in the reality that is goodness itself. To the extent that one succeeds in responding to the pull of that transcendent reality, the nature of its order is more and more fully disclosed. At the end of the process we begin to discern the familiar shape of the perspective on reality that has emerged.

Meditation on the crisis of our civilization is the means toward this realization. It provides the occasion not for despairing depression at the blind alley we have reached, but for the opening toward the truth that we have known yet strenuously sought to avoid for so long. We begin to recognize, with Nietzsche and Dostoevsky, that humans are incapable of grounding an autonomous morality on the basis of their own assertion of will. Without a transcendent foundation, the new order is quickly transformed into the "everything is permitted." From there, Camus shows us, we become responsible for the practical application of the principle, including the limitless justification it provides for the horrors of Dachau and Karaganda. Already in the characterization of such expressions of freedom as murder we experience the sense of revulsion that directs us back toward the limits that humans have not erected and cannot cross with impunity. By responsively following this direction we discover the order of reality independent of human will; from there it is evident that the inner spiritual growth of the person is only possible through submission to this order; and finally we encounter the divine presence whose deepest self-revelation is its desire to raise us up to participation in divine Being itself. The remarkable feature of this progression is that none of it has been based on discursive argument. It has been a meditation on the truth of experience that in some sense everyone knows.

The crisis through which we have passed has made it impossible for us to escape the recognition of our situation any longer. An explosion of spiritual and political disorder has detonated the false premises from which it has derived. At the same time it has demonstrated the truth of the opposite conception, that human beings participate in an order of which they are not the creator, and thereby the truth of all of the consequences that follow from it. Only because we have not utterly lost this awareness are we capable of recognizing the murderous dehumanization for what it is. However much we may wish to deny any limits to human freedom, we continue to live in a cosmos ordered from its transcendent ground. Now we have begun to recognize that what is at stake in our acceptance or refusal of participation in that order is nothing less than our humanity itself. By closing ourselves off from that source we do not make ourselves lord of the universe, but sink into the abyss of evil that is identical with the experience and reality of hell. There is no shortcut to the spiritual perfection for which we long. It is only to be won at the price of surrender, of dying to self, and ultimately of sacrificing all without condition or qualification to God, who is goodness and reality itself. There is no other way for humans to become God, to share the divine being, except to become like God. "Be ye perfect as your heavenly Father is perfect" (Matt. 5:48). Even if our goal is the more modest objective of living in freedom, we are obliged to acknowledge that true freedom consists in freely living in accordance with what is ultimately good. Anything less is a loss of freedom and a decline to the slavery of the passions—no matter how much we may convince ourselves that our choices are still free.

None of this any longer remains a matter of speculation for us. The descent into inhumanity from the pinnacle of self-aggrandizement is an empirical phenomenon within that prolonged historical experiment known as modernity. What reason could not accomplish by way of demonstration has now become clear through the force of reality itself. Only someone completely ignorant of our civilization's history could continue to maintain that humans create the order of their own existence. We have been brought to a powerful new awareness of the reality in which we participate, through our confrontation with the possibility of its total destruction and the loss of everything it means to be human. Knowledge of this order is primarily and fundamentally derived from our participation within it. We become aware of it as the powerful undertow of resistance that moves us to oppose "the abolition of man." The dimensions of this knowledge reveal themselves ever more completely as we open ourselves to the existential reformation of our lives in accord with its intimations. The focus of this book has been the example of those who have followed out this concrete meditative unfolding of truth to the point of its fullest elaboration. But it is a knowledge that continues to exist, even when it is pushed to the borders of consciousness within those who seek to deny it. Indeed, paradoxically, there is often a more intense awareness, as we have noted, among those who would deny the very reality of order most completely. We may conclude, therefore, that here we have the bedrock of knowledge or spiritual substance on which the plurality of individuals and traditions can be formed into a political community.

The catharsis of our time has meant that the prospect of a definitive loss of our humanity has called forth in response a heightened awareness of its reality. There has been an exploration of the depths of what it means to be human, with a correlative ascending articulation of ex-

periential truth equal to the great spiritual discoveries of the past. As
such we now have the recovery of foundations that ought to have occurred at the beginning of the modern world. When the symbols of
philosophy and Christianity had become opaque, the way toward the
recovery of order should have been the descent into the experiential
truth from which they emerged. Instead that search was deflected by
the contemporaneous desire to found the new order of reality on the
basis of the closed self. In liberalism the authority of the isolated autonomous self, without reference to divine or human guidance, was rendered supreme. This underwent a metamorphosis into the "egophanic"
outburst of the ideological movements, in which the ego sought to impose its order on the whole of reality, not merely to live by its own
light. Now that these enterprises have become thoroughly discredited,
the movement of resistance to their deformations has called forth the
most profound recovery of experiential truth since the beginning of the
modern period. We have the opportunity to begin the modern world
again.

Our task now is to explore the possibilities that were present at the
very beginning of modernity, but were subsequently neglected in favor
of the liberal and ideological alternatives. The example of Jean Bodin is
highly instructive in this regard. In the midst of the wars of religion in
sixteenth-century France, he explored the possibility of a new experiential foundation to the civil theology of the state. Like so many others,
especially the *politiques*, he had become sickened by the cruelly destructive conflicts to which the dogmatic disputes had given rise. But instead
of attempting to ground tolerance and order on a liberal compromise of
indifference, he sought to uncover the deeper experiential unity within
the world religions. Bodin explored the mystical truth within the different spiritual traditions. This was the *vera religo* whose pristine truth
would require no other validation than the illuminative experience itself. It carried its own proof within itself. As such, it was the one truth
that lay behind all the more specific theological formulations, and therefore the one indisputable foundation on which public order can be
based. This vision he marvelously elaborated in the *Heptaplomeres*, his
dialogue between seven representatives of all the world religions as well
as atheism. Their conversation, while it did not succeed in reaching the
philosophia perennis or the *vera religio*, did succeed in showing how a
tolerant openness to mystery is capable of grounding a social order of
diverse spiritual traditions.[20] Regrettably, it was not a vision that became historically effective. Something of this *politique* notion of tolerance was absorbed by liberalism, but the justification for it tended

toward the deprecation of religion to the indeterminacy of private opinion. When concern for the religious truth of society again emerged in the ideological movements, the consequences were disastrous for the cause of tolerance.

A more contemporary example of the experimental approach to order is to be found in the work of Henri Bergson. In his *Two Sources of Morality and Religion* he distinguishes between the closed self-interested morality whose highest attainment is to secure the collective good, and the open universalist morality that transcends both self and society in love of all human beings. The latter is rooted in the mystic opening toward God, especially within Christianity, and the proof of its superiority is contained within itself. Religion wins souls over, according to Bergson, by the higher truth of its morality. It appeals to that prior sense of obligation in all human beings that is the true foundation of all morality. Reason can never provide a sufficient basis, "since one can always reason with reason."[21] In the same way, it is as the unfolding of this primary sense of right order that the truth of the mystical experience is recognized. We can all verify the movement in our own experience that the mystics have elaborated as the realization that God is love, a love so abundant that it overflows in love of creatures whom God makes in order that they may triumph over materiality to return God's love. Humans are made to participate in the divine love. This movement Bergson considered to have its political expression in democracy. It is precisely the call of a human being toward self-transcendence that is the ultimate foundation of his or her rights as a being possessing freedom and dignity.

What is remarkable about Bergson's reflections is the manner in which they are presented. No arguments or lengthy defense of first premises are produced. His book begins rather from the common starting point of the truth of order, moral and spiritual, that to a greater or lesser extent all human beings recognize. The persuasiveness of his account of open and closed conceptions of order derives from the intuitive truth of the knowledge it seeks to unfold. There is none of the characteristically modern attempt to stand outside the question of order, viewing the moral and political realm as a self-contained entity, and purporting to provide a novel rational foundation from the resources of the autonomous self. Instead there is the recognition that our perspective on order is our participation within it. When the symbolic formulations of that order have ceased to be transparent, then order cannot be invented *de novo*. We must return to the inarticulate or experiential order that has been there all along. As the history of modern philosophy has demonstrated, no sense of moral obligation can be extracted from rational principles unless we appeal to the sense of obligation that was present before reasoning began. It is this prearticulate or soul knowledge of order that has always formed the basis for order between human beings.[22] Bergson's mystical exploration is simply a way of making the presence of this knowledge of order explicit.

Now the catharsis of the modern age has accomplished the same result. What the mystic knows by plumbing the depths of the soul has been revealed by the unfolding of our world itself. At the point where we have been stripped to the simple human essence, we discover participation in an order of reality beyond the self. We recognize that it has been the attempt to turn away from this in order to derive everything from our own self that has brought us to the brink of the abyss. It has caused us to lose the very self we sought so much to preserve. Only by turning away from the madness and delusion of creaturely domination of creation, we now recognize, can we have any chance of preserving our true self in reality. We must submit to an order we did not create, allowing ourselves to be formed by its directives, if each of us is finally to become, in Solzhenitsyn's words, "a human being." The consuming fire through which we have passed has the inestimable benefit of purification. All false premises have been exposed and have fallen away. The cathartic meditation has brought us to the point where the living reality of existence can be appreciated anew. The crucifixion of the modern world has also meant the heretofore unheard-of possibility of resurrection. This has been the true significance of the contemporary crisis. The suffering that we refused to undergo in our aspiration for self-salvation, we have now undergone involuntarily. Its results are bearing fruit in what is probably the first undistorted and unencumbered resurgence of the spirit in the modern world.

The experience of having been shorn of all our illusions is the best inoculation against infection by them again. This is what provides the sense of having definitively overcome the deforming influences of egophany. The insights and discoveries of Dostoevsky, Camus, and the others represent an authoritative postmodern truth because they have emerged from the most penetrating critique of the forces that have dominated our world. They are not one more idiosyncratic jumble of voices added to the general babble. Their truth is one that is recognized by and has triumphed over the very movements by which they are opposed. It is in this sense the recovery of a publicly authoritative truth within a context where all such agreements appeared to have become impossible. MacIntyre's complaint about the interminability and incommensurability of contemporary moral debate no longer applies to the kind of living truth embodied in Solzhenitsyn and Camus, and philosophically elaborated by Voegelin. Central to the nature of the postmodern enterprise has been the appeal to the living knowledge of order within the human heart, which is prior to the adoption of all positions and counterpositions. Because the truth of these thinkers has emerged from the existential struggle with the spirit of the age, and often at the cost of great personal sacrifice, it speaks with a power affecting every human soul.

When dogmas and principles and ideologies have broken down, these thinkers have shown, the living source of order remains from which all such constructions ultimately derive their legitimacy. This is the common ground that we continue to share, for it is on the basis of their residual knowledge of transcendent moral order that the ideological disputants form their arguments. The difficulty is, as C. S. Lewis has noted, that the ideologues wish only to maintain a part of the Tao and jettison the rest.[23] Yet this does not mean that awareness of that remainder is absent. It is there to be revived and rearticulated by individuals who seek to live out its full extent. When that is done, the recovery of a lived experience of order is recognized as the engendering reality behind the great symbolic formulations, of which Christianity and philosophy are the most significant for the Western context. The authoritative and formative role that they have historically played becomes possible again once the full amplitude of the experiences behind them have again become a living reality. It is in this sense that the foundation for social and political order has been recovered within our own time.

The Spiritual Foundation of Liberal Democracy

The crucial question is how this living experience of truth can be translated into the principles and structures of political order. How can an event that is primarily experiential be embodied in ideas and institutions? Does it not run the danger of itself becoming one more ideology competing for power? Moreover, there are the objections that will inevitably be raised by the spirit of modernity itself. This world began in the effort to shake off theological and ecclesiastical authority, with its attendant superstitions and intolerances, and it continues to retain a good deal of anti-Christian prejudice. Will not contemporary society merely perceive this as one more reactionary attempt to assert religious controls? The suggestion of mixing religion and politics calls up all the ancient fears and hatreds. Surely the proscription of references to the divine is the minimum we have been able to achieve since the sixteenth century. Can this seriously be the way for modern men and women to go?

Such are the objections, and they should not be taken lightly. Yet on reflection I believe they miss the essentially *postmodern* perspective we have outlined. The cathartic rediscovery of truth establishes it as a truth definitively beyond dogmatic encapsulation. The truth of "living life," as Dostoevsky referred to it, has been so deliberately won from the ideological chaos that there is little likelihood of confusing it as one more doctrinaire absolute. Eric Voegelin has made the recovery of experiences and symbols the principal theme of his work; there is almost no possibility of treating him as a dogmatist unless one is ideologically bent on doing so. Camus and Solzhenitsyn appeal beyond all abstractions to the incarnate truth of experience, which it has been their special artistic mission to mediate to their contemporaries. Apart from these achievements, the necessity of recovering the pre-articulate sources of order is becoming so widely recognized that it might be regarded as the common premise of all serious theoretical reflection today.[24]

This is also the essential response to the traditional liberal fears of moral or theological absolutism. When the truth about human nature and the order of existence is recognized as primarily an experiential reality, discovered only through lived participation in it and communicated largely through the power of exemplary self-sacrifice, then there is little likelihood that a conformism of moral or theological compulsion will be imposed on society. It is difficult to envisage any of the thinkers we have studied lending their support to such a scheme. They understood the problem of modern civilization to be one of spiritual and moral regeneration, and understood it with such penetrating clarity that they are ever unlikely to confuse it with any such program of externally enforced compliance. The author of "The Legend of the Grand Inquisitor" can hardly be so weak-minded as to commit the very error that he himself exposed with such searing brilliance.

Where the impact of a postmodern political order is likely to be felt is in the correlative refusal to abide within the humanly restrictive and destructive dogmas of liberalism itself. There may not be a public requirement to subscribe to the classical and Christian understanding of reality, but there is a positive obligation to ensure that that profound perspective is not eliminated or dismissed. In place of the militantly secular brand of liberalism recently dominant, the alternative would seem to be the more expansively nonlegalistic form that prevailed in earlier years. The difference is well illustrated in the changing nature of the American church-state debate. We have moved from an era of separate but friendly and cooperative relations between the state and the churches, to an attitude of pronounced indifference and even hostility on the part of political authority toward religion. What is needed is a restoration of the earlier relationship of comity. This should exist not only between church and state, but also between the liberal political order and the whole spiritual world that ultimately sustains the inner order of the citizens. An acknowledgment of the incapacity of liberal democracy to provide and foster its own moral foundations is urgently needed. This would then prevent the exaggerated application of liberal principles, to the point that they openly oppose the very spiritual traditions that have been their own roots.

Again, I cannot emphasize too much that this is not some outmoded confessional longing for theocracy. There is no suggestion of an established religion or of religious tests for the exercise of civil rights. What I am referring to is primarily an opening of horizons to include the most embracing context for political order. Essentially, it comes down to the recognition that the constitutional order rests on a moral and religious reality. The resolution of disputes ought not to be pushed to the point, therefore, where it jeopardizes the very foundations from which the possibility of order ultimately arises. The highest truth about humanity cannot be identified with the formal prescriptive rights of the liberal state. Despite the plurality of spiritual traditions and viewpoints that are included within this public structure, it is imperative that the presence of such a dimension in existential depth be recognized. Agreement on principles and processes is made possible by the underlying spiritual openness that all human beings share. There would be no common understanding of justice, fairness, equality, or right order without this prior sense of transcendent moral truth, which is where political community is ultimately founded.[25] This is the recognition that implicitly informs the most influential accounts of liberal political thought today.

We are living in the midst of a profusion of efforts at rearticulating the theoretical essence of liberalism, in direct response to the prevalent perception of the crisis concerning the foundations of liberal democracy since the Second World War. This effort has engaged some of the brightest philosophical minds and given rise to one of the richest and liveliest discussions in liberal political thought since the seventeenth century. We have already alluded to some of this literature in a negative fashion in chapter 1; here we will attempt to extract some of the positive consequences from the same works. Fortunately, it is not necessary to delineate the variety and complexity of the various authors or to unravel their continuing debates with one another. For our purpose it is sufficient to examine the one aspect from which all the rest unfolds: their ultimate motivating source. The root inspiration or conviction of these efforts, which is often implicit and sometimes even explicitly denied, reveals more about the true nature of liberalism than all the extensive discussion of interpretations and applications. Contemporary liberal thinkers reveal that even when they fail to acknowledge it, they are fundamentally guided by their sense of a transcendent order of truth.

The first evidence for this assertion is the almost-universal abandonment of any attempt at a utilitarian justification for the liberal conception of rights. The consensus that now prevails is that an intrinsic rationale, rooted in principle, must be uncovered. A widespread recognition of the amoral, manipulative, and totalitarian possibilities of utilitarianism and egoism has largely discredited such foundations. What is currently sought is some form of rights-based liberalism that emerges from the combination of two ideas—the customary liberal rejection of moral or religious first premises as inappropriate to a pluralistic order, and the acknowledgment of the need for a principle of respect for the inviolable dignity of the individual. This has been given one of its clearest formulations in John Rawls's dictum that "in justice as fairness the concept of right is prior to good." He is convinced that if the justification of individual rights is argued in terms of our mutual moral obligations, it will flounder irretrievably in subjectivism and hedonism and eventually collapse without support. To rescue the concept of rights from this chaos he tries to withdraw it entirely from the realm of moral debate. Rights ought to become, he contends, the first principle from which all further social and philosophical discourse is to proceed. "It is not our aims that primarily reveal our nature but rather the principles that we would acknowledge to govern the background conditions under which these aims are to be formed and the manner in which they are to be pursued."[26]

The problem is that the foundation he goes on to establish is in marked contrast to the high moral aspirations from which he began. Instead of meditatively unfolding his pre-articulate sense of fairness (along the lines pursued in the *Republic*, for example), Rawls launches into his now-famous thought experiment with the original position, the veil of ignorance, and finally the social contract to explain the genesis of our expectation of rights. The result is for the reader a distinct sense of disappointment. What he has provided is an ingenious explanation of how our concept of rights can be derived from a starting point of undiluted self-interest. It has nothing to do with the concept of fairness, that which we pursue irrespective of whether it serves our self-interest or not. As opposed to a theory of justice, Rawls has provided us with a theory of injustice. It is necessary to state the problem so bluntly in order to bring out the starkness of the contrast between his aspiration and his realization. When this is done we begin to recognize a bit more clearly what Rawls is really trying to do. He is providing a myth of self-interest that is intended to form a public consensus to support the order that he knows to be right. In the absence of a truly moral explication he furnishes an appeal to rational egoism.

His own explanation, in terms of the original social contract rooted in a calculation of self-interest, does not adequately account for the passion and intensity of his concern for individual rights. Why should Rawls or anyone else who has benefited so handsomely from the distribution of wealth, talent, and privilege care any longer for those who have not? Why should he continue to abide by the social contract? After all, there is little likelihood now that he will be reduced to the deprivation of a starving Ethiopian child. The same observation could be made of the majority of liberal political thinkers. Their intentions and inspirations have been better than their theories. In the contemporary context, this contrast is more dramatically in evidence than ever before, because of the intense awareness of the necessity of providing an authoritative foundation to rights. Ronald Dworkin, to refer to only one other recent example, wants us to take rights seriously, although he can provide no more of a justification for them than Rawls. Dworkin too refuses to leave them to the vagaries of moral debate, where all that we regard as precious in human life might conceivably be endangered.[27]

The situation is reaching a kind of lucidity where liberal thinkers themselves will have to confront the spiritual sources of their conviction. It has nothing to do with calculations of self-interest or with the bald assertion of rights, but with a sense of the unique irreplaceable worth of every human person. There is something incommensurable about a human being, from the tiny fragile baby to the sturdy mature adult, from the feeblest and weakest to the most intelligent and most powerful, that makes him or her a being of infinite value in himself or herself. A mystery and a depth dwells at the heart of every person; it prevents all our efforts to reduce, define, and determine the limits of our existence. No matter what the achievements, no matter how limitless or limited the contributions, a man or a woman is always something more.[28] The radical openness to transcendence, the dimension of what is beyond all space-time boundaries, endows a human being "with certain inalienable rights." Behind all the ponderous elaborations, this conviction is what animates men like Rawls, Dworkin, Nozick, von Hayek, and others who best represent the liberal tradition. In different ways each of them is moved by a passionate sense of what Camus called rebellion, revolt at the forces that threaten to negate the utterly irreplaceable worth of every human person.

All that is needed for a remarkable transformation of liberalism to occur, therefore, is a recognition of where its true inspiration lies. The real source, participation in transcendent reality, is virtually on the surface. Very little more is required to bring this knowledge to thematic recognition. This would definitively resolve the blind alley of trying to base unconditional respect for the rights of the individual on perpetually inadequate foundations, with consequent ill effects on the very sense of rights that we wish to preserve. The variety of traditions—religious, humanist, and agnostic—that acknowledge the validity of liberal political forms need only examine the roots of that assent within themselves. Beyond their symbolic and conceptual differences, they share a common foundation in human experience. There, rather than in self-interest, is where the real source of legitimacy lies. The underlying sense of right order may be more or less explicitly developed, and different traditions and individuals have unfolded it to a greater or lesser extent, and often in quite varied fashions, but it is the one existential reality that makes community possible. The common foundation is a fundamental humanism, but deeper than any propositions about humanity; it is the sense of human openness toward the whole of reality that is identical with the transcendent dimension of our existence. Rather than agreeing on dogmas or principles, the various traditions that uphold liberal democracy agree on questions and, more concretely, on the questioning nature of the human person. Thus, while a tradition of skepticism or agnosticism can be accommodated within this unity, the kind of militant atheism that in principle rejects the question of the ground of existence, cannot. The reason is that such a position represents a spiritual deformation of human nature that all too easily extends to its physical destruction as well.

In part this revision of liberalism is already well under way. The contemporary exponents of liberalism are confronted by an array of critics who might best be characterized as postliberal rather than illiberal. The postmoderns whom we have examined represent the most profound challenge to liberalism. But their voice is considerably amplified by the extensive spectrum of thinkers who have called for an infusion of ethical and spiritual substance into the often hollow structures of liberalism. Critics like Leo Strauss, Hannah Arendt, Michael Oakeshott, Reinhold Niebuhr, John Courtney Murray, Jacques Maritain, Yves Simon, John Hallowell, Peter Berger, Alasdair MacIntyre, George Parkin Grant, and others have forged something approaching a consensus concerning the need to found the liberal conception of rights in the understanding of community, citizenship, and what is owed to humans as moral beings. As we indicated in chapter 1, many of these thinkers are part of the postmodern revolution of thought, although they do not explore the dimension of the cathartic experience to the extent of a Dostoevsky or a Camus. There is, however, solid agreement on the fundamental direction that must be followed. Liberalism, all recognize, cannot long continue on its theoretically flimsy foundations. It must take up the core political problem of inculcating the principle of right order within the souls of the citizens. Liberal forms enable this to occur, but that does not eliminate the responsibility of the public authority to see that the process of moral education actually occurs. It is in the interest of liberal democracies to at least ensure that their citizens have the moral prudence to continue the process of self-government.

This philosophical reconsideration has already begun to bear fruit to some extent in the various postliberal political movements of recent years. Its most visible expression has been the rise of conservative parties and candidates, although this is by no means the sole ingredient of the process. Conservatives are only one element of a much larger phenomenon that also includes a range of disaffected liberals, transformed radicals, moderated activists, chastened technocrats, and others. The profusion of political labels by which they identify themselves and one another does not concern us here. What is significant is that all derive in one way or another from a disillusionment with liberal politics in either its individualist or statist manifestations. Gone is the blind faith in the capacity of private enterprise and initiative to solve our social-economic problems; equally absent is the unthinking optimism about the power of government programs to free individuals from oppressive conditions of existence. Liberal societies have been forced to confront the limits of liberal political action and, more important, to recognize the corrosive impact of liberal patterns of thought and action on themselves. A new awareness is beginning to dawn that the most profound social problems cannot be solved by political means. The influential books are the ones that call attention to this quandary of liberal democracy: its inability to form the inner order of the souls of its citizens.[29] Reality appears to confirm the critique of the spiritual bankruptcy of liberalism, and the desire to take up the challenge to struggle against the decline has become a widespread public mood. The response is in itself powerful evidence of the nondormant status of liberal democracy.

Whether any lasting revision of liberalism will arise from this self-examination, something that will prevent a repetition and continuation of the same desultory descent, is very much an open question. In large part the answer depends on our ability in the West, and in the modern world generally, to comprehend the fundamental nature of the problems. The redirection of a long-standing historical course is not an easy matter. All of the inherent dynamics tend toward a reversion to the familiar pattern. The sequence by which movements of reform and revision become co-opted by the very forces they seek to change, has been played out with monotonous regularity. Or there is the even more likely outcome that unfamiliar ideas, not easily assimilated into established mores, will simply be ignored. This is especially the case when what one is calling for is as undefinable as existential openness to the transcendent. It is not a new set of dogmas (yet another ideology would be all too easy), but a recognition of the living spiritual movement from which all our ideas about human nature, the order of existence, and the nature of reality as a whole ultimately spring. The essence of the postmodern persuasion is an appeal not to prematurely or peremptorily cut off this experiential movement. It points toward the commonality that all human beings share in the meditative unfolding of their questions. The various answers they have reached are all related to one another along the continuum of more or less differentiated elaborations of the same questions. None have a privileged knowledge. All have valid and valuable perspectives to contribute. Only those who arbitrarily dismiss the questions remain outside the community constituted by this conversation.

The Institutional Expression

To establish a truly open society requires the institutional embodiment of the reality behind it. In contrast to the historically liberal pattern of the state holding the monopoly on public authority and the relegation of all other associations to a strictly subordinate private status, a postmodern liberal democracy would be based on the acknowledgment of its own spiritual insufficiency.[30] It would recognize the profound incapacity of a liberal individualist ethos to create the virtues so essential to good citizenship. As a consequence, it would acknowledge the need of the public order for those other associations and institutions in which the moral development of the members takes place. In doing so the liberal regime would endow such ancillary social forms with a public status. No more would they be regarded as purely private associations, intended for the private satisfactions of their members. Now they would be seen as an integral feature of the polity, entitled both to full respect for their institutional freedom and also to exercise authoritative influence on the formation of policy. The liberal regime would continue to wield ultimate political power. The only difference would be that it would give explicit recognition to what it has implicitly recognized all along: that it depends on the ethically formed conscience of the citizens, and that its final purpose is to serve the ends of the person that transcend society itself.

A postmodern regime would, for example, recognize the family, with its basis in lifelong marriage, as the preferred interpersonal foundation of society. It is primarily within the family that individuals acquire the kind of love and care that enables them to become mature adult citizens. At the same time it is within the family that the unique precious infinity of each person receives its most concrete embodiment. Married family life is not merely one "lifestyle," but a preferred one that does not necessarily prejudice the freedom to pursue others. The churches and religion generally also play a fundamental role in the formation of the person, and therefore require a public acknowledgment of their status. Liberal states should recognize the mysterious connection that exists between the sacred and the practical moral order. For most human beings, participation in the transcendent is the animating source of their moral aspirations. In religion, too, we receive the most explicit statement in principle of our radically transpolitical value and destiny. The dangers of religious divisiveness virtually disappear when all are accepted equally by the state, but the indisputable contributions all make to the political order still remain.[31] A third institutional stratum deserving of special recognition are the centers and organizations of learning in society. Their autonomy must be guaranteed and their authority respected if the state is to benefit from them. But most important of all, their institutional freedom is indispensable to the contemplative enlargement of the human mind. Finally, the state must acknowledge the more diffuse yet crucial role played by all forms of voluntary associations. It is through such forms of mutual cooperation that the moral and political virtues are acquired; it behooves the state to encourage their operation without placing unnecessary restrictions in the way. Wherever possible, a function should be performed by a lower-level or private organization, rather than through the heavy-handed centralization of state bureaucracy. In this way the maximum of individual freedom and responsibility will be exercised.[32]

None of these ideas are new. They have been components of the most successful liberal regimes since the eighteenth century; they have been central to Christian social and political thought since the Church Fathers. The only difference is the clarity and universality with which they have returned to our attention. It has become evident, even within the most stable Anglo-American form of liberalism, that the inexorable drift is toward ever more extreme expressions of liberty. Without an authoritatively public recognition of such intermediate institutions as I have indicated, both their special role and the principles they reflect are doomed before the relentlessly expansive demands of individual liberty. To accommodate the unrestricted exercise of free choice, neither marriage nor church can be accorded any special position in society. They are reduced to wholly private associations, neither more nor less valuable than any of a range of other organizations and lifestyles. Politically this signifies a devaluation of the values embodied in these institutions, and, more generally, it leads to what Nietzsche termed the devaluation of all values. Eventually the only value that can be sustained is that of free choice—which is tantamount to the elimination of all moral truth.[33]

The insight that has to intervene is that liberal political order cannot be sustained on the basis of a centrifugally private ethos. Principles of fairness, justice, equality, liberality, compromise, and self-sacrifice are indispensable ingredients. They cannot be obtained from a preoccupation with individual self-gratification. Even respect for the equal liberty of others demands a basis in principle, rather than personal convenience or caprice. For this reason, an accommodation must be reached between the desire to enlarge the scope of individual liberty and the public endorsement of those principles and institutions that advance moral and spiritual growth. Every effort to respect the right of self-determination must be expended, even to the point of permitting private immorality to occur, as long as it causes no direct harm to others. But such permission must not be erected into a principle; it can remain a prudential exercise of discretion. Above all, the polity must retain the ability to distinguish between the moral character of human actions. There must remain the capacity to publicly differentiate between good and evil. Without maintaining a preference for the principles and institutions that are the source of its own order, the liberal political order cannot long survive. If liberal societies fail to preserve their own foundations, then all talk of protecting individual liberties becomes obsolete.

The expression of public preference for certain institutions or ways of life, for the encouragement of virtue and the disapproval of vice, cannot be regarded as fatal to individual liberty. The latter remains as inviolable as before, because of the absolute emphasis placed on the necessity of a free response. A postmodern liberal order would be founded on the conviction that it is preferable to permit human beings to commit evil, rather than to compel a false conformism that corrupts the moral impulse at its core. The state would turn a blind eye to evil as long as no imminent harm were likely, before it would promote the lie of hypocrisy. Reverence for the unconditional worth of each person makes any coercive interference with their autonomous growth in responsibility unthinkable. Nevertheless, the state has an affirmative obligation to promote those institutions and convictions that make this respect possible. If it is serious about the preservation of liberty, it cannot neglect the task of persuading its citizens concerning the value of liberty. By thus confining its role to one of *persuasion*, where the freedom of response is the sine qua non of the enterprise, the state avoids the danger of jeopardizing private liberty.

This is not to deny that individuals will experience both political and social pressure. When the state seeks to encourage religious participation, or provides special protections to the institution of the family, or promotes independent centers of learning, or recognizes the political value of voluntary associations, it clearly intends to influence the actions of the citizens. In this sense such preferences do seek to limit the absolute freedom of individuals. What justifies the reinforcement of preferences is the realization that there is no possibility of neutrality. The failure to publicly endorse these goals is tantamount to asserting their unimportance. Whatever remains wholly a matter of subjective inclinations is without objective merit of its own. Its value is whatever we subjectively assign to it. The political justification for intervention is that it tilts the balance in the direction of those principles and institutions that make liberty concretely possible. In other words, such constraints are ultimately justified as necessary to preserve the liberty of those who are most negatively affected by them. When faced with the choice of supporting those institutions that sustain liberty or promoting those that would undermine it, liberal democracy must always opt for the former.

Prospects

The real question is whether the liberal democracies are capable of such a profound political reorientation. Or are they doomed to drift in an ever-downward spiral toward chaos and tyranny? Fitful halts and adjustments may be made along the way, but is it realistic to expect that they can reverse the direction of a process that has been unfolding since the inception of modernity? Are the liberal democracies capable of becoming *postmodern*? The answer to that question depends on their ability to confront and resolve the core modern crisis. If the reflection does not penetrate to the depths, then it will not finally break free of the patterns and inclinations that have enveloped it to the present. There will still be a tendency to view the problem in terms of a wholly man-made order that is intended to maximize our individual and collective convenience. The issue will not be conceived in its starkest light, as the problem of doing good and avoiding evil, and the necessary clarity of perspective will not be attained. All too readily we will yield to the temptation to consider the difficulties soluble through new techniques and institutional reforms. The root problems, by contrast, lie within ourselves. Our spiritual and intellectual weakness is the source of the problems of liberal democracy. Thus, any true reorientation must begin within ourselves.

This is why the catharsis exemplified by Dostoevsky, Solzhenitsyn, Camus, Voegelin, and others is of such inestimable value. They have confronted the full magnitude of the darkness unleashed by the humanist dream of totally subordinating reality to the service of humanity. Contrary to the prospect of limitless power and the brave new world it seemed to promise, they have recognized the abyss of tyranny and destruction that opens up when humanity arrogates to itself lordship over all things. Our liberty is not enlarged through the conceit that we are utterly free to choose the life before us. Instead, this empty freedom recoils on our own heads. Without our attachment to an order of reality beyond ourselves, we become prey to all that erupts from the chaos of our passions. When absolute autonomy becomes the principle of political power, then no barriers remain to limitless cruelty and caprice. The pinnacle of our greatest triumph turns out tragically to be the moment of our greatest defeat.

But the postmodern thinkers have also shown us how this extremity of deprivation can become the starting point of an ascent toward a new life for individuals and society. All of the despair and desolation of modern human beings abandoned to the illusory world of their own power has been fully experienced by them, yet has not proved ultimately victorious. These thinkers have not sunk down toward the subhuman level. At the point of the modern world's loss of everything, they have discovered a reality within that draws them upward toward the lasting and true. We are not simply hollow men and women, empty husks of humanity wandering without guidance, capable only of inflicting unlimited misery on one another. Within us is a movement of resistance, rooted in the reality of our transcendent dimension, and capable of filling our lives with its truth and direction if we responsively follow its promptings. Humanity is not alone. We are part of a community of the spirit that mysteriously reaches its apex in the divine Being itself. For this reason the sufferings of human beings, the utter loss of all that has supported and sustained them, is not simply the pain of humanity alone. It is one with the sacrificial way of existence in which human sufferings are a participation in the divine suffering of evil as well. Modern men and women discover their unity with the God who empties himself of divinity so completely, to the point of forsakenness, in order that we might become sharers in the life of God's divinity. The crucifixion of humanity in our own era shows its meaning in continuity with the crucified Christ. When that occurs, the oppressive bonds of power slip away, and the reality of sacrificial love is revealed as the true power that triumphs over evil and death. The final truth about the modern deprivation of all meaning is not despair, but the glory of resurrection.

The viability of liberal democracy is very much dependent on its capacity to absorb these insights. It must break free of the temptation to derive all things from the logic of the closed autonomous self. Liberal democracy cannot long survive if it nurtures a view of human existence that runs contrary to its own principles and institutions. We have seen that the path of neutrality is impossible; it leaves us without defenses against the very influences whose corrosive effect we seek to avoid. But the question is whether the spiritual traditions that are most consonant with the liberal conception of politics will retain enough persuasive power to win broad social support. That is the concern that has animated this book. It was undertaken in the conviction that individuals who have made an experiential recovery of the Judeo-Christian and philosophic traditions, in the face of the utter loss of spiritual direction in our world, hold the greatest hope of making a universally persuasive appeal. They speak to us without ideological preconceptions and they possess no authority other than the exemplary truth of their own lives. Within them the modern world can again behold the transforming power of participation in transcendent reality in a direct and immediate way. The abyss of destruction and disorder that beckons us, they have shown, is not the only reality. It can be surmounted by the man or woman who responds to the pull of truth within. For all of us, the possibility remains that their paradigmatic witness can become the means for our own meditative ascent from the depths.

NOTES

1. See also his "Repentance and Self-Limitation in the Life of Nations," *Under the Rubble*, 105–143.

2. The confusion and uneasiness we experience in erecting memorials to the Holocaust or to "the victims of Stalinism" (significantly not Leninism) arises from this inability to transcend the roots of the problem. As long as we do not understand the causes, we will be forever uncertain what we ought to memorialize.

3. The responses to his Harvard Address are contained in *Solzhenitsyn at Harvard* (Washington, DC: Ethics and Public Policy Center, 1980).

4. This sympathetic relationship is well illustrated in the following passage from the liberal political scientist Harold Laski: "It is, indeed, true in a sense to argue that the Russian principle cuts deeper than the Christian since it seeks salvation for the masses by fulfillment in this life, and, thereby, orders anew the actual world we know. . . . Lenin was surely right when the end he sought for was to build his heaven on earth and write the precepts of his faith into the inner fabric of a universal humanity. He was surely right, too, when he recognized that the prelude to peace is a war, and that it is futile to suppose that the tradition of countless generations can be changed, as it were, overnight." *Faith, Reason and Civilization* (New York: Viking, 1944), 143, 184. A more recent expression of nihilist liberalism is to be found in B. F. Skinner's exhortation *Beyond Freedom and Dignity* (New York: Knopf, 1971).

5. T. S. Eliot, *The Idea of a Christian Society* (New York: Harcourt, Brace, 1940), 65.

6. Even a liberal statesman with the impressive literary talent of a Winston Churchill nowhere provides, in all of his voluminous writings, a reasoned statement of what it is that makes liberal democracy worth defending against the forces of totalitarianism. See George Parkin Grant, *English-Speaking Justice* (Notre Dame, IN: University of Notre Dame Press, 1985), 54–55. John H. Hallowell, *The Moral Foundations of Democracy* (Chicago: University of Chicago Press, 1954).

7. Voegelin, *Enlightenment to Revolution*; Niemeyer, *Between Nothingness and Paradise*; John H. Hallowell, *Main Currents in Modern Political Thought* (New York: Holt, 1950).

8. Claes G. Ryn, *Democracy and the Ethical Life*. 2nd rev. ed. (Washington, D.C.: Catholic University of America Press, 1989) chaps. 5–8.

9. Quoted in Walter Berns, *The First Amendment and the Future of American Democracy* (Chicago: Gateway, 1985), 162–63.

10. Ibid., 164. Or we might consider the following passage from Justice Holmes, 158: "If in the long run, the beliefs expressed in proletarian dictatorships are destined to be accepted by the dominant forces of the community, the only meaning of free speech is that they should be given their chance and have their way."

11. A more reflective critic, Richard J. Neuhaus, has expressed the difficulty thus: "When religion in any traditional or recognizable sense is excluded from the public square, it does not mean that the public square is in fact naked. This is the other side of the 'naked public square' metaphor. When recognizable religion is excluded, the vacuum will be filled by *ersatz* religion, by religion bootlegged into the public space under other names."*The Naked Public Square* (Grand Rapids: Eerdmanns, 1984), 80.

12. Berns, *The First Amendment*, 79. See also George Goldberg, *Reconsecrating America* (Grand Rapids: Eerdmanns, 1984).

13. John H. Hallowell, *Decline of Liberalism as an Ideology* (Berkeley: University of California Press, 1943); *Moral Foundations of Democracy*.

14. Berns, *The First Amendment*, 226. See also Francis Canavan, *Freedom of Expression* (Durham: Carolina Academic Press, 1984), for the historical evolution of these conceptions.

15. This is dramatically indicated in the title of John Powell's popular book *Abortion: The Silent Holocaust* (Allen, TX: Argus, 1981). For the process by which abortion became acceptable see the excellent study by Nanette J. Davis, *From Crime to Choice* (Westport, CT: Greenwood Press, 1985).

16. Grant, *English-Speaking Justice*, 71. See also his *Technology and Justice* (Notre Dame, IN: University of Notre Dame Press, 1986). "In negating all rights to the foetuses, the court says something negative about what they are, namely that they are such as to warrant no right to continued existence. And because the foetus is of the same species as the mother, we are inevitably turned back onto the fundamental question of principle: what is it about the mother (or any human being) that makes it proper that she should have rights? Because in the laws about abortion one is forced back to the stark comparison between the rights of members of the same species (our own), the foundations of the principles behind rights are unveiled inescapably. What is it about our species that gives us rights beyond those of dogs or cattle?" (18). The fact that the abortion debate has still not been settled is powerful evidence for the unease that is widely sensed concerning the practice. This has been reflected in recent shifts in mood by the Supreme Court, as in *Webster v. Reproductive Health Services* (1989). But like slavery, abortion will never be finally resolved until a full acknowledgment of the rights of all human beings involved has been made.

17. Neuhaus, *Naked Public Square*, 159. The American Medical Association has accepted the principle of withholding food and water as an acceptable form of passive euthanasia. Recently the *New England Journal of Medicine* has shown us the next step in the process by publishing a call for "harvesting" the organs of anencephalic infants (born without upper brains) for transplants. The contemporary language of "quality of life" does carry eerie overtones of the Nazi *Lebensunwertesleben*. See Robert J. Lifton, *The Nazi Doctors* (New York: Basic Books, 1986).

18. John Rawls, *A Theory of Justice*, is perhaps the clearest exemplar of this approach. A good recent example is Richard Rorty, *Contingency, Irony and Solidarity* (Cambridge: Cambridge University Press, 1989).

19. Francis Canavan, "The Dilemma of Liberal Pluralism," *Human Life Review* 5 (Fall 1979):15.

20. Jean Bodin, *Colloquium Heptaplomeres: Colloquium of the Seven about the Secrets of the Divine*, trans. M. D. Kuntz (Princeton: Princeton University Press, 1975). See also Paul Lawrence Rose, *Bodin and the Great God of Nature* (Geneva: Droz, 1980). The example of Bodin, of a mystical exploration of the roots of order, was enormously influential for Voegelin. "My careful study of the work of Bodin in the early thirties gave me my first full understanding of the function of mysticism in a time of social disorder. I still remember Bodin's 'Lettre à Jan Bautru' [ca. 1562] as one of the most important documents to affect my own thought. In the twentieth century, when the dogmatomachy is no longer that of theological but of ideological sects, a similar understanding of the problem has again been reached by Henri Bergson in his *Les deux sources de la morale et de la religion*. I doubt that Bergson has the same stature as a mystic that Bodin has. Still, these two French spiritualists are for me the representative figures for the understanding of order in times of spiritual disorder" (*AM*, 113–14). For a parallel discussion of the nature of mysticism that is never reducible to a dogmatic unity along the lines of a *philosophia perennis*, see William Newell, *Struggle and Submission: R. C. Zaehner on Mysticism* (Washington, DC: University Press of America, 1981). On the importance of spiritual openness for a truly "open" society see Dante Germino, *Political Philosophy and the Open Society* (Baton Rouge: Louisiana State University Press, 1982).

21. Bergson, *Two Sources*, 89.

22. Socrates appeals to this underlying level of pathos, of common experiences, in his conversation with Callicles in the *Gorgias* (481–482). Ultimately he compels Callicles to acknowledge that virtue is better than vice, because Callicles cannot go against the reality that he "knows" in regarding courage as superior to cowardice.

23. Lewis, *Abolition of Man*, 56.

24. Other remarkable contemporary examples include the work of Michael Polanyi on "tacit knowledge" and Bernard Lonergan on "transcendental method." See Eugene Webb, *Philosophers of Consciousness* (Seattle: University of Washington Press, 1988).

25. "The search for modern constitutional order is comprehensible only when the willingness of the founders of such regimes to surrender their sovereign power, and

content themselves with exercising the constituent power on behalf of the people is seen as the expression of a profound conviction about the sanctity of the personal self. . . . Justice as resting upon this conviction is a reflection in persons and institutions of a divine justice that transcends the human undertaking." Carl J. Friedrich, *Transcendent Justice: The Religious Dimensions of Constitutionalism* (Durham, NC: Duke University Press, 1964), 19.

26. Rawls, *Theory of Justice*, 31, 560.

27. Perhaps the most extreme example is Isaiah Berlin: "Principles are not less sacred because their duration cannot be guaranteed. . . . 'To realize the relative validity of one's convictions,' said an admirable writer of our time, 'and yet stand for them unflinchingly, is what distinguishes a civilized man from a barbarian.'" *Four Essays on Liberty* (Oxford: Oxford University Press, 1969), 172. Clearly, he does not mean that his own convictions are groundless, for they seem to be invested with an almost transcendent importance in the passion with which he defends them. Richard Rorty, in *Contingency, Irony and Solidarity*, has sought to make a virtue out of this inability to provide a justification for his conviction of human solidarity. But there too the same difficulty arises. While rejecting the idea of a human essence that evokes our sympathy, he makes a moving appeal for concern for the suffering of others as the ultimate principle of our politics. His own performance refutes the content of his theory.

28. The old doctor in *Cancer Ward* yields himself more and more to the contemplation of this truth: "At such moments an image of the whole meaning of existence—his own during the long past and the short future ahead, that of his late wife, of his young granddaughter and of everyone in the world—came to his mind. The image he saw did not seem to be embodied in the work or activity which occupied them, which they believed was central to their lives, and by which they were known to others. The meaning of existence was to preserve unspoiled, undisturbed and undistorted the image of eternity with which each person is born. Like a silver moon in a calm, still pond" (*CW*, 428).

29. Recent best-sellers have included Allan Bloom, *The Closing of the American Mind* (New York: Simon & Schuster, 1987) and Paul Kennedy, *The Rise and Fall of the Great Powers* (New York: Random House, 1987). Other notable examples are Peter Berger, *The Homeless Mind* (New York: Random House, 1973) and *Facing Up to Modernity* (New York: Basic Books, 1977); Robert Nisbet, *The Quest for Community* (Oxford: Oxford University Press, 1953); Russell Kirk, *The Conservative Mind* (Chicago: Regnery, 1953); Stanley Hauerwas, *A Community of Character* (Notre Dame, IN: Notre Dame University Press, 1981); Richard Neuhaus, *The Naked Public Square*; and Robert Bellah, Richard Madsen, William Sullivan, Ann Swidler, and Steven Tipton, *Habits of the Heart* (Berkeley: University of California Press, 1985).

30. This admission has historically characterized the American democratic experiment until very recently. None of the militant anticlericalism and strident secularism so characteristic of European liberalism was ever much in evidence within the American tradition. Even in the most rationalist Enlightenment generation, the founders of the United States, strong expressions of concern for the moral and spiritual foundations of the republic were prominent features. A classic statement is to be found in Washington's Farewell Address: "And let us with caution indulge the supposition that morality can be maintained without religion. Whatever may be conceded to the influence of refined education on minds of peculiar structure, reason and experience both forbid us to expect that national morality can prevail in exclusion of religious principle."

31. John Courtney Murray, *We Hold These Truths: Catholic Reflections on the American Proposition* (New York: Doubleday, 1964), especially chaps. 2, 9.

32. This is, of course, the principle of subsidiarity championed by Catholic social thought, but it is also integral to the tradition of voluntary associations in American political history. See de Tocqueville, *Democracy in America* (1835).

33. Willmoore Kendall, "The Open Society and Its Fallacies," *American Political Science Review* 54 (1960): 972–79.

Index